Center for Humanistic Inquiry
Emory University
1715 North Decatur Road, NE
Atlanta, GA 30322

Michel de Montaigne

Accidental Philosopher

Michel de Montaigne, the inventor of the essay, has always been acknowledged as a great literary figure but has never been thought of as a philosophical original. This book is the first to treat Montaigne as a serious thinker in his own right, taking as its point of departure Montaigne's description of himself as "an unpremeditated and accidental philosopher."

Whereas previous commentators have treated Montaigne's *Essays* as embodying a skepticism harking back to classical sources, Ann Hartle offers a fresh account that reveals Montaigne's thought to be dialectical, transforming skeptical doubt into wonder at the most familiar aspects of life. The essay is the new philosophical form of this dialectical thought, in which the world is presented as radically contingent but where the divine is present in an incarnational and sacramental way.

This major reassessment of a much admired but also much underestimated thinker will interest a wide range of historians of philosophy as well as sholars in comparative literature, French studies, and the history of ideas.

Ann Hartle is Professor of Philosophy at Emory University.

To my son, Robert Wyman Hartle, Jr.

Michel de Montaigne

Accidental Philosopher

ANN HARTLE

Emory University

PUBLISHED BY THE PRESS SYNDICATE OF THE UNIVERSITY OF CAMBRIDGE
The Pitt Building, Trumpington Street, Cambridge, United Kingdom

CAMBRIDGE UNIVERSITY PRESS
The Edinburgh Building, Cambridge CB2 2RU, UK
40 West 20th Street, New York, NY 10011-4211, USA
477 Williamstown Road, Port Melbourne, VIC 3207, Australia
Ruiz de Alarcón 13, 28014 Madrid, Spain
Dock House, The Waterfront, Cape Town 8001, South Africa

http://www.cambridge.org

© Ann Hartle 2003

First published 2003

Printed in the United Kingdom at the University Press, Cambridge

Typeface ITC New Baskerville 10/12 pt.   *System* LaTeX 2$_\varepsilon$ [TB]

A catalog record for this book is available from the British Library.

Library of Congress Cataloging in Publication data

Hartle, Ann.
    Michel de Montaigne : accidental philosopher / Ann Hartle.
        p.   cm.
    Includes bibliographical references and index.
    ISBN 0-521-82168-1
    1. Montaigne, Michel de, 1533–1592. Essais.   2. Montaigne, Michel de,
1533–1592 – Philosophy.   3. Philosophy in literature.   I. Title.
PQ1643 .H29 2003
844′.3 – dc21   2002073615

ISBN 0 521 82168 1 hardback

Contents

v

Acknowledgments

This study of the philosophical life has kept me mindful of the debt that I owe to Joseph Carpino, Gerald Galgan, Brother Pascal Kelly, Nino Langiulli, and Francis Slade, who first made manifest to me the integrity of the philosophical life and the life of faith. I want to acknowledge that debt here and to express my deepest gratitude for the example and the friendship of each of them.

I am grateful for conversations over the years with Donald Livingston, Carl Page, and Donald Verene, conversations that never failed to shed light for me on the nature of philosophy and the worth of the philosophical life. Each of these friends read an earlier draft of this book and gave me valuable suggestions for improving it. My thanks are also due to Gregory Johnson, whose comments on an earlier draft were very helpful to me. The Research Committee of Emory University provided funding for a leave during which much of my research was done. My thanks are due to Michelle Brady for her assistance with the research, and to Christopher and Susan Anadale for their editorial assistance. I owe a debt greater than I can express to my husband, Robert, for the many conversations that helped me to clarify my project, for the many hours spent in preparing the manuscript, and for his unfailing encouragement.

An earlier version of the section on skepticism from Chapter 1 appeared as "Montaigne's Scepticism," *Montaigne Studies* 12, nos. 1–2 (2000): 75–90. "The Dialectic of Faith and Reason in the *Essays* of Montaigne," *Faith and Philosophy* 18, no. 3 (July 2001): 323–36, is based on sections of Chapter 5. Some of the ideas developed in Chapter 8 were first published in *Philosophy and Literature* 24, no. 1 (April 2000): 138–53, as "Montaigne's Accidental Moral Philosophy."

Note on the Texts

References to the French text of the *Essais* are to the edition by Pierre Villey and V.-L. Saulnier, 3 vols., 2nd ed. (Paris: Presses Universitaires de France, "Quadrige," 1992). The English translation is that of Donald Frame, *The Complete Essays of Montaigne* (Stanford, Calif.: Stanford University Press, 1943). The citation (VS16; F9), for example, refers to p. 16 of the Villey-Saulnier edition and to p. 9 of the Frame translation. In some instances, I have emended Frame's translation. I have consulted the translation by M. A. Screech, *The Essays of Michel de Montaigne* (London: Penguin Press, 1991). References to the Screech translations are cited by the letter S and the page number – (S614), for example.

Introduction

This book is intended to show that Michel de Montaigne is a philosopher – that is, that he takes up the most fundamental philosophical questions in a profoundly original, comprehensive, and coherent way. Although his *Essays* have always been acknowledged as the origin of a new literary genre, they have never been recognized as philosophical in the deepest sense. Montaigne invented the essay because his thought could not be expressed in the traditional philosophical forms.

Those who have written on the philosophical aspects of the *Essays* have generally placed Montaigne in one or more of three categories. They have seen him as a skeptic of some kind, as a humanist, or as having evolved in his thought through Stoic, Skeptical, and Epicurean stages. Each of these views does capture something of the tone and substance of the *Essays*, but all are partial and none is as radical as Montaigne's own thought.

The interpretation I present here is based on the moment of self-discovery that occurs in the "Apology for Sebond." Montaigne is "a new figure: an unpremeditated and accidental philosopher!" I take him at his word: what he is doing in the *Essays* has never been done before.

Montaigne, then, breaks with both ancient philosophy and medieval theology. Is he, therefore, the first modern? If modernity is essentially the progress of autonomous reason that culminates in the Enlightenment, then Montaigne is not a modern philosopher. His philosophical position and the essay form in which it is embodied constitute a rejection of the claim to authority of autonomous reason, a claim that he recognized in its earliest stirrings.

Because Montaigne is a critic of modernity, can we then say that he is, as Lyotard has it, a postmodern thinker?[1] There are indeed several aspects of Montaigne's critique of modernity that postmodernists would find attractive and sympathetic. But Montaigne is deeply at odds with the most fundamental claims of postmodernism. His rejection of the authority of autonomous reason does not imply a rejection of the possibility of truth.

1

His affirmation of human diversity does not entail a denial of a common
bond of truth.

It would not, then, be appropriate to characterize Montaigne as either
modern or postmodern. It would be more accurate to locate him within
the premodern tradition of classical thought and Christianity.[2] That is, his
break with ancient philosophy and medieval theology is the kind of break
that actually carries the tradition forward by deepening it.

George Steiner's critique of modern and postmodern hermeneutics can
be taken, in reverse, as a description of Montaigne's relation to the premodern tradition: "What we have done since the masked scepticism of Spinoza,
since the critiques of the rationalist Enlightenment and since the positivism
of the nineteenth century, is to borrow vital currency, vital investments and
contracts of trust from the bank or treasure-house of theology. It is from
there that we have borrowed our theories of the symbol, our use of the
iconic, our idiom of poetic creation and aura. It is loans of terminology and
reference from the reserves of theology which provide the master readers
in our time (such as Walter Benjamin and Martin Heidegger) with their
license to practice. We have borrowed, traded upon, made small change of
the reserves of transcendent authority. At its key points of discourse and inference, hermeneutics and aesthetics in our secular, agnostic civilization are
a more or less conscious, a more or less embarrassed act of larceny."[3] The
Essays are unintelligible apart from the context of transcendent authority.

Steiner's account of "true reading," on the other hand, captures precisely
the ontological condition for the *Essays*: "To be 'indwelt' by music, art, literature, to be made responsible, answerable to such habitation as a host is
to a guest – perhaps unknown, unexpected – at evening, is to experience
the *commonplace mystery of a real presence*. . . . Where we read truly, where the
experience is to be that of meaning, we do so as if the text . . . *incarnates* (the
notion is grounded in the sacramental) *a real presence of significant being*. This
real presence, as in an icon, as in the enacted metaphor of the sacramental bread and wine, is, finally, irreducible to any other formal articulation,
to any analytic deconstruction or paraphrase. It is a singularity in which
concept and form constitute a tautology, coincide point to point, energy to
energy, in that excess of significance over all discrete elements and codes of
meaning which we call the symbol or the agency of transparence. These are
not occult notions. They are of the immensity of the commonplace."[4]

At the end of the preface to his historical study of Montaigne, Hugo
Friedrich invites philosophers to provide a philosophical interpretation of
Montaigne's thought. That is what I attempt to do here. My account of
Montaigne locates him in relation to the philosophical tradition, especially
because he himself defines his originality in relation to that tradition. But
this book is not a historical study or a work in the history of ideas. I do
not attempt to understand Montaigne within the historical context of the
Renaissance and, in particular, I do not claim to treat his views on faith and

religion within the full context of Renaissance and medieval theology. My interpretation is conceptual rather than historical.

Part I takes up the ways in which Montaigne breaks with the philosophical-theological tradition and presents himself as a "new figure." In Chapter 1 I discuss the differences between Montaigne and the ancient skeptics, and I show that there is indeed a skeptical moment in Montaigne's mode of thought but that this is a moment of openness to the possible rather than a suspension of judgment. In particular, I argue that Montaigne's apparent credulity, especially with respect to the stories he borrows from Plutarch, is compatible with this skepticism. Montaigne incorporates the skeptical moment into the dialectical movement of his thought: the moment of openness to the possible allows him to find the strange in the familiar.

The mode of philosophy from which Montaigne distinguishes himself most explicitly is what I refer to as "deliberate philosophy" (in contrast with his own accidental philosophy). Deliberate philosophy is the exercise of reason as rule within the soul, a place and function that reason claims for itself on the basis of its superiority within the hierarchy of nature. Indeed, reason asserts its own divinity insofar as it sees itself at one with the divine ruling principle within the whole. Montaigne criticizes and ridicules the deliberate philosophers' pretensions to divinity by reminding them in vivid and often comic terms of their bodies, of the most base and shameful bodily functions, of their vulnerability to all of the accidents of human life, and thus of the human condition that they share in common with the lowliest and most ignorant.

I conclude Chapter 1 with a preliminary account of what accidental philosophy is. First, in contrast with deliberate philosophy, accidental philosophy is nonauthoritative and purely human. Accidental philosophy implies that truth is prephilosophical and prereflective: the truth that is discovered is just the truth that was already there. Second, accidental philosophy is circular dialectic: thought moves from the common and familiar to the rare and strange, then returns to find the rare in the common and the strange in the familiar. Third, accidental philosophy involves getting beyond what Montaigne calls "the appearance of the first sense." Those who stop at the first sense remain in error. The essay uncovers, through circular dialectic, a deeper, second sense. The struggle with error that is implicit in the dialectic suggests that the meaning of Montaigne's title, *essai,* is "temptation": the essays are Montaigne's way of living the life of the intellect, the examined life, within the inescapable condition of the temptations of the intellect. Finally, what must being be if philosophy is accidental? Accidental philosophy implies that the world is a radically contingent, created world.

Chapter 2 deals with Montaigne's treatment of the traditional metaphysical categories: being and becoming, nature, causality, the particular and the universal. In each case, he transforms the meaning of the terms, not by stipulating or inventing new definitions, but by "lowering" them, that is, bringing them back to their prephilosophical meanings. In the minds of the learned, being is an abstract notion, far removed from what is common and familiar. In the *Essays*, being is revealed as the accidental particular. Nature has become the ideal of perfection from which we have fallen and the measure against which we must be judged. Montaigne blurs the distinction between nature and custom, including habit in the meaning of nature. The primary distinction for him is not between nature and custom but between nature and learning, especially philosophy. Nature is just how we are here and now. "Human nature" becomes "the human condition." With respect to the metaphysical category of causality, Montaigne contrasts himself with Aristotle from the very beginning of the *Essays*. In "To the reader" he takes up Aristotle's four causes – final, formal, efficient, and material – and presents himself as deficient and defective in each case. He cannot reveal himself apart from his imperfections. His own accidental philosophy is not the search for causes: he distinguishes the search for causes from the discovery of truth. Finally, Montaigne resists the philosophical tendency to ascend to universals. The essays stay at the level of particulars, and Montaigne uses the language of images more than the philosophical language of universals. And yet, "each man bears the entire form of the human condition." Montaigne's presentation of his own particular – and very imperfect – self communicates the universal human condition. Why does Montaigne lower or weaken each of the traditional metaphysical categories? His way of inquiring into "that which is" presupposes that truth is present in the imprecision and richness of common language and opinion, not in the abstract metaphysical jargon of the schools.

The third chapter deals with the form of the essay as the proper mode for Montaigne's accidental philosophy. The meaning of *essai* as "trial" or "test" is explored in relation to the essay's circular mode of thought, and to the way in which the essay articulates "that which is." Montaigne presents several formulations of his purpose throughout the *Essays*: to tell his *mœurs*, to communicate himself, to encourage others to liberty, to give authority to accidental opinion, and to make his mind ashamed of itself. All of these formulations reveal a unity of intention, namely, an attack on a certain kind of rationalism.

Montaigne's audience, then, is that "middle region" of men who are prone to error but who are able to come through error and the presumption of the learned and to think for themselves. In this regard, Montaigne is the best example of an educated man who engages fully in what Oakeshott calls "the conversation of mankind." The metaphor of conversation raises the issue of Montaigne's practice of quotation. I identify three levels of quotation in the *Essays* and I argue that Montaigne's stance of quotation, as he moves among the three levels, reveals what it means to think for oneself. So also, the dialectic of history and poetry that runs through the essays implies a necessary relationship between "borrowed" truth and the ability to witness what is before one's own eyes. The apparent disorder of the essays manifests an oracular origin in opinion; it is a daemonic-poetic order that allows to the accidental its role of discovery, in contrast to the premeditated outcome of the syllogism and the treatise.

Part II takes up the question of the meaning of accidental philosophy and the way in which Montaigne deepens the tradition. In Chapter 4 I set out the circular dialectic of accidental philosophy and show how it is circular, dialectical, accidental, and philosophical. I begin by discussing five essays and the first essay of each of the three books in order to trace out Montaigne's circular movement of thought. That circular movement might be described as a movement from low to high to low, from familiar to strange to familiar, from common to rare to common. Thought returns to its starting points and possesses those beginnings in a new way. Circular dialectic does not ascend from opinion to new knowledge. Rather, it brings to light the truth that was already there in opinion. Here I contrast Montaigne's circular dialectic with the skeptical mode of thought of Sextus Empiricus and Hume.

Montaigne refers to presumption as "our first and original malady" and as the greatest obstacle to wisdom. He recognizes two kinds of presumption, the presumption of the ignorant and the presumption of the learned. Circular dialectic overcomes both kinds of presumption and incorporates each of those moments of overcoming into its circular form. In order to see how Montaigne comes to terms with presumption, we must consider the ways in which he deals with the errors of presumption and the role of memory and imagination in overcoming presumption. His "monstrously deficient" memory is actually his freedom from the unexamined authority of both prephilosophical and philosophical opinion. His rich imagination allows him to be open to the unfamiliar and thus not subject to the presumption of the learned who dismiss as false whatever seems impossible to them. The imagination, when properly disciplined, is also essential for the proper formation of the judgment. Essay I.27, "It is folly to measure the true and the false by our own capacity," is one of the very few places where Montaigne reveals a decisive change in himself. That change is presented in terms of the two forms of presumption and it allows us to see that the circular dialectic is always a return to Montaigne himself: circular dialectic is the dialectic of self-knowledge.

The question about Montaigne over which there has been the deepest disagreement concerns his sincerity in religious matters. Some have argued that he is really an atheist who veils his atheism for rhetorical and political purposes. Others have seen him as a devout, orthodox (although perhaps weak) Christian. Between these extremes are the views of Montaigne as an unorthodox Christian, an indifferent Christian, and an agnostic. In Chapter 5 I begin to examine "what it means to believe" for Montaigne. The first section deals with the way in which Montaigne blurs the traditional theological distinction between nature and grace. Montaigne's attitude toward "the world," death, and repentance and his criticisms of the Reformation reveal not an indifference to religion but his own way of understanding the life of faith. Montaigne's faith is present in the *Essays* at a level deeper than the level of learning: it is present as the pretheoretical background in terms of which the *Essays* are intelligible. Montaigne blurs the distinction between nature and grace not because he denies the presence of the sacred in human life but because he sees the presence of grace everywhere. Or, to put the matter in skeptical terms, human reason cannot make the distinction between nature and grace. In this sense, Montaigne's skepticism is his faith: faith cannot presume to know and does not need to know whether the cause of any given action is nature or grace.

In the second section I discuss the "Apology for Sebond," the essay that addresses most explicitly the question of faith. I argue that, in the "Apology," Montaigne works through the dialectic of faith and reason, a dialectic that is expressed in terms of the two objections to Sebond's natural theology and Montaigne's replies to those objections. The first objection is usually seen as the objection that faith makes to the project of natural theology: reason is a threat to faith. The second is usually seen as the objection that reason makes to faith: faith cannot command universal assent and, therefore, cannot defend itself before the court of reason. The tendency has been to see Montaigne as either an atheist (placing him on the side of the second objection) or as a fideist (placing him on the side of the first objection) or as a skeptic-fideist (placing him on the side of the first objection and interpreting his response to the second objection as a skeptical response to the claims of reason). Montaigne, however, responds to both objections, so that any attempt to place him simply on one side would be an inadequate account of his position. In interpreting the "Apology" as a dialectic, we can see how the understanding of faith expressed in the first objection (faith is belief held by particular divine inspiration) is transformed through the dialectic with the second objection, and how the understanding of reason expressed in the second objection is reformed through its dialectic with the first objection. Faith is not particular inspiration, and reason is not autonomous. The dialectical understanding of the "Apology" leads to the conclusion that the essay is indeed a defense of Sebond, but a defense of a transformed version of Sebond's most fundamental premise concerning the harmony of faith and reason.

In Chapter 6 I discuss the ontological dimension of Montaigne's thought by working out what is implied in the beginning and end of the circular dialectic of accidental philosophy. Circular dialectic begins in opinion and testimony. This implies a prereflective harmony of thought and being, the location of the mind in the human world of opinion, and a notion of experience as participation in custom. Beginning in testimony also suggests an openness to mystery, to truth that cannot be fully articulated because it cannot be fully comprehended by the witness. Heidegger's discussion of "true humanism" is helpful in bringing out the ontological aspects of the *Essays*: for Heidegger, true humanism means that "the essence of man is essential for the truth of being." In its beginnings in opinion and testimony, we can identify an oracular and daemonic quality in thought itself in its openness to the essential mystery of being.

Circular dialectic ends in wonder at the most familiar. This implies an absolutely contingent, created world, a world created out of nothing and, at the same time, a world in which the divine is somehow present. Contingency is the fundamental condition for being and for thought. Montaigne's reconciliation to nothingness shows itself especially in the way he embraces our temporal condition. Creation out of nothing implies the ontological primacy of contingency and possibility. Therefore, being must be such as to allow for the most radical transformation, the "divine and miraculous metamorphosis" that Montaigne refers to at the end of the "Apology." Creation out of nothing also entails the complete absence of the divine from nature – that is, the divine is not a part of nature. This, in turn, means that the ancient hierarchy within nature, the ordering of nature in relation to the divine principle that is highest, can no longer be maintained. Accidental philosophy is the mode of philosophy in a world where the divine is present in the world in an astonishing way; that is, it implies a created and "incarnational" world. Distinctions can be made within this world but they are not the same kinds of distinctions that are made within a hierarchically ordered world: distinctions are made and the divine is made manifest only in the encounter with the particular and with the most familiar.

Part III deals with the character of the accidental philosopher, a character that is different in several important ways from the character of the deliberate philosopher. Chapter 7 argues that Montaigne presents himself in the *Essays* as a new possibility, the great-souled man without pride. A character such as that could not be expressed in terms of the ancient categories: for Aristotle, the great-souled man is necessarily proud. Montaigne's character is his graceful response to contingency, the harmonization of classical magnanimity and Christian humility. This harmonization is possible because Montaigne separates self-love from self-esteem and thus relocates the great-souled man from the public arena to the private realm.

Montaigne wrote his *Essays* because he was seized by the desire to tell his *mœurs*.[5] Those ways of being, he says, are "a bit new and unusual." In Chapter 8, I take up the subject of Montaigne's moral philosophy and focus on what is new in his character. Although Montaigne's admiration of classical heroic virtue is sincere, he does regard certain aspects of the self-mastery required by deliberate philosophy as excessive. In particular, he seems to associate the extremes of self-discipline with cruelty. He distinguishes between virtue, which involves inner conflict, and natural goodness or innocence, which does not involve inner struggle and which is, therefore, unworthy of honor. But it turns out that the heights of virtue, where struggle has

been transcended, look remarkably like natural goodness. Montaigne locates himself among the innocent rather than the virtuous. His character is
what it is not on account of any philosophical discipline but on account of
his nurse's milk. What is new in Montaigne's *mœurs* is his reordering of the
vices. He hates especially both lying and cruelty. The vices associated with
the weaknesses of the flesh, such as drunkenness, are ranked as lesser vices
than those that are all in the soul, such as ambition. Montaigne's reform is
not reform by "new opinions" but is rather a return to what he learned in
the nursery.

In Chapter 9 I draw out the political implications of Montaigne's presentation of his *mœurs*. I do this against the background of modern political
philosophy, especially as articulated by Rousseau in his account of the conflict between Christianity and politics. Three principles of modern political
philosophy emerge from that account: the subordination of religion to politics, the privacy of religion, and the rule of autonomous reason. Montaigne
is at odds with each of these principles. The nonauthoritative character of
the *Essays* implies Montaigne's denial of the claims of autonomous reason
over tradition. Montaigne's defense of the private life is not a preference
for "bourgeois individualism" but is rather his resistance to the tendency of
the state to crush all intermediary sources of institutional authority.

Montaigne belongs to two worlds – this world and the other world – but
both occupy the same space of appearances. Christianity and politics are
in conflict because politics is the realm of mastery and subjection whereas
Christianity is the realm of sociability. For Montaigne, Christianity provides
in a preeminent way the conditions of sociality – that is, truth, goodness,
and beauty. Christianity is the religion of public truth. Montaigne's criticisms
of the Reformation are directed at what he sees as the dangers it poses to
the conditions of sociality. Although Montaigne's skepticism concerning
the ability of politics to secure the human good makes him conservative in
some respects, if we follow out what is implicit in the conditions of truth
and goodness, we arrive at a political possibility – a Christian republic – that
Rousseau regards as impossible.

PART I

A NEW FIGURE

"That Is Where He Got It!"

Montaigne's Caprices and the Humors of Ancient Philosophy

Montaigne is surprised by himself. While making his collection of the "asinine stupidities," the absurdities and whims of the ancient philosophers, he comes upon himself quite by accident. "So I let fly my caprices all the more freely in public, inasmuch as, although they are born with me and without a model, I know that they will find their relation to some ancient humor; and someone will not fail to say: 'That is where he got it!'"(VS546; F409). He will appear to others as the mere collector of the opinions of the ancients, the consummate borrower, dragging out the most obscure quotations from the storehouse of his prodigious memory. But here is the moment of self-knowledge: "A new figure: an unpremeditated and accidental philosopher!"

Montaigne, of course, was entirely correct. He invented the form of the essay, and his literary genius has never been in question. But, from the point of view of philosophy, the tendency has been to place him within one or another or some combination of the ancient schools. The essay form itself, as Montaigne anticipated, does make it difficult to identify his distinct philosophical voice.

Readers of Montaigne are familiar with Pierre Villey's view that Montaigne's thought developed through three stages, roughly corresponding to the three books of essays: an early "Stoical" period, a skeptical crisis, and a final period in which Montaigne's design is to portray himself. Villey's thesis may capture something of the changing tone of the three books, but it cannot stand as an accurate account of Montaigne's thought, even if one believes him to be simply a philosophical follower, for he quotes dozens of philosophers with apparent approval throughout all three books.

Among some of those who recognize the limitations of Villey's reading (and those limitations are now widely recognized), there is still a tendency to look for a development or change in Montaigne's thought.[1] Donald Frame, for example, speaks of a new sense of human unity emerging in Book III of the *Essays*.[2] Again, this may capture something of the tone of Book III as

distinguished from the earlier books. But to say that there is a change of
tone is not necessarily to say that Montaigne's thought "developed." If he
had changed his mind about such things as his own purpose by the time he
wrote Book III, he could have expressed this development in his revisions
of Books I and II, thus changing their tone as well.[3]

The current tendency is to see Montaigne as ultimately a kind of skeptic.
Once again, this description captures what would seem to be the underlying skeptical tone of the *Essays* taken as a whole, and it finds support
in Montaigne's highly favorable accounts of the ancient Skeptics and the
absence of any explicit criticisms of the skeptical position.[4] One of the difficulties that this view faces is the fact that there are clearly nonskeptical
aspects of Montaigne's thought. For example, he does make assertions and
definitive moral judgments that, from the skeptical standpoint, appear to be
dogmatic. He does not seem to pursue the skeptical version of the highest
good, *ataraxia* or the calm that comes from true suspension of judgment,
whereas he does pursue the nonskeptical goal of self-knowledge.[5]

In an effort to do justice to this underlying skeptical tone while recognizing these difficulties, interpreters such as Conche have sought to attribute to
Montaigne a skeptical "method" that amounts to a refusal to "absolutize" his
own beliefs or to presuppose any stable truth and fixed essences of things.
Consistency requires that this refusal be extended to Montaigne's Christian
belief, and here this view of his thought as a moderated skepticism shows
its limits most clearly, because Montaigne does seem to hold that there is
indeed truth and that it resides in God, who has revealed it in part to man.

Some have tried to reconcile Montaigne's skepticism with his apparent
faith by attributing to him a kind of Christian skepticism. Human reason,
on its own, can do nothing. The recognition of this impotence prepares
the heart and mind to receive the truths of faith. This view of Montaigne
finds support especially in the "Apology," where the tone is strongly skeptical
concerning the powers of human reason and where Montaigne's purpose
seems to be a defense of Christian belief. But this interpretation leaves
us with a faith that is a kind of irrational clinging to beliefs just to have
something to believe, a faith for which we can find no grounds and for
which we can seek no understanding. In other words, this would seem to be
simply a skepticism that has not the courage to go all the way. Thus, some
interpreters have held that Montaigne is really a skeptic and an atheist who
hides his atheism behind a facade of perfunctory declarations of religious
belief and submission.

Each of these ways of describing and classifying Montaigne finds evidence
and support in the text of the *Essays.* My purpose here is not to give an exhaustive account of the full range of such descriptions. Nor do I claim to
have so easily refuted any of them. My point is that either Montaigne is
a philosophically inconsistent and even incoherent thinker – that is, he is
not a philosopher at all – or a way must be found to go somehow beneath

the philosophical chaos of the *Essays* and to locate Montaigne's distinct philosophical voice. That distinct philosophical voice is best expressed in Montaigne's own self-discovery: "A *new* figure: an unpremeditated and accidental philosopher!" Montaigne invented the essay because he needed this new form to express not a "teaching" or a "system of thought," but a way of being. Montaigne is a philosopher, but a philosopher of a certain kind. He cannot be located in any of the sects or schools of ancient philosophy: his "caprices" are "without a model."

In this chapter I begin to examine Montaigne's relationship to ancient philosophy. The first section will take up the question of his skepticism. I show that there is a kind of skeptical moment in Montaigne's mode of thought but that this skeptical moment is a transformation of ancient Skepticism: Montaigne incorporates the transformed skeptical moment into the dialectical movement of accidental philosophy. The second section deals with that aspect of ancient philosophy that Montaigne contrasts most explicitly with his own accidental philosophy: ancient philosophy is "deliberate philosophy." That is, ancient philosophy understands itself as the rule of reason within the soul of the philosopher, a rule that is achieved through the harmony of the philosopher's mind with the divine ordering principle within the whole. Deliberate philosophy directs the thoughts and actions of the philosopher to a single end, divine impassibility. In the third section, I provide a preliminary account of what Montaigne means when he calls himself an accidental philosopher.

Skepticism Transformed

Of all the attempts to locate Montaigne within the sects of ancient philosophy, the view that he is a skeptic would seem to find the greatest and most consistent support in the text. First, the repeated display of the diversity of opinion and of the disputes among the ancient sects contributes to the impression of the skeptical tone of the *Essays*. Second, Montaigne's own voice could plausibly be described as at least that of a "common sense" skepticism, the healthy dose of self-doubt that keeps one from being opinionated and stubborn and, more important, that moderates one's response to those who disagree. Third, Montaigne repeatedly and consistently speaks favorably of the skeptics. So it would seem that both the tone and the content of the *Essays* are skeptical.

As might be expected, the sheer diversity of philosophical opinion is made most manifest in the "Apology" and, in fact, constitutes one aspect of the response to the second objection against Sebond. Montaigne speaks of "the liberty and wantonness of those ancient minds which produced in philosophy and the knowledge of man many schools of different opinions, each undertaking to judge and to choose" (VS559; F420). In one section of the "Apology" he proposes to examine whether human reason has achieved any clarity about natural and human things (VS536; F400). Here he makes his collection of philosophical opinions concerning the soul, some of them "moderate" and some of them "dreams and fantastic follies." He provides numerous examples of arguments that are not only false but inept "in the reproaches that the philosophers make to each other in the dissensions of their opinions and of their schools" (VS545; F408). On the question of divine things, the situation is the same. After running through a long list of philosophical opinions on the divine, Montaigne concludes in an exasperated tone: "Now trust to your philosophy; boast that you have found the bean in the cake, when you consider the clatter of so many philosophical brains!" (VS516; F383). Philosophical disagreement extends even to the most important question of all: "There is no combat so violent among philosophers, and so bitter, as that which arises over the question of the sovereign good of man, out of which, by Varro's reckoning, two hundred and eighty-eight sects were born." And as Cicero tells us, if we disagree on the sovereign good, we disagree on all philosophy (VS577; F435).

Even if Montaigne does not see himself as a skeptic in the strict sense, there is an undeniably skeptical tone, a "commonsense" skepticism, sometimes made explicit in the *Essays*. When Montaigne considers the question of the movement of the heavens, he notes that for three thousand years it was believed that the stars moved; then Cleanthes or Nicetas maintained that it is the earth that moves. In his own time, Copernicus had so well defended this latter view that it served to account for all astronomical effects. "What are we to get out of that, unless that we should not bother which of the two is so? And who knows whether a third opinion, a thousand years from now, will not overthrow the preceding two?" The consequence to be drawn extends well beyond the matter of astronomy: "Thus when some new doctrine is offered to us, we have great occasion to distrust it, and to consider that before it was produced its opposite was in vogue; and, as it was overthrown by this one, there may arise in the future a third invention that will likewise smash the second" (VS570; F429).

This kind of healthy commonsense skepticism also has important practical consequences, especially evident in Montaigne's attitude toward sorcerers and witches. "To kill men, we should have sharp and luminous evidence; and our life is too real and essential to vouch for these supernatural and fantastic accidents" (VS1031; F789). There are numerous places in the *Essays* where Montaigne recommends moderation based on past experience of one's mistaken beliefs. This skepticism is a version of the recognition of one's ignorance and it extends even to one's speech: "I like these words which soften and moderate the rashness of our propositions: 'perhaps,' 'to some extent,' 'some,' 'they say,' 'I think,' and the like." If he had children to educate, he would teach them to speak this way, preferring that they keep "the manner of learners at sixty than to represent learned doctors at ten" (VS1030; F788).

Besides the skeptical tone of the *Essays*, there is the even stronger and more compelling evidence of Montaigne's very sympathetic accounts of ancient Skepticism and of his admiration for the Skeptics themselves, especially Pyrrho. Of the three kinds of philosophy that Montaigne distinguishes in the "Apology," he takes the trouble to spell out quite fully just what the position of the Skeptics is because, he says, many people find it difficult to understand, and even the Skeptical authors are somewhat obscure and diverse (VS505; F374). The skeptical manner of speaking is especially attractive to him. His own personal emblem, a scale with the motto "What do I know?" is meant to capture the desirability of this mode of speech, best expressed by the interrogative rather than the affirmative (VS527; F393). But the most compelling evidence for seeing Montaigne as a skeptic and, further, as a Christian skeptic is the way he concludes his full and sympathetic account of skepticism in the "Apology": "There is nothing of man's invention that has so much verisimilitude and usefulness [as Pyrrhonism]. It presents man naked and empty, acknowledging his natural weakness, fit to receive from above some outside power; stripped of human knowledge, and all the more apt to lodge divine knowledge in himself, annihilating his judgment to make more room for faith; neither disbelieving nor setting up any doctrine against the common observances; humble, obedient, teachable, zealous; a sworn enemy of heresy, and consequently free from the vain and irreligious opinions introduced by the false sects. He is a blank tablet prepared to take from the finger of God such forms as he shall be pleased to engrave on it" (VS506; F375). It does seem quite clear that, of all the sects of ancient philosophy, Montaigne prefers the Skeptics. It is also clear that, in his uncharacteristically long response to the second objection to Sebond's natural theology, he does speak in a decidedly skeptical voice. But is Montaigne himself a skeptic? Does skepticism provide us with a complete and adequate understanding of Montaigne's philosophical activity?

Montaigne is not a skeptic. First, he does not conform to the most important teachings of skepticism. Second, his own mode of thought is not skeptical but dialectical. Third, his reply to the second objection in the "Apology" cannot stand on its own as a statement of Montaigne's position.

Ancient Skepticism took two forms, one that looks to Pyrrho of Elis as its founder and one that emerges out of the Academy of Plato. There are differences between these forms that center around such issues as the practice of argument to achieve suspension of judgment and the role of probability in the conduct of life. Nevertheless, the three fundamental teachings of Pyrrho define the Skeptical school: we can know nothing of the nature of things; hence, the right attitude toward them is to withhold judgment; the necessary result of suspending judgment is imperturbability.[6]

Montaigne does not conform to these skeptical teachings. The first teaching refers primarily to our inability to know whether anything is good or evil by nature. That inability leads to the suspension of judgment. Montaigne throughout the essays is always making judgments about good and evil. The essays are, he says, the essays of his judgment (VS653; F495). With respect to the third teaching, Montaigne's end or goal is not imperturbability or indifference. He insists on his changeability, and the consistency that he does display is not dependent on his being unaffected by the accidents of life. It is a consistency that must be accounted for as the consistency of a being immersed in time. These aspects of his self-presentation are taken up especially in Chapter 7, where his character appears as his response to contingency, and in Chapter 8, where his moral judgments and innovations are discussed.

Second, Montaigne's thought is dialectical. He does often place arguments and opinions in opposition to each other but that does not lead to suspension of judgment. Rather, contradictions become part of a dialectical movement of thought that involves judgment about good and evil and that brings truth to light. This dialectical character of his thought emerges in a partial way in this chapter where I argue that Montaigne effects a kind of transformation of ancient Skepticism. In Chapter 4, I set out the dialectic more completely and also discuss the differences between Montaigne and the Skeptics with respect to the nature of the dialectic.

Third, the reply to the second objection against Sebond's natural theology (which is regarded as Montaigne's most explicitly skeptical statement) must be seen within the wider context of the "Apology" as a whole. In the first place, Montaigne himself draws attention to the rhetorical dimension of his reply by contrasting his harsh approach with the more gentle approach that he takes to those who put forward the first objection in the name of piety. Those who bring forward the second objection "insist on being whipped to their own cost and will not allow us to combat their reason except by itself" (VS449; F328). Montaigne sees himself as constrained here to argue in a certain way, within the limits of autonomous reason. Second and more important, the reply to the second objection cannot stand on its own but rather stands in a dialectical relation to the reply to the first objection. I set out this relationship in Chapter 5 as the dialectic of faith and reason.

Although I maintain that he is not a skeptic, I would argue that there is what might be called a "skeptical moment" in the movement of Montaigne's thought, a moment that resembles but transforms the doubt or suspension of judgment of ancient Skepticism. In this chapter, I follow out one aspect of that movement of thought in order to bring the skeptical moment to light.

We can begin by noticing one very curious fact about the essays and especially about the "Apology for Sebond." Here we have supposedly the most skeptical of all the essays, where attack after attack is made on the most universally held positions, where human reason is deflated to the point of nothingness. Here, in this most skeptical essay, we find instances of what appears to be an astonishing credulity. In their introduction to the "Apology," the editors Villey and Saulnier assure us that this essay contains numerous borrowings from the Skeptics and presents unequivocal statements of Montaigne's adherence to Pyrrhonism. But then they must try to explain the fact that, in the reply to the second objection against Sebond, Montaigne presents numerous stories about animals, many of which appear to be fabulous. For example, there are reports of ants negotiating with the enemy to ransom their dead, elephants contemplating and worshiping, the grateful lion who refuses to attack Androcles the slave who years before had removed a thorn from his paw, the halcyon's floating nest, and numerous dog stories. Montaigne seems simply to accept these stories. He repeats them without any evidence of disbelief on his part.

Villey and Saulnier explain his credulity in this way: "If in . . . (the comparison of man with the animals) one is astonished at finding so little of that critical sense, of which Montaigne shows so much in other parts of the same essay, one should not forget that these stories were guaranteed by the authority of Plutarch, from whom they are borrowed often almost verbatim, and that most of these legends were accepted without reserve by the scholars of the 16th century" (VS437). So, Montaigne's uncritical repeating of these stories, his apparent credulity, cannot really be reconciled with the otherwise overwhelmingly skeptical tone of the essay. His credulity must be explained as a lapse, a moment of thoughtless deference to the authority of Plutarch and a failure to rise above the prejudices of his century.

This interpretation is, to my mind, unsatisfactory: it denies to Montaigne's thought an elementary level of self-conscious consistency. On the other hand, if we see Montaigne's skepticism as a moment within a more comprehensive movement of thought, his skepticism turns out to be compatible with his credulity with respect to these stories.

In "Of the power of the imagination" Montaigne also repeats many stories that are, or at least may be, fabulous. But at the end of the essay, he says quite plainly that he is well aware of what he is doing and he gives us some hints as to why he does it. After reporting stories about a cat who, by its steady gaze alone, caused a bird to fall from a tree and about a falconer who brought down a bird from the air by the power of his gaze, Montaigne writes: "At least, *so they say*, – for I refer the stories that I borrow to the conscience of those from whom I take them" (VS105; F75, emphasis added). So, in spite of the fact that he himself is not certain of the truth of the stories, he reports them and even uses them as material on which to reflect and as examples from which to draw conclusions. Why does he do this? How could the truth of the stories be irrelevant to what he is doing? Montaigne provides this explanation: "In the study that I am making of our *mœurs* and motions of the soul [*mœurs et mouvemens*] fabulous testimonies, provided they are possible, serve like true ones. Whether they have happened or not, in Paris or Rome, to John or Peter, this is always some human potentiality [*de l'humaine capacité*] of which I am usefully advised by the telling. I see it and profit from it equally in shadow as in substance. . . . There are authors whose end it is to tell what has happened. Mine, if I knew how to attain it, would be to talk about what is possible to happen" (VS105–6; F75).

What does Montaigne mean by "possible"? What sense of "possible" can allow us to account for his apparent credulity? And what are the human capacities that are revealed in the telling of fabulous testimonies? There are two "levels" of possibility that Montaigne seems to be addressing. The first and more obvious is the possibility of human action, especially the achievements of the soul in heroic and extraordinary deeds. The second is the level of belief itself. What is revealed in the telling of fabulous testimonies is something about the nature and the possibilities of the human capacity of belief.

The believable is, on the whole, the familiar. We tend to believe or accept as true whatever fits with what we already believe or accept. So, for example, we have no difficulty believing a story about someone if it accords with our assessment of his character. That the coward once again acted like a coward is no surprise; it is just what we would have expected. What *would* be surprising and difficult to believe is that the coward did something courageous. This would not fit with what we already believe, and listening to the report of the deed would be hearing something outside our own experience. Then other factors would come into play, including, of course, the credibility of the reporter and the witnesses.

Now, the *Essays*, from beginning to end, are full of stories. (In the first essay, only three pages long, there are nine stories.) Most of these stories are borrowed from ancient historians, some from recent histories, and a few either from Montaigne's own experience or from witnesses close to home, for example, his household or his village. At least some of these stories are difficult to believe. Yet, almost without exception, Montaigne seems to believe and accept them as true.

"Of sleep" is a good example of Montaigne's way of proceeding. He begins by claiming that reason does not require the sage to be entirely immobile and impassable. "Even if Virtue herself were incarnate, I think her pulse would beat stronger going to the attack than going to dinner; indeed it is necessary that she should be heated and stirred. For this reason it has struck me as a rare thing to see sometimes that great men remain so entirely poised, in the loftiest undertakings and most important affairs, as not even to curtail their sleep" (VS271; F198). So he begins here by pointing to the rare, the extraordinary, to "great men," the lofty, and what is above the ordinary.

Then he tells several stories: first, Alexander the Great on the day appointed for the battle with Darius slept so soundly that he had to be called two or three times by name to wake him. Second, the emperor Otho resolved to kill himself and set about putting his affairs in order. While waiting to hear that his friends had reached safety, he fell into such a deep sleep that his servants heard him snoring. Third, the great Cato had decided to kill himself and was only waiting for word that his friends had gotten away from the port of Utica. He fell asleep until the first messenger came and woke him to tell him that a storm was keeping the ship in port. Then he went back to sleep until the second report came that the ship had sailed. The fourth story is also about Cato. The night before he was to confront Metellus in the public square (Metellus accompanied by the favor of the people and of Caesar, and by slaves and gladiators; Cato fortified only by his courage), Cato comforted his friends, his wife, and his sisters (who spent the night weeping and tormented), then he went to bed and slept soundly until morning.

The two stories about Cato are followed by this judgment: "The knowledge we have of the greatness of this man's courage from the rest of his life enables us to judge with complete certainty that his behavior proceeded from a soul elevated so far above such accidents that he did not deign to let them worry him any more than ordinary disturbances" (VS272; F199). Here it seems we have a clear case of what I mentioned earlier: these deeds of Cato are believable, even though they are rare and extraordinary, because they harmonize with the other aspects and deeds of Cato's life that we know about already. The principle here is consistency of character. Cato's character is itself extraordinary, and within the context of his extraordinary character, these deeds are believable.

The judgment on Cato is followed by two more stories. The first is about Augustus who, on the point of going into battle against Sextus Pompeius in Sicily, was overcome by such a profound sleep that he had to be wakened to give the signal for battle. The second is about the young Marius who, after having ordered his army and given the signal for battle against Sulla, lay down under a tree and fell asleep so soundly that he saw nothing of the combat and could hardly be awakened by the rout of his men. This is Montaigne's judgment on Marius and perhaps on Augustus as well: "They say that this happened because he was so extremely weighed down from work and lack of sleep that nature could hold out no longer" (VS272; F199).

If we compare the judgments, three things can be said. First, the judgment about Cato is made with "complete certainty" whereas the judgment about Marius is introduced with "they say." Montaigne presents the opinion but does not necessarily make it his own. Second, the metaphors heighten the opposition: Cato's soul is "so far elevated" above even the accident of death that he is able to sleep in its immediate presence, whereas Marius's soul is overcome or "weighed down" by sleep. Third, Cato's sleep is due to his courage, whereas Marius's sleep is due to nature. The essay then concludes in this way: "And, on this subject, let the doctors determine whether sleep is so necessary that our life depends on it. For we certainly find that they put to death King Perseus of Macedonia, when he was a prisoner in Rome, by preventing him from sleeping. But Pliny alleges that there are people who lived a long time without sleep. In Herodotus there are nations in which men sleep and wake by half-years. And those who write the life of the sage Epimenides say that he slept for fifty-seven years on end"(VS272–73; F199).

Perhaps the first thing to notice is the way these last stories are introduced: "And, on this subject, let the doctors determine whether sleep is so necessary that our life depends on it." What is the "subject" here? The subject is "nature." He had just reported that Marius was said to have fallen asleep because "nature could hold out no longer." It seems that in each case where "nature" is the cause, Montaigne distances himself from the truth of the assertion: "they say" that Marius fell asleep because nature could hold out no longer. In some sense, he even seems to want to put aside the question of nature: "Let the doctors determine whether sleep is so necessary that our life depends on it." That is a question for the "naturalists" and, as he says elsewhere, "I am not a good naturalist" (VS75; F52).

There is, then, a certain degree of doubt expressed in the way Montaigne reports some of these stories. One possible explanation of his complete acceptance of some stories and his distancing himself somewhat from others is that he trusts some sources more than others. The stories about Alexander, Otho, and Cato are all from Plutarch. The story about Augustus is from Suetonius. The stories about Marius and Perseus are from Plutarch. Of the stories that Montaigne seems to accept without question, all except one are from Plutarch. And certainly Plutarch is one of the authors Montaigne borrows from most frequently. It may be helpful then to consider Montaigne's views on the veracity and reliability of Plutarch. Here we can look especially to two essays, "Of the power of the imagination" and the "Defense of Seneca and Plutarch."

In "Of the power of the imagination" he writes: "Plutarch might well say to us...that the credit belongs to others if his examples are wholly and everywhere true; but that their being useful to posterity, and presented with a luster that lights our way to virtue, that is his work. There is no danger – as there is in a medicinal drug – in an old story being this way or that"(VS106; F76). Montaigne acknowledges that Plutarch, from whom he borrows, may himself have borrowed at least some of the stories he reports. But in the context of this essay, the fabulous testimony reveals some human capacity, some possibility.

In the "Defense of Seneca and Plutarch," Montaigne defends Plutarch against an accusation that Jean Bodin makes in his *Method of History*. Bodin accuses Plutarch "not only of ignorance...but also of writing incredible and entirely fabulous things" (VS722; F546). Montaigne does not object to the accusation of ignorance: "Let him [Bodin] have his say, for *that is not my quarry*" (emphasis added). What Montaigne objects to is the charge that Plutarch wrote "incredible and entirely fabulous things." If Bodin had simply said "things otherwise than they are," Montaigne would not object, for "that would have been no great reproach." It would be no great reproach "for what we have not seen we take from the hands of others and on trust."

Plutarch does not try to conceal the fact that he is often working with borrowed material and he does not pretend to report "things as they are." What
Montaigne objects to is Bodin's assessment of Plutarch's judgment: "[T]o
charge him with having taken incredible and impossible things as genuine
coin is to accuse the most judicious author in the world of lack of judgment"
(VS723; F546). Lack of judgment is here identified by Montaigne with the
failure to distinguish between the possible and the impossible.

Montaigne objects to Bodin's example of Plutarch's failure of judgment.
Bodin finds incredible and impossible the story of the Spartan boy who let
his stomach be torn up by a fox he had stolen and concealed under his
robe rather than be discovered in his theft. Montaigne says that he finds
Bodin's example badly chosen because "it is very hard to assign bounds to
the achievements of the faculties of the soul, whereas we have more chance
to assign limits to physical powers and to know them" (VS723; F546). If
Montaigne had had to come up with an example of something incredible
and impossible in Plutarch, he would have chosen an example having to
do with physical powers rather than with powers of the soul. And there are
indeed such examples in Plutarch.

But as for the story of the Spartan boy, Montaigne finds it entirely credible. The story is believable because it fits in with so many other stories about
Spartan endurance (just as the story about Cato is consistent with his character). Montaigne says "I find in his example no great miracle." In fact, he
says, "I am so steeped in the greatness of those people that not only does
Plutarch's story not seem incredible to me, as it does to Bodin, but I do
not find it even rare and strange. Spartan history is full of a thousand more
cruel and uncommon examples: by this standard it is all miracle" (VS723;
F547).

At this point in the essay, Montaigne makes a move that he makes repeatedly throughout the essays, a move that is most significant for understanding
his transformation of skepticism. After saying that the story of the Spartan
boy is entirely credible because it fits with a history that is full of such examples, Montaigne proceeds to recount three stories of amazing endurance
under torture, two from ancient Rome and one from his own day. He begins, in other words, to show that Spartan endurance is not so rare after
all. His non-Spartan examples are of two peasants and one woman: it is not
necessary to look for examples only among the great men.

Montaigne concludes these examples with a story that he says was made up
by someone. This is a story of a woman who, in the face of dire threats of punishment, refused to stop saying that her husband had lice. Finally, when she
was thrown into the water and drowning, she still raised her hands above her
head and made the sign of killing lice. This is an example, he says, of the stubbornness of women that we see every day and of which he has seen hundreds
of examples. What has this to do with Spartan endurance? "Stubbornness is
the sister of constancy, at least in vigor and firmness" (VS725; F548).

Montaigne concludes his defense of Plutarch against Bodin's accusation in this way: "We must not judge what is possible and what is not, according to what is credible and incredible to our sense. . . . It is a great error and yet one into which most men fall . . . to balk at believing about others what they themselves could not do – or would not do. It seems to each man that the ruling pattern of nature is in himself; to this he refers all other forms as to a touchstone. The ways that do not square with his are counterfeit and artificial. What brutish stupidity!" (VS725; F548).

In this connection, it is worth noting that the great modern "mitigated" skeptic, David Hume, makes a similar point. Hume is accounting for the fact that men are so unequal in the degree of understanding they achieve. He provides a long list of reasons, including this: "After we have acquired *a confidence in human testimony*, books and conversation enlarge much more the sphere of one man's experience and thought than those of another."[7] Both Montaigne and Hume recommend "a confidence in human testimony" for the enlargement of experience.

But certainly Montaigne is not suggesting that we should just accept and believe everything we are told. First of all, as he says in his response to Bodin, it is not difficult to judge that certain feats of physical strength are impossible. But, with respect to feats of the soul, consistency of character seems to be a guide in determining what we can accept. So the story of the Spartan boy is completely consistent with what we know about the Spartans. And in the essay "Of cruelty" Montaigne describes Cato's suicide, Cato tearing out his own entrails. He believes that Cato, in that noble act, found bliss and manly exaltation; that he not only endured it without disturbance but "enjoyed himself more in it than in any other action of his life." Were it not for Cato's goodness, which made him prefer the good of his country to his own, Montaigne believes that Cato would not have wanted to be deprived of the opportunity for this noble act occasioned by the ruin of his country. Here Montaigne goes out of his way to reject "the popular and effeminate judgments of some men" who claim that Cato's deed was prompted by some hope of glory. That consideration, he says, is "too base" to touch a heart like Cato's. Cato's action was undertaken for "the beauty of the very thing in itself" (VS425; F309).

Montaigne's judgment of Cato's death is, of course, at odds with the popular and effeminate judgments of some men and even goes further than the judgment that Cato endured his death without disturbance as the rules of Stoic discipline require. Montaigne arrives at this judgment because he does not judge what is possible by what he himself can do. This is the skeptical moment of the movement of thought displayed here. The skeptical act admits the possibility of what is incredible by the standards of the familiar, of one's own. "It seems to each man that the ruling form of nature is in himself, and to this he refers all other forms as a touchstone." Anything that is not like him is incredible and therefore impossible. The world is shrunk to the size of his own soul, whereas confidence in human testimony enlarges the sphere of experience. As Hume says, though, confidence in human testimony must be acquired. This is not simply what we might call "natural credulity." But it is an *education* of natural credulity.

The skeptical act with respect to human testimony is the initial suspension of the judgment that what I am hearing is impossible because it is incredible, and incredible because unfamiliar. It is an act of openness to the possible, to the unfamiliar. In this sense, Montaigne's credulity *is* his skepticism.

If we return now to that "most skeptical" of all the essays, the "Apology for Sebond," and in particular to the animal stories that prompted the editors to try to explain Montaigne's surprising credulity, we can perhaps move this account a step further. How do the animal stories fit into the "Apology"? Why are they there at all? Raymond Sebond was a Spanish theologian of the fifteenth century, whose book entitled *Natural Theology, or Book of Creatures,* was given to Montaigne's father, who asked his son to translate it from the Latin into French. Montaigne did so and later wrote this "Apology" as a response to two criticisms commonly made of this and other such works in natural theology. Montaigne suggests that Sebond's book may be a popularized version of Aquinas.

In the Prologue, Sebond claims that God has revealed himself clearly in two "books"; first, in the Bible, and, second, in nature. Sebond holds that man can know the truth about God and himself, insofar as it is possible for natural reason to know it, by reading these truths in the book of nature. In this book of nature, each creature is like a letter and man himself is the main, the capital letter. The two objections to Sebond that Montaigne addresses in the "Apology" are: first, that "Christians do themselves harm in trying to support their belief by human reasons, since it is conceived only by faith and by a particular inspiration of divine grace" (VS440; F321); second, that Sebond's arguments are weak and unfit to prove what he proposes (VS448; F327). The reason that there has been such debate over whether Montaigne's defense of Sebond is sincere (whether he is really defending him at all) is that Montaigne's response to the second objection is a skeptical attack on the ability of reason to know anything. But an attack on reason's claim to knowledge is as much an attack on Sebond's project as it is an attack on Sebond's critics.

The animal stories occur at the beginning of the long response to the second objection. The general intent of the response is to beat down human presumption. Montaigne begins by taking on man's exalted view of his place in nature, a view that ultimately amounts to the claim that man's reason is divine. (This is close to Sebond's own position: man is the image of God by virtue of his reason.) The animal stories are intended to bring man down to the level of the animals, to a recognition of his equality not with God but with the beasts. Montaigne introduces this long section on the animals with this question: "What sort of faculty of ours do we not recognize in the actions of animals?" (VS454; F332). He then takes us through just about every human capacity one could think of and points to its presence in the animals: reasoning, deduction, induction, calculation, cunning, contemplation, worship, moral virtue, and vice.

What Montaigne is displaying in this entire discussion is a certain mode of reasoning: he is moving from effect to cause, from appearances to an underlying reality, and his reasoning is based upon the principle "like causes produce like effects" or "from like effects we must infer like causes." When the fox goes out on the frozen river, brings his ear very near the ice to hear the water running beneath, then draws back or advances according as he finds the ice too thin or thick enough for his weight, why do we want to deny to him the faculty of reasoning, of ratiocination, and of drawing conclusions: "What makes a noise moves; what moves is not frozen; what is not frozen is liquid; what is liquid gives way under weight" (VS460; F337)? This is the process of reasoning that goes on in ourselves; therefore by the principle "like causes produce like effects" we must infer this faculty in the fox.

Montaigne's own mode of reasoning here is by analogy. And it must be noted that this is the mode of reasoning that Aquinas identifies as the way we are entitled to speak about God. Montaigne is showing that analogy cuts both ways: if we are justified in beginning from ourselves and inferring what God must be, then we must accept the appropriateness of this way of reasoning in the case of our relation to the animals. We are not entitled to engage in reasoning by analogy only when it flatters our pretensions to divine likeness. This willingness to liken ourselves to God is due to our presumption, which Montaigne refers to as "our first and original malady" (VS452; F330).

Our presumption is the first and most persistent obstacle to wisdom. Thus, it is presumption with which the activity of philosophy must first come to terms and where its skeptical moment must occur. The "brutish stupidity" of those who judge what is possible and impossible according to what is credible and incredible to them, who balk at believing about others what they themselves could not do, who take themselves as the touchstone of all forms of nature – this "brutish stupidity" is one of the most significant manifestations of presumption that Montaigne points to in the *Essays*. The stories about Cato, the Spartan boy, and the fox on the frozen river are all of a piece in this regard: they are all encounters with our presumption. The skeptical moment is not immediate disbelief but precisely the refusal simply to dismiss what is not familiar, what is not immediately recognized as being like us. Montaigne's "skepticism," then, is not the doubt of the ancient Skeptics, but rather an openness to what is possible and an overcoming of presumption at the deepest level. Montaigne incorporates the transformed skeptical act into his own mode of thought. How does he incorporate the skeptical moment, and what follows the skeptical moment in the movement of his thought?

If it were not for the fact that we prefer, in some sense, what is foreign and strange, Montaigne would not have spent so much time on this long list of animal stories from ancient sources. He would not need to go collecting stories from foreign lands and centuries, for he says, "in my opinion, whoever would observe up close what we see ordinarily of the animals who live among us, would find there facts just as wonderful as those we go collecting in remote countries and centuries." In the course of the long list of animal stories from Chrysippus, Plutarch, and others, he mentions the astonishing tricks that mountebanks teach their dogs. Then he says, "but I observe with more amazement the behavior, which is nevertheless quite common, of the dogs that blind men use both in the fields and in town; I have noticed how they stop at certain doors where they have been accustomed to receive alms, how they avoid being hit by coaches and carts. . . . I have seen one, along a town ditch, leave a smooth flat path and take a worse one, to keep his master away from the ditch" (VS463; F340). The movement of Montaigne's thought is first to open us to the possibility of the strange and foreign, then to lead us back to the familiar and let us see the extraordinary in the ordinary, in the familiar and the common.[8]

Montaigne's transformed skepticism, then, is fundamentally different from ancient Skepticism. The skeptical moment is incorporated into the more comprehensive dialectic of accidental philosophy. The differences between Montaigne's skepticism and ancient Skepticism will emerge more clearly in the discussion of circular dialectic in Chapter 4.

Deliberate Philosophy

One of the most persistent motifs of the *Essays* is Montaigne's apparent preference for the ancients and their works over the men and works of his own day. He sees in the ancient philosophers "man in his highest estate." These men "have regulated the world with governments and laws; they have instructed it with arts and sciences, and instructed it further by the example of their admirable conduct [*mœurs*]" (VS502; F371). When he turns to books, he finds that he prefers the ancient to the new, "because the ancient ones seem to me fuller and stronger" (VS410; F297). And when he compares himself to the ancients, he concludes that "the productions of these great rich minds of the past are very far beyond the utmost stretch of my imagination and desire. Their writings not only satisfy and fill me, but astound me and transfix me with admiration. I judge their beauty; I see it, if not to the utmost, at least enough so that I cannot aspire to it myself" (VS637; F482–83). His respect and admiration for the ancient authors is such that "they tempt me and move me almost wherever they please. . . . I find each one right in his turn, although they contradict each other" (VS569–70; F429).

The ancients are presented as "higher" and "stronger," as though men had become lower and weaker over the centuries. When Montaigne compares the ancient philosophers with those who call themselves philosophers in his time, the relation of philosophy to action seems most important to him. In the essays "Of pedantry" (I.25) and "On the education of children" (I.26), this distinction is especially clear with respect to the disdain that the vulgar have for the philosopher. The picture that Plato presents in the *Theaetetus*, that of the philosopher who appears to the nonphilosopher as ignorant of "the first and common things" and as presumptuous and insolent, is far from describing the philosophers of Montaigne's day. The ancient philosophers were envied as being above the common fashion, as despising public actions, as "having set up a particular and inimitable way of life regulated by certain lofty and extraordinary principles" (VS135; F98–99). The philosophers of Montaigne's day, on the other hand, are despised as being below the common fashion, incapable of public charges, as living a life of base and vile *mœurs*. The ancient philosophers were even greater in action than they were in knowledge, and if they were ever put to the test of action, they flew to marvelous heights. The ancient philosophers were both disdained and envied. The philosophers of Montaigne's day are simply disdained. Philosophy is "a thing of no use and no value, both in common opinion and in fact" (VS160; F118).

The worthlessness of contemporary philosophy and the contempt in which it is held are explained in this way: "I believe those [scholastic] quibblings... are the cause of this" (VS160; F118). Further, "this century in which we live... is so leaden that not only the practice but even the idea of virtue is wanting; and it seems to be nothing else but a piece of school jargon" (VS230; F169). Virtuous action is no longer even recognized. Montaigne sees it as his task and as part of his public purpose to place before his readers the vivid images of ancient virtue, the high and lofty actions that seem to have been so common in ancient times.

It would be easy to conclude that Montaigne is one of those people who feels so deeply dissatisfied and disgusted with the present that he tries to live in the past and tends to idealize that past, seeing it as a golden age, compared with which his own day looks pitiful and poor. Montaigne, however, sees his preference for the ancients as, in some measure, a manifestation of his own presumption. In "Of presumption" he tells us that there are two parts to the vice of presumption: esteeming oneself too much and esteeming others too little. "As for the first, ... I feel myself oppressed by an error of my soul which I dislike, both as unjust and, even more, as troublesome. I try to correct it, but uproot it I cannot. It is that I lower the value of the things I possess, because I possess them, and raise the value of things when they are foreign, absent, and not mine. This humor spreads very far" (VS633–34; F480). One of its manifestations is that "far-off governments and *mœurs* and languages delight me; and I realize that Latin, by its dignity, beguiles me more than it should, as it does children and common people" (VS634; F480). So at the very least, Montaigne is aware of this tendency in himself. But even more surprising, when we reach the last of the essays after having gone through so many instances of preference for the ancients, we find an explicit denial of this preference. Here Montaigne expresses his distaste for those who give credit only to what they read in books, and who do not believe the truth if it is not of sufficient age. "But I, who do not disbelieve men's mouths any more than their hands, and who know that people write just as injudiciously as they speak, and who *esteem this age just as if it were another that is past,* I quote a friend of mine as readily as Aulus Gellius or Macrobius, and what I have seen as what they have written. And, as they hold that virtue is no greater for being of longer standing, so I consider that truth is no wiser for being older. I often say that it is stupidity that makes us run after foreign and scholarly examples" (VS1081; F828, emphasis added). Montaigne is a man at home in the present, a man whose mind is not tyrannized by the authority of the ancients. Nevertheless, his admiration for the ancients is undeniably sincere, and that admiration centers on what I call the deliberate philosophy of the ancients (in contrast with Montaigne's accidental philosophy).

Montaigne himself does not use the term "deliberate philosophy." I use it as a term of distinction, derived from the passage in the "Apology" where he describes himself as an accidental philosopher in contrast with the ancient philosophers who ruled their lives by reason. "Deliberate philosophy," then, does not refer to the intentions of the philosophers in their writings. It refers first and foremost to the rule of reason in the soul of the philosopher. "Philosophy does not think it has used its resources badly when it has given to reason the sovereign mastery of our soul and the authority to hold our appetites in check" (VS728; F550). Perhaps the most obvious examples of deliberate philosophy in the *Essays* involve the Stoics and Epicureans, but the term applies to the ancient philosophers in general. Deliberate philosophers conform their actions to the precepts of philosophy. Emperor Julian the Apostate "was a very great and rare man, being one whose soul was deeply dyed with the arguments of philosophy, by which he professed to regulate all his actions; and indeed there is no sort of virtue of which he did not leave very notable examples" (VS669; F507). Pyrrho tried, "like all others who were truly philosophers, to make his life correspond to his doctrine" (VS705; F533). Seneca, speaking to his friends and his wife as he is about to cut his veins, asks "Where are those fine precepts of philosophy? What has become of the provisions against the accidents of fortune that we have been laying up for so many years?" The hour has come where he must show, no longer by discourse and disputes, but by acts, the fruit that he had taken from his studies (VS748; F566).

The goal of the deliberate philosopher is the divine *stasis.* This can be seen in the Milesian philosophers' search for the divine source of all that is, the Parmenidean attempt to articulate being as permanence and sameness; the Heraclitean union of the mind with the *logos;* the Platonic ascent to the eternal forms; the Aristotelian ascent to contemplation of the eternal

and unchanging first causes; the Stoic, Epicurean, and Skeptical striving
for divine imperturbability. The philosophers all agree that the sovereign
good is tranquillity of mind and body (VS488; F360). The sign of the true
philosopher is the conformity of his life to his teachings. And one of the
principal signs of this conformity is constancy or unity of life, a condition
achieved by very few: "In all antiquity it is hard to pick out a dozen men who
set their lives to a certain and constant course, which is the principal goal
of wisdom. For, to comprise all wisdom in a word, says an ancient [Seneca],
and to embrace all the rules of life in one, it is 'always to will the same things,
and always to oppose the same things'" (VS332; F240). It is not surprising
that the younger Cato is such a man: "[H]e who has touched one chord of
him has touched all" (VS334; F241).

The rare excellence of the philosopher who always rules his passions and
inclinations by reason is achieved only through a kind of practice. Instruction and belief are, by themselves, insufficient to lead to action. The soul
must be formed by experience to face the evils of life; otherwise, when the
moment for action comes, the soul will be unable to do what it knows it
should do: "That is why, among the philosophers, those who have wanted
to attain some greater excellence have not been content to await the rigors
of Fortune in shelter and repose, for fear she might surprise them inexpe-
rienced and new to the combat; rather they have gone forth to meet her
and have flung themselves deliberately into the test of difficulties" (VS370;
F267). The ancient philosophers anticipate the vicissitudes of fortune, deliberately imposing upon themselves the evils to which all men are subject
(e.g., pain and poverty), and testing themselves to measure how they stand
with respect to the rules of their discipline.

Why, though, is the perfect rule of reason in the soul so extremely rare,
so rare that it is hard to name even a dozen men among the ancients who
actually succeeded? The inability to rule is associated with the fact that the
philosophers can never capture the whole man. Some aspect of him will
always be left out or left over after the system of causes and explanations is
neatly constructed. Even in the account that they give of the human body,
which is closest to them, the philosophers' accounts do not really get at what
is: rather, their accounts stand somehow alongside, outside, what they are
trying to explain. "There is no more retrogradation, trepidation, accession,
recession, reversal, in the stars and heavenly bodies than they have fabricated
in this poor little human body." After telling us how the philosophers have
"forged another body" to grasp the human body, he says: "Not only in reality,
but even in daydreams they cannot so regulate him that there will not be
some cadence or some sound that escapes their architecture" (VS537; F401).

One of the principal limitations on the claims of philosophy to achieve
the sovereign good is manifested in the case of the philosopher subjected
to the force of wine, who shows us that even the "best-regulated soul in the
world has only too much to do to stay on its feet" (VS345; F249); "Look at

Lucretius, that great poet, all the philosophizing and self-discipline cannot prevent him from being driven insane by an aphrodisiac. Is there anybody who believes that an apoplexy will not stun Socrates as well as a porter? Some have been driven by an illness to forget their very name, and a slight wound has overturned the judgment of others. For all his wisdom, the sage is still a man"(VS345; F249). The philosopher tends to forget his humanity, the humanity that he shares with the most lowly and common man. He overlooks and even disdains the lowly and bodily good things of life such as health: "[T]o the strongest and most rigorous arguments that philosophy would impress on us to the contrary, we have only to oppose the picture of Plato being struck with a fit of epilepsy or apoplexy, and on this supposition defy him to call to his aid those noble and rich faculties of his soul" (VS765; F580).

Here we can begin to see Montaigne's persistent "lowering" of philosophy, the persistent deflation of the pretensions of philosophy to be "higher," and in particular, its pretensions to be more than human. It seems that reason, of itself and by virtue of what it is, cannot help but regard itself as highest and therefore as entitled to rule.[9] It is on account of reason that we hold ourselves to be "masters and emperors" (VS55; F37) of all other creatures and call ourselves "master and ruler of the universe" (VS450; F329). The sciences that can claim the highest place, philosophy and theology, are the sciences that "regulate men's morals [*mœurs*]" (VS198; F147), and the role of ruling the beliefs that men hold in common belongs to "the theologians and philosophers, directors of consciences" (VS942; F720).

But in the "Apology for Sebond" we are told that "there is no philosophical wisdom of such great firmness" that would allow the philosopher to walk across a plank laid between the two towers of Notre Dame just as if he were walking on the ground. And, if a philosopher were placed in an iron cage suspended from the top of one of those towers, "he will see by evident reason that it is impossible for him to fall, and yet . . . he cannot keep the sight of this extreme height from terrifying and paralyzing him" (VS594; F449). In "Of vanity" Montaigne points to a lack of conformity between philosophical rules and practice: "In all the barracks of ancient philosophy you will find this, that the same workman publishes rules of temperance, and publishes at the same time amorous and licentious writings" (VS989; F757). Here he is addressing the question: "What is the use of these lofty points of philosophy on which no human being can settle, and these rules that exceed our use and our strength?" (VS989; F756).

Not only is the philosopher subject to all the accidents that threaten every man, but also there are accidents that he cannot withstand. Even Socrates and Cato are not exempt: the philosopher's faculties are stunned and overthrown by the mere bite of a sick dog, and his soul has "no such great stability or reason, no capacity, no virtue, no philosophical resolution, no tension of its powers, that could exempt it from subjection to these accidents.

The saliva of a wretched mastiff could shake all his wisdom and all his great and well-regulated ideas, and annihilate them in such a way that no trace would remain of his former knowledge." The soul of the philosopher can resist this venom no better than a child can, "venom capable of making all philosophy, if it were incarnate, raving mad, so that Cato, who twisted the neck of death itself and of fortune, could not have endured the sight of a mirror or of water, would have been crushed with terror or fright, if he had come down by the contagion of a mad dog, with the disease that the doctors call hydrophobia" (VS550; F412). What has happened to the sovereign good in all of this, the sovereign good kept always before the philosopher's mind, giving unity to his actions and his life? What has happened is that "this soul loses the taste for the sovereign good of the Stoics, so constant and so firm" (VS551; F413).

At this point, reason must surrender its arms. Philosophy can prepare the soul for the accidents of life, even for death, but its means can serve only a soul capable of discourse and deliberation, not a soul that has become mad, troubled, and lost. The subject of madness is one of the few places in the *Essays* where Montaigne lets us hear so explicitly and directly his own philosophical voice: "The philosophers, it seems to me, have hardly touched this chord" (VS551; F413). Unlike the deliberate philosophers, who cling to rationality as the defining characteristic of man, Montaigne insists on including every aspect of human life, even the extremes of madness, in his account of human being.[10] When Montaigne retires from public life, he expects that when his mind is alone with itself he will find the rest and tranquillity of deliberate philosophy. To his surprise and shame, his mind gives birth only to "chimeras and fantastic monsters" (VS33; F21).

There are two forms of madness, a bestial madness and a divine madness, the madness due to the bite of the mad dog and the madness through which we enter the cabinet of the gods. Montaigne discusses both in terms of the limitations on the philosopher's claim to the sovereign good: "Is there not some rashness in philosophy to consider that men produce their greatest deeds and those most closely approaching divinity when they are out of their minds and frenzied and mad? ... The two natural ways to enter the cabinet of the gods and there foresee the course of destinies are madness and sleep.... I never was more willing to believe philosophy. It is a pure transport that the sacred truth inspired in the philosophical spirit, which wrests from it, against its intention, the admission that the tranquil state of our soul, the sedate state, the healthiest state that philosophy can acquire for her, is not her best state" (VS568; F427). Even in those rare cases where the soul has attained complete mastery of itself, the cases of Cato and of Socrates, we do not see the best state of the soul, by philosophy's own reluctant admission.

Montaigne ridicules the philosophers' pretentions to divinity using the same argument as he does concerning philosophy's failures to achieve the sovereign good. Cicero's praise of the occupation of letters – the occupation through which we have discovered the infinity of things, the immense grandeur of nature, the heavens and lands and seas, which has taught us religion, moderation, courage, which has taken our souls out of darkness and shown us all things high and low, first and last – makes it seem that the philosopher is a god, all-living and all-powerful. But in reality, "a thousand little women in their villages have lived a more equable, sweeter, and more consistent life than his" (VS489; F360). Lucretius speaks of Epicurus as a god and of his wisdom as divine; Chrysippus judges that Dion was as virtuous as a god; Seneca recognizes that God has given him life and that he has courage like God's, but because his courage is in spite of human weakness, he is superior to God. Aristotle confers on us the title "mortal gods." These are magnificent words, but a slight accident can put the understanding of the philosopher in a worse state than that of the least shepherd (VS489; F360). As I noted earlier, Montaigne's long discussion of the animals in the "Apology" is intended as an attack on philosophical presumption. It is also possible to see the entire reply to the second objection as an attack on philosophical pretensions to the divinity of the intellect. "To make gods of ourselves, like antiquity, passes the utmost bounds of feeble-mindedness. . . . but to have made gods of our condition, the imperfection of which we should know . . . this must have come from a marvelous intoxication of the human intelligence" (VS516; F383). So Montaigne concludes the "Apology" with the assertion that it is not Stoic virtue but Christian faith that can aspire to the divine.

Some of the most vivid and delightful passages of the *Essays* are those in which Montaigne reminds the philosopher of his body: "I love to see these leading souls unable to shake off our common lot. Perfect men as they are, still they are men, and most heavily so" (VS835; F634). In "On some verses of Virgil" he writes: "The most contemplative and wisest of men, when I imagine him in that position [of making love] seems to me an impostor to put on wise and contemplative airs; here are the peacock's feet that humble his pride: 'Against truth said in laughing / Is there a law?'" [Horace] (VS877; F669). In "Of experience" he ridicules those who despise the pleasures of the body: "Won't they try to square the circle while perched on their wives!" (VS1107; F850). And he does not hesitate to use vulgar terms for bodily parts and functions: "Kings and philosophers shit, and so do ladies" (VS1085; F831). We are brought down, then, from the heights of the divine and impassible intellect of deliberate philosophy to the merely accidental philosophy of the *Essays*, essays that he describes as the "excrements of an aged mind" (VS946; F721).

At two places in the *Essays* Montaigne contrasts himself with the ancients in a striking way. In "That the taste of good and evil depends in large part on the opinion we have of them," he writes: "Plato fears our hard bondage to pain and pleasure, since it obligates and attaches the soul too much to the

body; I, on the contrary, because it detaches and unbinds it" (VS58; F39).
And in the "Apology" he qualifies his praise of Epicurean apathy in this way:
"Crantor was quite right to combat the apathy of Epicurus, if it was built so
deep that even the approach and birth of evils were lacking. I have no praise
for the insensibility that is neither possible nor desirable. I am glad not to
be sick; but if I am, I want to know I am; and if they cauterize or incise me, I
want to feel it. In truth, he who would eradicate the knowledge of evil would
at the same time extirpate the knowledge of pleasure, and in fine would
annihilate man" (VS493; F364).

Ancient philosophy's preference for the soul over the body and its identification of what is highest in man with the divine lead to a desire to annihilate, in some sense, the human in favor of the divine in him. When Aristotle
speaks of the life of contemplation, he says that it is "more than human," and
that "a man who would live it would do so not insofar as he is human but because there is a divine element within him. This divine element is . . . above
our composite nature" (*Ethics* 1177b25–30). Montaigne is relentless, vivid,
and bold in his attack on this attempt to rise above the human. In "On some
verses of Virgil" he says: "Each one of my parts makes me myself just as much
as every other one. And no other makes me more properly a man than this
one [his penis]. I owe a complete portrait of myself to the public. The wisdom of my lesson is wholly in truth, in freedom, in reality" (VS887; F677).
Against Aristotle's claim that the divine element of the intellect, which is
highest, is "each man's true self" (*Ethics* 1178a), Montaigne puts the lowly,
common, shameful, unmentionable penis.[11]

Near the very end of the *Essays*, Montaigne discusses those who want to
dissociate the soul from the body even during those few hours of the day
when the needs of the body have to be satisfied by food and drink: "They
want to get outside of themselves and escape from the man. That is madness:
instead of changing into angels, they change into beasts; instead of raising
themselves, they lower themselves. These transcendental humors frighten
me" (VS1115; F856). He seems to be referring to both excessive philosophical and Christian asceticism. To try to be an angel is a metaphysical failure,
a failure of being and of self-knowledge, not simply a practical mistake or
even moral error.

One of the few Christian beliefs that Montaigne mentions explicitly is
the belief in the resurrection of the body. He does this just with respect
to the question of the association of soul and body: "Christians are par-
ticularly instructed about this bond; for they know that divine justice embraces this association and union of body and soul, even to making the body
capable of eternal rewards, and that God watches the whole man in action
and wills that he receive, in his entirety, punishment or reward, according
to his merits" (VS639; F485). The difference between ancient philosophy
and Christian faith, as manifested in the difference between the philosophical argument for the immortality of the soul (based on the divinity

of the intellect) and the Christian belief in the resurrection of the body, requires a fundamental reconsideration of what the activity of philosophy can be.[12]

What Is Accidental Philosophy?

At this point a preliminary account of accidental philosophy is possible. First, we must see the context in which this description of Montaigne emerges. In the course of his response to the second objection against Sebond, Montaigne sets out his collection of the "asininities" of ancient philosophy, the absurd and witless claims that philosophers have made, especially concerning the human soul. His point here is to demonstrate the ignorance and imbecility of human reason, and to illustrate this point, he makes an analogy: he had once advised a man who was worried about how he could get by in Italy because he did not speak Italian. Montaigne advised him to "simply use the first words that came to his mouth," whether French, Spanish, Latin, or Gascon, and then to add the Italian ending. That way, he would never fail to hit upon some Italian dialect. It is here that he turns to himself: "I say the same thing about philosophy; it has so many faces and so much variety, and has said so much, that all our dreams or reveries are found in it. Human fancy cannot conceive anything good or evil that is not in it. *Nothing so absurd can be said that it has not been said by some philosopher* [Cicero]. And I let fly my caprices all the more freely in public, inasmuch as, although they are born with me and without a model, I know that they will find their relation to some ancient notion; and someone will not fail to say: 'That is where he got it!' My *mœurs* are natural; I have not called in the help of any teaching to build them. But feeble as they are, when the desire to tell them seized me, and when, to make them appear in public a little more decently, I set myself to support them with reasons and examples, it was a marvel to myself to find them, simply by chance, in conformity with so many philosophical examples and reasons. What rule my life belonged to, I did not learn until after it was completed and spent. A new figure: an unpremeditated and accidental philosopher!" (VS546; F408–9).

The context suggests that accidental philosophy is to be contrasted with deliberate philosophy and, in particular, with deliberate philosophy understood as the rule of reason. Montaigne's caprices and his *mœurs* are not derived from any philosophical teaching or deliberately conformed to any philosophical rule. He describes his thoughts as born with him and without a model; he describes his *mœurs* as natural. He had not called in the help of any teaching to build them. What surprises him is their conformity to philosophical teachings, especially because they are so "weak." That conformity is accidental and his surprise is a sign that the conformity is not deliberate. He has achieved by accident what the deliberate philosophers have achieved by reason.

Accidental philosophy, then, is nonauthoritative. Deliberate philosophy teaches and rules: it conforms thought and action to a rational principle. Accidental philosophy does not teach or form; it discovers and tells. We might describe accidental philosophy as the activity of the mind that discovers the truth that was already there: he sees his thoughts and *mœurs* in a new light. Whereas deliberate philosophy forms and molds thought and action so as to make them rational, accidental philosophy simply sees the truth that was there all along, before philosophy came on the scene. Accidental philosophy leaves everything just as it is. This aspect of accidental philosophy is captured in Adorno's description of the essay form as a kind of phenomenology.[13]

Montaigne marvels to see that his thoughts and *mœurs* are conformed to "so many" philosophical discourses and examples. No single philosophical system can capture his being or the meaning of what he is. This implies that truth is too great to be captured in any system and that, therefore, any philosophical system must be partial.[14] Accidental philosophy, because it leaves everything as it is, resists the pull toward system building and thus remains open to the whole. Here, too, Adorno's discussion of the essay form is pertinent: the essay is "not exhaustive" because, unlike the Cartesian "general survey," the essay does not presume to determine "in advance that the object in question can be fully grasped by the concepts which treat it; that nothing is left over that could not be anticipated by these concepts."[15]

Accidental philosophy also implies that truth is prephilosophical and prereflective.[16] Accidental philosophy brings out this truth, which is everywhere and common. It does not arrive at some "new" truth that could not exist without it. This mode of philosophy, then, appears as merely accidental – that is, in contrast with deliberate philosophy, it seems weak and lowly. Montaigne's thoughts are mere caprices, and his *mœurs* are weak: his conformity to reason's rule is merely accidental. Accidental philosophy is a "lowered" form of philosophy, but "lower" is, of course, ironic, because accidental philosophy is what philosophy truly is.[17]

In sum, then, accidental philosophy is, first, a mode of thought that discovers the truth that was already there in prephilosophical, nonphilosophical life. It does not rule. Thus it is nonauthoritative and, consequently, it leaves everything just as it is, escapes the partiality of deliberate philosophy, and remains open to the whole of all that is. Second, accidental philosophy is circular dialectic. We have seen one manifestation of this in the discussion of Montaigne's transformation of skepticism – that is, in his openness to the possible, the rare and the extraordinary, and his return to the common and familiar. Thought comes back to its starting point but only after having gone through a movement of departure and return, in this case, a dialectic of skepticism and credulity.

In "Of vain subtleties" the dialectical aspect of this circular movement is brought out more clearly. Here Montaigne gives us at least three versions of the dialectic. First, he refers to "an abecedarian ignorance that comes before knowledge" and "a learned ignorance that comes after knowledge," that is, "an ignorance that knowledge creates and engenders, just as it undoes and destroys the first." Second, he describes those good Christians who are reverent and obedient through simplicity, and those good Christians who believe and obey because their strong minds have led them, through long investigation, to a deeper understanding of faith. But in the middle, between these two kinds of believers, is a third group comprising two types of men: those who "stick to the old ways" and those who regard sticking to the old ways as a sign of simplicity and stupidity. The dialectical dimension of this version is seen in the fact that those in the middle who stick to the old ways have, in fact and to our surprise, reached "the extreme limit of Christian intelligence."

The third version of the dialectic is the one in which he mentions himself explicitly: "The simple peasants are good men, and good men the philosophers, at least what passes for philosophers in our time: strong and clear natures, enriched by a broad education in useful knowledge. The half-breeds who have disdained the first seat, ignorance of letters, and have not been able to reach the other – their rear-end between two stools, like me and so many others – are dangerous, inept, and importunate: these men trouble the world. Therefore, for my part, I draw back as much as I can into the first and natural stage, which for naught I attempted to leave" (VS313; F227).

The dialectical aspect of the circular movement of thought is seen especially in the way he describes the kind of struggle and failure that is involved in the ascent to knowledge. Thought comes back to its starting point after having gone through a dialectic of trial and failure. It is surprised to find that when it fails, it actually sees the truth it was seeking all along, without knowing that that was what it was seeking, that is, the truth that was always there. This surprise shows the accidental quality of the dialectic and is the same surprise that Montaigne experiences when he sees the conformity of his *mœurs* to so many philosophical discourses.

Circular dialectic also allows us to make sense of the fact that Montaigne seems to be so often contradicting himself and why he appears to be in agreement with so many different philosophical positions. He shows us that he is very much aware of his contradictions but at the same time he assures us that "I may indeed contradict myself now and then; but truth . . . I do not contradict" (VS805; F611). Truth is "large" enough to contain all contradiction. Or, to put it differently, truth is everywhere, all contradictions contain some truth, and his contradictions are resolved in the circular dialectic.[18] Adorno compares the essay form with the Hegelian dialectic. For Adorno, "the essay is more dialectical than the [Hegelian] dialectic as it articulates itself. The essay takes Hegelian logic at its word: neither may the truth of the totality be played off immediately against individual judgments, nor may truth be reduced to individual judgments; rather, the claim of the particular to truth is taken literally to the point where there is evidence of its untruth.... [T]he untruth in which the essay knowingly entangles itself is the element of its truth."[19]

The way in which this happens leads to the third description of accidental philosophy. The circular dialectic reveals the truth by getting beyond what Montaigne calls "the appearance of the first sense." He uses this expression in "Of vain subtleties" in connection with the middle group of men between the simple unlearned believers and the strong-minded educated believers. As I noted earlier, two kinds of men are within this middle group: those who stick to the old ways and those who regard sticking to the old ways as evidence of stupidity. Montaigne says that the latter are in a condition of "error" because they do not get beyond "the appearance of the first sense" (in Frame's translation, they "stop at the first plausible meaning"). In other words, they are wrong to regard sticking to the old ways as evidence of stupidity. Montaigne includes himself among those in the middle who stick to the old ways: "those of us who stick to the old ways."

Accidental philosophy is the mode of thought that gets beyond the appearance of the first sense to a "second sense" by way of the circular dialectic. Circular dialectic reveals the true meaning of things. What is *accidental* about this aspect of the dialectic? It cannot be known in advance what that second sense is. Hence the essay form is genuinely a process of discovery. Perhaps the most important instance of this uncovering of the "second sense" occurs in the "Apology," in what I call the dialectic of faith and reason. In his reply to the first objection against Sebond, Montaigne says that most Christians do not really understand "what it means to believe." The dialectic of the "Apology" moves him from the appearance of the first sense of faith (the sense expressed in the first objection to Sebond) through the "ascent" to autonomous reason and, finally, to the second (true) sense of "what it means to believe."

The struggle with error that is implicit in the dialectic reveals what I take to be the most fundamental meaning of the title that Montaigne gave to his work. An *essai* is a trial, a putting to the test. In religious terms, to be essayed is to be tempted, and Montaigne's essays are his temptations, his way of living with the inescapable human condition of temptation, especially the temptations of the intellect.[20] The ancient authors "tempt" him and move him almost wherever they please. The first or original sin is philosophy: Adam and Eve want to be as gods, knowing good and evil. Accidental philosophy is the mode of thought that struggles with and resists the philosophical desire for the divinity of the mind.

In "Of vanity" Montaigne writes, "I am no philosopher. Evils crush me according to their weight" (VS950; F725). This comment calls to mind what he says in "Of vain subtleties" concerning the stupid who bear evils well because they do not see them for what they are, and the wise who bear them well because they "rule and command" the evil. The philosophers weigh and measure the evil and rise above it by the strength of their courage. Men of "the ordinary and middle condition" see and feel the evils but are not able to bear them (VS312; F226). The deliberate philosophers seek out the struggle with evil, practice overcoming it, anticipate the evils that fortune may send, build up their strength for future struggles with the unknown. Montaigne's way is more like escape. In "Of husbanding your will" he makes this contrast: "I know that some wise men have taken another way, and have not feared to grapple, and engage themselves to the quick, with many subjects. Those men are sure of their strength, under which they take cover in all kinds of adverse events, making their power of endurance wrestle with the misfortunes. . . . Let us not tackle these examples; we would not come up to them. These men obstinately determine to see resolutely and without perturbation the ruin of their country, which possessed and commanded their will. For our common souls there is too much effort and harshness in that. Cato therefore abandoned the noblest life that ever was. We little men must flee the storm from further away; we must try to avoid feeling it, not try to endure it, and dodge the blows we cannot parry" (VS1015; F777). Here Montaigne explicitly ties his own weak and lowly way to his Christian faith: "And the Holy Ghost in like manner: *Lead us not into temptation.* We do not pray that our reason may not be combated and overcome by concupiscence, but that it may not even be tested by it, that we may not be brought into a state where we even have to suffer the approaches, solicitations, and temptations of sin; and we supplicate our Lord to keep our conscience tranquil, fully and perfectly delivered from dealing with evil" (VS1016; F777). In this way we can also understand the "lowering" of philosophy that Montaigne brings about: accidental philosophy is completely and radically human.

The philosopher who expresses most explicitly what Montaigne means by accidental philosophy is Michael Oakeshott. Oakeshott's account of the essay form and his account of the meaning of philosophy are identical. The essay is the form taken by philosophical reflection that sees itself as "the adventure of one who seeks to understand in other terms what he already understands and in which the understanding sought . . . is a disclosure of the conditions of the understanding enjoyed and not a substitute for it."[21] He elaborates on what he means by philosophical reflection: "All reflection begins with something assumed to be known, but in reflection what is assumed to be known is assumed also not to be known. We begin with knowledge which is nevertheless assumed to be ignorance. . . . The root from which all reflection springs is the paradox which . . . is not to be resolved by describing our situation as one of knowing but of not knowing *enough* and of wanting to know *more.*" Here I take Oakeshott to be acknowledging what I described as the beginning of accidental philosophy in the truth that is found in prephilosophical opinion. This is the beginning of dialectic: "[R]eflection presupposes doubt but not universal doubt. . . . The process in reflection is dialectical, a process of considering something recognized as knowledge and supposed to be true, yet considering it with the assumption that it is not true – an assumption that we sometimes improperly interpret as 'not wholly true' or 'not the whole truth.' "[22] Dialectic arrives at the truth that was already there. The essay is the perfect form of this circular dialectic.

The beginning of accidental philosophy in opinion suggests a kind of prereflective identity or harmony between being and thought such that truth is found in opinion, in "the first words" that come to the mouth. But what is this harmony and what is its ontological basis? *Accidental* philosophy implies that there is nothing about the structure of the whole that makes philosophy a necessary activity.[23] Deliberate philosophy assumes a divine ruling, ordering principle within the whole, at the "top," with which the mind of the philosopher strives to be in harmony. Accidental philosophy implies a radically contingent (i.e., created) world.

The radical contingency of being is the condition for the *telos* of accidental philosophy. The *telos* of deliberate philosophy is the divine *stasis*. Deliberate philosophy begins in wonder and ends in some form of divine impassibility, whether contemplation of the eternal or the *ataraxia* of skepticism. Accidental philosophy *ends* in wonder, not at the rare and extraordinary but at the most familiar: what is did not have to be at all. It is, then, what Adorno calls "the claim of the particular to truth" that accidental philosophy takes as its beginning and its end. The particular is the accidental: there is nothing necessary about the particular. The particular is the most familiar, which deliberate philosophy wants to leave behind in its ascent to the first cause. The particular is the embodied, which deliberate philosophy must escape in its ascent to the divine.

Thus, Montaigne's "self" is not present in the *Essays* as "substance" or as modern "subjectivity." It is present just as the most familiar. That is why the circular dialectic comes back to himself and why, in the end, he wonders most at himself: "I have seen no more evident monstrosity and miracle in the world than myself. We become accustomed to anything strange by custom and time; but the more I frequent myself and know myself, the more my deformity astonishes me, and the less I understand myself" (VS1029; F787). Accidental philosophy is the dialectic of self-knowledge.

2

Bending and Stretching the Categories
of Traditional Metaphysics

Latin was the language that Montaigne learned first, and when he dab-
bled for a time in composing verse, he did so in Latin. But his Latin
verse was always imitative, revealing the poet he had just been reading.
The *Essays* are written in French, his second language, and some of the
earliest essays "smell a bit foreign" (VS875; F667), suggesting perhaps the
beginning stages of breaking free from imitation.

French is "a weaker idiom," abundant in images but tending to give way
under a powerful conception (VS440; F320). So it is for able minds to give
value to a language, "not so much by innovating as by filling it out with
more vigorous and varied services, by stretching it and bending it. They do
not bring to it new words, but they enrich their own, give more weight and
depth to their meaning and use; they teach the language unaccustomed
movements, but prudently and shrewdly" (VS873; F665). He contrasts the
many French writers of his day with the great Latin poets: these French
writers care for nothing but novelty. "To seize a new word they abandon the
ordinary one, which is often stronger and more sinewy." Virgil, on the other
hand, "has the object more vividly imprinted in the soul," and Horace "sees
more clearly and deeply into the thing." His mind "unlocks and ransacks
the whole storehouse of words and figures in order to express itself. . . .
The sense illuminates and brings out the words, which are no longer wind,
but flesh and bone. The words mean more than they say" (VS873; F665).
The *Essays* present us with a particular, an accidental being. The words
to communicate this being are ordinary words, the ordinary words of the
streets and markets and taverns of Paris. Montaigne does not invent new
words. And he avoids almost entirely the jargon of scholastic learning. He
does use some of the terms of ancient philosophy, but he gives "more weight
and depth to their meaning and use." In his hands, the words are "no longer
wind, but flesh and bone."

In this chapter I consider Montaigne's treatment of some of the most important categories of "traditional" metaphysics. I use the term "traditional"

here, not because I think that Montaigne invents some new metaphysical system to rival or replace the traditional one, but because Montaigne is very self-consciously speaking out of an authoritative body of knowledge and using its immediately recognizable terms. The traditional metaphysical categories that I consider here are being and becoming, nature, causality, and the universal and the particular.

Montaigne takes up each of these categories and transforms it. The transformation that he effects is not a matter of inventing a new meaning for these terms so as to fit them into some new metaphysical system. Rather, he "lowers" these terms, bringing them back down from their metaphysical heights and closer to their prephilosophical meanings.

Being and Becoming

The *Essays* are principally and fundamentally concerned with the question of being. But if that is true, then it is all the more surprising that Montaigne says extremely little about being and becoming, the most fundamental metaphysical categories, in any explicit way. The first and perhaps only passage that comes immediately to mind occurs at the very end of the "Apology." The larger context is the entire reply to the second objection to Sebond's project, in which Montaigne seems to be concerned chiefly with undermining reason's pretensions to knowledge. The passage begins: "We have no communication with being, because every human being is always midway between birth and death"(VS601; F455). The discussion goes on for several pages, mostly elaborating on the distinction between being, which is permanent and unchanging, and becoming, which is temporal and changing: "What suffers change does not remain one and the same, and if it is not one and the same, it also *is* not.... But what then really *is*? That which is eternal.... [Therefore], God alone *is*...in an eternity immutable and immobile" (VS603; F456–57).

The passage is almost entirely a very close paraphrase of Plutarch, but Montaigne does not mention this borrowing until the end so that the reader could easily assume that this long speech is that of Montaigne himself. There is a rhetorical context that must be taken into account. Toward the end of the "Apology," Montaigne suddenly lets it be seen that he is especially addressing a princess (presumably Margaret of Valois), who must defend the old religion against the Reformers. He urges her not to abandon the accustomed modes of argument. Much of what follows this direct address to the princess is scholastic in tone, even though this section is strongly skeptical. My point is that it is difficult to know what to make of this long, explicitly metaphysical passage, which is unique in the *Essays*, unique not only because it dwells on the question of being and becoming, but also because it carries over into speculative theology.[1]

There are very few explicit statements about being and becoming besides this passage from the "Apology." In "Our feelings reach out beyond us" Montaigne is discussing Aristotle's reference to the saying of Solon that no one can be called happy before he dies. Montaigne responds that, "while we move about, we transport ourselves by anticipation wherever we please; but once out of being, we have no communication with what is [*ce qui est*]" (VS17; F10). The last clause, "we have no communication with what is," is very similar to the beginning of the passage from Plutarch. But in "Our feelings reach out beyond us" being (*l'être*) is associated with movement, with life: there is here no effort to link movement to nonbeing. And in "Of repentance" Montaigne writes: "I do not portray being; I portray passing [*le passage*], or, as the people say, not from seven years to seven years, but from day to day, from minute to minute" (VS805; F611). The third passage is found in "Of the affection of fathers for their children" and is also occasioned by something he has read in Aristotle: "[B]eing consists in movement and action" (VS386; F279). We seem to have traveled from the Parmenidian unchanging and immobile Same to the Heraclitean relentless flux. But there is not necessarily a contradiction in this. Becoming must in some sense be, and this is *our* being. "I cannot keep my subject still. It goes along befuddled and staggering, with a natural drunkenness. I take it in this condition, just as it is at the moment I give my attention to it" (VS805; F610–11).

The fourth passage occurs in "Of the art of conversing." For Montaigne, discussion is the "most fruitful and natural exercise of the mind..., and sweeter than any other action of our life" (VS926; F704). The contrast that is suggested here is perhaps the action of solitary contemplation. Montaigne refers to conversation as "setting out in quest of that which is [*ce qui est*]" and adds, "we do no wrong to the subject when we leave it in order to see about the way to treat it. I do not mean a scholastic and artificial way; I mean a natural way, that of a sound understanding" (VS926; F706).

If he were forced to choose, Montaigne would rather lose his sight than his hearing or speech (VS922; F704). Being reveals itself in speech, in "ordinary" speech, not in the jargon of the schools. We can go in search of "that which is" in conversation with the unlearned, or with those unspoiled by learning. It seems to me that this is one reason why there is no explicit discussion of the metaphysical categories of being and becoming: being, which is most common, has become, in the minds of the learned, an abstract metaphysical notion at the farthest remove from what is common. In the *Essays*, being is revealed as the accidental particular, Michel de Montaigne, in flesh and bone.[2] Being is revealed as what is nearest and most familiar.

Nature

If being and becoming are almost never mentioned explicitly, the opposite must be said of the second metaphysical category, nature, for nature is at least mentioned on almost every page of the *Essays*. And Montaigne is clearly among those philosophers who tell us that man ought to live "according to nature." But what does that mean? "Live according to nature" is an empty rule until one specifies what nature is.

I argue that nature, for Montaigne, is a prephilosophical condition, a condition of freedom from philosophy. In the hands of the deliberate philosophers, nature is a ruler against which our present condition is found wanting. Montaigne lowers the meaning of nature and takes the measuring rod away from deliberate philosophy by blurring the distinction between nature and custom.

We can begin to consider just what nature is for Montaigne by examining his treatment of a way of talking about nature that was familiar in his day, namely, the notion of natural law. One very obvious difficulty here is that Montaigne contradicts himself, or at least appears to do so. In some places he agrees that there are natural laws, and in other places he denies this. The term "natural law" in this context refers not to the laws of physics but to laws that should guide human conduct. The notion of natural law found in Aquinas is a good example of the understanding of natural law that would have been familiar to Montaigne's contemporaries.

In "On the punishment of cowardice" Montaigne writes: "In truth it is right to make a great distinction between the faults that come from our weakness and those that come from our malice." The latter involve our knowingly violating "the rules of reason that nature has imprinted in us," whereas with respect to the former, "we can call on this same nature as our warrantor, for having left us in such imperfection and weakness" (VS70; F48). It is not clear to me whether Montaigne is asserting this as his own view or whether he is simply presenting a view that is reasonable for consideration, as he often does. But in either case, he is pointing to what may be a tension within the Thomistic teaching on natural law. For Aquinas, there is an order of the natural inclinations from the lowest, which we share with all things, to the highest, which are uniquely human. The inclination to self-preservation would be an example of the first, and the inclination to live in society and to know God would be examples of the second. One can see immediately the possibility of conflict here: living in society can ultimately entail my fighting in a war and losing my life, and in that case the inclination to self-preservation must be put aside or overcome. The inclinations that are uniquely human are inseparable from reason, man's rational nature. Montaigne refers to "the rules of reason, that nature has imprinted in us."

The tension is spelled out more fully in "Of the affection of fathers for their children." Here he presents what I take to be the Thomistic response to the difficulty implied in this tension – the difficulty that nature would thus be in contradiction with itself, placing in man two contradictory inclinations. Montaigne is discussing the natural affection that fathers have for their children: "If there is any truly natural law, that is to say, any instinct that is seen universally and permanently imprinted in both the animals and ourselves (which is not beyond dispute), I may say that in my opinion, after the care every animal has for its own preservation and the avoidance of what is harmful, the affection that the begetter has for his begotten ranks second." Here natural law is defined as "instinct," and instinct might be characterized as prereflective, not chosen or deliberate.

Soon after this identification of natural law with instinct, Montaigne presents the familiar Thomistic introduction of reason into the complete picture of natural law: "Since it has pleased God to give us some capacity for reason, so that we should not be, like the animals, slavishly subjected to the common laws, but should apply ourselves to them by judgment and voluntary liberty, we must indeed yield a little to the simple authority of Nature, but not let ourselves be carried away tyrannically by her: reason alone must guide our inclinations" (VS387; F279).

He then goes on to criticize the kind of thoughtless following of instinct in which we are simply moved by the monkey tricks, games, and puerile frivolities of our children as if we loved them for our amusement, as if they were little monkeys. "A true and well-regulated affection should be born and increase with the knowledge children give us of themselves; and then, if they are worthy of it, the natural propensity going along with reason, we should cherish them with a truly paternal love; and we should likewise pass judgment on them if they are otherwise, always submitting to reason, notwithstanding the force of nature" (VS387; F280). This is to treat them as men, not as playthings. It is dangerous to allow mothers to judge, for example, which child should inherit because women do not have sufficient strength of reason to choose according to worth: "They most readily let themselves be carried away where the impressions of nature stand most alone; like the animals." Thus they tend to give themselves more to the weak and defective (VS399; F290). The emphasis in this discussion is on the rule of reason.

After having gone through this long and detailed defense of the subordination of instinct to reason, Montaigne introduces the factor of custom or habit: "Moreover, it is easy to see by experience that this natural affection, to which we give so much authority, has very weak roots." He cites the example of the wet nurse, who, for a small profit, gives over her own child to be fed by a goat. "And we see in most of them a bastard affection soon engendered by habit, more vehement than the natural" (VS399; F290). The goats, in turn, develop a stronger attachment to the wet-nurse's children than to their own. "Animals alter and corrupt their natural affection as easily as we" (VS399; F291). The lowering of the philosophical meaning of "nature" is accomplished in the dialectic of nature and custom.

In "Of experience" he is discussing the futile multiplication of civil laws in an effort to cover all possible cases. "This number bears no proportion to the infinite diversity of human actions. Multiplication of our imaginary cases will never equal the variety of the real examples. . . . there is little relation between our actions, which are in perpetual mutation, and fixed and immutable laws. . . . Nature always gives us happier laws than those we give ourselves. Witness the picture of the Golden Age of the poets, and the state in which we see nations live which have no other laws" (VS1066; F816).

The link between natural law and the New World is made explicitly several times in the *Essays*. The most sustained discussion is found, not surprisingly, in "Of cannibals." Montaigne is considering the presumption that leads to the judgment that the Old World is superior to the New World, that the new world is barbarous: "These nations, then, seem to me barbarous in this sense, that they have been fashioned very little by the human mind, and are still very close to their original naturalness. The laws of nature still rule them, very little corrupted by ours." The purity of natural law that we see in these nations surpasses not only all the portraits of the golden age of the poets but even "the conception and the very desire of philosophy." Plato would find his imagined republic to be far from this newly discovered perfection. The philosophers could not have imagined or believed, for example, that "our society could be maintained with so little artifice and human solder." There is here "no knowledge of letters, no science of numbers, no name for a magistrate or for political superiority" (VS206; F153). This is only part of a long list of differences between the Old World and the New World and even between the philosopher's imaginings and the newly discovered real world.

Montaigne specifies what the natural laws manifested in the inhabitants of the New World are in this way: "Their whole ethical science contains only these two articles: resoluteness in war and affection for their wives" (VS208; F154), a formulation clearly reminiscent of Plato's formula for the education of soldiers in the *Republic*: they must be gentle to their own and ferocious to the enemy. "Their warfare," unlike wars of conquest for exploitation and expropriation, "is wholly noble and generous, and as excusable and beautiful as this human disease can be; its only basis among them is their rivalry in valor" (VS210; F156).

As I noted earlier, Montaigne is attacking the presumption of those who would say that these barbarians are inferior to themselves: "So we may well call these people barbarians, in respect to the rules of reason, but not in respect to ourselves, who surpass them in every kind of barbarity." Even in judging the practice of cannibalism, Montaigne admonishes us to look at ourselves: "I am not sorry that we notice the barbarous horror of such acts, but I am heartily sorry that, judging their faults rightly, we should be so blind to our own. I think there is more barbarity in eating a man alive than in eating him dead . . . and what is worse, on the pretext of piety and religion" (VS209; F155).

The general impression created by Montaigne's comparisons is that of the moral superiority of those who live under the laws of nature. But it is important to notice that this nature, while simple, pure, noble, and valiant, is also extremely harsh and cruel. Montaigne describes the life of the canni- bals' captive: he is treated well so as to make his life more dear to him and he is constantly threatened with his approaching horrible death, all for the purpose of making him show terror, of forcing him to acknowledge that his heart and his will have been subdued. And the act of cannibalism is not, as is often thought, for the sake of nourishment, but rather to manifest an extreme vengeance. So, in some ways, the cannibals are just as bad as we are, and nature is not sweet, innocent, and gentle.

In "Of the custom of wearing clothes" Montaigne wonders whether it is due to the warm temperatures of the newly discovered nations that their inhabitants go naked or whether it is "the original way of mankind" (VS225; F166). He says that "men of understanding," who realize that "all things under heaven . . . are subject to the same laws, . . . distinguish natural from artificial laws, and are wont to have recourse to the general order of the world, in which there can be nothing counterfeit. Now, since everything else is furnished with the exact amount of thread and needle required to maintain its being, it is in truth incredible that we alone should be brought into the world in a defective and indigent state, in a state such that we cannot maintain ourselves without external aid. . . . [Therefore] it is easy to see that it is custom that makes impossible for us what is not impossible in itself [i.e., by nature]" (VS225; F166–67). This makes it seem as if custom does indeed cover over the natural and conceal it, but that it is still possible to uncover it, in particular by looking at the New World.

In the "Apology" Montaigne provides a further characterization of "our natural state." Responding to those ancient philosophers who tell those who doubt the reality of heat to throw themselves into the fire, Montaigne writes that these responses "are most unworthy of the philosophical profession. If they had left us in our natural state, receiving external impressions as they present themselves to us through our senses, and had let us follow our sim- ple appetites, regulated by the condition of our birth, they would be right to speak thus. . . . This answer would be good among the cannibals, who enjoy the happiness of a long, tranquil, and peaceful life without the precepts of Aristotle and without acquaintance with the name of physics." But it is from the philosophers themselves that "we have learned to make ourselves judges of the world; it is from them that we get this fancy, that human rea- son is controller-general of all that is outside and inside the heavenly vault, embracing everything, capable of everything" (VS541; F404). The philoso- phers renounced the domination of "natural law," which was still "pure and simple," and which we share with all the animals (VS541; F405). Hence, the philosophers are not entitled to appeal to natural law against those who doubt the senses. Our natural state is presented here as a prephilosophical condition.[3]

Finally, in "Of the useful and the honorable" Montaigne affirms, but without elaboration, the idea of a "justice in itself, natural and universal," which must be distinguished from and is higher than "that other, special, national justice, constrained to the need of our governments" (VS796; F604). (The formulation "natural justice" is more Aristotelian than the Thomistic "natural law": Aristotle does consider the notion of natural justice in the *Ethics*, a justice that is the same everywhere, but he does not really discuss "natural law" as such.) The idea of a universal justice also comes up in the "Apology" within the context of Montaigne's discussion of the variety and confusion of ancient philosophical opinion. In the end, reason can only tell us to obey the laws of our own country. But Montaigne sees this as a most unsatisfactory state of affairs. Universal justice, justice in its true essence, ought not to be attached to the customs of this or that country. That would mean that our duty is by chance, changing and arbitrary, and justice is constantly at the mercy of the changing opinions of a people or a prince. Montaigne says of himself: "I cannot have my judgment so flexible" (VS579; F437).

Is it possible, then, to find a way out of this variety and contradiction? The philosophers are "funny when, to give some certainty to the laws, they say that there are some which are firm, perpetual, and immutable, which they call natural, which are imprinted on the human race by the condition of their very being. And of those, one man says the number is three, one man four, one more, one less: a sign that the mark of them is as doubtful as the rest." There is not a single law that is not contradicted by many nations. Universal approbation is the only sign by which it is possible to argue that there are natural laws, "for what nature had truly ordered for us we would without doubt follow by common consent. And not only every nation, but every individual would resent the force and violence used on him by everyone who tried to impel him to oppose that law." There is not even one such law. There is "nothing in short . . . so extreme that it is not accepted by the usage of some nation" (VS579–80; F437).[4]

We have moved from nature to custom, and that move seems to be complete: "The laws of conscience, which we say are born of nature, are born of custom. Each man, holding in inward veneration the opinions and the behavior [*mœurs*] approved and accepted around him cannot break loose from them without remorse" (VS115; F83). But has Montaigne contradicted himself, sometimes affirming and sometimes denying that there are natural laws? Can his consistent and unambiguous appeal to nature as a standard be reconciled with his apparent rejection of natural laws?

The Thomistic response to Montaigne's argument against the existence of natural laws (i.e., the argument that there is no law that can claim universal acceptance) would proceed along the following lines: in response to the question of "whether the natural law is the same in all men" Aquinas distinguishes between the general principles of the natural law and the conclusions that must be drawn from these principles. He claims that the general principles are the same for all men "both as to rectitude and as to knowledge." The conclusions drawn from the first principles are the same for all in the majority of cases but in some few cases the proper conclusions will not be reached because of certain obstacles – for example, the perversion of reason by passion, or evil habit, or an evil disposition of nature. His example is that theft was not considered wrong among the Germans.[5] Aquinas takes the same approach in answering the question of "whether the law of nature can be abolished from the heart of man." The general principles cannot be abolished but the conclusions or secondary precepts can be blotted out by evil persuasions, vicious customs, and corrupt habits.[6]

Whereas Aquinas sees a few exceptions to conclusions that are reached in the majority of cases, Montaigne sees almost nothing but "exceptions." The Germans who approved of theft are not an isolated instance. The Spartans held theft in high regard, and to attribute this to corruption is to begin to undermine seriously the argument for universality: the Spartans simply have to count as a virtuous and noble people. Even cannibalism is not an isolated practice, and it was defended by Chrysippus and Zeno, leaders of the Stoic sect (VS209; F155).

Whereas Aquinas sees the agreement of reason on the most basic principles and the success of reason in arriving at the proper secondary precepts, Montaigne sees reason as the problem: "It is credible that there are natural laws, as may be seen in other creatures; but in us they are lost; that fine human reason butts in everywhere, domineering and commanding, muddling and confusing the face of things in accordance with its vanity and inconsistency." This is how customs arise in all their extreme diversity: "One nation looks at one side of a thing and stops there; another at another" (VS581; F438).

The difficulties that arise with respect to the Thomistic teaching on natural law are due, in part, to the fact that Aquinas holds both "instinct" and reason to be natural, and these often come into conflict. The difficulty is supposed to be overcome by an ordering, a subordination of instinct to reason, of the lower to the higher. The lower is that which man shares with all the animals, the higher is what is unique to the human species, namely, reason. Reason is universal to the species; thus all men would know the same general principles and come to the same conclusions unless led astray by vicious and corrupt habits or the perversion of reason by passion.

Aquinas accepts the hierarchical ordering of nature from Aristotle, and there is, I believe, a very basic tension in Aristotle's notion of nature, or at least in his treatment of man. There seem to be two senses of "nature" in Aristotle: nature defined as "what is almost always the case" and nature defined as what is highest and thus rare. This tension does not really show up or make much difference with respect to other species, but it does make a difference when we talk about the human species.

If we take nature as "what is almost always the case," we can say that sight, for example, is natural to man. Blindness is a rare exception; sight is common. But if we take nature as "what is highest," we must confront the great inequalities that exist among men, especially with respect to intelligence. If nature is seen in terms of final cause, if the highest is the defining characteristic, the "specific difference," (i.e., reason), then only those very few men who actualize the natural potentiality for contemplation are most fully human. Now, I do not mean that, for Aristotle, only the philosopher is truly human. He seems to me to be looking at the species as a whole, and the full actualization of the capacity for reason in only a few men is, for him, a success of nature. Further, the undeniably great inequalities in intelligence among men do not simply translate into political inequality for him. My point here is that, within the hierarchical structure of nature, man is defined by what is highest in him; what is highest is intellect; and, for Aristotle, intellect is divine, at least in some sense. Aquinas follows Aristotle as far as the superiority of the intellect; but he cannot hold that the intellect is in any way divine. Yet there is a kind of confidence in human reason in Aquinas, a confidence manifested in his teaching on natural law concerning the ability of reason to know the general, first principles of the natural law and to reach the correct conclusions from them.

Now, if we compare Montaigne on this issue, we could say that, whereas Aquinas and Aristotle tend to define man in terms of what is highest, Montaigne tends to define him in terms of what is lowest and most common. And it is important to note here that the hierarchical picture of nature does identify the most common as the "low." I do not mean to imply that Montaigne reduces what is higher to what is lower or that he denies the distinction between higher and lower. (For example, in the "Apology," he considers the philosophers as having attained man's highest state [VS501–2; F371], and he presents Cato as nature's display of what is highest [VS231; F171], of the best that nature can do.) But the stronger tendency throughout the *Essays* is to identify the natural with the most common and thus the lowest.

This can be seen clearly in the "Apology," where Montaigne is intent upon bringing man "down," finding all our most prized faculties in the lowliest animals, where the philosopher is finally brought down to the "naïve, frank confession" that he would rather be a fool in the body of a man than wise in the body of an ass (VS486; F358). But it is not simply in the "Apology" that we see this "lowering" of nature. We are often told that we must look to the animals to see what is truly natural in us: "We must seek in the animals evidence of... [nature] that is not subject to favor, corruption, or diversity of opinion. For it is indeed true that they themselves do not always go exactly in Nature's road, but they deviate from it so little that you can always perceive the ruts" (VS1050; F803). And although at times he says that we can see nature in children, "who quite spontaneously follow nature" (VS234; F173), at other times he denies this: "The young of bears and dogs show their natural inclination, but men, plunging headlong into certain habits, opinions, and laws, easily change or disguise themselves" (VS149; F109).

But in a movement of thought that is characteristic of the *Essays*, Montaigne brings the reader back to man, first to men who are far away and strange, then gradually closer, and finally to himself. The discussions of the cannibals and of the inhabitants of the New World are intended, at least in part, to reveal what nature is and how it has been covered over. "These nations...have been very little fashioned by the human, and are still very close to their original naturalness. The laws of nature still rule them, very little corrupted by ours" (VS206; F153). What is essential to Montaigne's portrait of this "state of nature" is the lack or absence of learning. This world is "so new and so infantile that it is still being taught its A B C" (VS908; F693).

When Montaigne describes "our natural state," he speaks of a condition in which philosophy has not yet taught us that we are judges of the world, that human reason is ruler of the world (VS541; F404). But the condition of the inhabitants of the New World is not a condition of stupidity. It is a condition of ignorance, but "they... [are] not at all behind us in natural brightness of mind and pertinence" (VS909; F693). Once again, we begin to see that Montaigne is, in the end, talking about nature as a condition that is prephilosophical.

His chief criticism of the philosophical treatment of nature is expressed in this way: "The philosophers with much reason refer us to the rules of Nature; but these [rules] have no concern with such sublime knowledge. The philosophers falsify them and show us the face of Nature painted in too high a color, and too sophisticated, whence spring so many portraits of so uniform a subject" (VS1073; F821–22). And later in the same essay: "I seek... [Nature's] footprints everywhere. We have confused them with artificial tracks, and for that reason the sovereign good of the Academics and the Peripatetics, which is 'to live according to nature,' becomes hard to limit and express" (VS1113; F855).

Montaigne wants to take away from the philosophers the yardstick by which they measure the world. That is to say, he rejects the notion of nature as a *higher* standard against which we can measure man as he is. The philosophical inventions of natural law and the state of nature are the kinds of explanation that stand alongside the thing to be explained and always reveal it to be less than it should be. Nature, on this view, is a standard of reform, a goal to be achieved so as to make man be what he ought to be. It is the standard of "deliberate" philosophy, philosophy as rule.

At one point in the "Apology," in the long section on what the philosophers have held about the soul, Montaigne discusses Plato's "doctrine of recollection." What Montaigne says about Plato can be taken as his response to those teachings on nature that place nature either in some otherworldly realm or in the distant past. The doctrine that knowledge is recollection is an expression of our desire to believe that we are really and essentially perfect and only accidentally and temporarily imperfect. "For to value the condition of our souls as highly as we want to, we must presuppose them to be wholly knowing when they are in their natural simplicity and purity" (VS548; F410). Montaigne's response to the idea of a perfect natural state from which we have somehow fallen and which shows us what we truly are is this: "It is here in us, and not elsewhere, that the powers and actions of the soul should be considered. All the rest of its perfections are vain and useless to it" (VS549; F411). It is "the present state" of man by which he must be judged.

In his "Conversation with de Sacy" Pascal discusses the merits and the shortcomings of Epictetus and Montaigne in terms of how each supports and leads to or is at odds with Christian belief. Pascal is reported to have said: "It seems to me that the source of the errors of these two sects [Stoics and Skeptics] is that they have not known that the state of man at present differs from that of his creation, so that the one [Epictetus], noticing some traces of his first grandeur and unaware of his corruption, has treated nature as healthy and without need of reparation, which leads him to the acme of pride; whereas the other [Montaigne], experiencing the present wretchedness of man and unaware of his primal dignity, treats nature as necessarily infirm and irrecuperable, which throws him into despair at arriving at a true good, and thence into an extreme apathy."[7]

Pascal is referring to the understanding of that teaching concerning original sin which holds that man was created by God in a very different condition from his present one, that he was created as good, and that evil and error result from the first sin, the sin of disobedience. This state is described by Saint Augustine in Book IV of *The City of God*. Not only was man created good – a view that seems necessary if we are to preserve the belief in God's goodness, which entails the belief that God cannot be the source or origin of evil – man was created with a perfect intellect, and was not subject to any of the evils of human life in its present state. Pascal locates man's dignity in this first condition. The fall of man from this condition of perfection brought with it not only man's estrangement from God but also a significant change in his entire state: a "darkening" of the intellect, a weakening of the will, pain, disease, toil, and death.

But the price of exonerating God from the charge that he must be the cause of evil is the difficulty of accounting for that first sinful act. Why did Adam and Eve sin? If one assumes they were created good and that God had placed no seed of evil in them, where did evil come from? Saint Augustine struggles with this question in both *The City of God* and the *Confessions*. If God is just, as we believe him to be, then his punishment of man must be justified by the deliberateness of man's act. Man therefore cannot be held to sin because of his "nature." His original nature is perfect. Augustine's answer is that the locus of evil is the will: it is not evil "by nature" but can be evil in its "direction." (See especially *Confessions,* Bk. VII.) In *The City of God* (Bk. XIV, ch.13), he says that man sinned because he was created out of nothing. The original sin is pride, man's trying to make himself a god: "Ye shall be like gods, knowing good and evil."

It seems to me that Pascal is correct in claiming that Montaigne does not hold that "the state of man at present differs from that of his creation," at least insofar as that difference implies a higher state of perfection in the distant past to which we can now aspire, but this does not mean that Montaigne rejects entirely any belief concerning "original sin." He says that presumption is our "original malady," and his assessment of our "present state" is certainly in accord with much of the content of Pascal's "fallen state." But Montaigne does seem to reject or ignore the historical, narrative account that sets up two distinct historical conditions and thus a standard of perfection outside our present condition for judging what we are and what we ought to be.[8]

Montaigne's characterization of his own project is tied very closely by him to the issue of nature. And the *Essays* are a "lowering" of philosophy itself. In his very brief direct address "To the reader," Montaigne sets forth the purpose and the subject matter of his book. He will present to the reader his "natural" form, his simple, natural, and ordinary way of being. This must be contrasted with two other possible conditions: the studied posture of the learned and the condition of those who are said still to live under nature's first laws. Here Montaigne presents himself in a kind of middle position. The metaphor that Montaigne uses sometimes in the *Essays* is that of clothing: the learned man is "all dressed up," the man in the state of nature is naked, and Montaigne is in "shirt sleeves," an expression he uses in the essays to refer to the condition in which we can really see a man for what he is (VS259; F190). If Montaigne had wanted to present himself in a studied posture to seek the world's favor, he would have dressed himself up in borrowed knowledge. And "had I been placed among those nations which are said to live still in the sweet freedom of nature's first laws, I assure you I should very gladly have portrayed myself here entire and wholly naked" (VS3; F2). The freedom of nature's first laws is a freedom from deliberate philosophy: an excessive engagement with the occupation of philosophy interferes with our "natural liberty" (VS198; F146). It is important to notice that there are two notions of "nature" in "To the reader": nature as the condition of men in the New World and nature as his own middle way of being. Toward the end of the *Essays,* in "Of physiognomy," Montaigne mentions his many borrowings, his borrowed trappings. But he does not intend that they cover and hide him; that is the very opposite of his design. He wants to show only "what is naturally my own" (VS1055; F808).

The meaning of "nature" throughout the *Essays* is associated with a condition of ignorance. Ignorance is not stupidity or lack of natural vitality, but rather the absence of learning. There are two places in the essays that are

especially significant in this regard. The first occurs in "Of vain subtleties."
Here again we see Montaigne in a kind of middle position: "The simple peasants are good men, and good men the philosophers, at least what passes for
philosophers in our time: strong and clear natures, enriched by a broad education in useful knowledge. The half-breeds who have disdained the first
seat, ignorance of letters, and have not been able to reach the other – their
rear end between two stools, like me and so many others – are dangerous,
inept, and importunate: these men trouble the world. Therefore for my
part I draw back as much as I can into the first and *natural* stage, which
for naught I attempted to leave" (VS313; F227, emphasis added). The second is the passage I quoted earlier that provides the immediate context for
Montaigne's claim that he is an accidental philosopher. The passage begins:
"My *mœurs* are *natural*; I have not called in the help of any teaching to build
them" (VS546; F409; emphasis added).

At the beginning of "Of fear" Montaigne says: "*I am not a good 'naturalist'*
(as they call it) and I hardly know by what springs [*ressorts*] fear acts in us"
(VS75; F52, emphasis added). Then, in "Of physiognomy" he writes: "*We
naturalists* judge that the honor of invention is greatly and incomparably
preferable to the honor of quotation" (VS1056; F809; emphasis added). In
claiming that he is not a good naturalist, he seems to be distancing himself
from the practice of "natural philosophy" in the sense of physics: the pre-
Socratic natural philosophers were called "physicists," and Montaigne often
refers to the kind of causal explanations given by the "physicians." When
he later places himself among the naturalists, he seems rather to be distancing himself from the learned who seek only the honor of quotation. In
other words, the meaning of "naturalist" has changed. How has this change
occurred?

Natural philosophy rests on the traditional philosophical distinction between nature and convention. Convention can be described in several ways:
as custom, as agreement among men, as habit, as what is acquired, as artificial. Thus the conventional always has the connotation of being arbitrary
and changeable. Nature, on the other hand, is necessary and unchangeable.
Custom or convention can be expressed in laws, and the rightness or justice
of these laws is judged against the standard of natural justice or natural law.
Nature in this sense is higher than custom because it is the standard against
which custom is measured; nature is authoritative. So there is always a gap
or a tension for the philosopher between nature and custom or convention.
Nature is the yardstick by which the philosopher rules the world.

How does Montaigne deal with this traditional philosophical distinction?
In "Of repentance" he discusses repentance along with its corollary, reform,
and the possibility of moral reformation: "Natural inclinations gain assistance and strength from education; but they are scarcely to be changed and
overcome. A thousand natures, in my time, have escaped toward virtue or
toward vice through the lines of a contrary training. . . . We do not root out

these original qualities, we cover them up, we conceal them." The example he uses here is language: "Latin is like a natural tongue to me." He had heard and spoken only Latin until the age of five, but now it has been forty years since he has spoken it. Yet, in the grip of extreme and sudden emotion, "I have always poured out my first words from the depths of my entrails in Latin; Nature surging forth and expressing herself by force, in the face of long habit" (VS810–11; F615). What this example of Latin as "natural" seems to suggest is a meaning of nature as what is first learned, first acquired, not as what precedes all acquiring.

In "Of age" Montaigne considers what we ordinarily call a "natural" death: "What an idle fancy it is to expect to die of a decay of powers brought on by extreme old age, and to set ourselves this term for our duration, since that is the rarest of all deaths and the least customary! We call it alone natural, as if it were contrary to nature to see a man break his neck by a fall, be drowned in a shipwreck, or be snatched away by the plague or a pleurisy, and as if our ordinary condition did not expose us to all these mishaps. Let us not flatter ourselves with these fine words: we ought rather to call natural what is general, common, and universal. Death of old age is a rare, singular and extraordinary death, and hence less natural than the others" (VS326; F236–37).

The tendency to soften or blur or even eliminate the sharp line between nature and custom is especially evident in Montaigne's treatment of human action. In "Of pedantry" he is speaking of the effect that learning ought to have on the soul: precepts should not be mere words, learning must not be merely a knowledge in the soul "but its character and habit," not an acquisition "but a natural possession" (VS142–43; F105). In "Of presumption" he tells us that in his early childhood some people noticed in him a certain bearing that witnessed to a vain and foolish pride. "I want to say this first, that it is not unbecoming to have characteristics and propensities so much our own and so incorporated into us that we have no way of sensing and recognizing them. And of such natural inclinations the body is likely to retain a certain bent, without our knowledge or consent.... Such gestures can arise in us unperceived" (VS633; F479). Here, he calls these "natural inclinations," but the line is blurred between nature and what is acquired without our awareness – for example, the way Alexander held his head, the slight lisp of Alcibiades, Caesar's habit of scratching his head with one finger, Cicero's wrinkling of his nose. And in "Of vanity" he reaches a point where he does not seem to care whether nature or art is the cause of certain dispositions: "Whatever it is, whether art or nature, that imprints in us this disposition to live with reference to others, it does us much more harm than good" (VS955; F729).

So Montaigne, like the other philosophers, admonishes us to live according to nature and to take nature as our guide. But what does this mean now? How is it possible to sort out what is due to nature and what is due to custom and art since "habit is a second nature, and no less powerful"? (VS1010; F772). In "Of physiognomy" he talks about how we have abandoned nature as our guide in favor of learning (*science*). Human reason, "always finding some diversity and novelty, leaves in us no apparent trace of Nature. And men have done with Nature as perfumers do with oil: they have sophisticated her with so many arguments and far-fetched reasonings that she has become variable and particular for each man, and has lost her own constant and universal countenance" (VS1049–50; F803). And in "Of experience," he writes: "It is for habit to give form to our life, just as it pleases; it is all-powerful in that; it is Circe's drink, which varies our natures as it sees fit" (VS1080; F827). As he nears the end of his life, Montaigne writes: "In short, here I am in the act of finishing up this man, not of making another out of him. By long usage this form of mine has turned into substance, and fortune into nature. So I say that every one of us feeble creatures is excusable for considering as his own what is comprised under this measure" (VS1011; F773). Why is it that Montaigne refers to himself and those like him as "feeble" in this context? Perhaps he is implying that remaking or reforming oneself according to some higher standard of nature is a harsh and difficult task. So he makes this concession to his weakness. "If what Nature flatly and originally demands of us for the preservation of our being is too little ... then let us grant ourselves something further: let us also call the habits and condition of each of us *nature*; let us rate and treat ourselves according to this measure, let us stretch our appurtenances that far" (VS1009; F772). The meaning of "nature" has been lowered and weakened to include our habits and condition: the dialectic of nature and custom has arrived at a second sense of "nature" that includes both terms of the dialectic.[9] The line between nature and custom is blurred. This blurring implies a lowering of the concept of nature because living according to nature has been presented by the philosophers as something far more difficult and therefore higher than simply living thoughtlessly in the comfort of habit. Nature is just what we are now in our present condition. That is to say that, through the dialectic of nature and custom, "human nature" has become "the human condition." Whereas "human nature" suggests an ideal essence, "the human condition" is just our common subjection to all "human accidents" (VS1074; F822).

Causality

The metaphysical category of cause is closely related to the category of nature – that is, the philosopher thinks he knows what something is, what its "nature" is, when he has found the cause or the reason why it is the way it is. Philosophy, then, is seen as the search for causes. It will be helpful to consider three such cases of the search for causes as reported by Montaigne. The essay "Of smells" begins with the example of the sweat of Alexander the Great: "It is said of some, as of Alexander the Great, that their sweat emitted a sweet odor, owing to some rare and extraordinary constitution of theirs, of which Plutarch and others seek the cause" (VS314; F228). In the "Apology" he reports the story of Democritus and the figs. Democritus was eating some figs at dinner when he realized that they tasted of honey. He "began to seek out in his mind whence came this unaccustomed sweetness; and to clear up the matter, he was about to get up from the table to see the situation of the place where these figs had been gathered. His maidservant, having heard the cause of this stir, laughed and told him not to trouble himself about it, for the reason was that she had put them in a vessel where there had been some honey. He was vexed that she had deprived him of this occasion for research and robbed him of matter for curiosity: 'Go along,' he said to her, 'you have made me angry; I will not for all that give up seeking the cause as if it was a natural one'" (VS510–11; F378). And in "Of cripples" he considers the Italian proverb that "the cripple does it best!" – that is, that the most perfect sexual pleasures are only experienced with a cripple. Here Montaigne would have ventured a cause, "but I have just learned that ancient philosophy, no less, has decided the question. It says that since the legs and thighs of lame women, because of their imperfection, do not receive the food that is their due, the result is that the genital parts, which are above, are fuller, better nourished, and more vigorous" (VS1033–34; F791). The explanation is attributed to Aristotle, and Montaigne's tone is gently mocking.

The feature of philosophy that I want to focus on here is the way that the search for causes proceeds. First, something strange and unfamiliar is noticed. This strange and unexpected odor, or taste, or notion prompts the philosopher to look for the cause. He is not prompted to seek the cause of what is ordinary and familiar. Aristotle describes this movement of thought in the *Metaphysics*: "All men begin ... by wondering that things are as they are, as they do about self-moving marionettes, or about the solstices or the incommensurability of the diagonal of a square with the side; for it seems wonderful to all who have not yet seen the reason, that there is a thing which cannot be measured even by the smallest unit. But we must end in the contrary and ... the better state, as is the case in these instances too when men learn the cause; for there is nothing which would surprise a geometer as much as if the diagonal turned out to be commensurable" (983a15–20). Finding the cause, then, satisfies the philosopher's initial wonder and thereby eliminates that wonder, replacing it with the knowledge of why the matter is the way it is.

In contrast to the philosophers who seek the causes, Montaigne seems to be indifferent for the most part to the knowledge of causes.[10] So, for example, at the beginning of "Of fear" he writes: "I am not a good 'naturalist' (as they call it) and I hardly know by what springs [*ressorts*] fear acts in us" (VS75; F52). He is especially critical of those who pretend to be able to find the causes of events in the will of God. It is easy, he says, to deceive in matters about which we know least. So alchemists, astrologers, prognosticators, and medical doctors have a free hand, saying whatever they please, because the matter is so hidden. To these types Montaigne would add "interpreters and controllers-in-ordinary of God's designs, claiming to find the causes of every incident and to see in the secrets of the divine will the incomprehensible motives of his works" (VS215; F160). But his skepticism about causes extends much further. In the description of his sufferings from kidney stones and his dealings with doctors, he refers to "the uncertainty and ignorance of those who presume to explain the workings [*les ressorts*] of Nature and her inner processes, and all the false prognostications of their art" (VS1095; F840). Even "the great authors, when they write about causes, adduce not only those they think are true but also those they do not believe in, provided they have some originality and beauty." For "we cannot be sure of the master cause" (VS898–99; F685).

But if Montaigne is not concerned with seeking the causes of things, how does he understand his own philosophical activity? The distinction he makes in this regard is the distinction between the search for causes and the inquiry into truth. In "Of cripples" he writes: "I was just now musing, as I often do, on how free and vague an instrument human reason is. I see ordinarily that men, when facts are put before them, are more ready to amuse themselves by inquiring into their reasons than by inquiring into their truth. They leave aside the cases and amuse themselves by treating the causes. Comical prattlers! [*Plaisants causeurs!*] The knowledge of causes belongs only to Him who has the guidance of things, not to us who have only the enduring of them, and who have the perfectly full use of them according to our nature, without penetrating to their origin and essence" (VS1026; F785). Seeking the causes is associated with knowledge of the origin and the essence of things and with seeking the reason why things are as they are. Both are distinguished from "the truth." In this context, the search for causes appears to be an attempt to explain the thing in question by leaving it behind and talking about something, namely, the cause, that is outside of it. Truth, on the other hand, seems to be a matter of inquiring into the actual particulars in a way that takes them and leaves them just as they are.[11] This aspect of Montaigne's thought is presented in a striking way at the very beginning of the *Essays*, in "To the reader." Here he makes reference to the Aristotelian four causes, but he does so in a way that preserves and even emphasizes the disproportion between the particular in question (himself) and the ideal assumed in the causal explanation.

This book was written in good faith, reader. It warns you from the outset that in it I have set myself no goal but a domestic and private one. I have had no thought of serving either you or my own glory. My powers are inadequate for such a purpose. I have dedicated it to the private convenience of my relatives and friends, so that when they have lost me (as soon they must), they may recover here some features of my habits and temperament, and by this means keep the knowledge they have had of me complete and alive.

If I had written to seek the world's favor, I should have bedecked myself better, and should present myself in a studied posture. I want to be seen here in my simple, natural, ordinary fashion, without straining or artifice; for it is myself that I portray. My defects will here be read to the life, and also my natural form, as far as respect for the public has allowed. Had I been placed among those nations which are said to live still in the sweet freedom of nature's first laws, I assure you I should very gladly have portrayed myself here entire and wholly naked. Thus, reader, I am myself the matter of my book; you would be unreasonable to spend your leisure on so frivolous and vain a subject. (VS3; F2)

All four causes are here, but each is presented in a way that is weak and defective. His goal or end (final cause) is not the high purpose of public service and his own glory: "My powers are inadequate for such a purpose." He wants to be seen as he is "without straining," without striving toward any achievement.[12] He portrays himself in his simple, natural, ordinary fashion, in his natural form (formal cause), and that means that his defects must be included in his self-portrait. As he says in "Of repentance," he does not "form" man but simply tells of him. He portrays only "a particular one, very ill-formed" (VS804; F610). He is himself "the matter" of his book (material cause), and he is, of course, the author of his book (efficient cause), but the reader is warned: "[Y]ou would be unreasonable to spend your leisure on so frivolous and vain a subject."

In making the issue of causality the most prominent feature of his introduction to the entire book, Montaigne shows how central this issue is to his project and how crucial his weakening and lowering of such ideal explanations is to his account of human being.[13] This is especially clear in the case of final causality. In the discussion of deliberate philosophy in Chapter 1, I presented deliberate philosophy as a kind of striving toward the goal of the divine *stasis*, achieved in the rule of reason within the soul of the philosopher. But, as Montaigne tells us in "Of the inconsistency of our actions," it is difficult to find even a dozen men among the ancients who have achieved this goal. By this standard of final cause, manifested so perfectly in deliberate philosophy, almost all human life and action would have to count as failure and defect. What good are such explanations in that case?

Montaigne presents his own life, in comparison with the deliberate philosophers, as a life of weakness, laxity, and nonchalance. There is no hint of striving for perfection. However, his laxity actually attains the same consistency of action as Stoic strength does. This can be seen in the very first essay, in the first words that Montaigne says about himself: "I am marvelously lax in the direction of mercy and gentleness." Like the Stoics, he is consistent in his mercy to the afflicted. Unlike the Stoics, he does feel compassion, and that places him in the category of the weak. Montaigne achieves by accident what the Stoic achieves deliberately; he achieves by laxity what the

Stoic achieves by straining. Hence the "second sense" of his title, "By diverse means we arrive at the same end." Montaigne's lowering of the traditional metaphysical category of causality allows us to see more clearly why he calls himself an unpremeditated and accidental philosopher.

The Universal and the Particular

The fourth metaphysical category to be addressed in this chapter is the universal. In a rough way, we can state the origin of the universal as follows: when the intellect has encountered many particulars of the same kind, it grasps the universal, what is the same in each particular regardless of the many differences in the appearances. So, for example, in spite of the considerable differences between a beagle and a great Dane, both are dogs. Each possesses essential characteristics that make each equally a dog. Thus, in a sense, the universal is what is most "real" about the particular. In Aristotelian terms, the "form" is the same and the matter differentiates. Form, in the primary sense, is the "what" of *this* dog. In the secondary sense, form is the species. The particular is what it is by virtue of the species to which it belongs. All of the capacities and potentialities of the individual are determined by its species. For example, dogs can run but do not have the ability to fly.

During the Middle Ages, the controversy between "realists" and "nominalists" concerned the question of the mode of being or the "reality" of universals. The nominalists held that only particulars truly "are," and that universals are simply names. Ultimately, this controversy is theological and concerns the power of God to create particulars. Does God, so to speak, "need" universals to somehow mediate the bringing into being of particulars? Montaigne, of course, does not explicitly enter into this scholastic debate. But there does seem to be a deliberately nominalist slant to the *Essays*. In the first place, Montaigne is always reluctant to move from particulars to universals. This can be seen from the very first essay where he attempts to ascend to universals, then presents counterexamples, and finally concludes that "man is a marvelously vain, diverse, and undulating object" (VS9; F5). We cannot even locate a universal characteristic in one single man: "No quality embraces us purely and universally" (VS234–35; F173). Ironically, our most universal characteristic is difference.

What ought to count as universal, if anything does, are the features captured in the definition of man. If we take the definition "man is a rational animal," there are two essential qualities, both of which belong to every man. "Animal" is the genus to which he belongs, and rationality is the "specific difference," the property that differentiates the human species from all other animal species. Rationality, then, is the strongest candidate for the status of universal. This is precisely where Montaigne makes his most direct attack on universality, and it is especially strong in his reply to the second objection against Sebond's natural theology. In the course of showing human reason to be weak he also shows it to be diverse and variable: "Fortune herself is no more diverse and variable than our reason" (VS516; F383).

"Of experience" is set very plainly against an Aristotelian background directly concerned with the issue of universals. The first sentence of this essay, "There is no desire more natural than the desire for knowledge" (VS1065; F815), seems to be a very deliberate echo and restatement of the first sentence of Aristotle's *Metaphysics*: "All men by nature desire to know." If we follow Aristotle a bit further, we can trace the ladder by which we ascend to universals. We begin with sense perception and then move up to the memory of what is given in perception. From memory we climb to experience: "Experience is produced in men from memory, since many memories of the same thing produce the effect of a single experience" (*Metaphysics* 980b27). What Aristotle means by experience, then, is not the discrete "sense data" of certain empiricist accounts of knowledge but rather an important step on the way to the higher universal. Experience is the first act of unifying particulars.

From experience we move to art (e.g., medicine) and then to science (e.g., biology). "Art comes into being when, from many notions derived from experience, one universal judgment is formed about things that are alike" (*Metaphysics* 981a5). In actually performing a particular task, the man who has experience may well be preferable to the man who has studied the art but has no experience with particulars. But art and science are higher than experience because art and science know the causes and the universals, whereas experience does not really get much beyond particulars; the man who has only experience and not science knows *that* something is the case but not *why* it is the case (*Metaphysics* 981a30). For Aristotle "knowledge of everything necessarily belongs to the man who more than any other has knowledge of universals, since such a man knows in a way all the individuals that are included in them" (*Metaphysics* 982a21).

Where does Montaigne stand on this Aristotelian ladder? Not surprisingly, he stands on the lower rung, experience.[14] He is unwilling to move up to the universal: "The inference that we try to draw from the resemblance of events is uncertain, because they are always dissimilar: there is no quality so universal in this aspect of things as diversity and variety.... Resemblance does not make things so much alike as difference makes them unlike. Nature has committed herself to make nothing separate that was not different."

Montaigne's illustration of this is worth noting because it reveals the level at which he is really operating. "Both the Greeks and the Latins, and we ourselves, use eggs for the most express example of similarity. However there have been men, and notably one at Delphi, who recognized marks of difference between eggs, so that he never took one for another; and although there were many hens, he could tell which one the egg came from" (VS1065; F815). There are really two levels of example here, eggs

and men. The man from Delphi and others like him are counterexamples
to the universal claim that human beings cannot tell one egg from another.
Montaigne is really interested in the human. The peculiarity of the man
from Delphi removes our focus from the biological question about eggs
to the diversity of human possibilities and to the presumption entailed in
the act of universalizing: we move so easily and presumptuously from the
Greeks, the Latins, and ourselves, to "all men."

The kind of experience Montaigne is most concerned with is the experience by which he comes to know himself: "When I find myself convicted
of a false opinion by another man's reasoning, I do not so much learn what
new thing he has told me and this particular bit of ignorance – that would
be a small gain – as I learn my weakness in general, and the treachery of my
understanding; whence I derive the reformation of the whole mass. With all
my other errors I do the same. . . . I do not regard the species and the individual, like a stone I have stumbled on; I learn to mistrust my gait throughout,
and I strive to regulate it" (VS1074; F822). This is not a discussion along
biological lines about a universal property or quality or a metaphysical discussion about how he sees himself as an individual within the species "man."
It is rather a description of how a particular occurrence is taken up into his
self-understanding of his own, particular being.

Later in "Of experience" Montaigne modifies somewhat his original picture of diversity: "As no event and no shape is entirely like another, so none is
entirely different from another. An ingenious mixture on the part of nature.
If our faces were not similar, we could not distinguish man from beast; if they
were not dissimilar, we could not distinguish man from man. All things hold
together by some similarity; every example is lame, and the comparison that
is drawn from experience is always faulty and imperfect; however, we fasten
together our comparisons by some corner" (VS1070; F819).[15] What holds
things together is not some universal and essential property but just "some
corner." Again Montaigne's example is significant. The human face rather
than the human mind functions here as something close to universal. This
"lowering" from the mind to the body is also seen in the "Apology," where
the philosopher chooses to be a fool in the body of a man rather than wise
in the body of an ass: "What? So our philosophers abandon this great and
divine wisdom for this corporeal and terrestrial veil? Then it is no longer by
our reason, our intelligence, and our soul that we are superior to the beasts;
it is by our beauty, our fair complexion, and the fine symmetry of our limbs,
for which we should abandon our intelligence, our wisdom, and all the rest"
(VS486; F358).

Montaigne does indeed emphasize human difference and is very reluctant to ascend to any affirmative universals. And the *Essays* are about himself,
his weak and lowly self, which apparently can claim no exemplary status.
Nevertheless, the human condition is universal. In "Of repentance" he
writes: "I set forth a humble and inglorious life; that does not matter. You

can tie up all moral philosophy with a common and private life just as well as with a life of richer stuff. Each man bears the entire form of the human condition. Authors communicate with the people by some special extrinsic mark; I am the first to do so by my universal being, as Michel de Montaigne" (VS805; F611). The universal has become particular.[16]

In sum, then, Montaigne takes each of the traditional metaphysical categories and lowers it or weakens it. He takes the terms of the metaphysical distinctions, places them in a dialectical relationship with each other, and allows them to recombine in a way that restores their prephilosophical harmony. He restores to ordinary language the metaphysical content that philosophy had abstracted from it. His own inquiry into truth requires the imprecision of mere ordinary opinion.[17] This mode of inquiry is the essay.

3

The Essay as Philosophical Form

In *The Age of Cathedrals*, Georges Duby traces out the conditions and causes that ultimately brought into being the great Gothic cathedrals of France. The economic and social conditions were right, of course, but the true cause was theological. The abbot of Saint-Denis, Suger, pushed forward the transformation from monastery to cathedral in an attempt to express his belief that God is Light. This is especially evident in the choir of Suger's new church: here "the mutation in aesthetics took place ... at the culmination of the liturgical procession turned toward the rising sun." At that point, Suger "decided to take away the walls and urged the master builder to make fullest use of the architectonic resources of what until then had been merely a mason's expedient, the ribbed vault." Duby's account reveals that the creation of a new art form is not essentially the result merely of technical advances. The cathedrals do not come into being simply because the art of architecture now has the wherewithal to construct buildings of such great height, with walls of stained glass. Indeed, the very impetus for the architectural developments comes from outside the art. The master builders are urged on by the demands of faith to transform the mere mason's expedient, the ribbed vault, into "the glowing center" where the liturgical celebration takes place. Suger "revolutionized accepted notions of architecture by transforming an edifice into the tangible demonstration of a theology of light."[1]

A new art form with enduring meaning begins to form thought, and emerges necessarily as the sole mode of expression of thought that cannot be expressed in the available forms. As Jules Brody puts it: "Montaigne's unsettling, unorthodox, cavalier, etc. way of writing is not a problem waiting to be solved, it is, rather, the solution to problems that he as a thinker and writer perceived and that, in publishing his *Essais*, he invited his eventual readers to confront with him and through him."[2] So Montaigne invents the essay, not as a mere novelty, but as the perfect form of his accidental philosophy. What, then, is this thought that cannot be contained within the customary forms? Why does Montaigne invent the essay?

The Meaning of "Essay"

We can begin to answer this by considering the meaning of Montaigne's title, *Essays,* and some of the characterizations of the essay form that follow from the meaning of "essay." Erich Auerbach maintains that the meaning of the title *Essays* is rendered as "Tests upon One's Self," or "Self-Try-Outs." The word "essay" comes from *essayer,* which means to try or to attempt. Joseph Epstein notes that "in bringing up this etymology most people wish to understand the tentativeness of the form," but as Epstein points out, "such modesty does not at all apply to Montaigne." He prefers to take "essay" in Screech's sense of "assay": the essays are assays "of himself by himself." Marcel Conche's interpretation emphasizes not the tentativeness but the boldness of the form: *s'essayer* means "to try to think by oneself."[3]

The characterization of the essay that seems to best describe it as a philosophical form is the one proposed by Michael Oakeshott that I mentioned in Chapter 1. In his preface to *On Human Conduct,* Oakeshott refers to the essay as the most appropriate expression of philosophical reflection understood in a certain way, namely, as "the adventure of one who seeks to understand in other terms *what he already understands* and in which the understanding sought . . . is a disclosure of the conditions of the understanding enjoyed and not a substitute for it."[4]

Oakeshott's characterization captures the circular mode of Montaigne's thought, a movement in which we begin with what is already understood and "ascend" to an understanding in other terms but an understanding that actually returns to the first understanding and acknowledges its authority. This first understanding is opinion, and opinion is the oracular beginning of the essay. Perhaps this is what Merleau-Ponty has in mind when he says that for Montaigne we find "the fixed point we need . . . in the [sheer] fact that there is opinion, the appearance of the good and true."[5]

In Chapter 1 I also claimed that the meaning of the title *Essays* allows for the interpretation that the essays are trials in the sense of temptations. Oakeshott's description of the essay form suggests that the meaning of the temptation can be put in this way: the temptation for the intellect is to ascend from opinion to an understanding that does substitute for the understanding already enjoyed and that does not acknowledge the authority of the prephilosophical understanding. This is the temptation to deliberate philosophy, for deliberate philosophy seeks to replace opinion with knowledge and to rule over the prephilosophical rather than acknowledge its authority.

The term "essay" also conveys the sense of an attempt or a striving toward some goal. As we saw in the discussion of causality in Chapter 2, Montaigne includes all four Aristotelian causes in "To the reader" where the purpose of his book is made explicit. There he tells us that his "end" is merely domestic and private, that his powers are not great enough for a public "design." He also tells us that he wants to be seen in his natural form "without striving or artifice." The essay form displays an attempt that, by the standards of deliberate philosophy, fails to attain knowledge. Yet, in the return of thought to its starting point, having gone through the attempt, thought finds the truth that was already there.

The essay form articulates "that which is." The arguments of deliberate philosophy "are all the time running alongside the matter and sidestepping it, and barely brushing the crust of it" (VS834; F634). And "the sciences treat things too subtly, in a mode too artificial and different from the common and natural one. My page makes love and understands it. Read him Leon Hebreo and Ficino: they talk about him, his thoughts and his actions, and yet he does not understand a thing in it. I do not recognize in Aristotle most of my ordinary actions: they have been covered and dressed up in another robe for the use of the school. God grant these men may be doing the right thing! If I were of the trade, I would naturalize art as much as they artify nature" (VS874; F666). The great Pascal can recognize himself in the *Essays* – "It is not in Montaigne but in myself that I find everything I see there"[6] – but so too can the page, the shopboy, and the shepherd.

This attempt to articulate "that which is" accounts, in some measure, for the language of the *Essays*. There is no jargon of the schools, no specialized vocabulary: "I follow common usage in language" (VS796; F604). His style is a way of speaking that is "a formless and undisciplined way of talking, a popular jargon" (VS637; F483). He frequently uses obscenities, and in one such place (after reporting that the Romans wiped their ass with a sponge and that is why *spongia* is an obscene word in Latin), he says that "we must leave that vain squeamishness about words to women" (VS298; F217).

Montaigne wrote the *Essays* in French, not in his fluent Latin, and he wrote them at home, "in a backward region" (VS875; F666), where the people around him understand only the Latin of their Paternoster. When he is criticized for the language of the *Essays*, he responds that he avoids none of the terms and phrases in use in the streets of France; "those who would combat usage with grammar make fools of themselves" (VS875; F667). In "Of the education of children" he attributes to childish and pedantic ambition the search for novel phrases and little-known words: "Would that I might use only those that are used in the markets of Paris!" (VS172; F127). And in "Of the art of discussion" he refers to conversation as the way of seeking "that which is" (*ce qui est*), and he mocks the professional logicians who have learning but not understanding: "Do we witness more of a jumble in the chatter of fishwives than in the public disputations of the professional logicians? I would rather have my son learn to speak in the taverns than in the schools of talk" (VS926–27; F707). Montaigne's use of the vulgar language is not simply a rhetorical move but an ontological necessity: truth is more manifest in the chatter of fishwives than in the disputations of professional logicians.

The contrast of the essay form with deliberate philosophy can be drawn out a bit further with respect to the issue of final cause. In keeping with his claim in "To the reader" that his powers are inadequate for public service, at the very beginning of "Of repentance" he writes: "Others form man; I tell of him" (VS804; F610). He is persistent throughout the essays in his denial that he is able or even wants to rule anyone or teach anyone. How, then, are we to understand the purpose of the *Essays*?

Purpose

Several very different formulations of Montaigne's purpose are scattered throughout the *Essays*. The immediate cause and the ultimate purpose of the *Essays* are given precisely in the place where Montaigne tells us that he is an accidental philosopher: "The desire to tell my *mœurs* seized me" (VS546; F409), or, in Screech's translation: "I was seized with the desire to give a public account of [my ways of life]" (S614). This is, I believe, the most fundamental claim that Montaigne makes about why he wrote the *Essays* at all.

The desire that seizes him is the desire to tell his *mœurs*, his ways of life and being. This in itself is somewhat surprising because, as he often says, only a man who has done great deeds would seem to be excusable in presuming to talk about himself in public. In "On some verses of Virgil" he tells us that "St. Augustine, Origen, and Hippocrates have published the errors of their opinions; I, besides, those of my conduct [*mœurs*]" (VS846; F643). At one point, in "Of the resemblance of children to fathers," he suggests a development: "I want to represent the course of my humors [*le progrès de mes humeurs*], and I want people to see each part at its birth" (VS758; F574).

It is also important to note that the desire is to tell his *mœurs* in public – a desire that generates an implicit challenge and even accusation against him, an accusation of presumption that always stands in the background and is often brought forward by Montaigne to set in relief the strangeness of his enterprise. Why would a man who has done no great and glorious deeds and who does not claim to offer any authoritative teaching presume that the public would be interested in him? True, he begins "To the reader" on a "domestic and private" note but, before the end of that brief address, he is clearly assuming a public audience. And the passage in which he says that he was seized by this desire to tell his *mœurs* makes it clear that he turns to philosophy in order to "appear in public a little more decently" (VS546; F409).

And what are we to make of the desire itself? How can a desire that seizes him justify the entire project of the *Essays*? The origin of this desire remains mysterious. In referring to the impetus as a desire that seized him, Montaigne

is suggesting something irrational and daemonic. He is taken over by a desire
for which he gives no reason or explanation. But, even further, this desire
is authoritative for him, authoritative but unjustified rationally.

The second formulation of Montaigne's purpose elaborates on the oracular beginning of the essays. At the conclusion of "Of prognostications"
Montaigne writes: "The daemon of Socrates was perhaps a certain impulse
of the will that came to him without awaiting the advice of his reason. In a
well-purified soul such as his, prepared by a continual exercise of wisdom
and virtue, it is likely that these inclinations, although instinctive and undi-
gested, were always important and worth following. Everyone feels within
himself some likeness of such stirrings of a prompt, vehement, and accidental opinion. *It is for me to give them some authority,* since I give so little to our
wisdom. And I have had some as weak in reason as violent in persuasiveness –
or in dissuasiveness, as was more ordinary in Socrates – by which I let myself
be carried away so usefully and fortunately that they might be judged to have
in them something of divine inspiration" (VS44; F29–30, emphasis added).
Montaigne, then, sees his task as giving "some authority" to prompt, vehement, accidental opinion.

I believe that we are entitled to infer that the desire that seized him to
tell his *mœurs,* the desire that is the impetus for the *Essays,* is just such an
opinion or impulsion of the will, an opinion that he clearly does recognize
as authoritative for him. And it is important to notice that he says that each
man experiences such movements of the soul or, more precisely, an "image"
of the daemon of Socrates. Montaigne is willing to call this a kind of "divine
inspiration."

The third purpose of the *Essays* is mentioned in "Of idleness." When he
tries to engage his mind with itself alone, the result is a wild burst of chimeras
and other fantastic monsters that the mind generates "without order or
purpose." In an effort to contemplate their strangeness, he puts them in
writing, "hoping in time to make my mind ashamed of itself" (VS33; F21).[7]

Montaigne wants to show himself as he truly is, in all his strangeness and
defectiveness. There are several places in the *Essays* where he refers to his
self-revelation as confession: "In honor of the Huguenots, who condemn
our private and auricular confession, I confess myself in public, religiously
and purely." He does this because the evils of the soul become stronger for
being hidden. Therefore, we must expose them to the light of day, "we must
tuck up this stupid rag that covers our conduct [*mœurs*]" (VS846; F643).
But why a *public* confession? "I am hungry to make myself known, and I
care not to how many, provided it be truly. Or to put it better, I am hungry
for nothing, but I have a mortal fear of being taken to be other than I am
by those who come to know my name. . . . I am pleased to be less praised,
provided I am better known" (VS847; F643–44).

From this we can begin to see that his self-revelation is not for the purpose
of securing him honor or glory. This comes out clearly in "Of presumption."

After going through a list of his ineptitudes, he concludes in this way: "From these lines of my confession you can imagine others at my expense. But whatever I make myself known to be, provided I make myself known as I am, I am carrying out my plan. And so I make no excuse for daring to put into writing such mean and trivial remarks as these. The meanness of my subject forces me to do so. Blame my project if you will, but not my procedure. At all events, I see well enough, without others telling me, how little value and weight all this has, and the folly of my plan. It is enough that my judgment is not unshod, of which these are the essays" (VS653; F495). Both his imperfections and his lowliness preclude the attainment of honor and glory. This implies that his self-revelation is potentially humiliating and shameful: he lifts the rag that covers his private parts.

Yet there is also an aspect of openness and generosity to Montaigne's self-revelation, an aspect that he refers to as "communication." In "To the reader," it is expressed as nourishment: he wants his relatives and friends to have his book so that they may recover in it some features of his habits and temperament, and by this means nourish the knowledge they have had of him (VS3; F2). In "Of three kinds of association" the aspects of self-display and self-communication are joined in his very being: "My essential form is suited to communication and revelation. I am all in the open and in full view, born for company and friendship" (VS823; F625). As Virginia Woolf said, "the essays are an attempt to communicate a soul."[8]

Montaigne's self-revelation is intended not to put forward an object of theoretical knowledge but to give himself in an act of friendship. In "Of the affection of fathers for their children" he recalls his friendship with La Boétie and finds consolation for his loss in the fact that he had had with him "perfect and entire communication." He opens himself to his friends as much as he can: "I hasten to bring myself out and put myself forth" (VS396; F287–88).

One of the most explicit assertions of this aspect of the *Essays* occurs in "Of repentance," where he explains the complete harmony and unity of himself and his book: "Authors communicate with the people by some special extrinsic mark; I am the first to do so by my entire being, as Michel de Montaigne, not as a grammarian or a poet or a jurist" (VS805; F611). In order to realize perfectly the end he has proposed, he need only bring to his work a sincere and pure fidelity. Thus, "it cannot happen here as I see it happening often, that the craftsman and his work contradict each other . . . in this case we go hand in hand and entirely in step, my book and I" (VS805; F611–12).

But what is involved in this communication of being? For he is claiming to communicate not simply some mark or product of himself but his very being, entirely, universally. One of the principal justifications for Montaigne's claim to the perfect communication of his being is his discovery of the fundamental quality of the human condition: "I set forth a humble and inglorious

life; that does not matter. You can tie up all moral philosophy with a common and private life just as well as with a life of richer stuff: Each man bears
the *entire* form of the human condition" (VS805; F611, emphasis added).
Montaigne can completely and perfectly communicate his very being because he has located that which makes him one with every human being.

Here it is necessary to raise the question of whether it is ever possible
either to know or to communicate oneself entirely and perfectly. Is there
not some fundamental sense in which all communication of the self in
speech must be mediated? Yves Delègue, in his *Montaigne et la mauvaise foi:
L'écriture de la vérité*, examines Montaigne's first words in the *Essays*: "This
is a book of good faith." Delègue takes the very disorder of the essays as
evidence of Montaigne's good faith. Nevertheless, he argues that life cannot
be completely captured in words.[9] The subject is always escaping himself and
is discovered by and in the movement of his own loss. In the end, *la bonne
foi* amounts to playing a ruse on oneself with language, a ruse in which *la
mauvaise foi* is legitimated.[10]

Montaigne certainly acknowledges the problem of portraying a being that
is constantly changing: the essay form itself is a response to that difficulty.
But more important, the being that he is attempting to reveal is ultimately
mysterious to itself. What he arrives at in his repeated returns to himself is
always something astonishing and strange, not transparent or fully comprehended and self-possessed. Montaigne's engagement with the *on dit* reveals
a kind of acknowledged tension between speaking at the level of unexamined common opinion and speaking at the level of the truthfulness of "good
faith." The daemonic order of the essays displays a consciousness that comes
upon itself by accident and that can never be simply, naively familiar to itself.
Later in this chapter, I discuss Montaigne's practice of quotation and the
daemonic order of the essays, as both of these features have a bearing on
the issue of mediation.

We saw that in "To the reader" Montaigne alludes to the difficulty of
rationally justifying his public display of himself: it would be "unreasonable"
to spend one's leisure on so frivolous and vain a subject (VS3; F2). In "Of
repentance" he raises the issue of reasonableness again: "But is it reasonable
[*est-ce raison*] that I, so fond of privacy in actual life, should aspire to publicity
in the knowledge of me?" (VS805; F611). How and why does he move from
private to public? He does not begin from a public purpose; his end is
domestic and private, neither the public good nor his own glory. But he
does move to public visibility, even in "To the reader." The desire that seizes
him is to tell his *mœurs* in public.

One of the few explicit justifications for Montaigne's public display of
himself occurs in "Of practice," where he tells the story of his near-fatal
fall, an accident that brought him close to death and allowed him to famil-
iarize himself with it. "This account of so trivial an event would be rather
pointless, were it not for the instruction that I have derived from it for

myself.... What I write here is not my teaching, but my study; it is not a lesson for others but for me.... And yet it should not be held against me if I publish what I write. What is useful to me may also by accident be useful to another" (VS377; F272). There is no "necessary" lesson here: it is just possible that his experience might help someone else. "By accident" has the force of "nonauthoritative." He has not derived a universal rule from his experience, a rule or proof accessible to the reason of anyone. Experience is particular: the effect of one man's experience on another would have to be accidental.

In that same essay, Montaigne also refers to his "design" in terms of making his *mœurs* public: "[B]ut even if it were true that it is presumptuous, no matter what the circumstances, to talk to the public about oneself, I still must not, according to my general design, refrain from an action that openly displays this morbid quality, since it is in me" (VS378; F273). Now we can begin to see that Montaigne does have a "public purpose" in publishing the *Essays*, but we can also say that his public purpose is not a "teaching" in any conventional sense.

There are two places where Montaigne speaks about publishing his essays in terms of obligation. In "On some verses of Virgil" he writes: "*I owe* a complete portrait of myself to the public. The wisdom of my lesson is wholly in truth, in freedom, in reality" (VS887; F677, emphasis added). Here he is willing to call his work a "lesson" and to claim some wisdom for it. The context is his discussion of his sexual appetite and his locating his humanity in his genitals, the "lowering" of the properly human from the divine intellect to the shameful penis. In "Of the disadvantage of greatness" he writes: "But if my heart is not great enough, it is compensatingly open, and it *orders* me boldly to publish its weakness" (VS917; F700, emphasis added). The context is set by the title, "Of the disadvantage of greatness," and he is describing himself as a man of the "middle state." Here again, what he is obliged to publish is his weakness, his lowliness. This passage also reveals one of the most important "lessons" of the *Essays*: Montaigne's openness is presented as a form of greatness of soul, and it is this openness of heart that orders him to publish his weakness.

There is a further reason why Montaigne publishes his *mœurs*. It is because they are "new," thus not found in any previous philosophy, and hence not easily recognized. "The uniformity and simplicity of my behavior [*mœurs*] produces an appearance easy to interpret, but, because the manner of it is a bit new and unusual, it gives too fine a chance to calumny" (VS980; F749). His *mœurs*, then, must have some relevance for others, such that it is important for him to articulate them, to point them out and differentiate them from the "old" *mœurs*. Presumably, his new *mœurs* are the standard against which he judges the actions of others. In "Of giving the lie" he goes so far as to say that he *does* intend to "instruct" the public by these judgments: "How many times, irritated by some action that civility and reason kept

me from reproving openly, have I disgorged it here, not without ideas of
instructing the public!" (VS665; F504).

What, then, is Montaigne's public teaching and how, after all his protestations of his lowliness, can his public teaching have any authority? The most
explicit statement of Montaigne's public teaching occurs in "On some verses
of Virgil." Montaigne shows clearly that his making public what is by convention private is itself one of the most important aspects of the meaning of
the *Essays*: "I know well that very few people will frown at the license of my
writings who do not have more to frown at in the license of their thoughts.
I conform well to their hearts, but I offend their eyes.... I have ordered
myself to dare to say all that I dare to do, and I dislike even thoughts that
are unpublishable. The worst of my actions and conditions does not seem to
me so ugly as the cowardice of not daring to avow it. Everyone is discreet in
confession; people should be so in action. Boldness in sinning is somewhat
compensated and bridled by boldness in confessing. Whoever would oblige
himself to tell all, would oblige himself not to do anything about which we
are constrained to keep silent. *God grant that this excessive license of mine may
encourage our men to attain freedom, rising above these cowardly and hypocritical
virtues born of our imperfections; that at the expense of my immoderation I may
draw them on to the point of reason*" (VS845; F641–42, emphasis added). The
freedom that he wants to encourage is a kind of greatness of soul, an openness that rises above "cowardly and hypocritical virtues." The way Montaigne
displays his own freedom is through his very unconventional speech about
himself.[11]

There seem to be three reasons why speaking about oneself in the way
he does would be so rare. First, our gaze is naturally turned "outward" to
things outside ourselves. This is asserted at the end of "Of vanity," where
he says that anyone who looks at himself attentively will find that he is full
of inanity. We see in ourselves only misery and vanity, so that, in order not
to discourage us, "Nature has very appropriately thrown the action of our
vision outward" (VS1000; F766). The second reason has to do with the
prohibition against boasting. "Custom has made speaking of oneself a vice,
and obstinately forbids it out of hatred for the boasting that seems always
to accompany it" (VS378; F273). The third reason involves the very deep-
reaching prohibition against revealing the shameful and the private – that
is, it involves the way in which the private is the shameful. This means that not
only boasting but any speech about oneself is unacceptable: "I find myself
entangled in the laws of ceremony, for she does not allow a man either to
speak well of himself, or to speak ill" (VS632; F479).

Montaigne breaks with custom in all three ways: he makes the turn back
to himself, he puts ceremony aside, and he reveals the lowly and shameful
being that he is. Montaigne's break with custom is presented as a kind of
liberty: "We must pass over these common rules of civility in favor of truth
and liberty. I dare not only to speak of myself, but to speak only of myself"

(VS942; F720). And, as we have seen, this liberty is essential to his public purpose. In "Of some verses of Virgil," where he speaks of sexual matters freely and sometimes indecently, he alludes to Genesis and refers to God as "that great Judge who tucks up our rags and tatters from around our shameful parts and does not merely pretend to see us throughout, even to our inmost and most secret filth. Our virginal modesty would be a useful propriety if it could keep him from making this discovery. In short, whoever would wean man of the folly of such a scrupulous verbal superstition would do the world no great harm. Our life is part folly, part wisdom. Whoever writes about it only reverently and according to the rules leaves out more than half of it" (VS888; F677–78).

The liberty that Montaigne is displaying and encouraging must be understood in contrast to what he calls a "deformed liberty" (VS991; F758). That is the liberty of those whose actions and discourse go their separate ways. The discrepancy between actions and words is perhaps allowed to those who write about things other than themselves, but it cannot be allowed to those who write only of themselves as Montaigne does.

Montaigne's liberty is not the freedom of autonomous reason, hence, the *Essays* are not authoritative. Oakeshott says of the essay form that, "although it may enlighten, it does not instruct."[12] The *Essays* do not command others: "I do not make it my business to tell the world what it should do – enough others do that – but what I do in it" (VS192; F142). Montaigne does not even want to be taken by others as authoritative: "I myself . . . am singularly scrupulous about lying and . . . scarcely concern myself with giving credence and authority to what I say" (VS1028; F786). His assertions are simply his own opinions, not the authoritative pronouncements of the learned: "[T]hese are my humors and opinions; I offer them as what I believe, not what is to be believed. . . . I have no authority to be believed, nor do I want it, feeling myself too ill-instructed to instruct others" (VS148; F108–9).

True, Montaigne does have a public purpose, but still he does not claim authority for his beliefs. In "Of the useful and the honorable" he tells us that, when a great and powerful man once complained to him about the asperity and vehemence of his exhortations, Montaigne responded that his advice was given "to enlighten your judgment, not to compel it. . . . I am not so presumptuous as even to desire that my opinions should tip the scales in a thing of such importance" (VS1033; F790–91). Montaigne's nonauthoritative position is consistent with his attempts to recognize and resist the very fundamental human tendency to presumption.

In what is perhaps the strongest statement on his nonauthoritative stance, he writes: "If anyone should put my musings into account to the prejudice of the pettiest law, or opinion, or custom of his village, he would do himself a great wrong, and as great a one to me." His thoughts are nothing more than musings, fantasies, caprices. But now we can begin to see the other side of the coin. For it is precisely Montaigne's nonauthoritative status that gives him his freedom: "I would not speak so boldly if it were my right to be believed" (VS1033; F790).

There are three places in the *Essays* where Montaigne publicly submits to an authority outside his own reason. In "Of repentance" he writes: "Let me here excuse what I often say, that I rarely repent and that my conscience is content with itself – not as the conscience of an angel or a horse, but as the conscience of a man; always adding this refrain, not perfunctorily but in sincere and complete submission: that I speak as an ignorant inquirer, referring the decision purely and simply to the common and authorized beliefs. I do not teach, I tell" (VS806; F612). In "Of a custom of the Isle of Cea," concerning the custom of suicide, Montaigne begins: "If to philosophize is to doubt, as they say, then to play the fool and follow my fancies, as I do, is all the more to doubt. For it is for the learners to inquire and dispute, and for the master to decide. My master is the authority of the divine will, which rules us without contradiction and has its place above these vain and human wranglings" (VS350; F251). Finally, "Of prayers" begins: "I put forward formless and unresolved notions, as do those who publish doubtful questions to debate in the schools, not to establish the truth but to seek it. And I submit them to the judgment of those whose concern it is to regulate not only my actions and my writings, but even my thoughts. Equally acceptable and useful to me will be condemnation or approval, since I hold it as execrable if anything is found which was said by me, ignorantly or inadvertently, against the holy prescriptions of the Catholic, Apostolic, and Roman Church, in which I die and in which I was born. And therefore, always submitting to the authority of their censure, which has absolute power over me, *I meddle rashly with every sort of subject,* as I do here" (VS317–18; F229, emphasis added).

All of the formulations of the purposes of the *Essays* that I have discussed are fundamentally linked to each other. The desire that seized him to tell his *mœurs,* his gratuitous self-communication, his encouraging men to liberty, his giving authority to prompt, accidental opinion, and his making his mind ashamed of itself – all of these formulations reveal a profound unity of intention. Montaigne is attacking and undermining (in himself first of all) a certain kind of rationalism, a rationalism that is the form of presumption found in the learned.

Audience

In order to understand Montaigne's purpose, we must consider the audience that he identifies for himself. On one level, of course, the *Essays* are addressed to all men. In "A consideration upon Cicero" he tells us that he would have willingly adopted the form of the letter to publish his thoughts if only he still had his friend, La Boétie, to address them to. "I would have been more attentive and confident, with a strong friend to address, than

I am now, when I consider the various tastes of a *whole public*" (VS252; F186, emphasis added).[13] There are also instances in the *Essays* where he addresses directly a particular individual. But there are at least two places where he identifies a certain kind of individual as his primary addressee. In "Of vain subtleties" he says that the *Essays* "might get by in the middle region [of men]." In that same essay, the middle region is identified as the place of error, but error from which and through which it is possible to arrive at "the extreme limit of Christian intelligence" (VS313; F227). In "Of presumption" he asks, "And then, for whom do you write?" The learned value only science, erudition, and art. The common souls cannot appreciate the grace of an elevated and fine discourse. "Now, these two types fill the world. The third class into whose hands you come, that of minds regulated and strong in themselves, is so rare that for this very reason it has neither name nor rank among us; it is time half wasted to aspire and strive to please this group" (VS657; F498).

Montaigne's primary addressees are those who are prone to error on account of reason and who, at the same time, are not incurably learned, learned in the purely conventional sense. They are independent and capable of self-rule. These are the individuals who are susceptible to reformation, who "will not fail to come back to themselves and very discreetly let themselves be managed by the common faith and examples" (VS446; F325).

In "Of Essay-Writing" Hume distinguishes between the "learned" and the "conversible": the learned who labor in solitude and the conversible who are sociable and enjoy conversation. Hume claims that the separation of the learned from the conversible world is a great defect: when learning is shut up in colleges and monks' cells, *belles-lettres* become barbarous and enslaved. "Even Philosophy went to Wrack by this moaping recluse Method of Study," for experience is to be found only "in common life and conversation."[14] The essay form is intended to bring the learned and the conversible into conversation with each other, to the benefit of both. Pascal also describes Montaigne's style as "totally composed of thoughts born out of the ordinary conversations of life."[15] And Auerbach claims that Montaigne was the first author who wrote for the nonspecialized but educated reader: "[B]y the success of the *Essays* the educated public first revealed its existence."[16]

Montaigne's address to this "middle region" is not for the sake of elevating them to the level of the merely and incurably "learned." Rather, he places before them an example of what the outcome of education ought to be. In the words of Michael Oakeshott, the outcome is participation in "the conversation of mankind." Oakeshott says that "this conversation is not only the greatest but also the most hardly sustained of all the accomplishments of mankind. Men have never been wanting who have had this understanding of human activity and intercourse, but few have embraced it without reserve and without misgiving, and on this account it is proper to mention the most notable of those who have done so: Michel de Montaigne."[17]

The Practice of Quotation and the Essence of Thought

The metaphor of conversation leads us to ask about the place of quotation in the form of the essay and its significance for Montaigne's thought. The manner of Montaigne's participation in "the conversation of mankind" requires taking on the thoughts of others in the stance of quotation. There are what I would call "levels" of quotation in the *Essays*. The first level is that of direct quotation of a particular author, usually in Latin, sometimes in Greek or French, and usually set off on the page from the flow of his writing. The second level is that of the *on dit*, "they say," one of the most frequently used expressions in the *Essays*. The third level is that of common opinion, the least obvious but deepest level of quotation. Each level is a kind of quotation on account of the stance that Montaigne takes with regard to it.[18]

On the one hand, direct quotation of particular authors conveys a sense of borrowed authority. Montaigne mentions this in "Of presumption" when he tells us that he has begged his quotations and examples at the doors of the well known and famous, "not content with their being rich unless they also came from rich and honorable hands; in them authority and reason concur" (VS651; F494). In "A consideration upon Cicero" he refers to the "authority" of his examples and quotations (VS251; F185). And in "Of experience" he introduces a Latin quotation from Seneca in this way: "Authority alone has power over the common intelligences, and has more weight in a foreign language" (VS1114; F856). So also, quotation from the greatest authorities can elevate the tone of one's speech. Before paraphrasing a long section from Plato's *Laws*, Montaigne says, "The amusing dialogue between Plato's lawgiver and his fellow citizens will do honor to this passage" (VS398; F289).

On the other hand, he contrasts his own borrowings with those of "the undiscerning writers of our century," who scatter through their pitiful works entire passages from the ancient authors to do themselves honor.[19] But the contrary happens because their own work pales against the great writers (VS147; F107). In his "Defense of Seneca and Plutarch" he says "my book, built up entirely from their spoils, oblige[s] me to espouse their honor" (VS721; F545). But when Montaigne borrows he often changes the meaning a bit, putting the borrowed passage to his own use. And in "Of books" he says that his borrowings are usually from such well-known ancient works that they are recognizable without his identifying them. "In the reasonings and inventions that I transplant into my soil and confound with my own, I have sometimes deliberately not indicated the author, in order to hold in check the temerity of those hasty condemnations that are tossed at all sorts of writings. . . . I want them to give Plutarch a fillip on my nose and get burned insulting Seneca in me. I have to hide my weakness under

these great authorities" (VS408; F296–97). But what often becomes manifest when Montaigne transplants in this way is his equality with or superiority
to these great authors. When it is possible to identify those places, their writing seems less alive and vivid than Montaigne's. At the end of the "Apology"
for example, there is a long passage from Plutarch on being and becoming
that Montaigne does not identify as borrowed until the very end. It creates a jarring break in the conversational flow of his writing. Earlier in the
"Apology," Montaigne is beginning the section where he calls into question
the claim that the senses are the sure foundation of knowledge: "All that is
known is doubtless known through the faculty of the knower" (VS587; F443).
Although no source is indicated for this passage, it seems to be an imitation
of Aquinas's style put to Montaigne's own use. Again, there is a jarring shift
to the comparatively stilted scholastic style. Montaigne says of his practice
of quotation of the greatest authors, "I well know how audaciously I always
attempt to match the level of my pilferings. . . . If I were a match for them I
would be a good man, for I take them on only at their stiffest points" (VS148;
F108).

What, then, is the significance of Montaigne's practice of quotation, if not
simply to bring honor and give authority to his book? Montaigne's practice
of quotation, on all its levels, has to do with the essence of thought itself.

In "Of the education of children" Montaigne writes about the young man
who is to be educated: "Truth and reason are common to everyone, and no
more belong to the man who first spoke them than to the man who says
them later. It is no more according to Plato than according to me, since he
and I understand and see it in the same way. The bees plunder the flowers
here and there, but afterward they make of them honey, which is all theirs;
it is no longer thyme or marjoram. Even so with the pieces borrowed from
others; he will transform and blend them to make a work that is all its own, to
wit, his judgment. His education, work, and study aim only at forming this"
(VS152; F111). And elsewhere in that same essay, he writes: "I do not speak
the minds of others except to express myself better" (VS148; F108). In "Of
pedantry" he criticizes those who work only to fill their memory and leave
their understanding and conscience empty. "Isn't it doing the same thing,
what I do in this composition? I go about cadging from books here and there
the sayings that please me, not to keep them, for I have no storehouses, but
to transport them into this one, in which, to tell the truth, they are no more
mine than in their original place" (VS136; F100).

Montaigne's quotations, however, are not the *source* of his beliefs: "Since
then [childhood] I have established and fortified [my first beliefs] by the
authority of others and the sound arguments of the ancients, with whom
I found my judgment in agreement. These men have given me a firmer
grip on my ideas and a more complete enjoyment and possession of them"
(VS658; F499). The same point is made when he writes: "I have not studied
one bit to make a book; but I have studied a bit because I had made it, if it is

studying a bit to skim over and pinch, by his head or feet, now one author, now another; *not at all to form my opinions*, but certainly to assist, second, and serve those which I formed long ago" (VS666; F505, emphasis added).

Montaigne's stance of quotation at this first level is a stance of independence, not of dependence and derivation of his opinions. Robert Sokolowski, in his analysis of the phenomenon of quotation, brings out many of the features of quotation that we see in Montaigne's practice. "I can . . . be related to things either on my own cognitive authority or refractedly, through the authority of another speaker. When I quote someone, I have the quoted state of affairs as proposed by someone else; but in principle it is always possible for me to go on to possess the state of affairs by myself without an intermediary, to register the situation on my own. . . . When, after having quoted, I thus see for myself, I do not just register the situation; I register it as confirming or disconfirming what someone else has said. . . . The immediacy of my own cognitive possession of a situation becomes itself a qualified immediacy because I now know that I can be cognitively related to it not only by myself but also through another. *By myself* takes on a deeper hue." Sokolowski goes on to say that "the flexibility introduced by quotation can fail to be appreciated by two kinds of people or two characters of mind: by the gullible person who always just takes over, repetitionally, as his own and as being the case, anything the others say; and by the obstinate person who is so saturated with his own point of view that the statements of others are seen either as little more than the echoes of what he says, or else as rather foolish fancies that he never really entertains as opinions."[20] Distinguishing Montaigne from both the gullible and the obstinate helps to explain what I have been calling his stance of quotation, not only at the first level of quotation, but at the other, deeper levels as well.

By his practice of quotation at the first level, Montaigne locates himself in a tradition of learning and in a community of learners that goes back to the ancients. But he does not simply take over and repeat what others have said. His thought is not dominated by these opinions. By quoting in Latin or Greek he shows even more emphatically that he recognizes these statements as expressions of the opinions of others. Even when he agrees with the quoted statement, he is not under the authority of the speaker. As Sokolowski puts it, he gets out from under the domination of the speaker by the very act of attributing the statement to him.[21]

But when we move to the deeper levels of quotation, the authority of quoted opinion becomes more subtle and more powerful. As I noted earlier, *on dit*, or "they say," is one of the most frequently used expressions in the *Essays*. Montaigne's use of this expression shows that he recognizes the statement as a quotation and that he takes the stance of quotation toward it, the stance of allowing the possibility of its truth without accepting it as true on account of its presumed authority. The *on dit* confers upon the statement the added authority of numbers, whereas the direct quotation of a particular speaker makes the tentative posture toward the statement a more immediate response. It takes more independence of thought to distance oneself from the *on dit*.

Finally, when we reach the deepest level, that of common opinion, it becomes difficult to take the stance of quotation at all. The tendency here is for the mind to be so dominated by this anonymous opinion that it simply takes it as its own, not by a deliberate act but as the experience of what is first for it. Common opinion is so powerful and so pervasive that it becomes difficult to imagine that thought can be anything other than movement within its domain. This is how Montaigne describes the power of custom. It is not as if we first have a "natural" stance toward the world and then custom comes along and obscures it. Rather, custom is there from the start.

The level of common opinion is the level at which the *Essays* seem to come closest to being the voice of Montaigne himself. This, I believe, is the level at which the many instances of contradiction take place, for common opinion is not consistent. Montaigne's statement concerning his contradictions, "I may well indeed contradict myself now and then; but truth, as Demades said, I do not contradict" (VS805; F611), suggests that common opinion is contradictory, that truth is found in common opinion, and that the essay form is the mode of discovery. Montaigne's practice of quotation leads us deeper and deeper into the mind's stance of quotation until finally we must wonder whether thought is anything more than quotation, whether there is any such thing as "thinking for oneself." It is here that philosophy comes on the scene. The deliberate philosopher recognizes the domination of the mind by common opinion and seeks to escape that domination. He seeks to escape the contradictions of common opinion, the contradictions that perhaps led him to see common opinion as questionable in the first place. Sokolowski's discussion of Descartes is especially pertinent here because Descartes is the exemplar of the deliberate and definitive attempt to put common opinion aside. "The Cartesian enterprise is established by a shift in the way we are to understand intentionality and in the way we are to be able to quote everything said and presented in the prephilosophic attitude." Descartes's detachment of the mind from the senses means that "the manifest is disqualified" and so there is an "extreme and total opaqueness of reference between the ordinary speech used to articulate the manifest image of the world and the speech of Cartesian science and philosophy."[22] Descartes's bracketing or quoting of the world as it is manifest in common opinion has the effect of making philosophy the authoritative voice, authoritative because most deliberate.

Montaigne's stance of quotation toward all previous philosophical opinion and toward common opinion might appear to be the first step of the Cartesian project of refounding philosophy on autonomous reason. But, for Montaigne, common opinion is not simply false: we do not arrive at the truth by bracketing or quoting the prephilosophical and substituting a higher truth. His relationship to common opinion is inescapable; truth is somehow found in this relation to common opinion. Philosophical opinion only gives him a more complete possession of what he always knew. And so we come back to Oakeshott's definition of the essay as the philosopher's attempt "to understand in other terms what he already understands," an attempt in which "the understanding sought . . . is a disclosure of the *conditions* of the understanding enjoyed and not a substitute for it." *That condition is truth.* Truth is not some other higher, foreign, and learned explanation that replaces the understanding we thought we had. Rather, it is disclosed as the already present condition for the understanding we do have.

If we return now to Sokolowski's description of the gullible and the obstinate, we can spell out a bit further how Montaigne is distinguished from both. Montaigne takes quotation from its most obvious to its deepest level. But his mind is not dominated either by learned or common opinion: it is not constituted as a collection of quotations from any level. He addresses this very point in "Of repentance," where he criticizes those who do not "essay" their own natural faculties, preferring to borrow from others. "Even so someone might say of me that I have only made a bunch of other people's flowers, having furnished nothing of my own but the thread to tie them. Indeed I have yielded to public opinion in carrying these borrowed ornaments about on me. But I do not intend that they should cover and hide me; that is the opposite of my design, I who wish to make a show only of what is my own, and of what is naturally my own" (VS1055; F808). And in "On some verses of Virgil" he says of his book that "its principal end and perfection is to be precisely my own" (VS875; F667). Montaigne is not gullible, but neither is he obstinate. Both characters of mind are held in the unrecognized grip of presumption. Although the *Essays* are precisely his own, they are not the effort of a presumptuous autonomous reason. In the terms of Oakeshott's definition, the understanding achieved through the essay is not a substitute for the understanding already enjoyed in opinion. Rather, the essay brings to light the truth that was already there.

The Dialectic of History and Poetry

The second characteristic of the essay form to be considered here is Montaigne's use of examples. Examples keep us at the level of particulars, resisting the upward pull toward universals. Only through attention to examples can the unfamiliar strike us, can we be open to the possible and then return to the familiar to find the strange in the familiar. Examples are the mirror in which we can see ourselves.

Montaigne refers to examples as "the quarry for weak-backed people like myself" (VS58; F39). He gives the appeal to examples a lowly and weak status because the ascent to universals is, at least by conventional standards, a higher use of the mind. Also, examples are, for him, at the level of experience, and again, by conventional standards, experience is "lower" than reason (see VS105; F75). There is, of course, a difficulty at the level of examples. How do we appropriate examples? How do we learn from them without the mediation of the universal, without subsuming both ourselves and the example under the common universal? As Montaigne says, "Example is a hazy mirror, reflecting all things in all ways" (VS1088; F834). It seems that examples are useful only "by accident," just as he says that he publishes the story of his near-fatal fall because it might, by accident, be useful to someone else. Examples have only accidental authority. Most of Montaigne's examples are from the ancient historians and almost all of his examples are based on testimony. They are, as he puts it, "borrowed truth" (VS106; F76).

In "Of the education of children" Montaigne refers to history as "the skeleton [*l'anatomie*] of philosophy, in which the most abstruse parts of our nature are penetrated" (VS156; F115). History allows us to associate with the great souls of the past.[23] The education that Montaigne proposes is one in which the judgment is formed, not simply the memory. History gives us the *mœurs* of such men as Hannibal and Scipio: "That, in my opinion, is of all mattters the one to which we apply our minds in the most varying degree" (VS156; F115). And in "Of books" he again makes clear why he values the histories so highly: "The historians come right to hand. They are pleasant and easy; and at the same time, man in general, the knowledge of whom I seek, appears in them more alive and entire than in any other place – the diversity and truth of his inner qualities in the mass and in detail, the variety of the ways he is put together, and the accidents that threaten him. Now those who write biographies, since they spend more time on plans than on events, more on what comes from within than on what happens without, are more suited to me" (VS416; F303).

But histories are written by all sorts of people, and it is necessary to judge the historians themselves. Montaigne prefers those who are either very simple or very intelligent. The simple do not mix in anything of their own: they record everything faithfully and leave the judgment to the reader. The excellent historians select what is worth reporting and rightly assume the authority to judge. Those who fall between these extremes presume to judge for us. They slant their stories and thus often conceal a private word or action that would be most useful for our instruction. And they "omit as incredible things they do not understand" (VS417; F304).

Montaigne certainly does not accept everything that every historian writes: he does not subject his judgment easily. For example, he does not believe the testimony of Dion concerning the character of Seneca, in part because of Dion's inconsistencies (VS722; F545). But he trusts Plutarch, even with respect to such reports as the nest of the halcyon. And he says of Socrates: "It happened fortunately that the man most worthy to be known and to be presented to the world as an example should be the one of whom we have the most certain knowledge. We have light on him from the most clear-sighted men who ever lived; the witnesses we have of him are wonderful in fidelity and competence" (VS1038; F793).

In "It is folly to measure the true and false by our own capacity," he defends certain histories against the presumption of the learned. Froissart and Bouchet are witnesses whose rank perhaps does not give them authority over our belief, but are we to say that Plutarch, Caesar, Pliny, and Saint Augustine are simple people deceived just like the vulgar, that they are not so clear-sighted as we are? Shall we accuse them of ignorance and simplicity or of malice and imposture? He dismisses Bouchet's stories about all the miracles done by the relics of Saint Hilary, "but to condemn wholesale all similar stories seems to me a singular impudence" (VS181; F134). And at the end of a long discussion of Tacitus, he writes, concerning a seemingly fantastic story, "I have been accustomed in such things to bend under the authority of such great witnesses" (VS942; [F720], sentence omitted in F).

It is noteworthy that Montaigne is interested not only in the actions and *mœurs* of great men but also in the rumors that were spread during the times the historians write about. When he distinguishes among the three kinds of historians, he praises the simple ones, like Froissart, "who presents to us even the diversity of the rumors that were current and the different reports that were made to him. This is the material of history, naked and unformed" (VS417; F304). And he says of all good historians that "they keep a record of important events; among public incidents are also popular rumors and opinions. It is their part to relate common beliefs, not to regulate them. That part concerns the theologians and philosophers, directors of consciences" (VS942; F720). So, although Tacitus was writing at a time when the belief in prodigies had begun to wane, "he says he does not want for all that to fail to insert them in his *Annals*, and give a footing to things accepted by so many good people with such reverence for antiquity. That is very well said. Let them deliver history to us more as they receive it than as they see fit" (VS943; F720). For Montaigne, the very fact that something is accepted by many good people has some weight and cannot be simply dismissed. As Merleau-Ponty says, Montaigne finds significance in the sheer fact that there is opinion at all. That something is or has been believed reveals the nature of the human capacity for belief.

Although Montaigne refuses to simply dismiss reports of fantastic occurrences, he does not easily believe them, either. This is especially true with respect to accusations of sorcery. "To kill men, we should have sharp and luminous evidence; and our life is too real and essential to vouch for these supernatural and fantastic accidents" (VS1031; F789). In the matter of such accusations, a man ought to be believed about what is human but only God can authorize a supernatural effect. Someone is accused of being a sorcerer because witnesses say that one day he was in the east, the next day in the west. "Truly, I would not believe my own self about this. How much more natural and likely it seems to me that two men are lying than that one man should pass with the winds in twelve hours from the east to the west! How much more natural that our understanding should be carried away from its base by the volatility of our untracked mind than that one of us, in flesh and bone, should be wafted up a chimney on a broomstick by a strange spirit! ... It seems to me that we may be pardoned for disbelieving a marvel, at least as long as we can turn aside and avoid the supernatural explanation by non-marvelous means" (VS1032; F789). The distinction that he makes between physical powers (where it is easier to know our limits) and the possibilities of the human soul (where it is very difficult to assign limits) is the distinction that allows him to defend Plutarch against the skepticism of Bodin, and it would seem relevant to the way he evaluates such testimony.

In his presentation of examples, Montaigne sometimes alters, adds to, or omits details from the historical accounts. For instance, he adapts and adds details to the stories he takes from Plutarch;[24] he adds to the biblical story of the Jew Rasias that he pulled out his entrails; he invents the cannibal's song, which is not found in his source. In the story of the man who could recognize individual eggs, told at the beginning of "Of experience," Montaigne says that the man was from Delphi, whereas Cicero had written that the man was from Delos.[25]

The story of Alexander's treatment of Betis, recounted in "By diverse means we arrive at the same end," is taken from Quintus Curtius. Montaigne changes the account of the way in which Betis was bound to the chariot: Quintus Curtius says that he was bound with thongs, whereas Montaigne says that his heels were pierced. Montaigne simply omits the observation of Quintus Curtius that Alexander was "exulting with insolent joy" over his conquest of Betis (IV.vi.26) and focuses entirely on his anger. Montaigne also omits the final detail of Quintus Curtius's report – that is, that while Betis was being dragged around the city of Gaza, Alexander "boasted that in taking vengeance on an enemy he had imitated Achilles, from whom he derived his race" (IV.vi.29).

This last omission is especially striking because, even among the several possible causes of Alexander's rage that Montaigne offers, he does not include the one that the historian regards as foremost and that he attributes to the mouth of Alexander himself. In omitting this detail, Montaigne is deliberately silent about the power of poetry to affect human action, although he does mention in "Of the most outstanding men" that Alexander regarded Homer as his best counselor in military matters (VS753; F570). The omission is suggestive because Montaigne's transformations of the stories that he borrows are themselves poetic. This is especially significant in the case of Epaminondas, the man who, along with Homer and Alexander, is presented as a most outstanding man. I suggest that, just as Homer is the poet of Achilles (the exemplar for Alexander), Montaigne is the poet of Epaminondas (the exemplar that Montaigne places before his prince for imitation).

In his *Montaigne and the Quality of Mercy*, David Quint notes that Montaigne's picture of Epaminondas turning away from his Spartan friend in the heat of his most glorious battle is almost entirely invented by Montaigne. No such detail is reported in the ancient sources. So also, there is no direct textual evidence for Montaigne's assertion that Epaminondas spared the lives of all those whom he vanquished.[26] In "Of the most outstanding men" Montaigne goes so far as to rank Epaminondas as the greatest of all the men he has ever known, placing him above Alexander, Cato, and even Socrates. Yet it seems that the character of Epaminondas is largely his own invention. Montaigne's essay form incorporates a poetic dimension, a dimension that must be taken into account when we try to understand how the essay is the form of accidental philosophy.[27]

At the end of essay I.21, "Of the power of the imagination," Montaigne presents us with two different notions of truth. The first is what might be called poetic truth: "So in the study that I am making of our *mœurs* and motions of the soul, fabulous testimonies, provided they are possible, serve like true ones. Whether they have happened or no, in Paris or Rome, to John or Peter, they exemplify, at all events, some human potentiality.... There are authors whose end is to tell what has happened. Mine, if I could attain it, would be to talk about what can happen." The second notion of truth might be called historical truth. In this regard, Montaigne says of himself: "I surpass all historical fidelity, being scrupulous to the point of superstition. In the examples that I bring in here of what I have heard, done, or said, I have forbidden myself to dare to alter even the slightest and most inconsequential circumstances. My conscience does not falsify one iota; my knowledge, I don't know." Here he contrasts himself with the theologians and philosophers who cannot accept the testimony of unknown and ordinary witnesses and who would refuse to testify themselves concerning what happens before their own eyes (VS105–6; F75–76).

Montaigne's standard of truth is different from the standard of the theologians and (deliberate) philosophers. They will neither accept borrowed truth nor trust that truth is being revealed in their presence. Montaigne connects the two notions of truth. His openness to testimony, to borrowed truth, and to possibility allows him to see the truth that reveals itself to his own eyes. Through this dialectic of poetic truth and historical truth, Montaigne incorporates poetry and history into his accidental philosophy.

This discussion of poetry and history in relation to philosophy recalls Aristotle's discussion in the *Poetics* (1451a35–1451b10): "The poet's function is to describe, not the thing that has happened, but a kind of thing that might happen, that is what is possible as being probable or necessary. The distinction between the historian and poet is not in the one writing prose and the other verse; ... it consists really in this, that the one describes the thing that has been, and the other a kind of thing that might be. Hence poetry is something more philosophic and of graver import than history, since its statements are of the nature rather of universals, whereas those of history are singulars. By a universal statement I mean one as to what such or such a kind of man will probably or necessarily say or do – which is the aim of poetry." Although Aristotle regards poetry as more philosophical than history, he does not incorporate the poetic or the historical into philosophy: the universal that philosophy arrives at is "above" the particulars and abstracted from images. Montaigne, on the other hand, does incorporate poetry and history. History is borrowed truth and it is only through his openness to borrowed truth that he can possess the truth for himself. Poetry is the truth of the possible and it is only on condition of his openness to the possible that the actual can reveal itself to him in its true being.

Daemonic Order

One of the most puzzling aspects of the essay form is the initial impression that there is no order. Montaigne seems to begin just anywhere, to often wander off the topic, sometimes hardly even to get to the topic.[28] One of the terms that Montaigne uses most frequently to describe his order is "accidental." In "Of books," shortly after advising the reader to pay more attention to the form than to the matter of the essays, Montaigne writes: "I have no other marshal but fortune to arrange my bits. As my fancies present themselves, I pile them up; now they come pressing in a crowd, now dragging single file. I want people to see my natural and ordinary pace, however off the track it is" (VS409; F297). At the beginning of "Of friendship" he asks: "What are these [essays] of mine, in truth, but grotesques and monstrous bodies, pieced together of divers members, without definite shape, having no order, sequence, or proportion other than accidental?" (VS183; F135).

There is, of course, a numerical ordering of the *Essays*, but, for the most part, that too seems accidental. The only hint of design that I detect in the numerical ordering is in essay I.29, "The twenty-nine sonnets of Etienne de La Boétie," where the number of the essay matches the number in the title. There are instances in which one essay is clearly related to another as is the case with II.16, "Of glory," and II.17, "Of presumption": the link is made explicit in Montaigne's introductory remarks to II.17.[29] But there are many places in the essays where an accidental, apparently nonsubstantive link can be made. Essay I.40, "A consideration upon Cicero," ends with a reference to inscriptions on the title pages of printed books; at the beginning of essay I.41, "Of not communicating one's glory," he cites Cicero on the fact that the very authors who write against the concern for glory make sure that their names appear in the front of their books. Essay I.3, "Our feelings reach out beyond us," ends with a reference to salted meats and essay I.4, "How the soul discharges its passions on false objects when the true are wanting," begins with the story of the man who cursed salted meats for his attacks of the gout. The thumbs of essay II.26, "Of thumbs," had already appeared in the "thumbs down" of the Roman gladiatorial combats in essay II.23, "Of evil means employed to a good end." These are trivial connections, but that is the point. The order is accidental, as if some nonessential remark in one essay leads him into the next. There is something artful about this because Montaigne does not place his essays in strictly chronological order – that is, we are not really being presented with a "stream of consciousness." Nevertheless, Montaigne clearly intends to emphasize a certain accidental quality in the way his mind works.

When we look at the chapter titles, what we see are apparently random topics without any deliberate order. Pascal refers to this as "Montaigne's muddle" and explains that Montaigne "certainly felt the lack of a rigid method," and "avoided it by jumping from one subject to another."[30] Montaigne begins from the first thoughts that come to his mind. Sometimes these thoughts are prompted by his reading, but they can come from anywhere and often there is no indication of how he came to take up a particular topic. What he says of conversation is also true of his writing: "[A]ll subjects are alike to me" (VS824; F625).

The accidental order of the *Essays* conveys a lack of design and an absence of premeditation. He says something similar about his reading: "I leaf through now one book, now another, without order and without plan, by disconnected fragments" (VS828; F629). The order of the essays is not determined by an end that is known in advance, that is put forward as the purpose of the book, and that therefore necessitates a structure and sequence that lead inevitably to that end. So Oakeshott describes the essay as having a course to follow but no destination at which one deliberately aims.

In "Of vanity" Montaigne digresses to comment on a digression: "This stuffing is a little out of my subject. I go out of my way, but rather by license than carelessness. My fantasies follow one another, but sometimes it is from a distance, and look at each other, but with a sidelong glance." Then he elaborates on his style by comparing it with Plato's and Plutarch's and ultimately placing it within the context of the daemonic: "I have run my eyes over a certain dialogue of Plato, a fantastic motley in two parts, the beginning part about love, all the rest about rhetoric. The ancients do not fear these changes, and with wonderful grace they let themselves be tossed in the wind, or seem to. The titles of my chapters do not always embrace their matter; often they only denote it by some sign. . . . I love the poetic gait, by leaps and gambols. It is an art, as Plato says, light, flighty, daemonic. There are works of Plutarch's in which he forgets his theme, in which the treatment of his subject is found only incidentally, quite smothered in foreign matter. See his movements in 'The Daemon of Socrates.' Lord, what beauty there is in these lusty sallies and this variation, and more so the more nonchalant and accidental they seem." The poetic order is daemonic. The poetic author (including philosophers like Plato and Plutarch) often seems to forget his own topic. But it is precisely here that Montaigne says that "it is the inattentive reader who loses my subject, not I." Beneath this appearance of digression upon digression there is an underlying subject. These poetic authors *seem* to be tossed in the wind, their sallies *seem* nonchalant and accidental: "My style and my mind alike go roaming. 'A man must be a little mad if he does not want to be even more stupid' say the precepts of our masters, and even more so their examples" (VS994; F761). There is an underlying oracular and daemonic quality that appears in the poetic sallies of Plato and Plutarch, and in the roaming of the *Essays*.[31]

What sense, then, can we make of the order of the essays? Montaigne's order is based on the nature of the human mind and on the order of thought itself.[32] In the "Apology," as we have seen, Montaigne goes through a long discussion of the animals, showing how we are not so superior to them as we might think. There are, of course, numerous stories about dogs and, after recounting one such dog story from Plutarch, Montaigne turns from dogs to stories of oxen, elephants, and birds. Then he writes: "I do not want to omit citing also this other example of a dog that the same Plutarch says he saw (for as for the order, I fully realize that I am disturbing it; but I observe none in arranging these examples any more than in the rest of my work)" (VS465; F341). He then goes on to tell another story of a dog that Plutarch claims to have observed. On one level and according to one meaning of "order," he has disturbed the order by suddenly going back to dogs after having finished with them to turn to oxen, elephants, and birds: this is the order of "things" that he has interrupted. But the other level of order that he has not really interrupted is the order of testimony and of witnesses, for the story of the magpie that precedes the intrusive dog story is also from Plutarch. Montaigne's mind is following not the order of things and kinds, but rather the order of human testimony and of conversation. This is the order of the human mind, not the order of the divine intellect of the deliberate philosophers.

What order there is in the *Essays* seems to be an attempt to bring under the mind's control the wild flow of chimeras and monsters that the mind gives rise to all on its own. "In order to train my fancy even to dream with some order and purpose, and in order to keep it from losing its way and roving with the wind, there is nothing like embodying and registering all the little thoughts that come to it" (VS665; F504). Montaigne thus stays close to the ordinary undisciplined flow of thought. As Merleau-Ponty says of Montaigne, "beneath clear ideas and thoughts he finds a spontaneity abounding in opinions, feelings, and unjustifiable acts."[33]

So where he begins does not really matter, for he is concerned not with "things" but with thought itself. He is always beginning "within" thought. And thoughts present themselves in a very undisciplined and accidental way: "I take the first subject that chance offers. They are all equally good to me" (VS302; F219). Why are they equally good? In a passage that Montaigne removed in his last revision of the *Essays*, he says that he would have chosen

richer and fuller topics, "if I had some other end proposed than the one I
have: any action is suitable for making ourselves known" (VS302n4). Whatever the topic, the subject is himself; something of his being is revealed in
his thought, something that would be obscured by what Pascal calls "a rigid
method."

At the beginning of essay II.8, "Of the affection of fathers for their children," he gives an account of the impetus for his writing that echoes the one
given in I.8, "Of idleness": "It was a melancholy humor, and consequently
a humor very hostile to my natural disposition, produced by the gloom of
the solitude into which I had cast myself some years ago, that first put into
my head this daydream of meddling with writing. And then, finding myself
entirely destitute and void of any other subject matter, I presented myself to
myself for argument and subject" (VS385; F278). He turns to books not in
order to arouse and exercise his mind, but rather to rest it because his mind
tends to become completely absorbed and tense when engaged within itself.
Idleness becomes painful for him because "the principal and most laborious
study" of his mind is "studying itself" (VS819; F621).

It is, then, widely recognized that Montaigne's primary concern in the
Essays is self-knowledge. He tells us that "I study myself more than any other
subject. That is my metaphysics, that is my physics" (VS1072; F821). We can
go even further and say that this is his sole concern: "I dare not only to speak
of myself, but to speak only of myself; I go astray when I write of anything
else, and get away from my subject" (VS942; F720).

Montaigne is always leading the reader back to himself, back to his own
strangeness. It is man himself, the most familiar, that is most strange. "Of the
affection of fathers for their children" is addressed to Madame d'Estissac:
"Madame, if strangeness and novelty, which customarily give value to things,
do not save me, I shall never get out of this stupid enterprise with honor; but
it is so fantastic and appears so remote from common usage that that may
enable it to pass. . . . Finding myself entirely destitute and void of any other
matter, I presented myself to myself for argument and subject. It is the only
book in the world of its kind, a book with a wild and eccentric plan. And so
there is nothing in this job worth noting but its bizarreness; for a subject so
vain and mean could not have been fashioned by the best workman in the
world into something worthy of notice" (VS385; F278).

The wild and eccentric plan of the *Essays* is due to the fact that Montaigne
always comes upon himself by accident: "This also happens to me: that
I do not find myself in the place where I look; and I find myself more by
chance encounter than by searching my judgment."[34] Sometimes he cannot
understand what he himself has written because he forgets what he meant,
whereas a stranger will discover his meaning. But at other times, "chance
will show me the light clearer than noonday and make me astonished at my
hesitation" (VS40; F26–27). In "On some verses of Virgil" he writes: "[B]ut I
am displeased with my soul for ordinarily producing its most profound and

maddest fancies, and those I like the best, unexpectedly and when I am least looking for them" (VS876; F668).

The order or rather the apparent disorder of the essays is meant to be contrasted with the "rigid method" that, according to Pascal, Montaigne regarded as inadequate to his purpose. Specifically, the essay must be contrasted with the way of deduction carried out in the syllogism, with the mode of disputation practiced in the schools, and with the form of the treatise.[35] Montaigne finds more truth in the chatter of fishwives and more order in the arguments of shopboys and shepherds than in the disputations of the logicians. "It is not so much strength and subtlety that I ask for as order; the order that we see everyday in the altercations of shepherds and shop boys, never among us. If they get off the track, it is by way of incivility; so indeed do we. But their turbulence and impatience never sidetrack them from their theme; their argument follows its course. If they get ahead of one another, if they do not wait for one another, at least they understand one another" (VS925; F706).

The syllogism, the disputation, and the treatise all constrain thought within the limits of a rigid method that requires precise definitions of one's terms, that assumes the truth of one's premises, and that aims at a predetermined conclusion. The essay, on the contrary, embraces the full range and depth of meaning of its terms and thus allows a deeper meaning, a "second sense," to emerge. The essay begins in opinion but does not treat that opinion as a premise – that is, opinion is taken as revealing truth but only after it is examined as if it were untrue. In Oakeshott's words, we begin with something assumed to be known but, at the same time, we assume it not to be known. The essay does not aim at a predetermined conclusion. It is rather a way of discovery that allows the accidental "some authority." What comes to light in the essay's movement of thought is the surprising character of thought itself and of the being who thinks.

PART II

ACCIDENTAL PHILOSOPHY

4

The Circular Dialectic of Self-Knowledge

Accidental philosophy is a form of dialectic. The dialectical movement of accidental philosophy is not, however, an ascent from opinion to knowledge; it is rather a circular movement in which thought returns to its beginnings and thus possesses those beginnings in a new way. Thought no longer simply presumes its starting points. What makes this circular movement dialectical is the reconciliation of opposites that takes place in the course of departure and return and the change that is brought about in the accidental philosopher himself. Each moment of the dialectical movement is preserved in the return to the beginnings. What makes this circular dialectic philosophical is the discovery that truth can only be found in the beginnings: we can only come to understand what we already somehow understand, and we can only see the truth that was already there.

In this chapter I first set out the circular movement of Montaigne's thought by considering several of the essays in which that movement seems especially clear and by tracing out the circular path that includes the first essay of each of the three books of the *Essays*. (The dialectic of the "Apology" is taken up in Chapter 5.)[1] A contrast is drawn between Montaigne's circular dialectic and skepticism. I then show how the circular dialectic is Montaigne's way of thinking within the pervasive and inescapable human condition of presumption, "our first and original malady," which allows us to recognize and make sense of the change in Montaigne's own being that turns him away from deliberate philosophy and to his own accidental philosophy.

Circular Dialectic

"Of vain subtleties"

As we saw in the preliminary account of accidental philosophy in Chapter 1, Montaigne does make explicit and elaborate on his circular movement of thought in "Of vain subtleties," the numerically central essay of all three books. This essay consists almost entirely of examples taken from a game that is played at his house. The game is a contest to see who can find the largest number of things that meet at their two extremes. So, for example, "Sire" is the title of the king and is also given to the vulgar, such as tradesman, but is given to no one else in between. Each of the examples gives two extremes, a high and a low that are alike or the same in some way, and a middle region that is different from both extremes.

Montaigne mentions himself in two of the examples. The first has to do with his practice of the philosophical life: "The simple peasants are good men, and good men the philosophers, at least what passes for philosophers in our time: strong and clear natures, enriched by a broad education in useful knowledge. The half-breeds who have disdained the first seat, ignorance of letters, and have not been able to reach the other – their rear-end between two stools, like me and so many others – are dangerous, inept, and importunate: these men trouble the world. Therefore, for my part, I draw back as much as I can into the first and natural stage, which for naught I attempted to leave" (VS313; F227). Montaigne's return or descent to the "low," to the condition of ignorance, is not and cannot be complete, as if he had never left it at all. He is caught in a kind of middle position, almost back to where he started.

The second example has to do with his Christian life. At one extreme we have the "simple souls, less curious and less learned . . . who, through reverence and obedience, believe simply and live under the laws." At the other extreme, we find the "great minds, more settled and clear-sighted . . . who, by long and religious investigation, sense the mysterious and divine secret of our ecclesiastical polity." Both extremes are "good Christians" and "good believers." The middle region, however, is the place where "error in opinion is engendered." What is this error? "Those in this [middle] range follow the first plausible meaning [the appearance of the first sense], and have some claim to regard our sticking to the old ways – those of us who are not versed in these matters by study – as simplicity and stupidity." There are two things to be especially noted in this description of the middle range. First, error is associated with "following the first plausible meaning." Second, another group of men emerges: those who stick to the old ways but who are neither versed in these religious matters by study (like the great minds at the highest extreme) nor simple and stupid (like the unlearned and incurious at the lowest extreme). Montaigne locates himself in this group: "*our* sticking to the old ways."

So now we have a fourth group that is difficult to place with respect to the higher and the lower. Belonging to neither of the extremes, this fourth group would seem to fit in the middle range along with those who are prone to error. Montaigne introduces a further complication. Immediately after his description of the highest, the "great minds" who have penetrated to a deeper understanding of Scripture and of the Church by way of long religious meditation, he writes: "However, we see some who have arrived at this last [highest] stage by way of the second [middle stage], with marvelous profit and confirmation, as at the extreme limit of Christian intelligence, and who enjoy their victory with consolation, active gratitude, reformed conduct, and great modesty." These people would seem to be our fourth group, those who stick to the old ways but who do so neither on account of simplicity nor on account of study. Those in the fourth group come through the middle region of error and arrive at the extreme limit of Christian intelligence by way of error: that is why they are described as grateful, reformed, and modest.

The middle region, then, consists of two kinds of men: those who remain in error, who follow the first plausible meaning and interpret sticking to the old ways as simplicity, and those who stick to the old ways because, through error, they have come to understand something about "the mysterious and divine secret of our ecclesiastical polity." The *Essays* are written primarily for those in that middle region. Montaigne concludes the essay by returning to its beginning, the game that produced all the examples: "But I find again, as ordinarily happens after the mind has opened up a passage, that we have taken for a difficult exercise and a rare subject what is not so at all; and that after our inventiveness has been warmed up, it discovers an infinite number of similar examples. And so I shall add only this one: that if these essays were worthy of being judged, I think they might not be much liked by common and vulgar minds, or by singular and excellent ones; the former would not understand enough about them, the latter too much. But they might get by in the middle region" (VS313; F227). Montaigne has "opened up a passage" for the mind, a passage back to the familiar. He is, at the same time, the philosopher who pulls back as far as he can to the condition of ignorance (his rear end between two stools) and the Christian at "the extreme limit of Christian intelligence" who, therefore, sticks to the old ways.[2]

"By diverse means we arrive at the same end"

The circular dialectic of accidental philosophy can be traced out in the first essay of Book I, "By diverse means we arrive at the same end." The editors Villey and Saulnier, in their introduction to this essay, tell us that Montaigne deliberately placed this essay at the very beginning. Apparently it was not written during the time when he began his work (1571–72), and so they conclude that it was not the date of its composition that caused him to place it first. Rather, the idea of the inconstancy of man was so important for him that he wanted it to be the first idea presented in the *Essays*.

The first sentence of this essay is: "The most common way to soften the hearts of those that one has offended, when, vengeance in hand, they hold us at their mercy, is to move them by submission to commiseration and pity." Montaigne begins this essay and thus the entire book from "the most common" (*la plus commune façon*). Here we can begin to see the circular movement of his thought. For he also ends the *Essays* with the most common:

"The most beautiful lives, to my mind, are those that conform to the common human pattern [*qui se rangent au modèle commun et humain*]" (VS1116; F857). Viewed as a whole, the essays begin and end with the most common.

Montaigne begins from the commonplace: submission is the most common way to soften the heart of the avenging conqueror. No examples of softening the heart by submission are given. This is so obviously true that no examples are needed. Its truth is presumed. So he turns immediately to the exceptions: "However, audacity and steadfastness – entirely contrary means – have sometimes served to produce the same effect." The commonplace is not universally true, but it still holds for the most part. The claim about contrary means requires some examples since it is not so obviously true. Montaigne gives three examples. First, Edward, prince of Wales, "having suffered much harm from the Limousins, and taking their city by force, could not be halted by the cries of the people and the cries of the women and children abandoned to the butchery, who implored his mercy and threw themselves at his feet – until, going farther and farther into the city, he saw three French gentlemen who with incredible boldness were holding out alone against the assault of his victorious army. Consideration and respect for such remarkable valor first took the edge off his anger; and he began with these three men to show mercy to all the inhabitants of the city." Second, Scanderberg, prince of Epirus, was pursuing one of his soldiers in order to kill him. The soldier had tried everything in the way of submission but to no avail. Finally, in a desperate attempt to save his life, he resolved to face Scanderberg with his sword. The prince was so struck by his resolution that his fury subsided and he received him back into his good graces. Third, the emperor Conrad III had besieged Guelph and could not be moved by any terms of surrender to spare the duke and his men. The only concession he made was that the noble women could leave the city on foot with only what they could carry on their persons. The women put their children, their husbands, and the duke on their shoulders and carried them out. When Conrad saw that, he was so moved that he wept, and his bitter hatred toward the duke died within him.

After giving those three examples, Montaigne does two things: first, he turns to himself, evaluating himself in terms of the commonplace and the exceptions; second, he makes an attempt at formulating a rule or principle under which the commonplace and the exceptions can be subsumed. When he turns to evaluate himself, we have the first words he says about himself in the *Essays*: "Either one of these two ways [submission or audacity] would easily move me, for I am wonderfully lax in the direction of mercy and gentleness. As a matter of fact, I believe I should be likely to surrender more naturally to compassion than to esteem. Yet to the Stoics, pity is a vicious passion; they want us to succor the afflicted, but not to unbend and sympathize with them."

However, he says, the other three examples seem more to the point, for they show the soul assailed and tested (*essayée*) by both submission and bravery, sustaining the first and bending under the second: Edward, Scanderberg, and Conrad cannot be moved by submission, but they are moved by esteem. Now Montaigne offers what might be a principle or rule to explain both the commonplace and the exceptions: "It may be said that to subdue your heart to commiseration is the act of easygoing indulgence and softness, which is why the weaker natures, such as those of women, children, and the common herd, are the most subject to it; but that having disdained tears and prayers, to surrender simply to reverence for the sacred image of valor is the act of a strong and inflexible soul which holds in affection and honor a masculine and obstinate vigor" (VS8; F4). This distinction is certainly plausible, perhaps the first plausible meaning that would suggest itself. It is not quite clear whether it is a distinction within nature (i.e., strong and weak natures) or a distinction between nature that is weak and discipline that makes the soul strong.

In any case, Montaigne does not simply accept this plausible account because there are instances where "the common herd" has responded to audacity with something like esteem: "However, in less lofty souls, astonishment and admiration can engender a like effect." He gives two examples. The people of Thebes put their generals, Pelopidas and Epaminondas, on trial for having continued in their posts beyond the prescribed limit. Pelopidas pleaded and made supplications to save himself and just barely escaped punishment. But Epaminondas came forward and proudly recounted the things he had done and reproached the people in a haughty and arrogant manner. The people "did not have the heart even to take up the ballots into their hands, and the assembly broke up, greatly praising the loftiness of this man's courage" (VS8; F4). The second example is that of the captain Phyto, who had valiantly defended the city of Rhegium against Dionysius the Elder. Dionysius decided to make Phyto an example of his vengeance, so he had him stripped and dragged through the streets while being whipped cruelly and ignominiously. But all the while, Phyto kept calling out loudly the honorable and glorious cause of his death, his refusal to submit his city to the tyrant. The rank and file of Dionysius's army, instead of growing angry at Phyto's defiance, began to be softened by astonishment at his great courage. When Dionysius perceived that his soldiers were about to mutiny and seize Phyto out of the hands of his executioners, he stopped the spectacle and had Phyto taken away and secretly drowned in the sea. "The people" and "the rank and file" display the same or a similar reaction to "the sacred image of valor" as do the "strong" natures.

Now, after offering and rejecting a principle that would subsume the commonplace and the exceptions, Montaigne draws a conclusion of sorts: "Truly man is a marvelously vain, diverse, and undulating object. It is hard to found any constant and uniform judgment on him" (VS9; F5). The essay concludes with examples of the difficulty of making uniform judgments. Pompey pardoned an entire city on account of the valor and magnanimity of

one man, who took the burden of guilt upon himself alone, but Sulla was unmoved by similar valor in similar circumstances. Finally, "directly contrary"
to the first three examples, Alexander the Great treated the valiant com-
mander Betis with great harshness and cruelty for the way he had defended
Gaza. And Alexander's desolation of the city of Thebes was carried out mer-
cilessly and completely in spite of the fact that the Theban soldiers, to the
last man, showed extreme courage and defiance.

As Villey and Saulnier point out, this essay does put before us the idea
of the inconstancy of man. Not only does the attempt at a principle fail but
also the unity of character of even a single individual cannot be maintained.
Alexander was "the bravest of men and very gracious to the vanquished"
(VS9; F5), yet in these two cases he shows himself to be out of control
with rage and vengeance. This reluctance to arrive at a universal and the
tendency to dissipate apparent unity of character is a persistent feature of
Montaigne's thought. But it is only a part of the movement of thought that
I want to describe here.

In essay I.1 "the most common" is assumed, accepted as true without example or any further justification, as a commonplace arrived at on the basis
of experience. Montaigne's first move is to show that this commonplace is
not universally true by giving three examples where bravery has produced
the same effect as submission. But also involved in this display of the inadequacy of the commonplace is a move from common to rare, from low
to high, from familiar to unfamiliar or strange. First, there is a move from
submission as the common and ordinary way of softening the heart of the
conqueror to defiance and constancy as the rare way. Second, there is the
change in the state of mind of the three princes: they ignore and are unmoved by the cries of common people and women and children, but they
are struck and moved by the sight of the extraordinary.

This movement of thought from low to high is captured in the principle
that Montaigne formulates as a plausible explanation of the commonplace
and its contrary: the weak and lowly are moved by common submission,
whereas the strong and lofty disdain weakness and pity but are moved by
the rare spectacle of virtue. For Montaigne, of course, this principle fails, but
what is expressed in it is the philosophical tendency to move from low to high
and to prefer the high. That, I take it, is why the lofty Stoics are brought in
here, condemning the passion of pity, and why Montaigne contrasts himself
with the Stoics.

The principle fails because there are cases in which the vulgar, the common herd, display the same response to extraordinary virtue as do the strong,
noble, and lofty. Montaigne does not remain content with the principle,
the universal, but comes back down to particulars. At the same time, he
finds the high in the low, the rare in the common: "[A]stonishment and
admiration are able to produce a similar effect" in the souls of the lowly

as esteem does in the souls of the princes. Finally, in the two concluding stories about Alexander the Great, he displays the extraordinary valor of Betis and of six thousand ordinary, nameless Theban foot soldiers, against which Alexander's rage and cruelty appear mean and petty: the ordinary is extraordinary, the common is rare.[3]

What has come about through the circular movement of this essay? What is the dialectical outcome? The commonplace that is the starting point of his thought identifies the most common with submission and thus with weakness and identifies the rare with defiance and thus with strength. Montaigne's examination of the commonplace includes an attempt to formulate a principle that would associate the strong, the rare, and the lofty, on the one hand, and the weak, common, and lowly, on the other hand. That principle expresses "the first plausible meaning" or "the appearance of the first sense." The principle cannot be maintained, however, because the examples that come to his mind show that the rare is found in the common, the extraordinary in the ordinary, and the high in the low. In the end, six thousand anonymous Theban soldiers show the same strength, courage, and defiance in the many that the first three princes so admired in the few.

Essay I.1 displays a dialectic of opposites: strength and weakness, esteem and compassion. Montaigne's statement about himself must be seen in the context of this dialectic: "Either one of these two ways [submission and defiance] would easily move me, for I am wonderfully lax in the direction of mercy and gentleness. As a matter of fact, I believe I should be likely to surrender more naturally to compassion than to esteem. Yet to the Stoics, pity is a vicious passion; they want us to succor the afflicted, but not to unbend and sympathize with them" (VS8; F4). By describing himself as extremely "lax" and as naturally prone to compassion, Montaigne associates himself with the weak, lowly, and common rather than with the strong, lofty, and rare. But he is the only example in the entire essay who combines compassion and esteem within himself. The dialectic of opposites results in their union in him. This union is made possible because Montaigne's esteem is not accompanied by pride (unlike the esteem of the princes): he has placed himself among the weak and lowly. Alexander's rage, on the other hand, shows that his esteem is accompanied by pride.

Further, Montaigne is as consistent and constant as the Stoics: he is consistently, in all cases, merciful and gentle. But he does not attribute his consistency to Stoicism or to any other philosophical discipline: the Stoics consider pity to be a vicious passion whereas Montaigne is naturally prone to compassion. Here we see the "second sense" of the title of the essay, "By diverse means we arrive at the same end." Montaigne has arrived, by other means, at the goal that the Stoics achieve by reason. The essay is, then, a dialectic of self-knowledge: Montaigne is "thinking through" or essaying his own *mœurs* and displaying them through a dialectic of examples.

"Of drunkenness"

Essay II.2, "Of drunkenness," begins with a discussion of the order and measure of vices: not all vices are equal, and to teach that they are equal is to give a great advantage to tyrants, traitors, and murderers. "Now drunkenness, among the others, seems to me a gross and brutish vice." Other vices require intelligence, or diligence, or boldness, but drunkenness is "all bodily and earthy." It completely overturns the understanding, and the "worst condition of man is when he loses knowledge and control of himself" (VS340; F245). Montaigne then recounts some stories of extreme drunkenness: "I would not have believed in a drunkenness so dead and buried, if I had not read ... this ... in the histories" (VS341; F246). And he considers the commonplace that wine loosens the tongue and makes the drunkard reveal the most intimate secrets. But there are exceptions to this: Augustus was never betrayed by Lucius Piso nor Tiberius by Cossus, both of whom sometimes became so drunk that they had to be carried out of the Senate.

In this essay Montaigne's opinion about drunkenness is in some way modified. He begins with what seem to be expressions of strong disgust. But then he reminds himself that the ancients, even the Stoics and other philosophers, did not strongly condemn this vice. "My taste and constitution are more inimical to this vice than my reason is." His natural reaction and his reason are not in perfect harmony on this subject. The process of thought that goes on in the essay brings them into accord. And this is not simply because he accepts the authority of the ancients: "For, quite aside from the fact that I easily submit my beliefs to the authority of ancient opinions, I find it [drunkenness] a weak and stupid vice, but less malicious and harmful than the others" (VS342; F247).

Now he is open to the pleasures of drinking: "The pleasure we want to reckon on for the course of our life should occupy more space in it. Like shop apprentices and workmen, we should refuse no occasion to drink, and have this desire always in our head." It seems that every day we cut back on our time for eating and drinking. "Could it be that in some respects we are moving toward improvement? Certainly not" (VS343; F247).

The essay ends with several accounts of what Montaigne calls "frenzy and madness." The disdain for suffering shown by the martyrs and the Stoic and Epicurean deliberate embrace of severe pain are examples of this. "And as Plato says that a sedate man knocks in vain on the door of poetry, so Aristotle says that no excellent soul is free from an admixture of madness" (VS347; F251). According to Plato, the faculty of prophecy is above us so that we must be taken outside ourselves. Our wisdom must be "lifted from its place by some celestial rapture" (VS348; F251). These are the last words of the essay. We have gone from gross, brutal drunkenness, from "the worst state of man" when he has "lost the knowledge and government of himself," to "celestial rapture," the state in which he is taken outside and above himself. Montaigne has come to see the high in the low, the celestial in the earthy.[4]

He is drinking with shopboys and laborers. And his discourse has in some way affected his manner of being: his taste and his reason have been brought into harmony.

"That to philosophize is to learn how to die"
Essay I.20, "That to philosophize is to learn how to die," displays the same circular movement, and it is especially significant because it deals directly with the practice of philosophy. Toward the beginning of the essay, Montaigne asserts that death is the goal of our life; if we are afraid of it, how can we go ahead without being always feverish? "The remedy of the common herd is not to think about it. But from what brutish stupidity can come so gross a blindness!" (VS84; F57–58). The philosopher, and indeed any man of understanding, cannot adopt such a stance toward death: "This brutish nonchalance, even if it could lodge in the head of a man of understanding – which I consider entirely impossible – sells us its wares too dear" (VS86; F59). We must learn to meet death steadfastly rather than avoid it. "And to begin to strip it of its greatest advantage against us, let us take an entirely different way from the common. Let us rid it of its strangeness, come to know it, get used to it" (VS86; F60). The philosophers and all men of understanding follow the way of constant premeditation of death, but, in the end, Montaigne leads us back to the common herd: "Since death is always the same, why nevertheless is there much more assurance against it among villagers and humble folk than among others.... We must strip the mask from things as well as from persons; when it is off, we shall find beneath only that same death which a valet or a mere chambermaid passed through not long ago without fear" (VS96; F68). Montaigne acknowledges the philosophical desire to rise above the common herd, to confront death with thought about death itself. The point of this premeditation is to take away the strangeness of death, to make it so familiar that it cannot surprise us. But this is to achieve the same result as mere nonchalance. By diverse means we arrive at the same end.[5]

"Of custom"
In "Of custom" Montaigne tells us of his own experience in examining a custom that he was supposed to defend and support. He did not want to support it simply by the force of the laws and example, so he proceeded to trace it to its origins. But he discovered the foundation of this custom to be so weak that he, who was supposed to confirm it in others, could hardly keep from becoming disgusted by it himself. Montaigne's experience is just what the philosopher experiences when he first examines custom, when he steps back from it and frees himself from its authority so as to see it in its origin. But Montaigne's response to this experience is presented in the terms of circular dialectic. "The first and universal reasons are hard to scrutinize, and our masters either skim over them lightly or, not even daring to touch them

at all, cast themselves immediately into the protection of custom, where they puff themselves up and enjoy a cheap triumph." That is the response of "our masters" who want to protect custom from the withering gaze of the philosopher. On the other hand, the philosophers trace custom back to its origin in nature and then refuse to submit themselves to custom. "Those who will not let themselves be dragged out of this original source err even more [than our masters] and bind themselves to barbarous opinions, like Chrysippus, who in so many places strewed his writings with remarks displaying the little account he took of incestuous unions, of whatever kind they might be" (VS117; F84). This is similar to the account he gives in the "Apology," where he says that the laws have their authority from custom, that it is dangerous to trace them back to their beginning for the source is like a little trickle of water that gives rise to a mighty river. "These people who weigh everything and refer it to reason, who accept nothing by authority and on credit, have judgments that are often far removed from popular judgments. Since they are men who take as their pattern the original image of nature, it is no wonder if in most of their opinions they deviate from the common way" (VS583; F440).

Montaigne's response is neither that of the masters who do not want to even touch the subject nor that of the philosophers who remain at the source and who find in nature a model of conduct far removed from the customary. Montaigne presents a third possibility. "Whoever wants to get rid of this violent prejudice of custom will find many things accepted with undoubting resolution, which have no support but in the hoary beard and the wrinkles of the usage that goes with them; but when this mask is torn off, and he refers things to truth and reason, he will feel his judgment as it were all upset, *and nevertheless restored to a much surer status*" (VS117; F84–85, emphasis added). Here again, we see Montaigne return to his beginning. He makes the same initial move as the philosopher who tears the mask away from custom, but he then has his judgment restored to a much surer state. This cannot mean that he simply takes refuge under the cover of custom as "the masters" do. Montaigne has already gone beyond that: he has stripped the mask from custom. Nor can it mean that custom has somehow been justified for him by its origin or by its source in original nature: like the philosopher, he sees the weakness of the source. The criterion is "truth and reason." This is what justifies and restores his judgment to a surer state. Truth and reason, then, are not defined in terms of some notion of original nature but rather in terms of returning to what was already there in one's starting points.

Essays I.1, II.1, and III.1
Readers of the *Essays* have long recognized the similarity between essay I.1, "By diverse means we arrive at the same end," and essay II.1, "Of the inconstancy of our actions." Villey and Saulnier (VS7) maintain that Montaigne

places these essays first because the theme of inconstancy is especially important for him. But in their introduction to II.1, they note that he also puts forward another idea that seems to contradict this all-pervasive inconstancy. In essay III.2, "Of repentance," he speaks of a "forme maîtresse" that is in each of us, a form that unifies our actions into some kind of coherent whole. My view is that this is not a contradiction, that the idea of a master form is already present in the first essay of Book III, and that it is arrived at in the third moment of the overarching movement that structures the entire work.

We can recall that in essay I.1, Montaigne explicitly introduces the theme of inconstancy: "Truly man is a marvelously vain, diverse, and undulating object. It is hard to found any constant and uniform judgment on him" (VS9; F5). Not only are there great differences among individuals but even within one single individual there is inconstancy to the point of contradiction: Alexander the Great, whose character we think we know to be lofty and magnanimous, surprises us with instances of rage and cruelty. In this first essay, we also find Montaigne's first statement about himself, which I discussed earlier: that statement is an assertion of Montaigne's own constancy compared with the rationally achieved constancy of the Stoics.

When we come to essay II.1, "Of the inconsistency of our actions," the theme of inconsistency is explicit in the title and throughout: "Those who make a practice of comparing human actions are never so perplexed as when they try to see them as a whole and in the same light; for they commonly contradict each other so strangely that it seems impossible that they have come from the same shop. . . . There is some justification for basing a judgment of a man on the most ordinary acts of his life; but in view of the natural instability of our conduct and opinions it has often seemed to me that even good authors are wrong to insist on fashioning a consistent and solid fabric out of us. They choose one general characteristic, and go and arrange and interpret all a man's actions to fit their picture; and if they cannot twist them enough, they go and set them down to dissimulation" (VS331–32; F239). Montaigne goes so far as to say that he finds it strange to see intelligent men trying to find consistency in human action because "irresolution seems to me the most common and apparent vice of our nature" and that "nothing is harder for me than to believe in men's consistency, nothing easier than to believe in their inconsistency" (VS332; F239). Indeed, "there is as much difference between us and ourselves as between us and others" (VS337; F244). As if to strengthen the link between this essay and essay I.1, he uses Alexander the Great as one of his principal examples. Alexander's valor, as extreme as it was, is not complete or universal: he becomes frantically worried at the slightest suspicion that his men are plotting against him, he behaves with violent and indiscriminate injustice and with a fear that subverts his reason, and his superstition bears the mark of pusillanimity.

Montaigne does not exempt himself from his description of extreme mutability: "Not only does the wind of accident move me at will, but besides,

I am moved and disturbed as a result merely of my own unstable posture; and anyone who observes carefully can hardly find himself twice in the same state.... All contradictions may be found in me by some twist and in some fashion" (VS335; F242).

Thus far, we seem to have only a horizontal movement, from the inconstancy of I.1 to the more fully articulated inconstancy of II.1. But when we consider Montaigne's explanation in II.1 for this inconstancy of action, we can begin to identify an ascent from low to high. "If it were by reasoning that we settled on a particular course of action we would choose the fairest course.... If any man could prescribe and establish definite laws and a definite organization in his head, we should see shining throughout his life an evenness of habits, an order and an infallible relation between his principles and his practice" (VS332–33; F240). If a man is not valiant on all occasions, then isolated instances of courage simply show that his is "a courage formed not by reason" but by mere circumstance (VS335; F242). "That is why, to judge a man, we must follow his traces long and carefully" (VS336; F243). Consistency of action is extremely rare and difficult, so that "in all antiquity it is hard to pick out a dozen men who set their lives to a certain and constant course, which is the principal goal of wisdom" (VS332; F240). The great example is Cato, in whom we find complete harmony and unity of life.

Montaigne's account of what is required for consistency of action is given in terms of reason and final cause: "A man who has not directed his life as a whole toward a definite goal cannot possibly set his particular actions in order. A man who does not have a picture of the whole in his head cannot possibly arrange the pieces.... No one makes a definite plan of his life; we think about it only piecemeal.... Our plans go astray because they have no direction and no aim" (VS337; F243). This is the goal of "deliberate philosophy," and it is a height that Montaigne himself never claims to have reached.

Montaigne concludes this essay on the same subject with which he began: the subject of those who try to explain human action. He circles back to his beginning. But there is an important difference between the beginning and the end. He no longer asserts that this is an impossible task, but that it is difficult and dangerous: "In view of this, a sound intellect will refuse to judge men simply by their outward actions; we must probe the inside and discover what springs [*ressorts*] set men in motion. But since this is an arduous and hazardous undertaking, I wish fewer people would meddle with it" (VS338; F244). Consistency achieved by means of reason deliberately aiming at one end is extremely difficult and rare. Such consistency would appear in "outward actions." But perhaps there is a "lower" kind of consistency discoverable only when we "probe the inside," a consistency that cannot be captured in the rules of deliberate philosophy.

Essay III.1, "Of the useful and the honorable," does not appear to take up the theme of inconstancy in the direct manner we find in I.1 and II.1. Montaigne begins from the observation that "our being" is held together by such sickly qualities as ambition, envy, vengeance, even cruelty (VS790; F599). Whoever would take away the seeds of these qualities "would destroy the fundamental conditions of our life." So in all governments there are offices that are necessary, abject, and even vicious. "If these vices become excusable, inasmuch as we need them and the common necessity effaces their true quality, we still must let this part be played by the more vigorous and less fearful citizens, who sacrifice their honor and their conscience, as those ancients sacrificed their life, for the good of their country. We who are *weaker*, let us take parts that are both easier and less hazardous" (VS791; F600, emphasis added).

Montaigne goes on to discuss such means as fraud, deceit, and betrayal that are often used to achieve the good of one's country. But in the course of this discussion of dishonorable actions, he tells us a good deal about himself, especially his conduct as negotiator between princes. He emphasizes his openness and candor, his hatred of betrayal and deception, his disinterestedness, and the limits of his engagement: he will not lie or dissimulate or even allow himself knowingly to be used as an instrument of deception for the sake of utility. "Double men" are useful but, in the end, they cannot be trusted. "This whole procedure of mine is just a bit dissonant from our ways. It would not be fit to produce great results or to endure. Innocence itself could neither negotiate among us without dissimulation nor bargain without lying" (VS795; F603). The suggestion here is that he wants to associate himself with the qualities of simplicity and innocence rather than with qualities that bring glory. And it is here that we see the third moment of the movement from low to high to low. "And if anyone follows and watches me closely, I will concede him the victory if he does not confess that there is no rule in their school that could reproduce this natural movement and maintain a picture of liberty and license so constant and inflexible on such tortuous and varied paths, and that all their attention and ingenuity could not bring them to it. . . . The way of truth is one and simple" (VS795; F603). This seems to be a direct reference back to essay II.1, to those who try to make our actions consistent by the standard of reason acting toward a final end: that higher standard, the standard of reason, cannot capture Montaigne's lower kind of constancy, which he describes as "the way of truth."

The circular movement that I have been following is this: in essay I.1 we do find the theme of the inconstancy of men but we also find there Montaigne's consistently marvelous laxity in the direction of mercy and gentleness. In II.1 we are presented with the necessity for the rule of reason for consistency of action as judged by the most plausible criterion: reason directed toward a fixed and single goal. In III.1 we see Montaigne's own lowly, "natural" consistency that cannot be captured by any rule. The movement is from low to high to low, from lowly weakness to the heights of the consistency of deliberate philosophy (which he falls short of) to the truth of his prereflective weakness.

Circular Dialectic and Skepticism

In Chapter 1 I set out the major differences between Montaigne's philosophical stance and that of the ancient Skeptics. Here, it is useful to elaborate on these differences in relation to Montaigne's circular dialectic. I consider the Pyrrhonian philosophy of Sextus Empiricus and Hume's "mitigated skepticism" as representative of ancient and modern forms of skepticism.

In his *Outlines of Pyrrhonism*, Sextus explains that the goal of Skepticism is quietude or tranquillity: "The originating cause of Skepticism is, we say, the hope of attaining quietude." Men who were philosophically inclined were "perturbed by the contradictions in things and in doubt as to which of the alternatives they ought to accept" (I.12).[6] The skeptic experiences disquiet because "the man who opines that anything is by nature good or bad is forever being disquieted: when he is without the things which he deems good, he believes himself to be tormented by things naturally bad and he pursues after the things which are, as he thinks, good; which when he has obtained he keeps falling into still more perturbations because of his irrational and immoderate elation" (I.27–28).[7] The Skeptics escape this torment because, as Sextus explains, "we live in accordance with the normal rules of life, undogmatically" (I.23–24).[8] And in contrasting Skepticism with the New Academy, he notes that the men of the New Academy use probability as the guide of life, whereas "we live in an undogmatic way by following the laws, customs, and natural affections" (I.231–32).[9]

The Skeptic, then, having become sated with philosophical debate, ends by relapsing into the customs and institutions of his own society. Common opinion has not been given a philosophical foundation and has not been replaced by philosophical reasonings. This chastened return to preexamined opinion and custom is also characteristic of Hume's mitigated skepticism.

In his *Enquiry concerning Human Understanding*, Hume seeks to reconcile two deficient modes of philosophy: abstruse philosophy that radically questions common opinion and custom, and the philosophy that simply tries to represent the common sense of mankind. He regards ancient Pyrrhonism as excessive, so that his own mitigated skepticism is the result of correcting the extreme skeptical doubts "by common sense and reflection."[10] In his view, "philosophical decisions are nothing but the reflections of common life, methodized and corrected."[11]

Donald Livingston has set out Hume's philosophy in terms of the distinction between true and false philosophy. False philosophy tries to use reason autonomously outside the authority of the demands of common life and thus generates sophistry and confusion. True philosophy accepts the authority of common life and the unexamined belief or custom that is its foundation. Livingston presents Hume as a dialectical thinker: "The relation between philosophy and common life, for Hume, is a dialectical one: the philosopher exists both within and without the world of common life. He exists within insofar as he presupposes the order as a whole. He exists without insofar as his thought is aimed at understanding ultimate reality." The true philosopher, however, must recognize "his cognitive alienation from ultimate reality." Therefore, skepticism is "internal to true philosophy."[12]

Montaigne's circular dialectic is significantly different from both ancient and Humean skepticism. Montaigne does not simply relapse into the customs and institutions of society or accept the authority of custom and common life. His circular dialectic is in some sense reformative and transformative, as we have seen already, for example, with respect to "Of drunkenness." Montaigne tells us that his *moeurs* are new and unusual and, as I argue in Part III, he transforms the moral tradition through a reordering of the virtues. Further, with respect to the ancient teaching that one should always obey the customs of one's country, Montaigne says "I cannot have my judgment so flexible." Montaigne's circular dialectic, then, cannot be understood simply as the chastened return to preexamined opinion and custom.

Montaigne identifies a "middle region" of men and, within that middle region, he distinguishes between two types: those who are and remain in error because they stop at the appearance of the first sense, and those who have come through error to the "extreme limit of Christian intelligence." As we have seen already in the discussion of "Of vain subtleties," this fourth type combines "sticking to the old ways" with the extreme limit of Christian intelligence, implying that there is more to the fourth position than simple acquiescence in custom.

Montaigne's return to his starting points, or his sticking to the old ways, involves a recognition of the truth of those starting points and first opinions. He does not simply accept and acquiesce on account of having become sated with and tormented by philosophical debate or having been caught up in the sophistry and confusion generated out of autonomous reason. The outcome of circular dialectic is not skeptical imperturbability or Humean acceptance of custom, but wonder at the most familiar.

Montaigne's movement of thought is genuinely dialectical in a way that ancient Skepticism is not. And although there are similarities between Montaigne's circular dialectic and Hume's dialectic of true and false philosophy, there are essential differences. The skepticism that is internal to Hume's true philosophy is the skeptical moment of doubt, whereas the skeptical moment internal to accidental philosophy is the moment of openness to the possible. Hume's philosophy remains a form of skepticism, that is, "mitigated scepticism," whereas Montaigne's philosophy is "accidental." At each moment of the movement of his thought, a kind of presumption is overcome and that overcoming is preserved in the final outcome of the revelation of truth. These aspects of Montaigne's dialectic are developed further in the next section.

The Dialectic of Presumption

The circular movement of Montaigne's thought might appear to be decidedly unphilosophical. In merely returning to his prephilosophical starting points, he does not seem to break the hold of presumption over his thought. We would expect the philosopher first to recognize that the initial sense of certitude about his unexamined opinions is irrational. We would then expect him to examine those opinions in the light of reason, to reject those that prove to be false and retain those that are now established on a rational foundation. Some version of this Cartesian method would seem to be requisite for any mode of thought that wants to call itself philosophical.

Judged against the background of these expectations, Montaigne's description of his own engagement with presumption is extremely puzzling because it seems strikingly unphilosophical. In "Of presumption" he writes: "This capacity for sifting truth, whatever it may amount to in me, and this free will not to enslave my belief easily, I owe principally to myself. *For* the firmest and most general ideas I have are those which, in a manner of speaking, were born with me. They are natural and all mine. I produced them crude and simple, with a conception bold and strong, but a little confused and imperfect. Since then I have established and fortified them by the authority of others and the sound arguments of the ancients, with whom I found my judgment in agreement. These men have given me a firmer grip on my ideas and a more complete enjoyment and possession of them" (VS658; F499). Montaigne is making the highly presumptuous and unphilosophical claim that what he has always believed is true because he has always believed it. Yet he is claiming an independence of thought and an ability to discover the truth. The circular dialectic of accidental philosophy must be understood in terms of the way in which he comes to grips with the pervasive human condition of presumption.[13]

Montaigne refers to presumption as "our first and original malady" (VS452; F330) and as the first tyranny of the evil spirit (VS449; F328), suggesting that presumption is, in fact, original sin. Presumption is first, and thus unrecognized. It is the unreflective milieu of prephilosophical certitude, the sea of opinion in which we are immersed. And this condition of immersion in prephilosophical presumption the philosopher seeks to escape and transcend through reason. For Montaigne, however, deliberate philosophy does not go far enough. Deliberate philosophy simply escapes to another form of presumption, philosophical presumption. His own circular dialectic is thus far more radical than the ascent of deliberate philosophy because it recognizes and engages both kinds of presumption. The return of circular dialectic to prephilosophical opinion preserves both the initial deliberate philosophical break with unreflective opinion and the break that accidental philosophy makes with philosophical presumption. Ancient philosophy has only given him a "firmer grip" and a "more complete possession"

of his first beliefs. Montaigne's return to his first beliefs gives him those beliefs in a new way. That is why he can say in "Of presumption" that he does
not easily enslave his belief and that he has the capacity to sift out the true.
He finds the truth of his first beliefs.[14]

How, then, does the circular path of accidental philosophy move through
the dialectic of prephilosophical and philosophical presumption? I begin
by giving a brief account of Montaigne's portrayal of reason, that reason
by which the deliberate philosopher seeks to escape the presumption of
opinion. Then I set out the kinds of error that Montaigne associates with
presumption. We can then see how he deals with these errors of presumption: reason is corrected by the "lower" faculties of memory and imagination. Finally, I discuss what I believe to be the most remarkable confession
of presumption that Montaigne makes in the *Essays*. This recognition of
presumption is the condition for a kind of "intellectual repentance" that is
essential to the dialectic of self-knowledge.

Montaigne's references to reason in the *Essays* are almost entirely cau-
tionary or critical. The great philosophers have "amused themselves with
reason as with a vain and frivolous instrument, putting forward all sorts of
notions and fancies" (VS545; F408). It is extremely difficult to impose order
and measure on the mind (VS559; F419), and "we shall never heap enough
insults on the unruliness of our mind" (VS24; F15). Those who will accept
only reason as the touchstone of truth must be made to see that "it is a
touchstone full of falsity, error, weakness, and impotence" (VS541; F405).
Finally, philosophy itself recognizes the unruliness of reason: "I am calling
reason our reveries and dreams, with the dispensation of philosophy, which
says that even the crazy man and the wicked man are mad with reason, but
it is a particular sort of reason" (VS523; F389).

One of the essential aspects of Montaigne's criticism of reason is its
double-edged quality. "Human reason is a two-edged and dangerous sword"
(VS654; F496). Reason can argue for the false as well as the true. In its
function of seeking the causes of things, it can arrive at the false as well
as the true. Reason "always goes its way, even though crooked, lame, and
broken-hipped and with falsehood as with truth. Thus it is not easy to discover its miscalculation and irregularity. I always call reason that semblance
of intellect that each man fabricates in himself. That reason, of which, by its
condition, there can be a hundred contradictory ones about one and the
same subject, is an instrument of lead and of wax, stretchable, pliable, and
adaptable to all biases and all measures" (VS565; F425). The true and the
false are so difficult to separate because "human reason is a tincture infused
in about equal strength in all our opinions and ways [*mœurs*]" (VS112; F80).
How are we to sift out the true when "truth and falsehood are alike in face,
similar in bearing, taste, and movement?" (VS1027; F785). How are we to
overcome the condition of error, a condition so fundamental to what we are?
Reason seems to tend so much more easily toward error than toward truth.

Montaigne most often, if not always, associates error with some form of presumption. The first kind of error is the failure to be open to the unfamiliar: "We are all huddled and concentrated in ourselves, and our vision is reduced to the length of our nose. . . . We are all unconsciously in this error, an error of great consequence and harm" (VS157; F116). The expansion of experience by getting to know men through the testimony of others is a corrective to vulgar presumption through education, especially through history whereby we come to know the whole range of human possibilities. The second kind of presumption consists in the error of not coming back to ourselves, to the most familiar. "The most common and universal error of men" is to fail to see in our own selves the very things for which we blame others: "Not only the reproaches that we make to one another, but also our reasons and arguments in controversial matters can ordinarily be turned against ourselves; and we run ourselves through with our own weapons. . . . Our eyes see nothing behind us. A hundred times a day we make fun of ourselves in the person of our neighbor and detest in others the defects that are more clearly in ourselves, and wonder at them with prodigious impudence and heedlessness. . . . Oh importunate presumption!" (VS929; F709). This second kind of error keeps us from ever knowing ourselves. The movement of circular dialectic always brings us back to the most familiar.

In order to see how Montaigne gets out from under the power of presumption and its errors, we need to turn to what he tells us about the capacities of his soul as they relate to thought, especially the capacities of memory and imagination. Montaigne's discussion of his memory is one of the most puzzling parts of the *Essays*. What he says seems so obviously false that many readers have concluded that he is guilty of false modesty of the highest order. The especially pertinent passage occurs at the very beginning of essay I.9, "Of liars": "There is no man who has less business talking about memory. For I recognize almost no trace of it in me, and I do not think there is another one in the world so monstrously deficient. All my other faculties are low and common; but it is in this one I think I am singular and very rare, and thereby worthy of gaining a name and reputation" (VS34; F21). The *Essays* are full of hundreds of quotations from dozens of authors and hundreds of stories full of detail. Obviously Montaigne has an excellent memory. But before we conclude that this is false modesty, we ought to take him at his word and try to make sense of this passage.

What does Montaigne mean by memory in the sense in which he is monstrously deficient? The distinction that must be made is the distinction between memory and understanding. Language itself makes this distinction difficult to see: "[I]f in my part of the country they want to say that a man has no sense, they say he has no memory" (VS34; F22). But Montaigne insists on the distinction between memory and understanding, even going so far as to point out that excellent memories are often joined to very weak judgment. He also distinguishes between memory and invention: thanks to his poor memory, his speech is brief, "for the storehouse of memory is apt to be better furnished with matter than that of invention" (VS35; F22). On the other hand, Montaigne is excellent in forgetting: "I am so good at forgetting that I forget even my own writings and compositions no less than the rest" (VS651; F494). Perhaps he is also unique among philosophers in "the science of forgetfulness" (VS494; F365).

What is the philosophical import of Montaigne's discussion of memory? Lack of memory is clearly connected with telling the truth: "It is not unreasonably said that anyone who does not feel sufficiently strong in memory should not meddle with lying" (VS35; F23). Montaigne does not have enough memory to sustain a deception in his role in negotiations between princes: "Therefore I give myself up to being candid and always saying what I think, by inclination and by reason" (VS649; F492). He no longer prepares himself to make speeches, for he then feels enslaved to his memory: "[M]y plan in speaking is to display extreme carelessness and unstudied and unpremeditated gestures, as if they arose from the immediate occasion" (VS963; F735), a description of his speaking that could easily be applied to his writing. Finally, lack of memory is directly associated with Montaigne's "ignorance" (VS651; F494). And he says of the *Essays* that "if I had wanted to speak from knowledge, I would have spoken earlier. I would have written at a time nearer to my studies, when I had more wit and memory" (VS1056; F809).

How is this monstrously deficient memory crucial to the truth of the *Essays?* The distinctions that he makes between memory and understanding and between memory and invention suggest that memory holds thought in its power by the unrecognized authority of remembered or "borrowed" opinions. Montaigne's deficiency of memory is his freedom from subjection to unexamined presuppositions. His intellect is not dominated by either philosophical or common authoritative opinion and is not a mere storehouse or collection of received opinions.[15]

One of the most important aspects of the freedom from presumption that is implied in his lack of memory is manifested in the way Montaigne is able to see the familiar in an unaccustomed light. Considering "the things that are right in our hands," he says that "it is rather familiarity than knowledge that takes away their strangeness." If these now familiar things were presented to us for the first time, we would be surprised by them and find them incredible (VS179; F132–33). It is memory that makes things familiar, that takes away their strangeness and causes us to assume that we understand them.

The philosophical significance of Montaigne's monstrously deficient memory, then, is his freedom from prephilosophical presumption. And the other side of this freedom is his openness to the new and unfamiliar, for he is not bound to what is stored in his memory. This openness to the new and unfamiliar is especially evident in his discussion of the imagination. Whereas Montaigne is deficient in memory, he is rich in imagination: "I am

one of those who are very much influenced by the imagination.... Its impression on me is piercing" (VS97; F68). The imagination is not entirely
"innocent," however. It is not trustworthy, and it needs to be disciplined. In
the "Apology" Montaigne actually associates the imagination with presumption: "Presumption is our natural and original malady.... It is by the vanity
of ... imagination that [man] equals himself to God," imagining himself as
ruler of the universe (VS452; F330–31). And it would seem to be the same
imagination that is implicated in what happens to Montaigne when he retires to his home to spend his life in occupying his mind with itself. What
he finds is that "in the vague field of imagination" there is no folly or mad
dream that is not produced in his mind and that "so many chimeras and
fantastic monsters [are born from it], one after another, without order or
purpose" (VS33; F21).[16]

While the imagination is implicated in the pervasive condition of presumption, it is at the same time essential to the overcoming of presumption.
In the course of working out the role of the imagination in Montaigne's
practice of philosophy, we can bring to light just what it is that disciplines
the imagination and restrains its tendency to produce chimeras. In my discussion of the skeptical moment of Montaigne's thought in Chapter 1, we
see that the skeptical moment is one of openness to the strange. Unlike
those who cannot believe that anyone else can do what they themselves cannot do, Montaigne's belief expands and is at least open to much that others
would reject as unbelievable. The imagination is the faculty that is essential
to Montaigne's openness. This can be seen clearly in "Of Cato the Younger."
Montaigne begins this essay by distinguishing himself from those who judge
everyone by what they find in themselves: "I do not share that common error of judging another by myself. I easily believe that another man may have
qualities different from mine ... and in contrast with the common run of
men, I more easily admit difference than resemblance between us." He goes
on to say that just because he is not continent in sexual matters he does not
doubt the sincere continence of the Feuillant and Capuchin monks: "I can
very well insinuate myself by imagination into their place" (VS229; F169).
In "Of repentance" he says, "I imagine numberless natures loftier and better
regulated than mine" (VS813; F617). And in "Of solitude" he says that when
he considers the poor beggar at his door, "I put myself in his place, I try to
fit my mind to his bias" (VS243; F179).[17]

The *Essays* are so rich in images and in vivid detail because Montaigne
wants to rekindle the imagination of his readers, especially with respect
to heroic men like Cato. In his century, he says, not only the practice
"but even the imagination of virtue is wanting; and it seems to be nothing
else but a piece of school jargon" (VS230; F169). That is why he uses all
his "ingenuity" (*invention*) to raise these heroic souls as high as possible
(VS231; F170). He wants to rekindle the imagination of his readers so that
the great men he portrays will serve as models and imagined witnesses to

our actions: "Keep ever in your imagination Cato, Phocion, and Aristides, in whose presence even fools would hide their faults; make them controllers of all your intentions. . . . that is the counsel of true and natural philosophy" (VS247–48; F183).

What is the philosophical import of Montaigne's discussion of the imagination? Whereas reason seeks the necessary and the universal, the imagination is the faculty that gives us access to the possible and the particular and that keeps us fixed on the particular. Reason may ascend from particulars to the universal and to universal rules, but the imagination moves only among particulars. Remaining open to the possible requires this attending to and moving among particulars rather than ascending to universals. The attempt to ascend to a universal from many particulars entails the presumption of the sameness of the individuals and the disregarding of differences. If the possible is to appear, the understanding must be able to recognize it. The possible would have to appear as the new, the unexpected, and the new and unexpected could only appear as a particular. That is, the concern with ascending from particulars to universals closes the mind to genuine possibility because the universal becomes a crippling presumption of sameness.[18]

Montaigne also relates the faculty of imagination to the capacity for judgment. He refers to the *Essays* as essays of his judgment: "Judgment is a tool to use in all subjects, and comes in everywhere. Therefore in the tests [*essais*] that I make of it here, I use every sort of occasion" (VS301; F219). "Of ancient customs" begins with his reference to "a common vice" that is found not only in the vulgar but in almost all men, the vice of having one's judgment enslaved to the authority of custom. Montaigne's purpose in this essay is to present examples of ancient customs, some of which are the same as those of his own day and some of which are different, so "that we may strengthen and enlighten our judgment by having in the imagination this continual variation of human things" (VS297; F216). The imagination allows us to have in mind the differences and variety, the particularity of human things. And this, rather than the universal, enables us to clarify and strengthen our judgment. In "Of the art of discussion" he makes his preference for particularity explicit: "These universal judgments that I find so common signify nothing. They are like men who salute a whole people in a crowd and in a body. Those who have a real acquaintance with them salute them and notice them by name and individually. But that is a hazardous undertaking" (VS936; F715).

"Of the power of the imagination" concludes with the claim that "in the study I am making of our behavior [*mœurs*] and motions [of the soul] [*mouvements*], fabulous testimonies, provided they are possible, serve like true ones. . . . There are authors whose end is to tell what has happened. Mine, if I could attain it, would be to talk about what can happen" (VS105–6; F75). In this essay Montaigne again presents himself as a third possibility. There are the vulgar who "think they see what they do not see" – for example, visions, miracles, enchantments (VS99; F70). This is due to the power of the imagination. And there are the theologians and philosophers, and "such people of exquisite and exact conscience" who refuse to testify concerning actions that occur in their own presence, right before their own eyes, and who refuse to answer for the fidelity (*la foi*) of any man. How could the theologians ever write history? "How can they stake their faith on a popular faith? How [could they] be responsible for the thoughts of persons unknown and give their conjectures as coin of the realm?" (VS106; F76). On the one hand, there are the vulgar who see what is not there; on the other, the learned who do not see what is there. If Montaigne is a third possibility, then he presents himself as seeing what is there. But what does that mean? His "seeing what is there" is consistent with the acceptance of testimony and with staking his faith on a popular faith. His is a seeing that is somehow conditioned by an imaginative openness to the possible.[19]

But what can put a check on the imagination? How is it kept from flying off to rule the universe, or from accepting as true any wild fancy or dream that happens to present itself? One of the principal checks on the imagination is testimony. The things that we ought to be open to are things that have been "testified to by trustworthy people [*gens dignes de foi*]" (VS180; F133). And the conclusion of "Of the power of the imagination" is set within the context of testimony: "[F]or I refer the stories that I borrow to the conscience of those from whom I take them" (VS105; F75). These are "borrowed truths."

The check on the imagination that is provided by testimony entails his being drawn back out of the solitary world of chimeras and fantastic monsters and into the world of other men, into the world of the *on dit*. The mind by itself and turned in on itself gives rise to the dreams or nightmares of reason. The world of the *on dit* is the common world.

Now we can turn to essay I.27, "It is folly to measure the true and false by our own capacity," where we find one of the very few places in the *Essays* where Montaigne makes explicit any significant change or decisive turning point in his life. He begins this essay by describing both the presumption of the vulgar and the presumption of the learned. The vulgar and women and children believe easily and are easily persuaded, whereas the vice of those who think they are superior to the common folk is to disdain and condemn as false whatever seems impossible to them. Now he tells us of the remarkable change in himself: "I used to do so once; and if I heard of returning spirits [ghosts], prognostications of future events, enchantments, sorcery, or some other story that I could not swallow,... I felt compassion for the poor people who were taken in by these follies. And now I think that I was at least as much to be pitied myself" (VS178–79; F132). I believe it would be true to say that this is the most radical change in himself that Montaigne ever mentions in the entire *Essays*. How did this change come about? "Reason has taught me that to condemn a thing thus, dogmatically, as false and impossible, is to assume the advantage of knowing the bounds and limits of God's will and of the power of our mother Nature; and that there is no more notable folly in the world than to reduce these things to the measure of our capacity and competence. If we call prodigies or miracles whatever our reason cannot reach, how many of these appear continually to our eyes! Let us consider through what clouds and how gropingly we are led to the knowledge of most of the things that are right in our hands; assuredly we shall find that it is rather familiarity than knowledge that takes away their strangeness" (VS179; F132). This is Montaigne's confession of presumption, a confession made publicly by a repentant reason.

As a result of this change in himself, Montaigne is always pulling back and directing the reader back to the familiar from the strange. In "Of evil means employed to a good end" he describes the furious spectacles of Roman gladiatorial combats. The first Romans used criminals in those combats, but gradually they began to use innocent slaves and freemen who had sold themselves for that purpose. "This I would consider very strange and incredible if we were not accustomed to see every day in our wars many thousands of foreigners engaging their blood and their lives for money in quarrels in which they have no concern" (VS685; F519). In the section on the animals in the "Apology" he takes up the argument that the animals are inferior because they cannot communicate with us: "It is no great wonder if we do not understand them; neither do we understand the Basques and the Troglodytes" (VS453; F331). To the argument that the animals are inferior because they allow themselves to be captured and made to serve us, he says: "This is only the same advantage that we have over each other. We have our slaves on this condition" (VS461; F337). And in "Of experience" he describes the very great differences in customs and ways of living having to do with eating and sleeping, citing the ancients, Seneca, Socrates, and Attalus. But then, "look at the difference between the life of my manual laborers and my own. The Scythians and Indians are in no respect more remote from my powers and ways" (VS1082; F829). In "Of physiognomy" he compares the noble behavior of the common people of his region during the plague to the loftiness of the Roman soldiers who, after their defeat at the battle of Cannae, suffocated themselves in holes they had dug with their own hands (VS1049; F803).

In some cases, the return to the familiar has a decidedly moral import. In "Not to counterfeit being sick" he quotes a letter from Seneca to Lucilius concerning Harpaste, his wife's "fool," who is her hereditary charge. Seneca writes: "If I have a mind to laugh at a fool, I do not have to look far for one, I laugh at myself. . . . Let us not look for our disease outside of ourselves; it is within us, it is planted in our entrails" (VS689; F522). So in "On some verses of Virgil," after agreeing with the complaints of men that women are changeable and unfaithful in love, he turns back on those men and on himself: "Those who are astonished at this and exclaim against it and seek out the causes of this malady in women as if it were unnatural and incredible, why don't they see how often they accept it in themselves without being appalled and calling it a miracle?" (VS885; F675). And in "Of the art of discussion" he writes "A hundred times a day we make fun of ourselves in the person of our neighbor and detest in others the defects that are more clearly in ourselves, and wonder at them with prodigious impudence and heedlessness" (VS929; F709).

Not only does he draw us back to the familiar, he also seems to have a clear preference for the low: "If anyone will sum us up by our actions and conduct, a greater number of excellent men will be found among the ignorant than among the learned: I mean in every sort of virtue" (VS488; F359). In "Of three good women" he remarks that "among people [of low estate] . . . it is not so novel to see some trait of rare goodness, [but among those who are noble and rich,] these examples of virtue rarely lodge" (VS745–46; F564). In "Of presumption" he writes: "The least contemptible class of people seems to me to be those who, through their simplicity, occupy the lowest rank; and they seem to show greater regularity in their relations. The morals [*mœurs*] and the talk of peasants I find commonly more obedient to the prescriptions of true philosophy than are those of our philosophers" (VS660; F501). And in the "Apology" he tells us: "I have seen in my time a hundred artisans, a hundred plowmen, wiser and happier than rectors of the university, and whom I would rather resemble" (VS487; F359). Montaigne does not deny the distinction between high and low. Indeed, as we have seen, he opposes those who would debase the motives of such men as Cato, and he is contemptuous of those who cannot admit anything as possible that they themselves could not do. He often insists on his own inability to reach the heights of virtue. But he does find the resolution of Cato in the village woman who, tormented by her husband's beating and difficult temperament, premeditates her suicide for a whole night and then calmly jumps off a bridge. And of the villager who cuts off his genitals and throws them at his jealous wife, he says, "If this had been for reason and religion, like the priests of Cybele, what should we not say of so sublime an enterprise?" (VS706; F534).

His discussion of Socrates in "Of physiognomy" focuses on the lowliness of Socrates. It is Socrates who is the model of human perfection, yet he "makes his soul move with a natural and common motion. So says a peasant, so says a woman. His mouth is full of nothing but carters, joiners, cobblers and masons. His are inductions and similes drawn from the commonest and best-known actions of men; everyone understands him. . . . It is a great thing to have been able to impart such order to the pure and simple notions of a child that, without altering or stretching them, he produced from them the most beautiful achievements of our soul. He shows it as neither elevated nor rich; he shows it only as healthy, but assuredly with a very blithe and clear health. By these vulgar and natural motives, by these ordinary and common ideas, without excitement or fuss, he constructed not only the best regulated but the loftiest and most vigorous beliefs, actions, and morals [*mœurs*] that ever were. It is he who brought human wisdom back down from heaven" (VS1038; F793). And later in the same essay, he answers those who might find fault with him for choosing Socrates as his example because they believe that the discourse of Socrates is so far above common opinions. Montaigne responds that he has chosen Socrates on purpose: "[F]or I judge otherwise, and hold that it is a speech which in its naturalness ranks far behind and below common opinions. In an unstudied and artless boldness and a childlike assurance it represents the pure and primary impression and ignorance of Nature." The speech that Montaigne is referring to is Socrates' speech to his judges concerning his "nonchalant and mild way of considering his death" (VS1054; F807).

In "Of physiognomy" he also speaks of the simplicity of Socrates. His point is that we would have only contempt and disdain for Socrates if it were not for the reverence in which he is held in public opinion. We admire Socrates not because we really see what is of value in him but simply on account of the authority of the learned. "We need a clear and well-purged sight to discover the secret light" of Socrates' hidden beauty, his naiveté and simplicity. For us, naiveté is not far removed from stupidity. "Under so mean a form we should never have picked out the nobility and splendor of his admirable ideas, we who consider flat and low all ideas that are not raised up by learning" (VS1037; F793). Montaigne identifies a "well-purged" vision with the ability to see the high in the low, the noble in the base.

Socrates, on the day of his death, speaks and acts as if it is no different from any other day. "But how many low-born people do we see led to death – and not a simple death, but mingled with shame and sometimes with grievous torments – bringing to it such assurance, some through stubbornness, others through natural simplicity, that we see no change from their ordinary manner . . . yielding in nothing to Socrates" (VS51; F34). And in one of the most moving passages of the *Essays*, Montaigne writes: "Let us look on the earth at the poor people we see scattered there, heads bowed over their toil, who know neither Aristotle nor Cato, neither example nor precept. From them Nature every day draws deeds of constancy and endurance purer and harder than those that we study with such care in school" (VS1040; F795). In the end, philosophy itself, after teaching us all its rules, must send us back to the example of the lowly and common, who, in their ordinary lives, show more firmness than those who are merely learned.

Montaigne's "lowering" is not a mere rhetorical strategy for striking at the pride of the philosophers. Besides the more obvious moral and political implications, his preference for the low and the ordinary is an essential feature of his "metaphysics" or "first philosophy."[20] He truly intends to articulate the lowest and the most common. In speaking about his admiration for the great men of Rome, he tells us how real and vivid their images are to him. He pictures their faces, their clothes, the places where they walked.

"Of things that are in some part great and admirable, I admire even the common parts. I would enjoy seeing them talk, walk, and sup" (VS997; F763). That is because "every movement reveals us. That same mind of Caesar's which shows itself in ordering and directing the battle of Pharsalia, shows itself also in arranging idle and amorous affairs" (VS302; F219). The philosophers who want to give an account of the human only in terms of the highest in man cannot give a complete account: "Among the functions of the soul there are some lowly ones; he who does not see that side of her also, does not fully know her" (VS302; F220). We must go even further than admitting the lowest and common parts of the great. For "the souls of emperors and cobblers are cast in the same mold" (VS476; F350). We presume that, because the actions of princes are so important, the causes of those actions are greater and weightier. But, in fact, the great are moved by the same springs (*ressorts*) as we are. The same cause that leads us to quarrel with a neighbor leads a prince to wage war; the same passion that brings us to the point of striking a servant brings the prince to the point of destroying a province.

Finally, Montaigne is very clear about where he locates himself in the hierarchy of high and low. Among the many places where he insists on his lowliness, we can point to the lowliness of "this plebeian stupidity of mine," which he contrasts with the "noble impassibility of the Stoics" (VS1020; F780). And in what are perhaps the most famous words of the *Essays*: "I set forth a humble and inglorious life; that does not matter. You can tie up all moral philosophy with a common and private life just as well as with a life of richer stuff. Each man bears the entire form of the human condition" (VS805; F611). In the end, "we are all of the common herd" (*nous sommes tous du vulgaire*) (VS570; F429).

One of the most important differences between deliberate philosophy and Montaigne's accidental philosophy is that deliberate philosophy begins in wonder and ends in the knowledge that replaces wonder, whereas Montaigne's accidental philosophy ends in wonder: he wonders at the most familiar. In the "Apology" the long section on animals that is a part of his reply to the second objection is full of strange and even amazing stories. At one point, Montaigne calls on Chrysippus as witness to the movements of a dog who was either following his master or pursuing some prey. The dog came to a crossroads where three roads met. He sniffed at one, then another, and then, without further sniffing, ran off down the third road. Chrysippus, who is as disdainful of the condition of animals as any other philosopher, is forced to admit that the dog must have gone through a process of reasoning that led him to conclude, without sniffing the third, that his master must have taken that road. Here again we see the philosophical disdain for the low and the forced admission based on a presumably rare occurrence. Montaigne, however, does not need the rare and extraordinary: "[B]ut I observe with more amazement the behavior, which is nevertheless quite common, of the dogs that blind men use both in the fields and in town; I have noticed how they stop at certain doors where they have been accustomed to receive alms, how they avoid being hit by coaches and carts.... I have seen one, along a town ditch, leave a smooth flat path and take a worse one to keep his master away from the ditch" (VS463; F340). "We admire more, and value more, foreign things than ordinary ones; and but for that, I should not have spent my time on this long list [of strange stories]. For, in my opinion, if anyone studies closely what we see ordinarily of the animals that live among us, there is material there for him to find facts just as wonderful as those that we go collecting in remote countries and centuries" (VS467; F342–43). Montaigne is amazed at the common and the familiar.

This is repeated many times and in many ways throughout the *Essays*: "We have no need to go picking out miracles and remote difficulties; it seems to me that among the things we see ordinarily there are wonders so incomprehensible that they surpass even miracles in obscurity" (VS763; F578). "In my opinion, from the most ordinary, commonplace, familiar things, if we could put them in their proper light, can be formed the greatest miracles of nature and the most wondrous examples, especially on the subject of human actions" (VS1081; F829).

As we have seen, in "It is folly to measure the true and false by our own capacity," Montaigne alludes to the remarkable change that occurred in him: he is now open to the "follies" of the vulgar, for he has come to see the greater "folly" of submitting God and nature to our measure. Then he goes on to say: "If we call prodigies or miracles whatever our reason cannot reach, how many of these appear continually to our eyes! Let us consider through what clouds and how gropingly we are led to the knowledge of most of the things that are right in our hands; assuredly we shall find that it is rather familiarity than knowledge that takes away their strangeness and that if those things were presented to us for the first time, we should find them as incredible as any others, or more so" (VS179; F132–33). But what are the monsters and miracles that Montaigne wonders at when he comes back to the most familiar? Here we see how his wonder differs from "vulgar" wonder and from philosophical wonder. For the vulgar wonder at visions, ghosts, and enchantments, and the deliberate philosophers wonder at what is not yet subsumed under the universal. But the wonder that Montaigne is preparing the reader for is the "miracle" of his friendship with La Boétie (VS191; F142), a friendship that surpasses the precepts of philosophy and that cannot be subsumed under the ancient categories. It is difficult for him even to articulate this friendship because, "beyond all my understanding, beyond what I can say about this in particular, there was I know not what inexplicable and fateful force that was the mediator of this union" (VS188; F139). In the end their friendship is a "mystery," and Montaigne can only say, "If you press me to tell why I loved him, I feel that this cannot be expressed, except by answering: Because it was he, because it was I" (VS188; F139). The friendship that Montaigne describes is so rare that he does not expect to find many good judges of what he is saying. In effect, he is asking the reader to be open to this possibility, this mystery and miracle.

The first time that Montaigne mentions himself in the *Essays* is in essay I.1: "I am marvelously lax in the direction of mercy and gentleness" (VS8; F4). He marvels at himself and at man: "Man is a subject marvelously vain, diverse, and undulating" (VS9; F5). The passage in which he describes himself as an accidental philosopher displays the same movement of Montaigne's thought. In his mere caprices he marvels to find the heights of ancient wisdom, and in his weak *mœurs* he marvels to find a conformity with so many philosophical examples. This wonder at the most familiar is never transcended in the *Essays*; it is only deepened by the movement of his thought: "I have seen no more evident monstrosity and miracle in the world than myself. We become accustomed to anything strange by custom and time; but the more I frequent myself and know myself, the more my deformity astonishes me, and the less I understand myself" (VS1029; F787).[21] Merleau-Ponty says that Montaigne finds in himself "the place of all obscurities, the mystery of all mysteries, and something like an ultimate truth."[22] Montaigne's being is not Cartesian mind or "subjectivity." He puts "not self-satisfied understanding but a consciousness astonished at itself at the core of human existence."[23]

We can now return to the remarkable claim that Montaigne makes in "Of presumption": he owes his capacity for sifting truth to the fact that his firmest and most general ideas were born with him. Montaigne's movement of thought overcomes both vulgar and philosophical presumption by its circular path from the familiar to the strange and back to the familiar. That is, he sees and recognizes his presumption at every step. His return or descent to the familiar allows him to see the familiar for what it is – that is, *presumed* truth – and thus the familiar is no longer simply presumed. He believes what he had first believed, but he no longer simply presumes the truth of what he had first believed.

There are two places where Montaigne explicitly points to his constancy of belief. In essay II.6, "Of practice," he tells the story of a near fatal fall from his horse and of what he experienced as he came so close to death. He describes this as a state of weakness and extreme lassitude, even mixed with the kind of sweetness we feel in drifting into sleep. He believes that this is really what those who are in the agony of death are feeling, not the grievous pains that most people think the dying are going through. One of the subtle but striking features of this discussion is Montaigne's refrain that this is what he has always thought: "This has always been my view, against the opinion of many.... Now I have no doubt, now that I have tried this out by experience, that I judged this matter rightly all along" (VS374–75; F270–71). His experience only confirms what he always believed.

In essay II.37, "Of the resemblance of children to fathers," he wants to explain why he holds doctors and medicine in such horror. "My ancestors had an aversion to medicine by some occult natural inclination; for even the sight of drugs filled my father with horror" (VS764; F579). It is possible that he received his natural aversion to medicine from his ancestors, "but had there been only this consideration, I would have tried to overcome it. For all those predispositions that are born in us without reason are bad; they are a kind of disease that we must combat. It may be that I had this propensity, but I have supported and fortified it by arguments which have confirmed me in my opinion" (VS765; F580). Twenty pages later, he comes back to this same point: "I have taken the trouble to plead this cause, which I understand rather poorly, to support a little and strengthen the natural aversion to drugs and to the practice of medicine which I have derived from my ancestors, so that it should not be merely a stupid and thoughtless inclination and should have a little more form; and also so that those who see me so firm against exhortations and menaces that are made to me when my sickness afflicts me may not think that I am acting out of plain stubbornness; or in case there should be anyone so unpleasant as to judge that I am spurred by vainglory. That would be a well-aimed ambition, to want to derive honor from conduct that I have in common with my gardener and my muleteer!" (VS785; F597). Montaigne makes his constancy of opinion explicit in at least two other places: "As a boy, a man, and graybeard, I have always thought and judged in the same way" (VS165; F122), and "in the matter of general opinions, in childhood I established myself in the position where I was to remain" (VS812; F616).

What does this mean? The circle of his thought carries him back to his first beliefs. There is something Aristotelian in this: knowledge always begins from what we already know. In order to begin at all, we must assume what we already know, but Montaigne's movement of thought comes back to what was initially assumed. Once again, Merleau-Ponty has captured what is going on: "[R]egaining nature, naïveté, and ignorance means regaining the grace of our first certainties in the doubt that rings them round and makes them visible."[24] Or, as Michael Oakeshott puts it, knowledge always means "reforming knowledge which is already there."[25] This is why Montaigne pulls back as far as possible to the first seat, that of ignorance, and why his rear end is always between two stools. What we have always believed is not simply visible but only becomes visible at the end of the circle of thought.

The remarkable statement from "Of presumption" – that his capacity for sifting out the true and his freedom in not easily subjecting his belief are due to the fact that his beliefs have always been the same – is further clarified in this statement from the "Apology": "Now from the knowledge of this mobility of mine I have accidentally engendered in myself a certain constancy of opinions, and have scarcely altered my original and natural ones. . . . thus I have, by the grace of God, kept myself intact, without agitation or disturbance of conscience, in the ancient beliefs of our religion, in the midst of so many sects and divisions that our century has produced" (VS569; F428). Unlike the authoritative philosophers and theologians, Montaigne *does* "stake [his] faith [*foi*] on a popular faith [*foi*]" (VS106; F76). Montaigne's accidental constancy, his integrity in the ancient beliefs of our religion, is not a practical or rhetorical strategy. The truths of faith are universal and common, accessible to the lowliest village woman and to the greatest theologian. Montaigne's movement of thought is a return to the most common and the recognition of his unity with all men.

5

"What It Means to Believe"

Isak Dinesen's story "Babette's Feast" is set in a nineteenth-century Norwegian village that is home to a small sect of very pious, God-fearing, and righteous Lutherans who are admired throughout Norway for their renunciation of the pleasures of this world. Since the death of their founder, dissension and discord have arisen in the community, and while the atmosphere of their life together remains austere and devout, it has become rather grim and joyless. Then Babette comes to town to cook for two elderly sisters who are the founder's daughters. And when the community decides to celebrate the hundredth birthday of their deceased founder, Babette takes all the money she has and plans a feast. Suddenly all kinds of wonderful things begin to arrive from France – fragrant and foreign things like spices and wines and even a live turtle. Sauces are prepared and aromas fill the air. The whole community is caught up in watching the preparations and warning themselves about the temptations of the senses. But at the feast, the wine flows freely, and, as the old animosities are forgotten, the stern faces open up and there is laughter and joy and affection.[1] Surely, before this, they had loved each other as God commands. This laughter, joy, and affection must simply be the wine. Or so "the naturalist" would say.

But the skeptic – if he is Montaigne's kind of skeptic – would not know and, in some sense, would not care what the cause is, whether the wine or divine grace. For Montaigne, what it means to believe is precisely not to know. This claim puts me, in a very limited way, on the side of those who say that Montaigne is a Christian skeptic, but I interpret his Christian skepticism to mean not that skepticism is a preparation for faith but that faith is a kind of skepticism that cannot know the distinction between nature and grace in a given act. Further, this inability to know the cause (whether nature or grace) is not a source of torment but rather a kind of doubt that is integral to faith itself, for this skepticism is inseparable from the recognition of the possibility of the sacred in the mundane. That is, the skepticism that is integral to faith is the skeptical moment of openness to the possible described in Chapter 1.

In this chapter I want to begin to explore "what it means to believe" for Montaigne. The first part of this chapter deals with the way Montaigne undermines and blurs the theological distinction between nature and grace. I begin by acknowledging those aspects of the *Essays* that have led some readers to see him, at best, as nonchalant about religion and, at worst, as an unbeliever and atheist. I show that Montaigne's stance toward this world, his "nonchalance" concerning Scripture and the sacraments and prayer, the pagan language of the *Essays*, his reluctance to attribute the events of his life to providence, and his apparent refusal of repentance are not signs of indifference to religion, but are actually manifestations of the way Montaigne lives the life of faith as he understands it. In the second part of this chapter, I discuss the dialectic of faith and reason as it is worked out in the "Apology." In particular, I differentiate my own position from the position of those who see Montaigne as a skeptic-fideist. The third part shows how the dialectic achieves the harmony of faith and reason: the "Apology" is indeed a defense of Sebond but a defense that transforms the meaning of Sebond's most fundamental assumptions.

Nature and Grace

This World

Montaigne rejects any attempt – whether religious or philosophical – to raise ourselves above our humanity. The "Apology" ends with a quotation from the Stoic Seneca and Montaigne's comment on it: "'O what a vile and abject thing is man . . . if he does not raise himself above humanity!' That is a good statement and a useful desire, but equally absurd. For to make the handful bigger than the hand, the armful bigger than the arm, and to hope to straddle more than the reach of our legs, is impossible and unnatural. Nor can man raise himself above himself and humanity; for he can see only with his own eyes, and seize only with his own grasp. He will rise, if God by exception lends him a hand; he will rise by abandoning and renouncing his own means, and letting himself be raised and uplifted by purely celestial means. It is for our Christian faith, not for his Stoical virtue, to aspire to that divine and miraculous metamorphosis" (VS604; F457).

Man can rise above humanity, but only through a "divine and miraculous metamorphosis," not through his own power and his own designs. Whatever the mode of being of man is, it must be such that it can undergo such a divine and miraculous metamorphosis, a change far more radical than the change brought about by the deliberate conformity of one's life to Stoic doctrine. The ancient categories of being and becoming are not adequate to account for this change, a change that cannot be deduced or inferred from the philosophical and natural possibilities.

This limitation of philosophical categories also comes out forcefully in Montaigne's discussion of philosophical views on life after death. "We cannot worthily conceive the grandeur of those sublime and divine promises, if we can conceive them at all; to imagine them worthily, we must imagine them unimaginable, ineffable, and incomprehensible, and completely different from those of our miserable experience. 'Eye cannot see,' says Saint Paul, 'neither can it have entered into the heart of man, the happiness which God hath prepared for them that love him' [I Corinthians]" (VS518; F385). Faith in these divine promises implies a recognition of our contingency, a contingency far more radical than what is captured in the ancient philosophical category of becoming. It implies a recognition of our nothingness, of creation out of nothing. What is death for Montaigne? It is not described in terms of the philosophical separation of the soul from the body, but rather in the promise of the Resurrection and in the words of Saint Paul: "I would be dissolved . . . and be with Jesus Christ" (VS445; F324). Montaigne breaks with the categories of ancient philosophy and goes even further than Saint Augustine in his acceptance of this world and of the contingent and bodily condition of human being.

Erich Auerbach, in his "L'humaine condition," uses the expression "creatural realism" to refer to Montaigne's outlook. This creatural realism, he says, "would be inconceivable without the preparatory Christian conception of man" developed in the Middle Ages. But Auerbach goes on to say that, although Montaigne's style is creatural and Christian, his attitude is no longer Christian and medieval: "[H]is creatural realism has broken through the Christian frame within which it arose." Auerbach comes to this conclusion because he sees in Montaigne the sense that "life on earth is no longer the figure of the life beyond; he can no longer permit himself to scorn and neglect the here for the sake of a there. Life on earth is the only one he has."

Although Montaigne's attitude is, according to Auerbach, no longer Christian and medieval, neither is it that of antiquity. "Montaigne's emancipation from the Christian conceptual schema did not – despite his exact knowledge and continuous study of antique culture – simply put him back among the ideas and conditions among which men of his sort had lived in the days of Cicero and Plutarch." What remains of the attitude of creatural realism is a rootedness in the realm of the concrete. Auerbach, then, sees Montaigne's outlook as creatural but not Christian or medieval. I agree that he does not express himself in the forms of medieval theology, but I believe that his outlook remains Christian. In part, this claim might be defended by considering just what is new in Montaigne, what makes it impossible for him simply to return to the ancient world of ideas and beliefs. Auerbach points to "his newly acquired freedom . . . directly connected with the feeling of insecurity," the insecurity of a world in which there are no "fixed points of support," but it seems to me that this is precisely the world created out of nothing, the absolutely contingent world in which Montaigne makes himself at home.[2] So, Nietzsche says of Montaigne: "If my task were to make myself at home on this earth, it is to him that I would cleave."[3] There seems to be nothing "otherworldly" about Montaigne: he is a man very much in *this* world; his entire being is here, present, and earthy.

This is perhaps why Pascal says that "Montaigne inspires indifference regarding salvation." His views on death are "completely pagan," for he is "without fear or repentance," and unwilling to die as a Christian. He thinks only of dying a death of cowardly ease.[4] So, is Montaigne a pious Christian or is he "completely pagan" and entirely at home in this world? Following Pascal's lead, perhaps the best way to consider this question is to begin with Montaigne's views on death. We would not expect to find in the *Essays* any philosophical arguments for the immortality of the soul. In fact, such attempts at proving our immortality are cited among the clearest cases of the impotence of reason to arrive at any certitude. We can know that the soul is immortal only through revelation : "Let us confess frankly that God alone has told us so, and faith; for a lesson of nature and of our reason it is not" (VS554; F415).

But even though our immortality can be known through revelation, Montaigne almost never mentions the "other world" or a life after death. Where, then, is his faith? The subject of death comes up repeatedly in the *Essays*, giving him many opportunities to display his belief in immortality, but he almost never takes these opportunities. Essay I.20, "That to philosophize is to learn how to die," is a good example of this silence. We find there a defense of sorts of the claim that philosophy is a preparation for death. There is a long speech by Nature placing the insignificant individual and his passage into nonbeing within its cosmic context, but there is no consolation offered from Christian belief. One of the greatest instances of a philosophical death, that of Socrates, is presented in "Of physiognomy." It is reason that makes Socrates courageous in death, "not because his soul is immortal but because he is mortal" (VS1059; F811). This is a puzzling statement. Is Montaigne expressing his own opinion or what he takes to be the opinion of Socrates, in spite of the arguments for immortality put forward in the *Phaedo*? But even more puzzling is a statement that he makes in "That the taste of good and evil depends in large part on the opinion we have of them" and that he explicitly acknowledges as his own view. This essay is concerned with the role of opinion in enduring the evils of life (death, pain, and poverty). Montaigne quotes Saint Augustine, "*Death is not an evil, unless that which follows it is.* And I should say, still more probably, that neither what goes before nor what comes after is an appurtenance of death" (VS56; F38).

What is Montaigne's stance toward death and toward this life? At first, his stance might appear as indifference concerning salvation. Unlike Saint Augustine, for example, he does not present himself as clinging to God who is unchanging. In his *Confessions*, Augustine addresses God with respect to his condition in this way: "Then I thought upon those other things that are less than You, and I saw that they neither absolutely are nor yet totally are not: they are, in as much as they are from You: they are not, in as much as they are not what You are. For that truly is, which abides unchangeably. *But it is good for me to adhere to my God,* for if I abide not in Him, I cannot abide in myself."[5] Montaigne, in contrast, seems to accept completely his immersion in the changeable.

One of the most striking examples of this contrast can be seen in the way each responds to the death of his friend. Augustine thought of his soul and his friend's soul as one soul in two bodies. When his friend died, he "raged and sighed and wept and was in torment, unable to rest, unable to think. I bore my soul all broken and bleeding and loathing to be borne by me; and I could find nowhere to set it down to rest."[6] He tries to flee from his sorrow by leaving Tagaste for Carthage. Augustine looks back at how he was then: "I was wretched, and every soul is wretched that is bound in affection of mortal things: it is tormented to lose them, and in their loss becomes aware of the wretchedness which in reality it had even before it lost them."[7] His judgment is this: "I had spilt out my soul upon the sand, in loving a mortal man as if he were never to die."[8] Now he sees that he must not cleave to things that are passing, "for they go their way and are no more; and they rend the soul with desires that can destroy it, for it longs to be one with the things it loves and to repose in them. But in them is no place of repose, because they do not abide."[9]

When Montaigne looks back on the death of his friend La Boétie, he expresses neither regret at having loved a mortal man as if he would never die nor consolation in turning to an immutable God: "[I]n truth, if I compare all the rest of my life . . . with the four years which were granted me to enjoy the sweet company and society of that man, it is nothing but smoke, nothing but dark and dreary night" (VS193; F143). And in "Of diversion" he tells us how he dealt with his grief: "I was once afflicted with an overpowering grief, for one of my nature, and even more justified than powerful. I might well have been destroyed by it if I had trusted simply to my own powers. Needing some violent diversion to distract me from it, by art and study I made myself fall in love, in which my youth helped me. Love solaced me and withdrew me from the affliction caused by friendship" (VS835; F634). As Augustine fled from grief to Carthage, Montaigne flees from grief to *l'amour*. But there is no regret or remorse expressed about this diversion, no apparent move from the sequence of mortal affections to a higher clinging to God.

It would not be fair to leave the impression that Augustine somehow becomes indifferent to his friend or somehow uses God as a way out of the trials associated with being mortal and changeable: "Blessed is the man that loves Thee, O God, and his friend in Thee, and his enemy for Thee. For he alone loses no one that is dear to him, if all are dear in God, who is never lost."[10] Nor, on the other hand, do I want to suggest that Montaigne's position is diametrically opposed to Augustine's, or that he wants to attack Augustine on philosophical or religious grounds. Rather, I would claim that

Montaigne sees himself as going further than Saint Augustine in working through "what it means to believe" and in following out the implications of creation out of nothing.

Montaigne is both attached to this world and detached from it.[11] The greatest example of his attachment is his friendship with La Boétie, which he describes as extremely rare, as a "miracle." The union of their wills and lives was so complete that "we went halves in everything; it seems to me that I am robbing him of his share. . . . I was already so formed and accustomed to being a second self everywhere that only half of me seems to be alive now" (VS193; F143). Montaigne says explicitly that their friendship surpasses the ancient descriptions of friendship and even the precepts of philosophy. The depth of his attachment cannot be explained in terms of the ancient categories.

Yet, in spite of the fact that Montaigne seems to be entirely at home in this world, he does also present himself as detached from this world: "Never did a man prepare to leave the world more utterly and completely, nor detach himself from it more universally, than I propose to do" (VS88–89; F61). And in this same apparently pagan essay, "That to philosophize is to learn how to die," he says: "Our religion has no surer human foundation than the contempt for life" (VS91; F64).

We saw that Pascal criticizes Montaigne for his "completely pagan" views on death and that this criticism is based at least in part on the fact that Montaigne does not discuss the "other world" or dwell on any life after death. But there are two places in the *Essays* where he does clearly assert the reality of the "other world." In "Of experience" he is discussing the search for knowledge as a never-ending search: "There is no end to our researches; our end is in the other world" (VS1068; F817). And in "Of vanity," which is largely about his travels and absences from his home, his thoughts turn to the subject of true friendship and the interplay of presence and absence: "Separation in space made the conjunction of our wills richer. This insatiable hunger for bodily presence betrays a certain weakness in the enjoyment of souls" (VS977; F747). Even the separation effected by death is not complete: "Are they not still wives and mistresses of the deceased, who are not at the end of this world, but in the other world? We embrace both those who have been and those who are not yet, not merely the absent" (VS976; F746).[12]

It is also important to note, in this context, that Montaigne does withdraw from "the world." He withdraws as much as possible from political life, and his project in the *Essays* must be understood in terms of his withdrawal.[13] True, he does not withdraw to a monastery or to a life of celibacy and asceticism. But in his judgment, the temptations to ambition are more serious than the temptations of the flesh. Perhaps Montaigne's deliberate withdrawal from politics could be interpreted as nothing other than the detachment of the philosopher from political life for the sake of the higher life of contemplation, but he never presents himself as detached for the sake of some higher and better world.

Montaigne's dual stance of attachment and detachment is one aspect of his understanding of "what it means to believe." He is both more deeply attached to this world and more profoundly detached from it than either the philosopher who despises this world or the saint who must acknowledge the goodness of this world, but who clings, in this life, to the eternal and unchanging.[14] That is, Montaigne's understanding of his created being goes further than Saint Augustine's because he is not held back by the ancient philosophical categories, and his acceptance of his created being is more complete.

True Repentance

Pascal says that Montaigne is "without fear and repentance." Is Pascal correct, or does Montaigne in fact go through a kind of repentance that transforms his entire being? The most obvious place to begin to take up this question is essay III.2, "Of repentance." The first sentence is this: "Others form man; I tell of him, and portray a particular one, very ill-formed, whom I should really make very different from what he is if I had to fashion him over again" (VS804; F610). This is a statement of the project of reformation. It assumes that we fashion ourselves, form ourselves, and can reform ourselves. Toward the end of the essay, we are confronted with what seems to be the exact opposite sentiment: "I have made no effort to attach, monstrously, the tail of a philosopher to the head and body of a dissipated man; or that this sickly remainder of my life should disavow and belie its fairest, longest, and most complete part. I want to present and show myself uniformly throughout. If I had to live over again, I would live as I have lived. I have neither tears for the past nor fears for the future" (VS816; F619–20).

This is not an inadvertent self-contradiction but a change that occurs in him. How does this change occur? The opening statement is one of regret, a statement of "disgust with things present." But regret is not repentance, and this is one of the main themes of the essay, to distinguish regret from repentance.[15] The context of the concluding sentiment ("If I had to live over again, I would live as I have lived. I have neither tears for the past nor fears for the future.") suggests that Montaigne has overcome regret, not repentance. And the regret he overcomes is regret at not having been an angel or Cato. "As for me, I may desire in a general way to be different; I may condemn and dislike my nature as a whole, and implore God to reform me completely and to pardon my natural weakness. But this I ought not to call repentance, it seems to me, any more than my displeasure at being neither an angel nor Cato" (VS813; F617). The movement of Montaigne's thought is from regret that he is a man, and a weak man, to acceptance of his humanity. And this is itself a kind of reform, but not deliberately undertaken. Perhaps it is even repentance for "disgust with things present." This is not reform by reason. Rather it is a reform of reason, of reason's presumption, and it goes much deeper than any reform by reason. But where does this reform or repentance come from? "God must touch our hearts" (VS816; F620). Such reformation requires the presence of grace: "This great and holy image could not be in so mean a domicile, unless God prepares it for that purpose, unless God reforms and fortifies it by his particular and supernatural grace and favor" (VS563–64; F423–24). But we cannot really distinguish between God's action and the natural reformation brought about by age: "The years lecture me every day in coldness and temperance. This body of mine flees disorder and fears it. It is my body's turn to guide my mind toward reform" (VS841; F638).

Montaigne is very mistrustful of all attempts at rational reform. Usually, he speaks ironically of them. Of the reform of the calendar by Pope Gregory XIII, he writes: "It has been two or three years since they shortened the year by ten days in France. How many changes were supposed to follow this reform!" (VS1025; F784). In "Of names" he asks, "will not posterity say that our reformation has been fastidious and precise, not only to have combated errors and vices, and filled the world with devotion, humility, obedience, peace, and every sort of virtue, but to have gone so far as to combat our ancient baptismal names, Charles, Louis, François, in order to populate the world with Methuselahs, Ezekiels, and Malachis, which smack much more of the faith?" (VS277; F202). And on more weighty matters he is opposed to the Protestant project of translating the Bible into the vernacular: "Comical folk, those who think they have made it fit for the people to handle because they have put it into the language of the people! Is it just a matter of the words, that they do not understand all they find in writing? Shall I say more? By bringing it this little bit closer to the people, they remove it farther" (VS321; F232). Real reform does not come through the mere changing of opinions: "Those who in my time have tried to correct the world's morals [*mœurs*] by new opinions, reform the superficial vices; the essential ones they leave as they were, if they do not increase them" (VS811; F615).

Montaigne is not a mere partisan of the Catholic side in the civil wars of his day. He is perfectly capable of criticizing it as harshly as he criticizes the Reformers when it comes to the conduct of the wars. He even tells us that he might well have been tempted in his youth by the ambition of the risk and difficulty of the enterprise of reform. Why, then, does he remain a Catholic?

In part, he remains a Catholic because of the reformation he himself has undergone as displayed in "Of repentance." That is, he has come to accept his humanity. This acceptance comes through in some of his most extended criticisms of the Reformation: "As for those who, in recent years, tried to construct for us a system of religious practice that is all contemplative and spiritual, they should not be astounded if there are some who think that religion would have melted away and slipped through their fingers if it did not hold fast among us as a mark, title, and instrument of division and faction rather than by itself" (VS930; F710). In the "Apology" he reminds us that of all the religions that Saint Paul found in Athens, it seemed that the one dedicated to a hidden and unknown divinity was most excusable. On the other hand, if Numa, the Roman king and legislator, tried to attach the piety of his people to a purely intellectual religion, he attempted something useless. "The human spirit cannot keep on floating in this infinity of formless ideas; they must be compiled for it into a definite picture after its own pattern. The divine majesty has thus let itself be somewhat circumscribed within corporeal limits on our behalf; his supernatural and heavenly sacraments show signs of our earthly condition; his worship is expressed by perceptible rituals and words; for it is man that believes and prays." With respect to the Reformers' attack on images, he says: "I leave aside the other arguments that are employed on this subject. But I could hardly be made to believe that the sight of our crucifixes and the pictures of that piteous agony, the ornaments and ceremonious movements in our churches, the voices attuned to the piety of our thoughts, and that stirring of the senses, do not warm the souls of the people with religious emotion very beneficial in effect" (VS513–14; F381). Montaigne's true repentance must be distinguished from both regret at not being an angel and reform that tries to turn men into angels. It is, as he says, a man, not an angel, that believes and prays.

The Underlying Presence of Faith
Montaigne does not give demonstrations or arguments for the articles of faith in the manner of the theologians. And he does not often appeal to Scripture as authoritative. He does not appear to be very pious in any conventional sense, and he does not engage in extended discussions of God, heaven, and hell. In the *Essays*, faith mirrors the way in which faith is present in Montaigne's life and the way it informs his thought and his character. It is present at a level that is deeper than the level of his learning displayed in direct quotation. Even those who hold that Montaigne is a Christian have the impression that his faith is of secondary importance to him and does not really inform his entire being.[16]

So, for example, Hugo Friedrich devotes more than forty pages of his masterful study to Montaigne's knowledge of antiquity but only one page to his "Christian sources."[17] There are indeed few quotations from Christian sources in the *Essays*. As Friedrich says, the Book of Ecclesiastes is perhaps the book of the Bible most frequently quoted. There are a few quotations from Saint Paul, one from Saint Bernard, and several from Saint Augustine's *The City of God*. In almost every case, a pagan source is quoted along with the Christian source – for example, Plato with Saint Paul (VS360; F260), Tacitus with Saint Augustine, Pliny with Saint Augustine (VS539; F402), and Heraclitus with Saint Bernard (VS543; F406).

Friedrich claims that "the nearly complete absence of the Gospels is note-worthy. They are only represented in four passages, and these are somewhat unimportant ones."[18] This judgment is, I believe, an instance of overlooking the level at which Montaigne's faith appears. In addition to several refer-ences to the Resurrection, there are many more or less obvious allusions to gospel stories throughout the *Essays* – for example, to the parable of the servant who buried his master's treasure in the story about Dionysius the Younger (VS65; F45), to the parable of the Prodigal Son (VS645–46; F490), to the betrayal and hanging of Judas (VS798; F606), and to "the poor in spirit" of the Sermon on the Mount (VS1009, 1039; F771, 794). These allusions to Gospel stories and parables often appear in context with sto-ries and examples from ancient sources, just as the direct quotations from Christian sources are almost always accompanied by quotations from pagan sources. There are also at least two references or allusions to the miracles of Christ recorded in the Gospels, but in both cases they are "spiritualized." In "Of pedantry" Montaigne writes: "The crippled are badly suited to the exercises of the body; and, to the exercises of the mind crippled souls are badly suited" (VS141; F104). And in "Of husbanding your will" he refers to a "spiritual leprosy" that has a false air of health (VS1014; F776).

I am not trying to claim that these allusions somehow prove that Montaigne is a Christian but only that the New Testament is at least part of the pretheoretical ground of his thought. In the same way, it is possi-ble to recognize the level at which and the way in which he mentions the sacraments and prayers of the Church. For example, Montaigne talks about the possibility of dying away from home and why he is not troubled by this thought. He has seen so many dying men besieged by a crowd of family and friends: "[O]ne torments your eyes, another your ears, another your tongue; there is not a sense or a part of you that they do not shatter. . . . If we need a wise woman [midwife] to bring us into the world, we certainly need a still wiser man to help us out of it" (VS978; F747–48). It would be difficult for a Catholic to miss the allusion to the sacrament of Extreme Unction, to the hand of the priest anointing the organs of sense. And a few pages later, Montaigne makes direct reference to this sacrament: "At the very beginning of my fevers and the maladies that lay me low, while still whole and in the neighborhood of health, I reconcile myself with God by the last Christian offices, and find myself thereby more free and unburdened" (VS982; F751). "On some verses of Virgil" sets a standard of fidelity in marriage, even in thought, that might well be described as the standard of the Christian sacra-ment (VS897; F684). Montaigne mentions that he has a chapel in his home and that the liturgy is celebrated there (VS828; F629). And in "Of experi-ence" he commends his father for giving him, from among the poorest of his village, the godparents who held him over the baptismal font.[19]

In "Of prayers" Montaigne expresses the wish that the Our Father be said on all occasions when it is customary to pray so that the people should have this prayer continually on their lips. "It is the only prayer I use in every circumstance; and I repeat it instead of changing" (VS318; F230). He disapproves of the custom of forbidding children to use the word "father" when addressing their fathers so as to foster reverence: "We call God Almighty father, and disdain to have our children call us that" (VS393; F284). And he often refers to phrases from the Our Father: "The Christian prays God that his will be done" (VS576; F434); "'Forgive us,' we say, 'as we forgive those who have trespassed against us'" (VS323; F234). We ask that we not even be led into temptation (VS1016; F777). And in the midst of the dangers of civil war, he goes to bed after saying the Our Father, wondering if he will be betrayed and slaughtered that very night (VS970; F741). The sign of the cross is a sign that he reveres and continually uses (VS319; F231), and he comes to worship "fully prepared": the "Sursum corda" of the Mass is lost on him (VS414; F301). And in the middle of the trials of life, he recalls the words of the psalm: "*[T]hy rod and thy staff they comfort me*" (VS577; F435). Once again, in at least some instances, the Christian prayer is accompanied by a pagan example: "The Romans used to say in their religion '*Hoc age*,' as we say in ours '*Sursum corda*'" (VS414; F301).

What conclusions can we draw at this point concerning the way in which Montaigne's faith is present in the *Essays*, and the way he addresses the question of "what it means to believe"? An example that Montaigne uses in "Of custom" is highly suggestive in this regard. He is discussing the fact that custom is extremely powerful, especially in the way it stupefies our senses. The example he gives is that of people who live near bell towers, who after a short time no longer notice the noise of their ringing. He himself has experienced this: "At home I live in a tower where at dawn and at sunset every day a very big bell rings out the *Ave Maria*. This jangling frightens my very tower; to me, it seems unendurable at first, but in a short time it has me tamed, so that I hear it without disturbance and often without awaking" (VS110; F78). The *Ave Maria*, sounded by the Angelus bell, is the prayer of the Annunciation and marks the moment of the Incarnation. The shocking newness of this announcement is blunted over time, through custom, and is now just there in the background, part of the pretheoretical rhythm of life. In this way, it has become no different from ordinary belief and custom.

We have also seen that Montaigne almost always has a pagan source or example alongside a Christian source or example. As Friedrich says, "the Bible is one source of quotations among others" for Montaigne.[20] So also, his Christian beliefs just seem to be "in there" with all the other beliefs, in the same way that the Christian religion is just in there with all the others, on equal footing. "[We] receive our religion only in our own way and with our own hands, and not otherwise than as other religions are received" (VS445; F324).

How, then, are other religions received? On the one hand, religion is received by natural means. We are born in a certain place and time, we are brought up in the religion of our parents, and we learn its teachings and practices just as we learn any other nonreligious beliefs and customs. "We are Christians by the same title that we are Perigordians or Germans" (VS445; F325). This line of argument is part of Montaigne's response to the pious objectors in the "Apology" who claim that faith is received through "a particular inspiration of divine grace."

On the other hand, there is a kind of divine inspiration that Montaigne does recognize. In his response to the "rationalists" (those who bring the second objection against Sebond), he writes: "In truth, considering what has come to our knowledge about the course of this terrestrial government, I have often marveled to see, at a very great distance in time and space, the coincidences between a great number of fabulous popular and savage customs and beliefs, which do not seem from any angle to be connected with our natural reason. The human mind is a great worker of miracles; but this correspondence has something or other about it that is still queerer: it is found also in names, in incidents, and in a thousand other things" (VS573; F431). He then goes through a long list of such coincidences – for example, circumcision, fasting, abstinence, crosses (even the particular style cross of Saint Andrew), celibate priests, belief in a perfect created state of which we were deprived by sin, the story of the flood, the formula used on Ash Wednesday ("You have come from dust, and you will return to dust"), belief in purgatory. Montaigne concludes that "these empty shadows of our religion that are seen in some of these examples testify to its dignity and divinity. It has insinuated itself to some extent not only into all the infidel nations on this side of the world by some sort of imitation, but also into these barbarous ones as by a common and supernatural inspiration" (VS574; F433). This line of argument begins from the course of "nature" and ends with "common and supernatural inspiration." And, although the pagan religions are "empty shadows of our religion," Montaigne does seem to believe that they are somehow inspired.

The language of the *Essays*, as Montaigne himself tells us, is entirely human: "I for my part allow it to say, *in unsanctioned terms* [Saint Augustine], 'fortune,' 'destiny,' 'accident,' 'good luck' and 'bad luck,' 'the gods,' and other phrases, in its own way" (VS323; F234). He avoids the theological language of "providence," preferring the pagan way of speaking. Montaigne's reluctance to attribute certain events to the direct and extraordinary intervention of God is apparent in "We should meddle soberly with judging divine ordinances." He is objecting to the way in which the success of the endeavors of his side in the civil war is taken as a sign of God's intentions and as a support for his religion. "It is enough for a Christian to believe that all things come from God, to receive them with acknowledgment of his divine and inscrutable wisdom, and therefore to take them in good part, in whatever aspect they may be sent to him. But I think the practice I see is bad, of trying to strengthen and support our religion by the good fortune and prosperity of our enterprises. Our belief has enough other foundations; it does not need events to authorize it. For when the people are accustomed to these arguments, which are plausible and suited to their taste, there is a danger that when contrary and disadvantageous events come, this will shake their faith" (VS216; F160).

Montaigne's blending of pagan religious and philosophical examples with Christian examples serves to blur the theological distinction between nature and grace, not in such a way as to imply the denial of grace but, on the contrary, to show that grace is everywhere. So, for example, the unspoken presence in "By diverse means we arrive at the same end" is Christ before Pilate. (It is perhaps not by accident but in imitation of Montaigne that Bacon begins his first essay with this image.) Images of Christ are scattered everywhere in this essay: the women of Guelph who carry their men on their backs, Phyto being whipped and dragged through the streets, Zenon offering to take on the guilt of the entire people, the silence of Betis before Alexander, Alexander's piercing of Betis's heels (a detail that Montaigne invents). In the horrible story of George Sechel that concludes "Cowardice, Mother of Cruelty" we can see the image of the Eucharist (VS701; F530). And in his own life, we see the images of events in the New Testament. For example, the story of his near fatal fall from his horse calls to mind the experience of Saint Paul on the road to Damascus: Montaigne was hit as though by a "thunderbolt" (VS373; F269). The sacred is not confined to the eternal or to the distant past or to the other world. Rather it is visible in the present and the mundane.[21]

This blurring of the distinction between nature and grace is also seen in the passage that is crucial for locating the starting points of Montaigne's thought: "I have accidentally engendered in myself a certain constancy of opinions, and have scarcely altered my original and natural ones.... Thus I have, by the grace of God, kept myself intact... in the ancient beliefs of our religion" (VS569; F428). The beliefs of faith are not distinguished from his natural opinions. This kind of repetition – saying something first in the language of nature and then in the language of faith – is frequent in the *Essays*.

In "Of physiognomy" he tells two stories, the first of which concerns a troop of soldiers of the opposing side who enter his house under false pretenses, presumably to take his house and his goods, and possibly to kill him. Suddenly, their leader gives the signal for them to leave, giving up the overwhelming advantage he had gained by his ruse. The second is about his capture in the forest by a large band of soldiers of the opposing side in the civil war. His horse and all his possessions are taken from him, and his captors try to determine how much ransom they will demand. After two or three hours, the leader suddenly changes toward him, speaks gently to him, returns to him the possessions he is able to recover, and sets him free. How does he understand what has happened? "The true cause of so unusual an about-face and change of mind, without any apparent motivation, and of such a miraculous repentance, at such a time, in a premeditated and deliberate enterprise which had been made lawful by custom (for from the outset I openly confessed to them what party I belonged to and what road I was taking), I truly do not even now well know. The most conspicuous among them, who took off his mask and let me know his name, repeated to me then several times that I owed my deliverance to my face and the freedom and firmness of my speech, which made me undeserving of such a misadventure; and he asked me to assure him of similar treatment should the occasion arise. It is possible that the divine goodness willed to make use of this vain instrument for my preservation" (VS1062; F813). Here is this skepticism that does not claim to know the true cause but is open to the possible. Perhaps it was simply his face that saved him, perhaps it was grace. Or perhaps the distinction cannot be made.

In "Of experience" he tells us that his father had him nursed in a poor village so as to accustom him to the lowest and most common way of living. "His notion aimed at still another goal, to ally me with the people and that class of men that needs our help; and he considered that I was duty bound to look rather to the man who extends his arms to me than to the one who turns his back on me. And this was the reason why he also had me held over the baptismal font by people of the lowliest class, to bind and attach me to them. His plan has succeeded not at all badly. I am prone to devote myself to the little people, whether because there is more vainglory in it, or through natural compassion, which has infinite power over me" (VS1100; F844). Is his compassion natural or is it the effect of the grace of baptism? Faith cannot presume to say and does not need to know. "What it means to believe" is to see the sacred in the natural.

The Dialectic of Faith and Reason

Faith is first present in the *Essays* as the pretheoretical background of Montaigne's thought and as the presupposition of his way of being. But what happens when faith is confronted with unbelief, when faith is challenged by reason to defend itself on the level of the theoretical?

Few questions about the *Essays* have given rise to such radically different interpretations.[22] On one side, there is the claim that Montaigne is really an atheist. Thus the passages where he does speak about the Christian faith must be explained away as merely rhetorical: the rhetorical dimension of the *Essays* would be intended both to couch his teaching in a form that can be acceptable to his largely Christian audience and to protect him from censorship and persecution by the Church. This view of Montaigne entails the claim that he writes in the tradition of the "noble lie," a tradition that he mentions several times in the *Essays*. This view also finds support in the highly ambiguous character of the "defense" of natural theology found in the "Apology."

At the other end of the spectrum, we have the interpretations of those who claim that Montaigne is a skeptic-fideist. In his *Le scepticisme de Montaigne*, Frédéric Brahami presents a compelling version of this interpretation. He shows clearly that Montaigne's is a *new* skepticism, that he breaks with the ancient Skeptics on the decisive issue of the sovereign good and goes further than the ancient Skeptics in his annihilation of the pretenses of human reason. Brahami argues that this new skepticism is made possible, or rather, necessary, by the introduction of the Christian concept of God.[23] Montaigne, then, would be a skeptic on the natural, philosophical level, and a "fideist" on the theological level. That is, he would deny the ability of reason to grasp or to ground the truths of faith, and he would deny that faith is itself a mode of thought that can give a public account of itself. "The fideist founds the faith on faith; he is, literally, one for whom there are no reasons to believe."[24]

The view of Montaigne as skeptic-fideist finds support in Montaigne's praise of skepticism as the most useful of all the philosophical teachings because it presents man as naked, empty, and weak, "annihilating his judgment to make more room for faith" (VS506; F375). It attempts to come to terms with Montaigne's assertion that the immortality of the soul cannot be established by reason but can be known only through faith (VS554; F415). And it accords with his defense of his practice of avoiding the theological language of divine providence. Montaigne puts forward his thoughts as simply human, not as celestial rules, as "matter of opinion, not matter of faith" (VS323; F234).

Both of these opposing views have the merit of seeing Montaigne as a man who takes religion and faith very seriously and who is deeply and thoroughly engaged in living an examined life. The kind of "compromise" view that sees him as "mildly religious" must, I think, be rejected as an account of Montaigne's intellectual and moral position (although it may be accurate as an assessment of his outward show of piety). It fails to acknowledge the depth and the seriousness of Montaigne's project. To be "mildly religious" would be to leave the most important questions of human life unexamined. I do not mean that a serious man could not *doubt*, but only that he could not be indifferent.

What, then, of the two extremes, that is, the view that Montaigne is an atheist and the view that he is a skeptic-fideist? The claim that Montaigne is really an atheist who hides his atheism is, on one level, impossible to refute. If the atheism is really hidden, then no interpretation can find it and bring it out into the open. If it is only partly hidden or thinly veiled, then some of the things that Montaigne says must be deliberately false. But how do we tell which things are false? Ultimately, the selection must be either arbitrary or determined by a priori criteria. Of course, this claim to a hidden meaning cannot be refuted by appealing to Montaigne's avowals of his sincerity, because these avowals themselves may be merely rhetorical. But one reason why many readers of Montaigne are so reluctant to accept the claim that he lies, even nobly, is that his lying would be a betrayal of the reader's trust: what is offered to us in the *Essays* is not a mere verbal puzzle but the man himself and a man of a certain character, a man for whom truth is a moral imperative. This is not a complete answer, but simply a statement of what I take to be some of the difficulties with the interpretation that Montaigne is really an atheist.[25]

With respect to many philosophical authors, it is possible to distinguish between the author's own personal religious beliefs (which may be difficult or even impossible for us to know) and the way he deals with questions of faith and religion in his writings. So, for example, it seems to me that an inference from Descartes's proofs for the existence of God to the claim that he is or is not an orthodox Christian in his own life would not be justified. Nor are we entitled to infer that Hobbes is or is not an atheist on the basis of what he writes about the need to subordinate religion to the state. With Montaigne, however, this distinction is more difficult to make, not simply because he says he is writing in "good faith," but more importantly because his very manner of thinking is grounded in his Christian pretheoretical beginnings which become self-consciously his through the essay form.

The difficulty I see with the claim that Montaigne is a skeptic-fideist has to do with what I take to be the way in which the skeptic-fideist must deliberately keep himself from thinking about the truths that are most important to him. I acknowledge that Montaigne rejects the mode of Sebond's natural theology, what Brahami calls Sebond's "rationalism." And I do recognize the need to make sense of both Montaigne's claim that his project is simply human and his apparently ambiguous defense of Sebond. But "rationalism" does not exhaust the meaning of thought. And it seems to me that the skeptic-fideist interpretation implies a frustration of the natural desire to think honestly about one's life and a condition of conflict within the self, neither of which is evident in the *Essays*. So Brahami says that faith cannot be formulated in terms of knowing, or even of thought. Man is a "believing thing," rather than a "thinking thing."[26]

Apart from the skeptical moment of openness to the possible, Montaigne's faith cannot be understood as the faith of a skeptic-fideist. While he does depart from the traditional forms of theology, his entire mode of thought and being is Catholic and self-consciously so. The discussion of the "Apology" that follows shows that Montaigne is engaged in a dialectic that culminates in a harmony of faith and reason. In Chapter 6 I argue that his very mode of thought is creational and incarnational. Chapters 7, 8, and 9 display a mode of being, a character, that is a harmony of classical magnanimity and Christian humility. Such a character would have been un-thinkable within the categories of ancient philosophy and it requires the essay form for its revelation.

Where, then, is Montaigne's faith? It must be nowhere (because he is re-ally an atheist) or somewhere outside the *Essays* (because faith is inarticulate and private) or somehow in the *Essays.* The first answer (atheism) places him on the side of the second objection to Sebond; the second answer (fideism) places him on the side of the first objection. The third, that Montaigne's faith is somehow in the *Essays,* is the answer that I want to show to be true. We can begin, then, with the "Apology for Sebond," because this essay deals so directly with the issue of belief.

Raymond Sebond was a Spanish theologian of the fifteenth century whose book, entitled *Natural Theology or The Book of Creatures,* was given to Montaigne's father, who then asked his son to translate it from Latin into French. Montaigne did so and then wrote this "apology" as a response to two criticisms commonly made of this and other such works in natural theology. Montaigne reports that someone told him that Sebond's book was actually a kind of distillation of the teachings of Thomas Aquinas.[27]

In the Prologue to his *Natural Theology,* Sebond claims that God has revealed himself clearly in two "books": first, in the Bible, and second, in nature. Sebond holds that man can know the truth about God and himself by reading these truths in the book of nature. In that book, each creature is like a letter and man himself is the main or capital letter. Montaigne describes Sebond's natural theology in this way: "His purpose is bold and courageous, for he undertakes by human and natural reasons to establish and prove against the atheists all the articles of the Christian religion" (VS440; F320). Montaigne's own task in the "Apology" is to defend Sebond against the two principal objections that are made to his work. By describing his task in that way, Montaigne is adopting the Scholastic terminology and mode of presentation, although his adaptation is very loose. The Scholastics, including Aquinas, usually wrote in a highly structured form based on the practice of disputation. A question is posed, for example, Does God exist? Objections to the writer's own position are stated, the writer presents his own view in the *corpus,* and finally he answers the objections each in turn. The entire "Apology," then, in spite of its length and its appearance of disorder, actually has a very simple underlying structure: the statement of and response to the first objection and the statement of and response to the second objection.

If we compare this with the Scholastic question, we see that what is missing is the "body" of the question, the author's own view or, in Scholastic terminology, the *corpus.* The highly structured form of the question is intended to require the author to state the authoritative objections to his own position and then to allow him the freedom to say what he himself thinks. Where, then, is Montaigne's own view? It seems that it must be found in what I call the "dialectic" between the two objections and responses. In other words, it would be illegitimate to identify Montaigne's own position with either of the two objections or even simply with his responses to both objections. No doubt the responses by themselves do reveal something of his own stance, but they do not give us the complete picture any more than Aquinas's replies to objections would allow us to reconstruct completely his own fully articulated answer. The replies are consistent with the answer and give some idea of what the answer must be, but they are incomplete and stated in a way that is determined by the objection. What I now attempt to do is to work out that dialectic.

The first objection to Sebond's theology is put forward in the name of piety by those who think of themselves as believers. They say that "Christians do themselves harm in trying to support their belief by human reasons, since it is conceived only by faith and by a particular inspiration of divine grace" (VS440; F321). The second objection is put forward by unbelievers and atheists. Sebond's arguments, they say, are "weak and unfit to prove what he proposes." And these unbelievers set out to shatter Sebond's arguments with ease (VS448; F327).

The first objection identifies faith with belief that is held by particular inspiration of divine grace. The second objection identifies understanding with autonomous reason, and thus with unbelief, because Sebond's arguments cannot command universal assent. As we have seen, most commentators have placed Montaigne himself entirely on the side of one or the other of these objections. Montaigne, however, refutes *both* objections, but also finds something true in each objection. Any interpretation of the "Apology" that places him simply on either side must be inadequate.

The two objections, as formulated by Montaigne, are usually regarded as opposites, as the opposing and contradictory voices of belief and unbelief. Brahami, for example, says that "the second objection is diametrically opposed to the first" and that "these two radical positions, that of belief and that of unbelief undermine the synthesis of Sebond."[28] But when these objections are exposed more fully, they show themselves to be related to each other and even dependent on each other at a deeper level. The first objection defines faith in terms of its origin: faith is "belief that is conceived only by faith and by a particular inspiration of divine grace." God inspires those whom it pleases him to inspire: that is why they believe and others do not. There is a direct communication by God to the mind of the believer. Faith, then, is taken to be private, inarticulate, and incommunicable. The second objection is a reaction against the possibility of faith, but it also accepts this understanding of what faith is. Unbelief must see faith as a private experience, an experience that it ultimately regards as illusory because it is publicly indefensible. Unbelief reacts against the first objection's claim to private knowledge and particular inspiration by putting forward as its standard what it takes to be the most public expression of the activity of the mind, autonomous reason.

Rationality prides itself in being both public and common. In the first place, it is completely transparent and communicable: when the demonstrations of Euclidian geometry are displayed, for example, they can be understood by any rational human being and they receive universal assent. The truths of faith, of course, do not receive universal assent. Second, rationality is universal, the defining characteristic of the human species, whereas particular inspiration is not universal. Therefore, in this view of reason, faith (understood as particular inspiration) cannot give a public account of itself. It is defenseless before the court of reason.

The first and second objections, then, share the same understanding of the meaning of faith. This shared understanding gives rise to the "dialectic" of the two objections, and it is this shared understanding that Montaigne refutes.

Further, the first and second objections also share the same understanding of the meaning of reason. The first objection takes faith to be belief, but belief that each is justified in holding because it comes from God by a direct and particular inspiration. The beliefs that are guaranteed by particular inspiration are elevated then to the status of knowledge and certitude. The second objection sets demonstration as the standard of knowledge: whatever cannot meet this publicly accessible standard must count as mere belief or private opinion. It demands, then, that faith be defined and justified within the terms of the philosophical categories of knowledge, certitude, and doubt. The doubt to which the first objection is susceptible is due to the fact that faith cannot command universal assent because it cannot be demonstrated or proved. In the doubt to which it is prey, the first objection concedes the definition of reason assumed by the second objection.

In other words, the second objection accepts the first objection's definition of faith, and the first objection accepts the second objection's definition of reason. It is to these shared understandings of what faith and reason are that Montaigne is really addressing himself. To the first objection he responds that faith is not belief held by particular divine inspiration. To the second objection he responds that reason is not autonomous and cannot secure universal assent.

The dialectic between the two objections and responses begins to come to light when we examine the three ways in which Montaigne responds to the first objection. Against the claim that Christian faith is held by means of particular inspiration of divine grace and that faith is therefore a private, incommunicable experience, Montaigne pushes in the direction of the public and the common. "We are Christians," he says, "by the same title that we are Perigordians or Germans." This takes the pious objector out of his own private certitude and confronts him with the fact that, had he been born in a very different place or time, had he not been brought up as a Christian, he would not believe as he does. Montaigne is also moving away from the claim of divine origin and toward the acknowledgment of the human origins of faith: "Another region, other witnesses, similar promises and threats, might imprint upon us in the same way a contrary belief" (VS445; F325). Little Moslem and Hindu babies do not grow up to find themselves somehow directly inspired by God to believe the articles of Christian faith. By moving in the direction of human origins, we come to the point where Christian faith looks no different from any other religious belief. If it is not of divine origin, how can it claim any superior status? It begins to appear "that we receive our religion only in our own way and with our own hands, and not otherwise than as other religions are received. We happen to have been born in a country where it was in practice" (VS445; F324).

Besides moving in the direction of the common and public, Montaigne is also moving in the direction of the natural and away from the supernatural. For Christian belief now appears no different from any other "natural" belief or custom. Just as custom varies from country to country or from culture to culture, so too do religious belief and practice. The terrible reproach to Christians, Montaigne says, is that we do not even believe in God to the same degree that we believe in the ordinary and natural. "If we believed in him, I do not say by faith, but [even] with a simple belief,... if we believed in him just as in any other story, if we knew him like one of our comrades, we would love him above all other things" (VS444; F324). Montaigne is here making a distinction between faith and "simple belief," precisely the distinction that the first objection fails to make: faith is belief held by particular inspiration. If confidence in its divine origin is shaken, what is left is ordinary belief, belief that is unexamined and presumptuous. Such belief begs for reason to step in because faith no longer has any definitive claim to truth. The first objection's view of faith is one that undermines itself and easily turns into unbelief. This is why Montaigne agrees with those who predict that the Reformation will degenerate into atheism and why he attributes the second objection to atheism. Once "personal consent" becomes authoritative, all of the ancient beliefs will be shaken off "as a tyrannical yoke" (VS439; F320).

The second way in which Montaigne responds to the first objection is by pointing to the lack of conformity between Christian belief and conduct. "All other signs are common to all religions: hope, trust, events, ceremonies, penitence, martyrs. The peculiar mark of our truth should be our virtue, as it is also the most heavenly and difficult mark, and the worthiest product of truth" (VS442; F322). Once again, Montaigne is calling the objectors into the public realm, demanding evidence of the presence of faith. But the actions of most Christians give no evidence of such faith: "[S]o divine and celestial a teaching as ours marks Christians only by their words.... Compare our morals with a Muhammadan's or a pagan's; we always fall short of them. Whereas, in view of the advantage of our religion, we should shine with excellence at an extreme and incomparable distance, and people ought to say: 'Are they so just, so charitable, so good? Then they are Christians'" (VS442; F322). Instead, we have civil war, extreme cruelty, vengeance, and hatred. Montaigne says: "There is no hostility that excels Christian hostility" (VS444; F324).

The failure of Christian moral action is a sign of the inadequacy of the first objection's understanding of what faith is. In some cases, the lack of conformity between belief and conduct entails hypocrisy and a deliberate attempt to deceive others. But in most cases, it is simply a matter of self-deception: "Some make the world [think] that they believe what they do not [really] believe. Others, in greater number, make themselves believe it, being unable to penetrate what it means to believe" (VS442; F322).

The third way in which Montaigne responds to the first objection is by appealing to the authority that the pious believer must acknowledge, the first great commandment: "Thou shalt love the Lord, thy God, with all thy heart, with all thy soul, and with all thy mind." God commands that we love him with our minds and this commandment justifies the project of theology. Theologians interpret the commandment, as Sebond does, along the lines of natural philosophy, seeking the truth about God in the book of nature and appealing especially to Saint Paul's claim that "the invisible things of God appear by the creation of the world, when we consider his eternal wisdom and his divinity in his works" (VS447; F326). So, then, Montaigne concludes his response to the first objection with an assertion of compatibility between faith and reason, a compatibility that the first objection denies.

Now if we consider the medieval definition of theology as "faith seeking understanding," we see that faith is primary. In the words of Saint Anselm's prayer: "Grant me to understand you to be as I [already] believe you to be."[29] As the formula of medieval theology puts it, philosophy is the "handmaiden" of theology. Montaigne's formulation of Sebond's project (that "he undertakes by human and natural reasons to ... prove against the atheists all the articles of the Christian religion") suggests that Sebond may actually be claiming something closer to the independence of reason from the first principles of faith, thus tending toward the reversal of Anselm's "unless I believe, I shall not understand" to "unless I can prove, I shall not believe."

But whether or not Sebond's mode of theology is an extreme and unorthodox rationalism (as some have described it), Montaigne's defense of the mind's place in the life of faith leads him directly into the second objection. It is here, I think, that we get a sense of the "Apology" not simply as a response to all those others "out there" who fall within the two categories of objectors, but rather as a dialectic within Montaigne himself. For in the process of responding to the understanding of faith in the first objection, he suddenly finds himself speaking in the voice of unbelief. He says: "I have already, without thinking about it, half involved myself in the second objection" (VS448; F327).

The way in which Montaigne falls into the second objection and the way he characterizes reason from the very beginning of his response suggest that once reason is invited in, it claims for itself an authority that ultimately admits no other authority. There are three related aspects of reason's self-assertion that Montaigne emphasizes: reason inevitably tends to see itself as what is highest in nature, therefore as entitled to rule, and therefore as autonomous. Those who put forward the second objection, he says, "will not allow us to combat their reason except by [reason] itself" (VS449; F328).

Reason is their only "touchstone" and they will neither receive nor approve anything except by way of reason (VS541; F405). First, Montaigne combats the arrogance of reason in the way it immediately sets out a hierarchy within nature and places itself at the top. Reason sees itself ordering nature, and man's reason is in harmony with this divine ordering principle. Montaigne asks: "Is it possible to imagine anything so ridiculous as that this miserable and puny creature, [man, the rational animal] who is not even master of himself, exposed to the attacks of all things, should call himself master and emperor of the universe, the least part of which it is not in his power to know, much less to command?" (VS450; F329). And he characterizes those who make the second objection as "these people, who think Sebond's reasons too weak, who are ignorant of nothing, who govern the world, who know everything" (VS538; F402).

Now it must be said that this presumption of reason is very similar to the position taken by Sebond's natural theology: man is said to be made in the image of God by virtue of his reason. This, of course, is why Montaigne's so-called defense of Sebond seems ambiguous or even ironic: an attack on reason is an attack on the second group of objectors but, at the same time, it is an attack on Sebond's entire project of natural theology. In attacking the arrogance of reason, Montaigne is acknowledging what is true in the first objection – namely, that Christians do themselves harm by seeking to support their faith by reason, if reason is presumed to be the autonomous reason of the second objection. So also, in demanding public evidence of faith, he acknowledges what is true in the second objection, namely, the indefensibility of claims to private inspiration.

How, then, does Montaigne respond to the second objection, expressed as the presumption and autonomy of reason? He responds in two ways. First, he brings reason down from its heights, from its presumed divinity to the level of the animals. The animal stories in the "Apology" are intended to bring man, the self-styled rational animal, to a recognition of his equality not with God but with the beasts. The thrust of Montaigne's line of argument here is to show reason to be, not the divine element in the human soul, but so common, so pervasive in all of animal nature, that the unbelievers who pride themselves on their rationality are forced to disdain this reason as lowly and base, by their own measure.

As we saw in Chapter 1, Montaigne's mode of reasoning in the discussion of the animals is analogical, the mode of reasoning that Aquinas identifies as the way we are entitled to speak about God. Montaigne is showing that analogy cuts both ways: if we are justified in beginning from ourselves and inferring what God must be, then we must accept the appropriateness of this way of reasoning in the case of our relation to the animals. We are not entitled to engage in reasoning by analogy only when it flatters our pretensions to divine likeness. This willingness to liken ourselves to God is due to the presumption that Montaigne refers to as "our first and original malady" (VS452; F330). With respect to natural theology's "arrogance of trying to discover God with our eyes" (VS528; F394) through analogical reasoning, Montaigne says that "our overweening arrogance would pass the divinity through our sieve" (VS528; F393) and it is "vain to try to make guesses about God from our analogies and conjectures, to regulate him and the world by our capacity and our laws" (VS512; F380).

The second way in which Montaigne responds to the objection of unbelief and the assertion of reason's autonomy is to point out and display in vivid detail what he calls the "unruliness" of reason, especially as that unruliness manifests itself in the wild diversity of human opinion. That diversity is especially acute and instructive in the case of philosophical opinion, for here we supposedly see man at his best, in his "highest estate." Yet all of the centuries of philosophical speculation have not produced a single opinion on which there is universal agreement. Montaigne says that "we shall never heap enough insults on the unruliness of our mind" (VS24; F15). Even the greatest thinkers have only "amused themselves with reason as with a vain and frivolous instrument, putting forward all sorts of notions and fancies" (VS545; F408). Philosophy itself recognizes the unruliness of reason: "I am calling reason our reveries and dreams, with the dispensation of philosophy, which says that even the crazy man and the wicked man are mad with reason, but it is a particular sort of reason" (VS523; F389). Finally, then, we must conclude that reason, to which we had turned for a common ground, to which we had turned as the universal and defining characteristic of the species, is so highly particularized that it cannot serve as the common, public ground we were seeking. Reason, Montaigne says, "always goes its way, even though crooked, lame, and broken-hipped and with falsehood as with truth. . . . I always call reason that semblance of intellect that each man fabricates in himself. That reason, of which, by its condition, there can be a hundred contradictory ones about one and the same subject, is an instrument of lead and wax, stretchable, pliable, and adaptable to all biases and measures" (VS565; F425). Autonomous reason does not simply and of itself arrive at what is true. It constructs arguments but cannot guarantee the truth of its premises. Autonomous reason *assumes* the truth that it demonstrates. In their failure to examine their own starting points in a radically philosophical way, the atheists show themselves to be just as much in the grip of presumption as the simple believers who put forward the first objection.

The inability of reason to secure universal assent is especially clear in Montaigne's criticisms of the theological view that there are "natural laws" that are or can be known by all men through reason. "Men," he says, "have done with Nature as perfumers do with oil: they have sophisticated her with so many arguments and farfetched reasonings that she has become variable and particular for each man, and has lost her own constant and universal countenance" (VS1049–50; F803). There may be natural laws that we can

see in other creatures, "but in us they are lost; that fine human reason butts
in everywhere, domineering and commanding, muddling and confusing the
face of things in accordance with its vanity and inconsistency" (VS580; F438.
There is nothing so absurd that it has not been said by some philosopher
and nothing so bizarre or evil that it has not been the custom or law of some
nation. The logic of his response to the first objection drove Montaigne to
the common, public, universal ground of reason. But autonomous reason,
instead of being the rock on which to build anything common, turns out to
be a mere dream or, worse, a nightmare that dissolves into chaos.[30]

The Harmony of Faith and Reason

Where, then, does Montaigne himself stand on the question of the relation
of faith and reason, at least insofar as his stand is revealed in the dialectic of
the two objections? We can begin to answer this by returning to the issue of
his sincerity in calling this essay a "defense" of Sebond. The tendency has
been to see Montaigne's apology for Sebond as either completely ironic
or as unselfconsciously ambiguous and self-contradictory because, if he is
either an atheist or a skeptic-fideist, then he must deny any harmony or
compatibility between faith and reason, and that compatibility is Sebond's
most fundamental assumption.

If we see the two objections in their relation to each other and follow
the movement of Montaigne's thought as he works his way through the
objections and their shared understandings of reason and faith, we find
that he is in fact defending a transformed version of Sebond's assumption.[31]
Montaigne calls this essay an apology for Sebond because he *does* affirm the
harmony of faith and reason – but not faith as defined in the first objection
and not reason as assumed in the second objection. For Montaigne, faith is
not belief held by particular divine inspiration, and autonomous reason is
not common and universal. The harmony that he recognizes and displays
in the *Essays* is a harmony of *true* faith and *reformed* reason.

What, then, is true faith and what is reformed reason? How are they in
harmony? Faith as defined in the first objection is incomplete, imperfect,
and even presumptuous: it is unexamined belief that must be completed and
in some way transformed in its dialectic with reason. The autonomous reason
of the second objection is proud and presumptuous: it must be reformed in
its dialectic with faith.

Montaigne's responses to the first objection tell us just how this unexamined faith must be transformed, and his responses to the second objection
tell us just how arrogant reason must be reformed. To those who maintain
that faith is belief held by particular divine inspiration, he answers, first,
that faith is acquired by natural means, that faith is inherited, that we are
Christians by the same title that we are Perigordians or Germans. Second,
the actions of most Christians do not give evidence of the presence of true

faith: most of those who call themselves Christians do not know "what it means to believe." Third, the refusal to think about the truth of faith is a failure to love God with all one's mind. To those who assert the autonomy of reason, he answers that autonomous reason cannot achieve universal assent and cannot give us a common world. Human reason is not divine and does not rule and measure the world.[32]

How does the dialectic transform unexamined belief and autonomous reason so as to bring them into harmony? We saw that in "Of vain subtleties" Montaigne refers to the error of those in the middle region (between the simple and the learned believers) who "regard our sticking to the old ways . . . as simplicity and stupidity." It turns out that Montaigne's sticking to the old ways is actually due to his having come through error to reach "the extreme limit of Christian intelligence." We also saw a similar change in "It is folly to measure the true and false by our own capacity." The presumption of the simple consists in believing too easily whatever they are told, whereas the presumption of the learned is more insidious: they disdain as false whatever seems impossible to them. Montaigne says "I used to do [that] once . . . I felt compassion for the poor people who were taken in by these follies. And now I think that I was at least as much to be pitied myself" (VS178–79; F132). Now Montaigne is subject neither to the unthinking credulity of the simple nor to the arrogant presumption of the learned.

That same circular movement of thought is just what occurs in the dialectic of the two objections in the "Apology": from simple inarticulate belief he ascends through doubt to autonomous rationality and then descends to the truth of faith. Of course, he cannot simply return to or deliberately adopt the stance of unthinking belief as if he had never ascended from it. He ends up in a kind of middle position that transcends both simple credulity and learned presumption, and that, in philosophical terms, would be called "learned ignorance." Perhaps this is what T. S. Eliot has in mind when he says that "what makes Montaigne a very great figure is that he succeeded . . . in giving expression to the scepticism of *every* human being. For every man who thinks and lives by thought must have his own scepticism, that which stops at the question, that which ends in denial, or that which leads to faith and which is somehow integrated into the faith which transcends it."[33] Montaigne's skepticism is integrated into the faith that transcends it. The faith that has transcended and transformed doubt is not an unthinking and inarticulate faith but Montaigne's way of living the examined life as a Christian.

The truths of faith are first revealed in the testimony of simple and ignorant witnesses. "The participation that we have in the knowledge of truth, whatever it may be, has not been acquired by our own powers. God has taught us clearly enough by the witnesses that he has chosen from the common people, simple and ignorant, to instruct us in his admirable secrets. Our faith is not of our own acquiring, it is a pure present of another's liberality"

(VS500; F369). The necessity for the learned to acknowledge that their belief ultimately rests on the testimony of the simple and ignorant is one way
in which reason is humbled and reformed: "I will destroy the wisdom of the
wise and crush the prudence of the prudent.... Has God not made stupid
the wisdom of this world?" [I Corinthians 1.18–20] (VS500; F370).[34]

In "Of the power of imagination" Montaigne's openness to the truth of
testimony is shown to be the condition for his ability to see what occurs
in his own presence. Once again, he distinguishes himself from both the
simple (who think they see what they do not see) and the learned theologians and philosophers (who refuse to accept the testimony of the ignorant,
who will not stake their faith on a popular faith, and who will not testify to
what happens before their own eyes). Montaigne's openness to testimony
allows him to see for himself: he sees the actual against the background
of the possible. His faith is not simply belief in events that are past. Nor
is it based on the evidence of visions and extraordinary occurrences such
as the simple are prone to see. The dialectic of poetic and historical truth
culminates in Montaigne's ability to see *in the present* the evidence of God
in creation. This is how he interprets Saint Paul's claim that "the invisible things of God appear by the creation of the world," the claim that he
cites in order to elaborate on what it means to love God with one's whole
mind.

One of the ways in which Montaigne responds to the first objection is to
challenge the presumptuous believer to manifest his faith in action. This
suggests that there is something hidden about faith, and his criticism of the
actions of those who call themselves Christians is meant to call them to a
public, common standard. What is action like when it proceeds from true
faith? There are two places in the *Essays* that are especially relevant here.
In "Of vain subtleties" Montaigne describes those who have come through
error to the extreme limit of Christian intelligence as enjoying their victory
"with consolation, active gratitude, reformed conduct, and great modesty."
And he distinguishes them from "those others who, to cleanse themselves
of the suspicion of their past error and make us sure of them, become extreme, injudicious, and unjust in the conduct of our cause [in the civil wars],
and stain it with infinite reproaches of violence" (VS313; F227). In his reply
to the first objection, Montaigne discusses the reasons why some men are
atheists. In a few cases, atheism is an opinion that they hold seriously. But
for many, it is "out of vanity and pride in conceiving opinions that are not
common and that reform the world." When these people are near death,
when they have a sword thrust in the chest, when fear or sickness beats down
their fervor for distinction, they lift their hands to heaven. Then, he says,
"they will not fail to come back to themselves and very discreetly let themselves be formed by the common faith and examples." But there is another
motive that he gives for returning to the common faith: "[W]e are brought
back to the belief in God either by force [the sword thrust in the chest]

or by love" (VS446; F325). Where is his example of returning to the common faith through love? This, I believe, is Montaigne himself.

In the passage where he describes himself as an accidental philosopher, he brings his caprices and his *mœurs* out of hiddenness and finds that he must clothe them in the garments of philosophy in order to make them visible. "When the desire to tell [my *mœurs*] seized me, and when, to make them appear in public a little more decently, I set myself to support them with reasons and examples, it was a marvel to myself to find them, simply by chance, in conformity with so many philosophical examples and reasons" (VS546; F409). Montaigne is struck with wonder at the way in which the dreams and reveries of his reason and his weak *mœurs* accidentally conform to so many philosophical discourses and examples. Faith is the synthesis of all that is true in philosophy. His "ascent" to philosophy in an effort to articulate his being publicly simply gives him a better understanding of what he already is. It allows him to bring to light what is hidden, but it does so in a way that does not eliminate the mystery of his being and the wonder that is his response to that mystery. The faith that is merely "inherited," that he has by the mere accident of being born in a particular time and place, is now revealed and possessed in its truth.

At the beginning of his reply to the second objection Montaigne says that the means he will take to beat down the pride and presumption of the second objectors is "to make them feel the inanity, the vanity and the nothingness of man" (VS448; F327). How will he do this? "Saint Augustine, arguing against these people, has good cause to reproach them for their injustice in that they hold those parts of our belief to be false which our reason fails to establish. And to show that there can have been plenty of things whose nature and causes our reason cannot possibly establish, he puts before his adversaries certain known and indubitable experiences into which man confesses he has no insight; and this he does, like all other things, with careful and ingenious research." Presumably Montaigne is referring to *The City of God* (especially Bk. XXI, ch. 5), where Augustine makes this argument and gives examples, mostly from Pliny, of such marvels as the salt of Agrigentum (which melts in fire), the spring in Epirus (which extinguishes but then rekindles the extinguished torch), and the trees of Tylon (which never lose their foliage).

But Montaigne does not propose to follow Augustine's procedure. Rather, he says, "*We must do more*, and teach them that to convict our reason of weakness, there is no need to go sifting out rare examples" (VS449; F328, emphasis added). Doing more means showing the ordinary to be extraordinary and beyond our powers to explain. The divine presence is both hidden and revealed in the ordinary. It is hidden there just by the ordinary: its strangeness is hidden by the familiarity of the ordinary. Montaigne's circular dialectic reveals the strange in the familiar, the extraordinary in the ordinary.

Faith, as it is understood in the first objection, must be transformed in its dialectic with reason. So also, reason must be reformed in its dialectic with faith. At the same time that the reply to the second objection destroys the common world for autonomous reason, it opens up the world for faith. The world is restored through true faith to its astonishing strangeness. That is, the world is now seen as what it must be for faith. A world created out of nothing, a world in which the Word was made flesh, is revealed as such in the philosophical activity that ends in wonder at the most familiar. Accidental philosophy is the harmony of reason and faith.

6

The Latent Metaphysics of Accidental Philosophy

Montaigne does not debate the great metaphysical questions. To the extent that there is any metaphysical content at all in the *Essays*, it would seem to be either merely presupposed or implied. Does this mean that Montaigne was just not interested in the question of being or that he regarded the Aristotelian teachings of the schools as sufficient and the great metaphysical issues settled?

The metaphysics of the *Essays* is a latent metaphysics. But in calling it latent I do not mean to suggest that Montaigne was either unaware of or uninterested in the metaphysical foundations of his own thought, rather that its latency is necessitated by the meaning and character of accidental philosophy. Accidental philosophy is purely human: it is not the activity of an intellect that sees itself as divine. Accidental philosophy is purely philosophical: it is not a theology that takes the truths of faith as its axioms or as simply presumed.

The revelation of being and the relation of thought to being, as displayed in the *Essays*, necessitate a latent metaphysics. Being is both revealed and hidden. It is revealed in the accidental movement of circular dialectic. But the fact that it must be revealed through dialectic implies that it is, of itself, hidden. The latency of the metaphysics of the *Essays* mirrors the revelation and hiddenness of being itself, and thus the *Essays* instantiate the condition of human being with respect to being as such.

In this chapter I discuss the ontological dimensions of Montaigne's thought. I consider what is presupposed in the way his thought begins in opinion and in testimony. Beginning in opinion implies the prereflective harmony of thought and being, the situatedness of the mind in the human world, and the character of experience as formed by custom. Relying on testimony as a source of truth implies that truth manifests itself without necessarily being fully understood. Testimony opens the mind to mystery and to the possible, allowing it to see the actual for what it is. Heidegger's description of "true humanism" captures some of the features of Montaigne's thought: true humanism means that "the essence of man is essential for the truth of Being." The place of the oracular and the daemonic in the *Essays* helps us to see the character of thought itself and how it allows the truth of hidden being to appear.

I also examine the metaphysical dimensions of the *telos* of the circular dialectic – that is, wonder at the most familiar. The philosophical activity that ends in wonder at the most familiar implies a world created out of nothing, an absolutely contingent world, and, at the same time, a world in which the divine is present. I first consider the way in which creation is the background of the *Essays*: the nothingness of man is our fundamental condition. Then I examine four implications of creation out of nothing: the temporal character of human life, the ontological priority of contingency and possibility, the absence of the divine from nature, and the collapse of the ancient philosophical hierarchy within nature. The incarnational aspects of Montaigne's metaphysics are considered in terms of the following issues: the presence of monsters and miracles in the *Essays*, the self as monster and miracle, the identity of the metaphysics of the *Essays* with the project of self-knowledge, the way in which the eternal is encountered in the temporal, the way in which distinctions can be made within a nonhierarchical world, and the primacy of the particular within a nonhierarchical world.

Thought Thinking Thought

What is presupposed and what is implied by the mode of thinking that begins in opinion and then simply returns to its beginnings? In Book XII of his *Metaphysics*, Aristotle presents that part of his metaphysics which is called theology. God, he writes, "is an eternal and immovable substance separate from sensible substances." This divine being is pure actuality and must therefore be engaged in a form of activity consistent with its being. The substance of the divine being is mind or thought. "The mind, then, must think of itself if it is the best of things, and its thought will be thought about thought" (1074b30–35). The human mind can attain to some semblance of this state at certain moments and over certain periods of time, and the philosopher strives for precisely this contemplation – a condition that is accessible to very few men.

Montaigne's circular dialectic is a "lowered" and purely human version of Aristotle's "thought thinking thought." In "Of three kinds of association" Montaigne discusses the activity of his mind. "At the first thoughts that come to it, it stirs about and shows signs of vigor in all directions, practices its touch now for power, now for order and grace, arranges, moderates, and fortifies itself. It has the power to awaken its faculties by itself. Nature has given to it as to all minds enough material of its own for its use, and enough subjects of its own for invention and judgment." He finds it difficult, he says, to shake off the importunity of his soul, "which cannot ordinarily apply itself unless it becomes wrapped up in a thing, or be employed unless with tension and with its whole being. However trivial a subject you give it, it is prone to enlarge and stretch it to the point where it must work on it with all its strength."

Whereas "most minds need foreign matter to arouse and exercise them," his mind needs foreign matter to rest itself : "[F]or its principal and most laborious study is studying itself." Here he mentions Aristotle: "There is no occupation that is either weaker or stronger, according to the mind involved, than entertaining one's own thoughts. The greatest minds make it their profession, *to whom living is thinking* [Cicero]. Thus nature has favored it with this privilege, that there is nothing we can do so long, and no action to which we can devote ourselves more commonly and easily. It is the occupation of the gods, says Aristotle, from which springs their happiness and ours" (VS819; F621–22).

Montaigne does not deny the distinction between weak and strong minds. Only the greatest minds make thinking their whole life. But he does transform and "lower" the sense of Aristotle's description of the life of contemplation. It is clear that in Book X of his *Ethics*, Aristotle is describing a life that is possible for only very few men. In contrasting it with the life of moral virtue and politics, he writes of the contemplative life: "Such a life would be more than human. A man will not live like that by virtue of his humanness, but by virtue of some divine thing within him. His activity is as superior to the activity of the other virtues as this divine thing is to his composite character. Now if mind is divine in comparison with man, the life of the mind is divine in comparison with mere human life. . . . As far as possible, we should become immortal and do everything toward living by the best that is in us. Even if it is small in bulk, in power and value it is far above everything. It may be that each individual is really this, since this is the master-part, the best thing in man. . . . The life of reason will be best for man, then, if reason is what is truly man. That sort of man, then, will be the happiest" (1177b25–1178a9).

Montaigne transforms and lowers this Aristotelian description by claiming, first, that "nature has given to . . . all minds" enough material and enough subjects of their own "for invention and judgment" and, second, that there is "no action to which we can devote ourselves more commonly and easily" than the action of thinking. He does not deny the distinction between weak and strong minds, but he does not want to claim that the difference is such that some men are divine through their thinking. He affirms something "common" to all human minds such that there is a kind of continuity from weak to strong that Aristotle would have to deny. Montaigne does not define the human in terms of Aristotle's "highest" and most rare activity (i.e., contemplation of the eternal) but in terms of a mode of thinking that is the most common of all actions. The thinking that is definitive of human being is everywhere.[1]

In "Of practice" he tells us that the only object of his thoughts is himself and his thoughts: "It is a thorny undertaking, and more so than it seems, to follow a movement so wandering as that of our mind, to penetrate the opaque depths of its innermost folds, to pick out and immobilize the innumerable flutterings that agitate it. And it is a new and extraordinary amusement, which withdraws us from the ordinary occupations of the world, yes, even from those most recommended" (VS378; F273). In that same essay, he addresses those who would accuse him of presumption and who would require that he testify about himself "by works and deeds, not by base words." His response is: "My trade and my art is living." But what does that mean? "What I chiefly portray is my thoughts [*cogitations*], a shapeless subject that does not lend itself to expression in actions. It is all I can do to couch my thoughts in this airy medium of words. Some of the wisest and most devout men have lived avoiding all noticeable actions. . . . It is not my deeds that I write down; it is myself, it is my essence" (VS379; F274).[2]

Montaigne's essence is his thought. This is an assertion that sounds very much like Aristotle's claim that a man's being is the "small part" of him that is divine, that contemplates and that thinks without the body. It also sounds like the precursor of the Cartesian distinction between mind and body: "I am . . . precisely only a thing that thinks; that is, a mind, or soul, or intellect, or reason. . . . I am not that connection of members which is called the human body."[3] But Montaigne does not separate soul and body. "Those who want to split up our two principal parts and sequester them from each other are wrong. On the contrary, we must couple and join them together again. We must order the soul not to draw aside and entertain itself apart, not to scorn and abandon the body (nor can it do so except by some counterfeit monkey trick), but to rally to the body, embrace it, cherish it, assist it, control it, advise it, set it right and bring it back when it goes astray; in short, to marry it and be a husband to it, so that their actions may appear not different and contrary, but harmonious and uniform" (VS639; F484–85). He is "intellectually sensual, sensually intellectual" (VS1107; F850). When Montaigne says that his essence is his thought, he does not mean that a part of him is his essence but rather that everything about him, everything he does, is thought. Thought is not a mode of being that escapes the human condition: thought *is* the human condition.

Montaigne begins and remains within the circle of thought. What are the metaphysical grounds for this? First, Montaigne's beginning in opinion and remaining within the circle of thought do not cut him off from being or reality. This does not mean that he subscribes to a "coherence theory" of truth. The metaphysical presupposition on which the beginning in opinion rests is the prereflective harmony between being and thought. Richard Regosin claims that: "the essayist affirms man's nullity and emptiness, and his own, in a way which challenges any notion of the self as an origin or ground from which truth is generated and imposed on the world.

The reality of man as nothing shows up the illusion of vanity and presumption which postulate human-centered meanings, meanings which in turn nourish man's false sense of self."[4] The truth of being is found in opinion and is brought to light through the circular dialectic.

Second, Montaigne's beginning in opinion also presupposes that mind is not isolated. Unlike Descartes, who deliberately isolates the mind from other men in order to overcome doubt and secure himself against all error, Montaigne remains within the world of other men's thoughts and thus within the prereflective mixture of truth and untruth that is opinion. Montaigne's break with presumption entails a recognition that one's initial condition was one of both truth and untruth. As Heidegger expresses it in his confrontation with Cassirer at Davos: "Because of its finitude, man's Being-in-the-truth is at the same time a Being-in-the-untruth. Untruth belongs to the inmost core of *Dasein*."[5]

Third, beginning in opinion must be distinguished from beginning in the evidence of the senses. The latter assumes that the senses are our link with being, with the real, and that thought takes off from this true experience to ascend to first causes. Montaigne begins his last essay, "Of experience," with the first sentence of Aristotle's *Metaphysics*: all men by nature desire to know. In terms of the Aristotelian ladder from sense perception up to "first philosophy," Montaigne remains close to the bottom: experience is low and common. But what is experience for Montaigne? It is not the sense data of the empiricist but rather what he calls "the ordinances of custom." As he says in "Of custom," "we drink them [the ordinances of custom] with our milk from birth . . . and the face of the world presents itself in this aspect to our first view. . . . And the common notions that we find in credit around us [are] infused into our soul by our fathers' seed" (VS115–16; F83). That is why "first philosophy" must begin not with things that are seen but with the *on dit*. As Oakeshott explains, the first appearances are not "the scientific minimum we can say . . . when we have purged our perceptions of the contingencies and irrelevancies of informal observation." The first appearances are "what we learned in the nursery."[6] Adorno's contrast between the essay form and Descartes's four rules presented in the *Discourse on Method* is relevant here. He writes: "The third Cartesian rule, 'to conduct my thoughts in such an order that, by commencing with the simplest and easiest to know, I might ascend by little and little, step by step, to the knowledge of the more complex,' is sharply contravened by the form of the essay in that it begins with the most complex, not the most simple, which is in every instance the habitual."[7]

A metaphysics of human being and human action, then, cannot proceed according to the manner of natural science.[8] Montaigne complains that the schools of his day simply accept without question the metaphysical first principles of Aristotle and these first principles are actually derived from physics: "[T]he metaphysicians take as their foundation the conjectures of physics" (VS540; F404). A metaphysics of human action that is derived from physics cannot discover or illuminate the possible. The possibilities of human action are available to us only through an openness to testimony.

Fourth, Montaigne regards testimony as an essential source of truth. He refers to testimony as "borrowed truth" but that is not a cause for rejecting it. As we have seen in the discussion of the dialectic of poetic and historical truth, Montaigne's openness to testimony allows him to see what is actually before him. Unlike the theologians and philosophers, he does stake his faith on a popular faith, a faith that is first grounded on the testimony of simple and ignorant men.

Montaigne's reliance on testimony shows us another aspect of how the truth of being is revealed. The truth that is witnessed does not have to be fully understood or even understood at all in order to manifest itself as true. The witness does not have to be able to explain what he has seen or to say why it is the way it is. Thus, the truth that is revealed is greater than can be known and reveals itself to be mysterious.[9]

Heidegger's discussion of humanism is especially helpful in bringing to light the relation of accidental philosophy to the truth of being. In his "Letter on Humanism" he both criticizes what he takes to be the unexamined assumptions of humanism and provides a description of what he means by true humanism. Montaigne's thought is just such a true humanism. According to Heidegger, false humanism simply assumes a metaphysical doctrine and never asks the most fundamental question about being. Man is "put within beings as a being amongst others" – that is, among plants, animals, and God.[10] The manner of being of the whole is assumed, man's place within that whole is assumed, and so man is defined in terms of his place. "The first humanism, the Roman, and all the humanisms that have since appeared, presuppose as self-evident the most general 'essence' of man. Man is considered as the *animal rationale*."[11] Heidegger criticizes the humanists' definition of man as "rational animal": "The essence of man ... consists of being more than mere man, insofar as this mere man is represented as a rational animal. 'More' must not be understandable in an additional sense, as if the traditional definition of man were to remain as the basic definition, in order to undergo an expansion through an addition of the existential. The 'more' means: more original and, therefore, ... more essential."[12] *True* humanism means that "the essence of man is essential for the truth of Being, and apart from this truth of Being, man does not matter."[13]

Heidegger explains the way in which the essence of man is essential for the truth of being by describing a kind of thought that is the action that "brings to fulfillment the relation of Being to the essence of man," not an action that makes or produces this relation.[14] Thought is the simplest form of action. "The strange thing in this thought of Being is its simplicity. This is precisely what keeps us from it. For we seek for the thought that in the name of 'philosophy' has its world-historical prestige in the form of the unusual, which is only accessible to the initiate. . . . We represent thought to ourselves in the manner of scientific knowledge and research. . . . through its simple essence the thought of being is disguised for us." We must, then, "become friends with the unusualness of the simple."[15]

The thought that is essential for the truth of being must overcome traditional metaphysics: "Thought does not overcome metaphysics by surpassing it and canceling it in some direction or other and ascending even higher: it descends into the nearness of the nearest. The descent, especially where man has ascended too far into subjectivity, is more difficult and more dangerous than the ascent. The descent leads to the poverty of the existence of the *homo humanus*."[16]

On the one hand, thought (as Heidegger presents it) produces nothing. "Such thinking results in nothing. It has no effect. It suffices its own essence, in that it is." On the other hand, this thinking "surpasses doing and producing, not through the magnitude of its performance, nor through the consequences of its activity, but through the humbleness of the achievement that it accomplishes without result."[17] It accomplishes the revelation of the most familiar. "Being is the closest. Yet its closeness remains farthest from man." Being is "closer than the closest and at the same time, for ordinary thought, farther than the farthest."[18] Montaigne's circular dialectic returns to the most familiar and common to find the truth there.

One other aspect of Heidegger's account can lead us a step further in our understanding of Montaigne. Heidegger considers the meaning of the "daemon" in connection with his discussion of thought. He says that the saying of Heraclitus – *ethos anthropō daimon* – is usually translated as "a man's character is his daimon." But Heidegger takes *ethos* in the wider sense of 'dwelling' or "abode." So he finds in this saying the idea that "the abode of man contains and maintains the advent of that to which man in essence belongs. This, according to Heraclitus's saying, is *daimon*, God. The fragment says: Man insofar as he is man, dwells in the nearness of God."[19] Man "stands outside himself within the truth of Being."[20]

In explaining his translation of Heraclitus's saying, Heidegger recounts the story of Heraclitus told by Aristotle. The story goes that Heraclitus is sitting at a stove in the kitchen warming himself. Some strangers approach but are surprised to see him sitting at a stove and so they hesitate to go in. Heraclitus bids them to come in with the words "for here too there are gods present." Heidegger interprets the story to mean that the strangers were disappointed because they believed that they "must find the thinker in conditions which, contrary to man's usual way of living, show everywhere traits of the exceptional and the rare." In sitting at the stove to warm himself, Heraclitus "betrays the whole poverty of his life at this spot which is in itself prosaic."[21]

Both the daemonic and the oracular play a significant role in Montaigne's thought. The daemonic is especially evident in poetry, which, at its best, astonishes and transfixes us (VS231; F171). The poet recognizes that his poetic sallies surpass his own abilities and strength and that they come from somewhere outside himself. The orator is pushed beyond his own design. The painter is astonished at his own work because it surpasses his conception. In all of these cases, the extraordinary grace and beauty of the production occur without the intention or even the knowledge of the worker (VS127; F93). We have seen in Chapter 3 that Montaigne attributes the leaps and digressions of the essays to the daemonic art (VS994–95; F761). And he takes pleasure in extracting from the deliberate philosophers the admission that men produce their greatest and most divine deeds not while engaged in the pursuit of philosophy but "when they are out of their minds and frenzied and mad" (VS568; F427).

It is true that at the very end of the *Essays* he says that it is difficult for him to digest Socrates' ecstasies and possessions by his daemon, specifically the days and nights that he spent in a contemplative trance. But these reservations occur within the context of his criticism of what he calls "transcendental humors." He is discussing the monstrous ways in which men despise their own being and especially their own bodies. "They want to get out of themselves and escape from the man. That is madness: instead of changing into angels, they change into beasts; instead of raising themselves, they lower themselves. These transcendental humors frighten me, like lofty and inaccessible places" (VS1115; F856).

In typical fashion, Montaigne finds the rare in the common. The daemonic appears throughout the *Essays* in very ordinary ways. This is especially evident in what Screech calls "everyman's ecstasies" such as sexual intercourse: "Wherefore to Socrates generation is a divine act; and love, a desire for immortality and itself an immortal daemon" (VS103; F73). In "That the taste of good and evil depends in large part on the opinion we have of them," Montaigne tells the story of his way of dealing with wealth and poverty. His attitude toward them went through three stages. The first, in which he was entirely dependent on fortune, was carefree: "I was never better off" (VS62; F43). The second, in which he had some money, was full of painful solicitude. But "I know not what good daemon cast me out of it . . . and sent into abandonment all this saving, the pleasure of a certain trip at great expense having overthrown this stupid fancy." Now, he says, "I live from day to day" (VS65; F45). And what is it that accounts for the way a man chooses, from a crowd of enemy soldiers, the one to whom he will trust his life? Why does he choose one face rather than another among men he does not even know? (VS1058–59; F811).

In my discussion in Chapter 3 of the purpose of the *Essays*, I referred to the conclusion of essay I.11, "Of prognostications," where Montaigne discusses "the daemon of Socrates" as a "certain impulse of the will that came to him without awaiting the advice of his reason." Here too we find the pervasive movement from rare to common: "Everyone feels within himself some likeness of such stirrings of a prompt, vehement, and accidental opinion." And this is followed by the surprising claim: "It is my business to give them some authority, since I give so little to our wisdom." He concludes this essay by revealing that he himself has experienced such "prompt, vehement and accidental opinions" by which he let himself be carried away. These opinions "might be judged to have in them something of divine inspiration" (VS44; F30). We can infer that it was just such a divine inspiration that brought the *Essays* into existence: "the desire to tell my *mœurs* seized me."

The conclusion that I draw from Montaigne's treatment of the daemonic and the oracular is that thought *always* has something daemonic and oracular about it. The condition in which Montaigne's thought begins – the condition of opinion – is oracular and daemonic, for opinion simply speaks itself without knowing what it is saying. It is always both understood and not understood; thus it requires dialectic to reveal its truth. The speakers do not know what they know until they say it. In that sense, the dialectic is accidental, not premeditated and deliberate. Finally, thought is always divinely inspired. Thought presupposes revelation: revelation is the condition of thought because it is the necessary condition for the truth of oracular opinion.

Revelation, in turn, implies hiddenness. In *Mystery and Philosophy*, Michael B. Foster contrasts the God of the Bible with the idea of the divine in Greek philosophy. God in the Bible is hidden, in contrast to the unhiddenness of being for Greek philosophy. The God of the Bible makes himself known, but by an act of will or grace: "[I]t is not his nature to be unhidden."[22] Foster, therefore, claims that "belief in a divine Revelation seems to involve something like a repentance in the sphere of the intellect"[23] and the requirement of repentance is "alien to our main philosophical tradition which has inherited from Greek philosophy the belief in the divinity of the intellect."[24] I am reminded of Montaigne's confession: "And now I think that I was at least as much to be pitied myself" (VS179; F132). The corollary of the conclusion that thought presupposes revelation is that truth is everywhere and common. It is not the exclusive possession of the few philosophers but belongs to man as such. The repentance of the intellect entails this humbling of philosophical pride.

Accidental Being

In this section I consider the metaphysical dimensions of the *telos* of circular dialectic. Wonder at the most familiar presupposes a world that did not have to be at all. The sheer fact of its being is amazing.[25] Ancient philosophy cannot ask the question "Why is there something rather than nothing?" because the absolute contingency of the whole cannot be thought if the whole is assumed to be all that is. The astonishing presence of being only reveals itself at the end of the circular dialectic. It is not obvious to a mind steeped in either prereflective or philosophical presumption.

For accidental philosophy, nothingness is not a condition in the distant past, replaced through creation by a new condition of being. Rather, nothingness is our present condition, the very condition for the appearance of the radically contingent. Thought must always occur against the background of nothingness. In "Of physiognomy" Montaigne makes this statement that captures the meaning of his entire project: "There is nothing I treat specifically except nothing" (VS1057; F809).

His frequent references to the nothingness of man are, then, not to be taken as hyperbole or as metaphor. In "Of practice," where he tells us that his essence is thought, he reminds us of "the nothingness of the human condition" (VS380; F275). In the "Apology" he says that he intends to make the atheists feel "the inanity, the vanity, and the nothingness of man" (VS448; F327). Scripture addresses the man who esteems himself: "Dust and ashes, what have you to glory in?" and Montaigne adds: "In truth, we are nothing" (VS499; F368). Protagoras had said that "man is the measure of all things" but when we consider the impotence of human reason, we must realize that this was "just a joke which led us necessarily to conclude the nullity of the compass and the compasser" (VS557; F418). Montaigne has the oracle at Delphi say to man: "There is not a single thing as empty and needy as you" (VS1001; F766).

Marcel Conche sees Montaigne's recognition of man's nothingness as "tragic." Montaigne's wager to live the best life possible is made not in the hope of the immortality of the soul but in the expectation of nothingness. Thus Conche concludes that Montaigne lives heroically in the face of nothingness and that the *Essays* "are not, then, a Christian book."[26] But it seems to me that Montaigne's living in the face of nothingness is precisely what makes the *Essays* a Christian book, "a book of good faith." Here I think that Oakeshott's characterization of religious faith comes closer to capturing the tone and the spirit of the *Essays*: "While religious faith may be recognized as a solace for misfortune and as a release from the fatality of wrong-doing, its central concern is with a less contingent dissonance in the human condition; namely, the hollowness, the futility of that condition, its character of being no more than 'un voyage au bout de la nuit.' What is sought in religious belief is not merely consolation for woe or deliverance from the burden of sin, but a reconciliation to nothingness."[27] This reconciliation is not a denial of the dissonances of the human condition but an acceptance, a "graceful" response.[28]

Montaigne does not simply accept the human condition of nothingness with resignation; he embraces it. This can be seen especially in the way he comes to terms with temporality, the condition opposed to divine permanence. In "Of vanity" he objects to a misinterpretation of his nonchalance: "This is not a philosophical scorn for transitory and mundane things; my taste is not so refined, and I value them at least at their worth" (VS953; F728). Contrary to the notion that the Christian despises this world and values only the other world, Montaigne values this world just for what it is. As C. S. Lewis says: "Because we love something else more than this world we love even this world better than those who know no other."[29]

In the way he accepts his temporal condition, Montaigne is carrying through on the admonition that he makes to himself in the "Apology," that "we must do more" than Saint Augustine. Augustine comes to terms with temporality and mutability through narrative and memory. The first nine books of *The Confessions* are the story of his life or rather the story of God's action in his life, a story that comes full circle in the death of his mother recounted in Book IX. Then in Book X, Augustine turns within to memory itself as mind. There are three aspects of Augustine's engagement with temporality that I want to set out so as to contrast them with what Montaigne does. First, Augustine finds through memory a coherence in his life over time: there is a coherent story in which changes occur and which is held together and given its unity by God's action. Second, there are decisive moments, turning points, in his life that he can point to, moments of such significant change that the coherence of the story has to be sustained by some force of unity outside himself. Third, although all of the moments of his life are ultimately dependent on God, the decisive moments make visible the action of God and his intentions.

Now if we compare Montaigne as he is presented in the *Essays* with Augustine's self-presentation, we see that the *Essays* are not the narrative of Montaigne's life. There are many stories told, and some of them are about himself, but there is no attempt to present a coherent, chronological narrative account of his life. As he says "there is nothing so contrary to my style as an extended narration" (VS106; F76). Second, Montaigne does refer to changes in himself (especially in "It is folly to measure the true and false by our own capacity"), but he does not locate those changes in relation to decisive moments in the temporal flow of his life. As Steven Rendall points out: "Autobiography generally assumes some crisis, some critical event that establishes a new perspective or even a new identity, and permits the author to see his life as a provisionally completed pattern."[30] Montaigne is not willing to assert that any particular event in his life is the effect of God's action or intervention, or that any particular event makes visible God's intentions.

In his discussion of Montaigne in *Studies in Human Time*, Georges Poulet describes the kind of duration that the essays give to Montaigne's thoughts, an "agitation... which preserves the mind from not being and from returning of itself to non-being."[31] He refers to the "astonishing novelty" of the claim that Montaigne makes in "Of repentance": "I do not portray being: I portray passing" (VS805; F611) and describes this passing as "the very movement by which being quits being, by which it flees away from itself, and in which it feels itself dying. This decision is thus joined to the deepest feeling of indigence. It is an acceptance of the human condition in the radical imperfection of its essence, which implies in Montaigne the presence of the same feeling of spiritual nakedness as that of the great Christian thinkers."[32]

The unity of the *Essays* is the unity of his life. In "Of physiognomy" Montaigne returns to the theme of philosophy as a preparation for death: "[D]eath is indeed the end, but not therefore the goal, of life; it is its finish, its extremity, but not therefore its object. Life should be an aim unto itself, a purpose unto itself" (VS1051–52; F805). The straight-line narrative unity of life from conception to death is here put aside. Instead we see life as valuable in itself, the moments of life not given value by virtue of their relation to anything else. As Oakeshott says of the life of religious faith: "Ambition and the world's greed for visible results, in which each stage is a mere approach to the goal would be superseded by a life which carried in each of its moments its whole meaning and value."[33] There is no "external" final cause that gives unity to Montaigne's life or, consequently, to the *Essays.* As Friedrich points out: "Autobiographical recounting has a teleological, final character" that is missing from the *Essays.*[34]

The first consequence of the complete acceptance of the condition of creation out of nothing is, then, the graceful response to temporality that the *Essays* display. The second consequence is the ontological primacy of contingency and possibility. Friedrich explains something of what is entailed in the primacy of contingency: "[W]hen what exists is seen as surrounded by the possibility that it can be revoked at any time, as something that can just as well be as not be, then no relationship to it is possible other than one of acceptance of its mere actuality. No judgment can be permitted to generalize this actuality into a knowledge of eternal laws. The skeptical spirit lives in the expectation of limitless possibility and in the reflective viewing of reality which is inexhaustible because it is contingent."[35]

Montaigne often speaks of himself in terms of the possible and the contingent. In fact, the very first instances in which he speaks about himself in the *Essays* are examples of this. In "To the reader" he presents his desire to be seen in his "simple, natural, ordinary fashion" in terms of what he might have done but did not do: "*If I had written* to seek the world's favor, *I should have bedecked* myself better, and should present myself in a studied posture." And "*had I been placed* among those nations which are said to live still in the sweet freedom of nature's first laws, I assure you *I should very gladly have portrayed myself* here entire and wholly naked" (VS3; F2, emphases added). In "By diverse means we arrive at the same end," the first time he speaks about himself in the *Essays* proper, he does so in terms of possibility. After telling us that there are two ways to soften the heart of the avenging conqueror – by submission and by defiance – he writes: "Either one of these two ways *would* easily win me . . . I believe I *should be* likely to surrender more naturally to compassion" (VS8; F4, emphases added). Montaigne's thinking about himself and his own self-understanding take place within the context of possibility, a context that is, at least in part, formed by the human possibilities available in stories and testimony.

The ontological priority of possibility also allows for a kind of transformation of human being that is more fundamental and more real than what can be expressed in the Aristotelian categories of potentiality and actuality. For Aristotle, the potential is always dependent upon and limited by the prior actuality. So, for example, the bird actualizes its potentiality for flying only because the ability to fly is an essential characteristic of the permanent species. There is no real novelty here even though there is change, and this is perhaps an adequate explanation for nonhuman and physical occurrences. As Montaigne says, it is not difficult to know the limits of the forces of the body and we can say without presumption that certain physical feats are impossible for a human being.

But for Montaigne, human being must be such that it can undergo the most complete transformation and yet still be. At the very end of the "Apology" he considers Seneca's claim that man is a vile and abject thing if he does not lift himself above his humanity. Montaigne's response is that this is "absurd," for it is "impossible and monstrous" that the handful be bigger than the hand. "Nor can man raise himself above himself and humanity; for he can see only with his own eyes, and seize only with his own grasp. He will rise, if God by exception lends him a hand; he will rise by abandoning and renouncing his own means, and letting himself be raised and uplifted by purely celestial means. It is for our Christian faith, not for his Stoical virtue, to aspire to that divine and miraculous metamorphosis" (VS604; F457). Montaigne allows for the possibility of a divine and miraculous transformation, a literal change of form.

So, he quotes Saint Paul: "I desire to be dissolved, to be with Jesus Christ" (VS360; F260 and VS445; F324). This, Montaigne says, is a "voluntary dissolution." And the desire does not issue from despair or lead to nonbeing. In the "Apology" he takes up the issue of immortality and the way in which the philosophers have tried to talk about the life after death. Human reason must say to the philosopher: "If the pleasures that you promise us in the other life are of the kind I have tasted here below, that has nothing in common with infinity. Even if all my five natural senses were filled to overflowing with delight, and this soul possessed of all the contentment it can desire and hope for, we know what it is capable of: that would still be nothing. If there is anything of mine in it, there is nothing divine. If it is nothing but what can pertain to this present condition of ours, it cannot be counted. All contentment of mortals is mortal" (VS518; F385). The philosophers, such as Plato, want to make us capable of divine beatitude by purification, but then the "reform and change" of our being "must be by so extreme and universal a change that, according to the teachings of physics, it will no longer be ourselves" (VS518; F385). And when Plato tries to make sense of immortality by saying that it will be only the spiritual part of man that will enjoy the rewards of the other life, we must acknowledge that "by that reckoning, it will no longer be man, nor consequently ourselves, . . . for we are built of two principal essential parts, whose separation is the death and destruction of our being" (VS519; F386). A metaphysics that takes its principles from physics cannot be adequate to the belief in the resurrection of the body and to the contingent and the possible as the Christian understands and believes them to be. "We cannot worthily conceive the grandeur of those sublime and divine promises, if we can conceive them at all." They must be "completely different from those of our miserable experience. 'Eye cannot see,' says Saint Paul, 'neither can it have entered into the heart of man, the happiness which God hath prepared for them that love him'" (VS518; F385). The meaning of being and of possibility must be such as to allow for these most radical senses of transformation.

For Montaigne, one of the most significant implications of the belief in creation out of nothing is the complete absence of the divine from nature. The ancient philosophers, who searched for the causes of all things, identified those first causes within nature with the divine. So, for example, Thales holds that all things are really water, water is the source and the divine ordering principle; Heraclitus holds that the *logos* is divine. Perhaps the clearest expression of the place of the divine in nature is given in Aristotle's *Metaphysics*. The divine is pure actuality and the final cause of all that is. It is here that we find his characterization of the divine as "thought thinking thought." For all of these ancient philosophers, the mind of the philosopher achieves a harmony with what is divine in nature. As Michael B. Foster explains, for the Greek philosophers, "contemplation was the union of the divine element in man with the divine nature of the universe." This is very different from the Christian theology of creation "according to which God *created* the world and man, so that both nature and man are creatures and not divine."[36]

Christianity introduces the most radical possible distinction between God and the world, between Creator and creation. Robert Sokolowski, in *The God of Faith and Reason*, explains the distinction in this way: "Christian theology is differentiated from pagan religious and philosophical reflection primarily by the introduction of a new distinction, the distinction between the world understood as possibly not having existed and God understood as possibly being all there is, with no diminution of goodness or greatness."[37] Thus, none of the distinctions that we are accustomed to make within nature can apply in exactly the same way to the far more fundamental distinction between God and nature.

There are, of course, important consequences for thought if the divine is no longer held to be a part of nature. For Aristotle, the divine orders the whole. It is, so to speak, the highest part of the whole, ordering everything beneath it. That ordering is in terms of likeness to the divine – that is, what is more like the divine is higher than what is less like it. Thus, the presence of the divine within nature and as a part of nature necessarily produces a hierarchy within the whole. And this hierarchy is reproduced in man: his faculties and parts are ordered hierarchically with reason as the highest and, therefore, entitled to rule, just as the divine *nous* rules and orders the whole. In his discussion of the classic experience of reason, Eric Voegelin describes the relationship of the mind to the divine in this way: "In the Platonic-Aristotelian experience, the questioning unrest [philosophy] carries the assuaging answer within itself inasmuch as man is moved to his search of the ground by the divine ground of which he is in search. The ground is not a spatially distant thing but a divine presence that becomes manifest in the experience of unrest and the desire to know. The wondering and questioning is sensed as the beginning of a theophanic event that can become fully luminous to itself if it finds its proper response in the psyche of concrete human beings – as it does in the classic philosophers."[38]

Now, what happens if the divine is removed from the whole and the apex of the whole disappears? The hierarchy collapses. There is no longer anything to sustain it. Its principle of order is no longer there to justify rationally the place of anything because place was determined relative to the divine, the highest. In his "Three Cosmologies" Joseph Carpino describes the way the cosmos looks when the divine has been removed: "There are still, within the world, some regularities to be observed, some structures that remain. But there is now no way of ranking them with any surety; 'higher' and 'lower' are simply no longer representationally functional."[39]

Foster says that Greek theology thought of the divine as dwelling with the nondivine within nature. But "for Biblical theology God is beyond nature, and therefore all elements of nature, whether of human or of cosmic nature, are equal in being not God. There can be no hierarchy of divine and non-divine elements in nature, nor in human nature." These consequences follow from "a renunciation of the inheritance of the Greek belief in the divinity of reason."[40] What Cassirer says of Nicholas of Cusa could be said as well of Montaigne. In the inherited Aristotelian-Platonic system of "graduated mediation," "the higher an element stands in the cosmic stepladder, the closer it is to the unmoved mover of the world, and the purer and more complete is its nature. But Cusanus no longer recognizes any such relationship of the proximity and distance between the sensible and the supersensible. If the distance as such is infinite, all relative, finite differences are annihilated. When compared to the divine origin of being, every element, every natural being is equally far and equally near to that origin. There is no longer any 'above' and 'below,' but a single universe, homogeneous within itself."[41]

This collapse of the ancient hierarchy is decisive for Montaigne, for his understanding of being and of the activity of philosophy itself. The collapse of the ancient hierarchy is the ontological ground of the "lowering" that is so characteristic of his thought, especially with respect to final causality. That is what Montaigne is pointing to in his relentless display of the irrationality of human life and action: in "Of the inconsistency of our actions" we are told that not even a dozen men among the ancients were able to order their lives in relation to a single end. Rational consistency requires a kind of striving and straining that is the opposite of Montaigne's own nonchalance. In contrast with the perfection of the Aristotelian causes, Montaigne presents himself as defective and deformed.

Here it must be said that the full import of the removal of the divine from nature, including the collapse of the ancient hierarchy, was resisted throughout the Middle Ages. The theologians who attempted to harmonize Christian faith with ancient philosophy were unwilling to abandon the notion of a natural hierarchy. In the *Essays*, this is exemplified in Sebond's natural theology: man is the image of God by virtue of his reason, which is highest in him. Carpino explains the theological attempt to preserve the hierarchical picture of the world: "Plato's Forms become the 'ideas' of God or the intentions of the Creator. . . . Nature is governed by Law. . . . Everything is as it was. . . . Hierarchical dominion is still very much the way of the world."[42]

Just as Montaigne says in the "Apology" that "we must do more" than Saint Augustine, so too we can infer that we must do more than Saint Thomas. That is, Montaigne sees himself as following out the implications of creation more completely and more radically than the theologians had done. He is a genuinely new figure. He is neither a deliberate philosopher nor a theologian: his accidental philosophy is the mode of thought that corresponds to the truth of created being.

If the ancient natural hierarchy can no longer be sustained, what does the world look like? How does being present itself for thought? Montaigne's first ontological presupposition is that the world is created. His second presupposition is that the world is "incarnational." The first implies that the divine is absolutely distinct from the world. The second implies that God is present in and revealed in the world. The Incarnation is a different kind of presence of the divine in the world from the presence of the divine as a part or a cause within the world. It is that incarnational kind of presence that Montaigne reflects in his thought and in his *mœurs*.

How does the incarnational presupposition manifest itself in the *Essays*? It would, I believe, be proper to apply to Montaigne the description that T. S. Eliot gives of the thought of Pascal: "The Christian thinker – and I mean the man who is trying consciously and conscientiously to explain to himself the sequence which culminates in faith, rather than the public apologist – proceeds by rejection and elimination. He finds the world to be so and so; he finds its character inexplicable by any non-religious theory: among religions he finds Christianity, and Catholic Christianity, to account most satisfactorily for the world and especially for the moral world within; and thus, by what Newman calls 'powerful and concurrent' reasons, he finds himself inexorably committed to the dogma of the Incarnation."[43] How, then, does Montaigne find the world to be inexplicable apart from the truth of the Incarnation?

First, we can turn to his stance with respect to the monsters and miracles that are so frequent in the *Essays*. He never ceases to see the monstrous and miraculous in the ordinary and familiar, especially in human action: "If we call monsters or miracles whatever our reason cannot reach, how many of these appear continually to our eyes! Let us consider through what clouds and how gropingly we are led to the knowledge of most of the things that are right in our hands; assuredly we shall find that it is rather familiarity than knowledge that takes away their strangeness" (VS179; F132). In "Of the resemblance of children to fathers" he refers to the presumption that consists in admitting our ignorance in many things but assuming that we do understand what is common: "We have no need to go picking out miracles and remote difficulties; it seems to me that among the things we see ordinarily there are strange things so incomprehensible that they surpass even miracles in obscurity. What a prodigy it is that the drop of seed from which we are produced bears in itself the impressions not only of the bodily form but of the thoughts and inclinations of our fathers! . . . If anyone will enlighten me about this process, I will believe him about as many other miracles as he wants" (VS763–64; F578–79).

The histories and the testimony of the ancients open us to possibilities of which we would not have even dreamt, but in the end we must come back to our own time and place and our own experience: "If we say that we lack authority to gain credence for our testimony, we say so without reason. By the same token, in my opinion, from the most ordinary, commonplace, familiar things, if we could put them in their proper light, can be formed the greatest miracles of nature and the most wondrous examples, especially on the subject of human action" (VS1081; F829). If there is a monster in nature, it is man himself: "What a monstrous animal to be a horror to himself, to be burdened by his pleasures, to regard himself as a misfortune!" In this we are truly unique: "We regard our very being as vice" (VS879; F670).

When he turns to the familiar, Montaigne ultimately turns back to himself to find the miraculous and the monstrous. We have seen that he refers to his friendship with La Boétie as a miracle and a mystery. And it seems to me that, in two other places where he describes a certain type of character as miraculous, he is really referring to himself. In the "Apology" in his reply to the first objection, he discusses the hatred, cruelty, and ambition that Christians show toward each other especially in the civil wars of his day. It is a "miracle" if some rare temperament displays goodness and moderation (VS444; F324). And in his reply to the second objection, he says that, in his day, the most excellent minds are almost all given over to unruliness in license of opinions and of *mœurs*: "It is a miracle if you find a sedate and sociable one" (VS559; F419).

The most significant statement that Montaigne makes in this regard occurs in "Of cripples" where he is discussing belief in miraculous cures: "To this moment all these miracles and strange events have eluded me. I have seen no more evident monstrosity and miracle in the world than myself. We become habituated to anything strange by use and time; but the more I frequent myself and know myself, the more my deformity astonishes me, and the less I understand myself" (VS1029; F787).[44]

We see here that Montaigne's metaphysics is identical with his project of self-knowledge: "I study myself more than any other subject. That is my metaphysics, that is my physics" (VS1072; F821). Montaigne's "self" is not substance, or mind, or subjectivity. It is the most familiar and, at the same time, "the place of all obscurities and the mystery of all mysteries."[45] Or as Friedrich says: "In proximity to himself, man becomes to himself the most alien being and the greatest of all wonders."[46] Just as Montaigne's circle of thought is the lowered and purely human version of Aristotle's "thought thinking thought," so his deformed, monstrous, and miraculous self is the lowered and purely human version of Aristotle's mind: the mind is nothing, yet the mind becomes all things (*De Anima* 429a20–430a).

Montaigne's wonder at the most familiar, his finding the monstrous and miraculous in the ordinary, is due not only to the supposition of creation but also to the supposition that the divine is revealed in the ordinary and is thus, in some way, present there. As C. S. Lewis says: "If a miracle means that which must simply be accepted, the unanswerable actuality which gives no account of itself but simply is, then the universe is one great miracle." Miracles are "focal points at which more reality becomes visible than we ordinarily see at once."[47] In the miracle at Cana in which water is changed into wine, we see one such focal point, for God always changes water into wine through "natural" processes: God creates the vine and the rain. "The miracles [of Christ] in fact are a retelling in small letters of the very same story which is written across the whole world in letters too large for some of us to see."[48] Lewis, like Montaigne, refers to the miracle of ordinary, common generation, and "every miracle," he says, "exhibits the character of the Incarnation."[49]

Michael Oakeshott, in his discussion of religious faith in *On Human Conduct*, provides a description of the way in which the divine is present in and manifested in a nonhierarchical world. "Religious faith is the evocation of a sentiment . . . to be added to all others as the motive of all motives in terms of which the fugitive adventures of human conduct, without being released from their mortal and their moral conditions, are graced with an intimation of immortality: the sharpness of death and the deadliness of doing overcome, and the transitory sweetness of mortal affection, the tumult of a grief and the passing beauty of a May morning recognized neither as merely evanescent adventures nor as emblems of better things to come, but as *adventures*, themselves encounters with eternity."[50] The poet expresses this religious sentiment: "Knit me that am crumbling dust." Oakeshott concludes: "The dignity of a religion lies in the intrepidity of its acknowledgement of this human condition, in the cogency of the reconciliation it intimates, and in the poetic quality, humble or magnificent, of the images, the rites, the observances, and the offerings (the wisp of wheat on the wayside calvary) in which it recalls to us that 'eternity is in love with the productions of time' and invites us to live 'so far as is possible as an immortal.'"[51]

Oakeshott's essay "Religion and the World" might well be, whether he intended it or not, a portrait of Montaigne. "To keep unspotted from the world means, not to have restricted the field of our experiences, but to have remained uninfluenced by a certain scale of values, to be free from a certain way of thinking. ... The other world of religion is no fantastic supernatural world, from which some activities and interests have been excluded, it is a spiritual world, in which everything is valued, not as a contribution to some development or evolution, but as it is itself."[52] The way in which Christianity is present in the *Essays* is captured here. "Religion, then, is not ... an interest attached to life, a subsidiary activity; nor is it a power which governs life from the outside with a, no doubt divine, but certainly incomprehensible, sanction for its authority. It is simply life itself, life dominated by the belief that its value is in the present, not merely in the past or the future, that if we lose ourselves we lose all."[53]

Distinctions can be made within the nonhierarchical world but they are not the same distinctions that one would make in a hierarchically ordered world. The situation in which distinctions are made is captured beautifully and simply by Pascal: "Just as Jesus remained unknown among men, so the truth remains among popular opinions with no outward difference. Thus the Eucharist and ordinary bread."[54] The world of faith is not a separate, higher, other world to which we hope one day to go. It is here in this world, with no outward difference. Again, C. S. Lewis points to the condition of the incarnational world: "Common bread, miraculous bread, sacramental bread – these three are distinct, but not to be separated."[55]

One of the most important implications of this "horizontal" picture is that the divine is revealed in the particular and the presence of God is experienced in the encounter with the particular. This helps explain Montaigne's persistent reluctance to ascend to universals and his insistence on remaining at the level of examples.

In *Fear and Trembling*, Kierkegaard gives us a description of the incarnational situation within which distinctions must be made and the particular encountered: "We are touched, we look back to those beautiful times. Sweet sentimental longing leads us to the goal of our desire, to see Christ walking about in the promised land. We forget the anxiety, the distress, the paradox. Was it such a simple matter not to make a mistake? Was it not terrifying to sit down to eat with him? Was it such an easy matter to become an apostle? But the result, the eighteen centuries – that helps, that contributes to this mean deception whereby we deceive ourselves and others. I do not feel brave enough to wish to be contemporary with events like that, but I do not for that reason severely condemn those who made a mistake, nor do I depreciate those who saw what was right."[56]

The incarnational world is a world in which God is both revealed and hidden. Michael B. Foster elaborates on Kierkegaard's insight: "God is hidden in his very revelation of himself. . . . the revelation of God is at the same time by its very thoroughness a veiling of God. . . . the Incarnation, as Kierkegaard said, is the assumption of an incognito, which obscures the person of the Incarnate, and lays it open to misinterpretation."[57] The situation of those who witnessed the life of Christ is not really different from our own, for how would they have known what they were actually seeing? But our situation is also no worse than theirs. Like Kierkegaard, Montaigne brings the question of belief into the present. Revelation is not in the past or from "on high." It takes place in the present, in the encounter with the most familiar.

PART III

THE CHARACTER OF THE ACCIDENTAL
PHILOSOPHER

7

Montaigne's Character

The Great-Souled Man without Pride

Montaigne is astonished at his own deformity. Astonishment, for him, does not occur because there has been a disruption of the ordinary flow of things, the unexpected emerging against the background of the ordinary. Not just the unexpected startles him by its chance happening: the customary and presumedly permanent background for the appearance of the unexpected is now itself seen as contingent. What astonishes him is the most familiar: the most familiar did not have to be at all. Contingency, not subjectivity, is the fundamental ontological category of Montaigne's self-understanding. Thus Auerbach can say of Montaigne that "among all his contemporaries he had the clearest conception of the problem of one's self-orientation; that is, the task of making oneself at home in existence without fixed points of support."[1]

Within that context, Auerbach claims that "the tragic is not yet to be found in Montaigne's work."[2] There is in the *Essays* nothing of the modern sense of the tragic, the highly personal tragedy of the individual unrestricted by ideas of the cosmos and fate. Auerbach tends to attribute the absence of the tragic to Montaigne's temperament. But it may be equally true to say that Montaigne's character is what it is because the tragic has been, in some ultimate sense, transformed within his self-understanding. Expressed in religious terms, he is presenting us with a picture of what it means to hope.

"Truth Said in Laughing"

Montaigne's orientation in an existence without fixed points of support is closer to the stance of Democritus than it is to the stance of Heraclitus: "Democritus and Heraclitus were two philosophers, of whom the first, finding the condition of man vain and ridiculous, never went out in public but with a mocking and laughing face; whereas Heraclitus, having pity and compassion on this same condition of ours, wore a face perpetually sad, and eyes filled with tears" (VS303; F220). Montaigne prefers the first humor "not because it is pleasanter to laugh than to weep, but because it is more disdainful, and condemns us more than the other, and it seems to me that we can never be despised as much as we deserve. . . . The things we laugh at we consider worthless" (VS303; F221). Montaigne finds us more inane than evil, more worthless than wretched. And he ends this essay with the judgment that "our own peculiar condition is that we are as fit to be laughed at as able to laugh," thus qualifying the definition of man as "the animal that can laugh" (VS304; F221).

Now it must be said that while Montaigne is closer to Democritus, his own stance is not identical with that of Democritus for Montaigne is not mocking and disdainful.[3] The first thing that he says about himself in essay I.1, "By diverse means we arrive at the same end," is that he is "marvelously lax" in the direction of mercy and compassion. Montaigne, then, combines the laughter of Democritus and the compassion of Heraclitus in a new way. But he is closer to Democritus because the fundamental ontological category for him is contingency, and laughter is the fundamental human response to contingency.

In his analysis of the meaning of laughter, Joseph Carpino shows that "temporality . . . as the 'structure' of human awareness, and fragility as an abiding part of its content, are both essential to laughter."[4] That is why laughter always entails surprise: a set of expectations is falsified by events and laughter is the sudden release and relief of the intellect when what happens is suddenly not as bad as we expected it to be. "Looked at 'structurally,' the central organizing theme of laughter and of a sense of humor in general is hope. . . . If there is no hope there can be no laughter."[5] So the question becomes: "What must being be for laughter to make sense?" None of the cosmologies offered to us by ancient philosophy can really make sense of laughter. It is rather the idea of creation out of nothing that provides the ontological basis for laughter and for hope: being must be contingent.

Merleau-Ponty says of Montaigne that he puts a consciousness astonished at itself at the core of human existence. His random life is a "fundamental accident."[6] Thus, "consciousness has an essential foolishness"[7] and is "mixed according to its very principle with the absurd and foolish."[8] For Merleau-Ponty the essential foolishness of consciousness has to do with the fact that consciousness is not Cartesian "mind." Montaigne's realm is rather the mixture of soul and body: "[H]e is interested only in our factual condition, and his book endlessly describes this paradoxical fact that we are."[9]

That is one reason why Montaigne so often reminds the philosopher of his body and why he does so in vivid and comical terms: "Won't they try to square the circle while perched on their wives!" (VS1107; F850). He ridicules the philosopher who disdains pleasure as if it were brutish and unworthy of the wise man: "The only pleasure he derives from the enjoyment of a beautiful young wife is the pleasure of his consciousness of doing the right thing, like putting on his boots for a useful ride. May [that philosophy's] followers have no more right and sinews and sap in deflowering their wives than her lessons have!" (VS1113; F855).

But Montaigne's is not the mocking laughter of one who despises the condition of man and who somehow thinks himself above it. After all, the *Essays* themselves are merely "the excrements of an aged mind." Montaigne's is rather a joyous laughter that comes from the sudden recognition that what-might-not-have-been-at-all *is*.[10] There are two aspects of being that are revealed in Montaigne's sudden recognition. The first is sheer particularity. We laugh when we picture the philosopher perched on his wife while trying to square the circle and when we imagine the collection of chamber pots to which Montaigne compares his essays. It is the philosopher's embodiment, most clearly displayed in the most base and shameful acts, that prompts the sudden release of laughter. That laughter is the recognition of being in its particularity. The reason that it is the philosopher, and not the muleteer, perched on his wife who makes us laugh is that the philosopher is trying to square the circle in this ridiculous position; his pretensions to universal and disembodied reason, while engaged in an act that is so completely bound to the particular and to the body, create a disparity that is comical.

The second aspect of being that is revealed in Montaigne's sudden recognition is its lowliness. It is not the divinity of his intellect that astonishes him; it is his deformity. That is the surprising thing, that the lowly and the base and the common should be.[11] So in the example of the philosopher perched on his wife we see not only his particularity but the lowering of his estimation of himself. He is, after all, human. This comes out vividly in "On some verses of Virgil" where he pictures "the absurd, witless, and giddy motions" of Zeno and Cratippus while they are in the act of making love, "that reckless frenzy" and "that grave, severe, and ecstatic countenance in so silly an action" (VS877; F668). Montaigne concludes that "it was in mockery that nature left us the most confused of our actions to be the most common, in order thereby to make us all equal and to put on the same level the fools and the wise, and us and the beasts. The most contemplative and wisest of men, when I imagine him in that position, seems to me an impostor to put on wise and contemplative airs; here are the peacock's feet that humble his pride: 'Against truth said in laughing, Is there a law?' [Horace]" (VS877; F668–69).

The idea of "truth said in laughing" is crucial here, for it tells us something about laughter but also something about truth. For Montaigne, truth means finding the strange in the familiar, the surprising in the ordinary. His laughter, then, is not the mocking laughter of disgust and contempt. It is the sudden recognition of being in the most common and the affirmation of the merely human in the face of nothingness. "The surest sign of wisdom," Montaigne tells us, "is constant cheerfulness" (VS161; F119). That is what it means to say that "our wisdom is folly" and that we must flee "worldly philosophy."

Against this background of creation out of nothing, of contingency, laughter, and hope, we can see and understand what the character of Montaigne is. As Auerbach says, the reader who has come to be at home in the *Essays* begins to feel that he can "hear him speak and see his gestures. This is an experience which one seldom has with . . . theoretical writers as strongly as with Montaigne."[12] The particularity of Montaigne comes through to us against the background of nothingness and allows us to recognize a genuinely new human possibility, the great-souled man without pride.

Readers as different as Oakeshott and Nietzsche are struck by the greatness of this man. In a letter written toward the end of his life, Oakeshott says that Montaigne and Saint Augustine are "the two most remarkable men who have ever lived."[13] In his *Schopenhauer as Educator*, Nietzsche says of Montaigne: "The fact that such a man has written truly adds to the joy of living on this earth."[14] What could it be that Oakeshott and Nietzsche and so many others see in Montaigne that elicits these reactions?

Montaigne is a new figure who cannot be adequately explained in terms of the traditional categories. Just as he had to bend and stretch those traditional categories to capture his ontological stance, so too the traditional moral categories must be used, but bent and stretched, in order to express what he is. My discussion of Montaigne's character here and in Chapter 8 is related most closely to the moral tradition of the virtues, that is, to the tradition that has its basis in Aristotle's ethics. In his *Vertu du discours, discours de la vertu: Littérature et philosophie morale au xvie siècle en France*, Ullrich Langer demonstrates that the Aristotelian tradition in moral philosophy was a vital aspect of the intellectual and practical moral life of Montaigne's day. This view is a corrective to the focus on neo-Platonism and neo-Stoicism that has dominated the contemporary perception of sixteenth-century France.[15] Langer locates Montaigne within the Aristotelian tradition, but he also claims that Montaigne presents us with a modification of classical virtue. Prudence is modified in its confrontation with chance and with the laughable. Montaigne's *magnanimitas* is modified by his preference for private life and his "nonchalance."[16] My own account of Montaigne's character is similar in some ways to Langer's portrait of him.

This characterization – the great-souled man without pride – is a bending and stretching because the quality of being great-souled would seem to require pride of a certain kind. The classic description of the great-souled man occurs in Aristotle's *Ethics*, Book IV, where Aristotle goes through the list of virtues and defines each in relation to its two opposite vices, one of excess and one of deficiency. The Greek term is transliterated as *megalopsychia*, which means literally "greatness of soul" and which was translated into Latin as *magnanimitas* from which "magnanimity" is derived. Martin Ostwald chooses to translate *megalopsychia* as "high-mindedness" because that "seems better suited to rendering the pride and confident self-respect inherent in the concept."[17] To say that someone is "great-souled without pride," then, seems to be a contradiction and to posit an impossible combination. In Aristotle's description, the great-souled man is actually defined in terms of the attitude that he has toward honor (just as the generous man is defined in terms of his attitude toward wealth). The great-souled man thinks he deserves and truly does deserve great things. The greatest of the "external goods" and the prize of the most noble achievements is honor, so the great-souled man regards himself as worthy of honor.[18]

The man who falls short of the proper attitude toward honor is "small-minded": he deprives himself of the good he deserves, for he does not think he deserves good things, especially honor. Aristotle says that this man "does not know himself" for, if he did know himself, he would desire what he deserves (*Ethics* 1125a20–25). Small-mindedness is not really evil, but the small-minded man is mistaken. Thus he must be distinguished from the man who thinks he deserves little and actually does deserve little. The latter is simply a man who knows his limitations (1123b5–10). The man who exceeds with respect to estimating the honor he deserves is vain. Such people "are fools and do not know themselves, and they show it openly" (1125a25–30). At this point, we might be inclined to locate Montaigne at the deficient end of the spectrum. His persistent characterizations of the essays as lowly and base and his self-mocking references to himself are the kinds of things that have led some to accuse him of false modesty.

What does the great-souled man deserve to be honored for? "Honor is the prize of excellence and virtue, and it is reserved as a tribute to the good. High-mindedness thus is the crown, as it were, of the virtues: it magnifies them and it cannot exist without them. Therefore, it is . . . impossible to be truly great-souled without goodness and nobility" (1124a1–5). So it is with respect to his moral character that a man would be described as great-souled or not. Now even here, Montaigne counts himself as lowly and especially as weak. In comparing himself with men such as Cato, he insists that he could never reach such heights. And in the crucial passage in which he calls himself an unpremeditated and accidental philosopher, he is careful to specify that his *mœurs* are weak (*imbéciles*).

In spite of all his protestations concerning his lowliness and weakness, the Montaigne who comes through the pages of the *Essays* is some version of the great-souled man (as Oakeshott and Nietzsche testify), and I want to claim that he is the great-souled man without pride. This claim is possible because Montaigne separates self-love and self-esteem. He makes a distinction that is not even possible to make in the classical version of the great-souled man, a distinction that arises out of a recognition of his createdness, that is, of his nothingness. What is displayed in Montaigne's character is the possibility of Christian magnanimity, the synthesis of classical greatness of soul and Christian humility. Montaigne loves himself but does not esteem himself.

We have to consider, then, just what the mode of Montaigne's self-love is and how and why he separates self-love from self-esteem.

The Friendship That We Owe Ourselves

The most obvious way that Montaigne's self-love is manifested is through the self-centeredness of the *Essays*. This self-centeredness can be contrasted, for example, with the openly God-centeredness of Augustine and Pascal. Montaigne himself is the principal subject matter of the *Essays*. But besides this absorption in the task of self-knowledge, Montaigne presents a picture of his life as centered entirely on himself. "I live from day to day, and, without wishing to be disrespectful, I live only for myself; my purposes go no further" (VS829; F629). And he is not at all interested in the affairs of anyone else: "Never did a man do less inquiring or less ferreting into other people's affairs" (VS364; F263). The contrast that comes to mind here is with Socrates who, like Montaigne, is concerned with self-knowledge but who is, at the same time, very much involved in the affairs of others, spending all his time in the marketplace, waylaying the passersby with his questions and challenges to the way they conduct their lives. Socrates is a "busybody." For all his admiration of Socrates, Montaigne minds his own business and is careful to present himself that way, especially in essay III.10, "Of husbanding your will," where he gives an account of his service as mayor of Bordeaux. "Those who know how much they owe to themselves, and for how many duties they are obligated to themselves, find that nature has given them in this a commission full enough and not at all idle. You have quite enough to do at home; don't go away" (VS1004; F767). Montaigne takes a very different attitude from the common one that would have us always busy and fully engaged in large and small matters: "I keep myself to myself" (VS1004; F768). He begins the essay by making it clear that his will is in some way centered on himself: "As much as I can, I employ myself entirely upon myself.... the passions that distract me from myself and attach me elsewhere, those in truth I oppose with all my strength. My opinion is that we must lend ourselves to others and give ourselves only to ourselves" (VS1003; F766–67). In "Of physiognomy," in the course of discussing the civil wars of his day, he makes this shocking admission: "I doubt if I can decently admit at what little cost to the repose and tranquillity of my life I have passed more than half of it amid the ruin of my country" (VS1046; F800).

How should Montaigne's self-centeredness be taken? Is it the equivalent of petty selfishness? Montaigne's self-centeredness must be seen first as a response to the "temptation" to ambition, which is why it is presented so forcefully within the context of his account of himself as mayor. The temptation of ambition is the temptation to politics. When he describes the course that our lives ought to take, the temptation to ambition is prominent: "The range of our desires should be circumscribed and restrained to a narrow

limit of the nearest and most contiguous good things; and moreover their
course should be directed not in a straight line that ends up elsewhere, but
in a circle whose two extremities by a short sweep meet and terminate in ourselves. Actions that are performed without this reflexive movement, . . . the
actions, for example, of the avaricious, the ambitious, and so many others
who run in a straight line, whose course carries them forward – are erroneous and diseased actions" (VS1011; F773).

That Montaigne is tempted by ambition is clear. "I have long been
preaching to myself to stick to myself and break away from outside things;
nevertheless I still keep turning my eyes to one side. Inclination, a favorable
word from a great man, a pleasant countenance, tempt me. . . . I still listen
without frowning to the seductions that are held out to me to draw me into
the marketplace, and I defend myself so softly that it looks as if I would prefer to succumb to them. Now a spirit so indocile needs some beatings; and
we need to knock together and tighten the hoops, with good mallet strokes,
on this cask that is splitting its seams, cracking up, and falling completely
to pieces" (VS1045–46; F800). In "Of vanity" he discusses the occupation
of politics and especially the aspect of rule: "By the little experience I have
had in that profession, I am just that much disgusted with it. I sometimes
feel rising in my soul the fumes of certain temptations toward ambition; but
I stiffen and hold firm against them" (VS992; F759). In "Of experience" he
admits that, although his thought has been purged of the desire for glory,
his temperament still retains some traces of it. Even in his old age, he feels
the attractions of a visible, public life, but he presents them as temptations
to be resisted, not as opportunities to do good for others and to enjoy the
honor and praise that visible good works might bring.

Aristotle's great-souled man knows that he deserves honor but prefers the
reality to the mere appearance of virtue. Thus, he is regarded as haughty because, while he knows what honor he deserves, he is indifferent to the opinions of others about himself (*Ethics* 1124a20). Two features of Montaigne's
character look something like the haughtiness of which the great-souled
man is accused. Montaigne has always had "a way . . . of avoiding justifying,
excusing, and interpreting myself, thinking that it is compromising my conscience to plead for it." When he is accused of something by his enemies
in the civil wars, he does not retreat from the accusation. Instead, he says,
"I advance to meet it and rather enhance it by an ironic and mocking confession, if I do not flatly keep silent about it as about something unworthy of an
answer." But this way of his is due neither to "an over-haughty confidence"
nor to the weakness of an indefensible cause. His description of the reaction
of "the great" to his manner is especially pertinent. For the great, "lack of
submission is the ultimate offense." They are "rough on any righteousness
[*justice*] that is aware of itself and does not feel itself to be abject, humble,
and suppliant. I have often bumped myself on that pillar." In the face of the
accusations that he had to endure, "an ambitious man would have hanged

himself." Montaigne, then, is not an ambitious man but his is a righteousness that is "aware of itself and does not feel itself to be abject, humble, and
suppliant" (VS1044–45; F799).

Second, Aristotle's great-souled man is "the kind of man who will do
good, but who is ashamed to accept a good turn, because the former marks
a man as superior, the latter as inferior.... It is, further, typical of a high-
minded man not to ask for any favors, or only reluctantly, but to offer aid
readily" (*Ethics* 1124b8–10, 16–20). In "Of vanity" Montaigne says of himself:
"I see no one freer and less indebted than I am up to this point.... Oh, how
much I am obliged to God that it was his pleasure that I should receive all
I have directly from his grace, and that he has kept all my indebtedness for
himself privately! How earnestly I beseech his holy mercy that I may never
owe thanks for essential things to anyone! Blessed liberty, which has guided
me so far! May it continue to the end! I try to have no express need of
anyone" (VS968; F739–40). In fact, it is with respect to this freedom from
indebtedness that Montaigne makes one of his strongest statements about
himself: "Those who know me, both above and below me, know whether
they have ever seen a man less demanding of others. If I surpass all modern
examples in this respect, it is no great wonder, for so many parts of my
character contribute to it: a little natural pride, inability to endure refusal,
limitation of my desires and designs, incapacity for any kind of business, and
my very favorite qualities, idleness and freedom. Through all these I have
conceived a mortal hatred of being obliged either to another or by another
than myself. I employ my power to the utmost to do without, before I employ
the kindness of another, however slight or weighty the occasion" (VS969;
F740–41).

These features of Montaigne's character do closely resemble Aristotle's
description of the great-souled man. But there are significant differences
that have a bearing on Montaigne's claim that he is a new figure. The kind
of self-sufficiency or self-possession that Montaigne displays in his reluctance
to justify himself, in his self-aware integrity, and his extreme lack of indebtedness is due less to pride or haughtiness than to the great value that he places
on freedom. Put somewhat differently, it has less to do with self-esteem than
it does with self-love.

What, then, is the nature of Montaigne's self-love? Just as Montaigne's
self-centeredness has to be seen not as a form of blind and petty selfishness
but as a form of resistance to ambition, so his self-love must be understood
as a form of resistance to self-hatred. Montaigne himself, of course, is a
master of the art of depicting human weakness and vanity, and so he is
closer to the stance of the laughing Democritus than to that of the weeping
Heraclitus. But he distances himself from Timon, who was called "the hater
of men" (VS304; F221). Hatred, like weeping, is a response that takes us too
seriously. Self-love, in its proper sense, must be a form of love that has taken
into account our vanity and nothingness.[19]

Perhaps it is the sight of our own weakness and vanity that disgusts us with ourselves and prompts us to hate ourselves. We despise ourselves because we are not angels or God. We are ashamed of our own humanity. And, in turn, our self-hatred is one of our great weaknesses and most bizarre qualities. "We are the only animal whose defectiveness offends our own fellows, and the only ones who have to hide, in our natural actions, from our own species. . . . it is a wonderful sign of our defectiveness that acquaintance and familiarity disgust us with one another" (VS484–85; F356–57).

Self-hatred often takes the form of hatred of the body and contempt for its pleasures. "Isn't man a miserable animal? Hardly is it in his power, by his natural condition, to taste a single pleasure pure and entire, and still he is at pains to curtail that pleasure by his reason: he is not wretched enough unless by art and study he augments his misery" (VS200; F148). We are truly ingenious when it comes to destroying our pleasure. "What a monstrous animal to be a horror to himself, to be burdened by his pleasures, to regard himself as a misfortune!" In all of these passages, Montaigne is insisting to man that he is an animal. "Are we not brutes to call brutish the operation that makes us? . . . We regard our being as vice" (VS878–79; F669–70).

It is against this background of vanity and self-hatred that we can see the quality of Montaigne's self-love. First of all, he does not think that he is exempt from the human condition: "I who spy on myself more closely, who have my eyes unceasingly intent on myself, as one who has not much business elsewhere . . . I would hardly dare tell of the vanity and weakness that I find in myself" (VS565; F425). But in response to those who criticize his vain pursuits, he writes: "'There is vanity,' you say, 'in this amusement.' But where is there not? And these fine precepts are vanity, and all wisdom is vanity. 'The Lord knoweth the thoughts of the wise, that they are vain.' These exquisite subtleties are only fit for preaching; they are arguments that would send us all saddled into the other world. Life is a material and corporeal movement, an action which by its very essence is imperfect and irregular; I apply myself to serving it in its own way" (VS988; F756).[20] And he concludes "Of vanity" with the acceptance of his vain condition: "If others examined themselves attentively, as I do, they would find themselves, as I do, full of inanity and nonsense. Get rid of it I cannot without getting rid of myself. We are all steeped in it, one as much as another; but those who are aware of it are a little better off" (VS1000; F766).

In "A custom of the isle of Cea" Montaigne addresses the subject of self-hatred directly: "As for the opinion that disdains our life, it is ridiculous. For after all, life is our being, it is our all. Things that have a nobler and richer being may accuse ours; but it is against nature that we despise ourselves and care nothing about ourselves. It is a malady peculiar to man, and not seen in any other creature, to hate and disdain himself. It is by a similar vanity that we wish to be something other than we are" (VS353; F254). That is why he can say in "Of repentance" that he rarely repents and that his conscience is content with itself "not as the conscience of an angel or of a horse, but as the conscience of a man" (VS806; F612).

In "Of moderation" Montaigne points to the fact that "human wisdom" is ingenious in the ways it finds to spoil our pleasures. Then he says: "If I were the head of a [philosophical] sect, I would have taken another course, one that would have been more natural – which is to say, true, practicable, and holy; and I might perhaps have made myself strong enough to set bounds to [philosophy]" (VS200; F148). Indeed, it is "absolute perfection and virtually divine to know how to enjoy our being rightfully. We seek other conditions because we do not understand the use of our own, and go outside of ourselves because we do not know what it is like inside" (VS1115; F857).

When Montaigne presents Socrates to us as the model of perfection, he shows us not only the Socrates who was seen standing in a trance for an entire day and night, who covered Alcibiades and rescued him from the enemy, and who came forward to rescue Theramenes who had been condemned by the Thirty Tyrants. He shows us also the Socrates who never refused to play at cobnut with children and to ride a hobbyhorse with them and to do so gracefully: "[F]or all actions, says philosophy, are equally becoming and honorable in a wise man." So Montaigne bends the meaning of "greatness of soul." He defines it precisely in contrast to "the most barbarous of our maladies," which is "to despise our own being." Greatness of soul, he says, is not so much pressing upward and forward: it "shows its elevation by liking moderate things better than eminent ones." For "there is nothing so beautiful and legitimate as to play the man well and properly" (VS1110; F852).

Montaigne hates that "inhuman wisdom" that would have us disdain the body (VS1106; F849), and he finds that "supercelestial thoughts and subterranean conduct" always go together (VS1115; F856). So, for him, "the summit of human wisdom" is to know and understand the friendship that we owe to ourselves. This is neither the false friendship that mistakes external goods such as glory and wealth for our true being nor the overindulgent and undiscriminating friendship that causes self-decay. True friendship is what we owe to ourselves. In religious terms, this is expressed in the "as thyself" of the second great commandment: "Thou shalt love thy neighbor as thyself."

The self-love that is true friendship with oneself is very rare. This is at first surprising because we quite naturally assume that self-love is among the most common and most familiar aspects of the human condition. And indeed it is. But in most men it is confused, immoderate, and indiscreet and manifests itself in the two vices that are opposed to magnanimity: small-mindedness and arrogance. Montaigne takes so much care in showing us what genuine self-love is because we do not just naturally and unthinkingly love ourselves in the proper way. In his discussion of friendship for oneself as the summit of human wisdom, he tells us that those who give us our rules and precepts (the philosophers and theologians) are always pushing us outside ourselves into the public square to be useful to society. "They thought to achieve a fine result by diverting and distracting us from ourselves, assuming that we were attached to ourselves only too much and by too natural a bond" (VS1006; F769).

Our first and original malady, the most pervasive and inescapable condition, is presumption. And presumption is defined by Montaigne as "an over-good opinion we form of our own worth" (VS631–32; F478). It is because we cherish ourselves with a thoughtless affection that we represent ourselves to ourselves as other than we are and more perfect than we are. Presumption, then, is a failure to separate self-love and self-esteem. We are so vain and wretched that we think we cannot love ourselves unless we can esteem ourselves. Montaigne achieves in his character the separation of self-love and self-esteem, and thus overcomes presumption to the extent and in the way that this is possible for us.

The separation is made explicit in two places in "Of presumption." Toward the beginning of that essay, he tells us: "It would be very difficult, it seems to me, for anyone else to esteem himself less, or indeed for anyone else to esteem me less, than I esteem myself. I consider myself one of the common sort, except in that I consider myself so; guilty of the commoner and humbler faults, but not of faults disavowed or excused; and I value myself only for knowing my value" (VS635; F481). Later, he repeats this self-appraisal in somewhat different terms, focusing on the separation of self-love and self-esteem. "I think my opinions are good and sound; but who does not think as much of his? One of the best proofs I have of mine is *the little esteem I have for myself*; for if these opinions had not been very firm, they would easily have let themselves be fooled by *the singular affection I have for myself*, being one who concentrates nearly all his affection upon himself and does not squander much of it elsewhere" (VS657; F499, emphasis added).

How, then, are we to reconcile Montaigne's rejection of self-esteem with his publication of his work? The *Essays* are his emergence out of the anonymity of the common. Why does he want to do something that would distinguish him, set him apart, and make him noticed, unless he does so for the sake of honor and pride?

Montaigne himself recognizes this objection to his project and responds to it in two related ways. First, the custom that forbids us to speak about ourselves does not really get to the source of pride: "The supreme remedy to cure it is to do just the opposite of what those people prescribe who, by prohibiting talking about oneself, even more strongly prohibit thinking about oneself. The pride lies in the thought; the tongue can have only a very slight share in it" (VS379; F274). It is precisely the "hidden and secret actions" that do not appear on the outside (the thoughts, intentions, and desires) that must be ordered (VS630; F478). Second, in publicly displaying what he is, Montaigne is not boasting. On the contrary, he is revealing his deformity, weakness, and ignorance.

Relocating the Great-Souled Man

Montaigne's separation of self-love and self-esteem is related to his choice of a private over a public life. At the end of "Of husbanding your will," in which he discusses his performance as mayor, he writes: "I had published elaborately enough to the world my inadequacy in such public management. I have something still worse than inadequacy: that I hardly mind it, and hardly try to cure it, in view of the course of life that I have designed for myself" (VS1024; F784). The life that he has designed for himself must be contrasted with what traditionally has been called "the active life." In "Of solitude" he makes this distinction: "There are some temperaments more suited to these precepts for retirement than others. Those whose susceptibility is weak and lax, and whose affection and will are fastidious and slow to enter service or employment – of whom I am one, both by natural disposition and by conviction – will comply with this advice better than will the active and busy souls who embrace everything and engage themselves everywhere" (VS242; F178–79).

Montaigne's choice of a private over a public life allows us to see what his stance is toward ambition and the life of honor, for the public arena is the place where honor is conferred. In "Of liars" he tells us of the monstrous deficiency of his memory. But he consoles himself for this lack of memory because "it is an evil that has shown me the way to correct a worse evil which would easily have developed in me – to wit, ambition; for lack of memory is intolerable in anyone who is involved in public negotiations" (VS34–35; F22).

He also consoles himself because his lack of memory means that he does not remember offenses received (VS35; F23). The man who values honor is strongly disposed to take offense when he is slighted and he is also strongly disposed to take revenge when the opportunity presents itself. This is what Aristotle says of the great-souled man: "He bears no grudges, for it is not typical of a great-souled man to have a long memory, especially for wrongs, but rather to overlook them" (*Ethics* 1125a3–5). Like Aristotle's great-souled man, Montaigne bears no grudges, and he is marvelously lax in the direction of mercy. "Vengeance is a sweet passion, whose impact is great and natural: I see this well enough, though I have no experience of it in myself" (VS835; F634). Even receiving what is, in justice, due to him is of little importance to Montaigne. He goes so far as to say: "Among men, as soon as an altercation over precedence in walking or sitting goes beyond three replies, it is uncivil. I have no fear of ceding or preceding unfairly to avoid such a bothersome argument, and never did a man covet my right to go first but that I yielded it to him" (VS980; F749). He is not a man who insists on his rights and prerogatives. But he takes no pride in his practice of forgiving, attributing it to a mere accident of temperament, to his deficiency of memory, to his "easy-going ways" (VS820; F622).

Indeed, this is one of the most important aspects of Montaigne's account of his character: he takes no credit for it because it is merely unpremeditated and accidental. It is here that we see clearly his humility, a humility that is the result of his "skepticism" concerning the causes of his actions. He is not concerned to "own" his actions by virtue of their "deliberateness."

Certainly it is not cowardice that causes him easily to cede his place and yield his rights: "Since we will not do so out of conscience, at least out of ambition let us reject ambition. Let us disdain this base and beggarly hunger for renown and honor which makes us grovel for it before all sorts of people . . . abjectly and at no matter how vile a price" (VS1023; F783). There may be some natural pride in his disdain for honor, but the reason that seems to be strongest is his love of freedom. He hates any form of subjection and even of obligation. He speaks of his "unruly humors" which make him hate all kinds of ties and obligations (VS852; F648). And he is especially wary of the obligations that honor imposes: "I avoid subjecting myself to any sort of obligation, but especially any that binds me by a debt of honor. . . . The tie that binds me by the law of honor [*la loi d'honnêteté*] seems to me much tighter and more oppressive than is that of legal constraint" (VS966; F738). He even goes so far as to say "I am so fond of throwing off burdens and obligations that I have sometimes counted as profit the ingratitude, affronts, and indignities that I had received from those to whom, either by nature or by accident, I owed some duty of friendship; taking the occasion of their offense as that much aquittance and discharge of my debt. . . . I see no one freer and less indebted than I am" (VS967–68; F739).

In his own home, he dispenses with the constraints of ceremony as much as possible: "As for me, I often forget . . . these vain formalities, just as I cut out all ceremony in my house. Someone takes offense: I can't help it. It is better for me to offend him once than myself every day; that would be per-petual slavery. What is the use of fleeing the servitude of courts if we drag some of it right home to our lair?" (VS48; F32). Montaigne was brought up in the rules of French civility: "I could run a school of it." But he refuses to be tyrannized by them: "I like to follow these laws, but not so timidly that my life would remain constrained. They have some troublesome forms, which a man may forget, provided he does so by discretion and not by mistake, without losing grace by his behavior" (VS48–49; F32). The knowl-edge of the laws of civility "opens the door for us to learning by the exam-ples of others, and to bringing forth and displaying our own example, if it has anything instructive and communicable about it" (VS49; F33). The guests in his home enjoy "an unusual freedom." The painful rules of cour-tesy are dispensed with and "everyone there behaves as he pleases; anyone who wants to, communes with his own thoughts; I remain mute, dreamy, and locked up in my thoughts, without my guests' taking offense" (VS824; F625).

The clearest expression of Montaigne's preference for the private life and its relation to freedom is found in "Of vanity": "I love a private life because it is by my own choice that I love it, not because of unfitness for public life, which is perhaps just as well suited to my nature. I serve my prince the more gaily because I do so by the free choice of my judgment and my reason" (VS988; F756). Montaigne does not need the public arena of politics in order to be (or to become) what he is. The sphere of the private allows him sufficient scope for his actions.

The discussion of action in Hannah Arendt's *The Human Condition* is most helpful in bringing to light the significance of Montaigne's choice of a private life. Arendt gives an account of action as distinguished from labor and work; she finds the phenomenon of action to be most clearly visible in the Greek *polis* and to depend upon the prior distinction between the public and private spheres of life (a distinction that she says has been blunted or even lost in the modern world).

Arendt begins her account of action from Dante's claim that "in every action what is primarily intended by the doer ... is the disclosure of his own image ... [and] in action the being of the doer is somehow intensified"[21] Action, then, is not the process of pursuing the means to an end, as production is. Rather, it is its own end, an end-in-itself, for its essence is the sheer self-disclosure of the being of the agent. So the paradigm of action shows itself in the "agonal spirit, the passionate drive to show one's self in measuring up against others that underlies the concept of politics prevalent in the city-states."[22] It is indeed only within the web of relationships that constitutes the city that action is real.[23] The prior distinction between public and private means that "there are things that need to be hidden and others that need to be displayed publicly if they are to exist at all."[24] The hidden things are those having to do with the body and the necessities of life, the servile realm of means and ends, of labor and work. The public realm is the realm of action in its proper sense, action as the mode in which human beings appear to each other in the public space of the city and where they distinguish themselves from each other by their deeds. "Because of its inherent tendency to disclose the agent together with the act, action needs for its full appearance the shining brightness we once called glory, and which is possible only in the public realm."[25] It is within this necessarily public arena that deeds give rise to stories.

How do the *Essays* show themselves against this background of action as glorious deeds captured in stories? There are at least four places where Montaigne addresses this issue directly and defines his project in terms of it. In "Of presumption" he defends himself for violating the prohibition against speaking of oneself that is so deeply rooted in custom: "Those whom fortune ... has caused to spend their lives in some eminent station, can testify to what they are by their public actions. But those whom she has employed only in a mass, and of whom no one will speak unless they do so themselves, may be excused if they have the temerity to speak of themselves to those who have an interest in knowing them" (VS632; F479). At the very beginning of "Of vanity" he refers to his writing as vain and then goes on to say: "Who does not see that I have taken a road along which I shall go, without stopping and without effort, as long as there is ink and paper in the world? I cannot keep a record of my life by my actions; fortune places them too low. I keep it by my thoughts. . . . Here you have . . . some excrements of an aged mind" (VS945–46; F721). And later in the same essay, he writes: "One man guides himself well who does not guide others well, and produces Essays, who cannot produce results" (VS992; F759).

"Of giving the lie" begins: "Yes, but someone will tell me that this plan of using myself as a subject to write about would be excusable in rare and famous men who by their reputation had aroused some desire to know them. That is certain; I admit it; and I know full well that to see a man of the common sort, an artisan will hardly raise his eyes from his work, whereas to see a great and prominent personage arrive in a city, men leave workshops and stores empty. It ill befits anyone to make himself known save him who has qualities to be imitated, and whose life and opinions may serve as a model. In the greatness of their deeds Caesar and Xenophon had something to found and establish their narrative upon, as on a just and solid basis. . . . This remonstrance is very true, but it concerns me only very little. . . . I am not building here a statue to erect at the town crossroads, or in a church or a public square." Then, quoting Perseus: "We two talk alone." He goes further in comparing himself with those who are justified by great deeds: "Others have taken courage to speak of themselves because they found the subject worthy and rich; I, on the contrary, because I have found mine so barren and so meager that no suspicion of ostentation can fall upon my plan. I willingly judge the actions of others; I give little chance to judge mine because of their nullity" (VS664; F503).

Caesar and Xenophon do not need to apologize for telling their great deeds. But Montaigne is writing about himself; and he has no great deeds to tell. The *Essays* are not about Montaigne's deeds: we learn very little from his writing concerning any role he might have had in public affairs, even his deeds as mayor of Bordeaux. The *Essays* are not the narrative of his life because what he is is not properly disclosed in his deeds. The essay, not the story, is the appropriate form of expression for what he is. So he acknowledges fully the force of the accusation that must be "out there," anonymous, in the *on dit* of public opinion: it is a vain, frivolous, and ridiculous presumption to write about oneself when one's deeds are nothing, when the artisan would not even lift his eyes from his work to see him pass by.

Instead of telling his deeds, Montaigne presents his *mœurs* and his thoughts – another aspect of the "lowering" so characteristic of the *Essays*.

In order to see how this is a lowering, we can look to Machiavelli's *Discourses*, Book III, chapter 34, entitled "What Fame or Word or Opinion Makes the People Begin to Favor a Citizen; and Whether It Distributes Magistracies with Greater Prudence Than a Prince." Machiavelli discusses the way the people judge the men who claim authority to rule them. The first way is to judge by the company a man keeps, including who his father is. The second way is by a man's practices (*mœurs*). The third is by the standard of "extraordinary and notable action." The first way, he says, is fallacious: reputation based on relatives and fathers is soon dissipated when the public has the chance to see that the reputation is not supported by the man's own virtue. "The second, which makes you known by way of your practices, is better than the first, but it is much inferior to the third, for until some sign is seen that arises from you, your reputation remains founded on opinion, which it is very easy to cancel." Machiavelli gives this advice to "those citizens who wish to acquire fame so as to obtain honors in their republic" and to princes who want to maintain their reputations in their principalities: "[N]othing makes them so much esteemed as to give rare examples of themselves with some rare act or saying conforming to the common good, which shows the lord either magnanimous, or liberal, or just, and is such as to become like a proverb among his subjects."[26] By this set of standards, Montaigne is presenting himself for judgment at the second level, the level of *mœurs*, a level much inferior to the highest standard of the great and glorious deed.

We see that he stands in a position that is difficult to articulate, a position somehow between public and private, a position without a name. That is because he is doing something new. He is the private man presuming to reveal himself in public. He brings the private realm out of its hiddenness into the public light and, at least in some respects, puts it on a par with the public realm. The common and undistinguished becomes, paradoxically, exemplary. "I set forth a humble and inglorious life; that does not matter. You can tie up all moral philosophy with a common and private life just as well as with a life of richer stuff. Each man bears the entire form of the human condition" (VS805; F611). The rare and illustrious loses its status as defining what it means to be human. This emergence of the private has, then, not only moral and political but ontological significance as well.[27]

Montaigne's relocation of the great-souled man to the private realm is entailed in his separation of self-love and self-esteem and is the overcoming of the pride in his character. He distances himself from the so-called agonal spirit, "the passionate drive to show one's self in measuring up against others that underlies the concept of politics" in the city, and thus opens up the possibility of magnanimity to the private, common man. So it would be a partial and mistaken view of Montaigne to see him as simply lowering the standards of moral action so as to build on the lowest but most solid base. Rather, he creates a space that did not exist before.[28] With pride and honor no longer elements of the character of the great-souled man, this character becomes possible for those whom fortune has not placed in a position to disclose themselves in actions visible to all. Or perhaps it would be more accurate to say, not that Montaigne creates a new space, but that he makes visible a space that was not visible before and that he gives to the invisible a voice and a mirror in which they can recognize themselves. What he does is to allow for a certain kind of character to emerge and to be conscious of itself.

Without doubt, there are important questions to be raised about the political implications of this shift. In particular, we must consider whether this is an instance of what Arendt describes as the antagonism between Christianity and the *res publica,* an antagonism provoked by the Christian requirement that goodness be hidden: "[G]oodness that comes out of hiding and assumes a public role is no longer good but corrupt."[29] Does Montaigne's removal of pride from the great-souled man really amount to a denigration of politics as such or does it perhaps allow for new political forms? I address those issues in Chapters 8 and 9.

The private life that Montaigne loves is the life of philosophy. But he is an unpremeditated and accidental philosopher. The life of philosophy as he presents it is a life of freedom and idleness. In other words, it is truly "useless." When Aristotle characterizes philosophy as useless he intends this as the highest praise: philosophy is useless because it serves no external purpose. It is useless because it is free, not servile, and therefore the best activity for a human being. It seems to me that Montaigne's practice of philosophy shows it to be a useless activity in the most radical possible sense. Rather than praise his activity, he calls it "frivolous and vain." Montaigne takes all the honor out of philosophy. Accidental philosophy does not rule anything. It is only when Montaigne wants to articulate his *mœurs* that he finds himself speaking philosophy: his *mœurs* are not formed by philosophy. Accidental philosophy leaves everything precisely as it is. That is what it means to say that it is nonauthoritative. The aim of accidental philosophy – if we can say that it has an aim at all – is to think philosophically, not to construct "a philosophy," an authoritative teaching.[30]

The character of Montaigne as I have sketched it thus far is captured, in somewhat different terms, by Michael Oakeshott in his essay "Religion and the World." Oakeshott puts aside as unsatisfactory the medieval dichotomy between the natural and the supernatural, but he maintains the idea of a world from which the religious man tries to escape. He is interpreting what Saint James could mean when he says that "Pure religion is to keep unspotted from the world." For Oakeshott, this means that the religious man remains uninfluenced by a certain scale of values and is free from a certain way of thinking. The worldly man measures the worth of life by its external achievements; his is the "careerist" ideal. The religious man, on the other hand, believes in "the fleetingness of the things men do and make and the permanence and value of sensibility and possession by insight."[31] The most important thing for him is integrity of character, both moral and intellectual. Thus, he "will inherit nothing he cannot possess by actual insight," and he measures the worth of life by its sensibility.[32] His virtues are candor, sincerity, and "the courage to know what belongs to his life" a courage by which he "steps outside the tedious round of imitation." The freedom that he seeks is "the sole condition of the intellectual integrity he values more than anything else."[33] In this portrait of the religious man, we can recognize the self-love, self-possession, and carelessness of honor that Montaigne displays in his *Essays*.

But our sketch of Montaigne's character is not yet complete. For what we have up to this point is a man who loves himself and is a friend to himself. But what can be said about the presence of "love thy neighbor" in the *Essays*?

Openness of Heart and Tongue

The most obvious instance of an acknowledged affection in the *Essays* is, of course, his friendship with La Boétie. Montaigne's description of this friendship, both in "Of friendship" and throughout the entire book, leaves no doubt about his capacity for the deepest and most unselfish love.[34] The second kind of human bond that is acknowledged in the *Essays* is compassion. As we have seen, the very first thing that Montaigne says about himself has to do with his compassion. This bond is spelled out more fully in the last of the essays where he tells us that he is so grateful to his good father who "sent me from the cradle to be brought up in a poor village of his, and kept me there as long as I was nursing, and even longer, training me to the humblest and commonest way of life." His father's intention was to toughen him but also "to ally me with the people and that class of men that needs our help. . . . And this was the reason why he also had me held over the baptismal font by people of the lowliest class, to bind and attach me to them." Montaigne's judgment is that his father's plan succeeded. "I am prone to devote myself to the little people, whether because there is more vainglory in it, or through natural compassion, which has infinite power over me" (VS1100; F844).

Montaigne does not deny or minimize the force of convention in inequalities among men, but neither does he mistake them for natural differences. This is a man who (we learn in passing) takes boys out of a life of begging into his service, who looks for them when they are drawn back to their accustomed life, who begs and threatens them to come back to his kitchen when he finds them picking up mussels in the dump heap for their dinner (VS1082; F829). He is unimpressed by erudition, wealth, and power; he is alert to any signs of intelligence, virtue, and beauty in the lowly and common.

How, then, might we complete our sketch of Montaigne's character? What must be added to this description of his mode of self-love and his lack of self-esteem in order to complete the portrait of the great-souled man without pride? The term that captures the essence of Montaigne's magnanimity is "openness," the term suggested by Montaigne himself. Openness includes elements of both friendship and compassion as I have presented them, that is, friendship as uncalculating self-giving and compassion without condescension. The meaning of "openness" is seen more clearly if we contrast it with its opposite: "lack of heart." What Montaigne means by "openness" is a courageous generosity of soul.

In "Of the disadvantage of greatness" Montaigne writes that "to eschew greatness is a virtue, it seems to me, which I, who am only a gosling, could attain without great striving" (VS916; F699). He is accustomed to a middle station both by fortune and by taste. "But if my heart is not great enough, it is compensatingly open, and it orders me boldly to publish its weakness" (VS917; F700). It is Montaigne's openness that explains his publication of his *Essays*. That is, he does not seek either authority or honor on account of his work: he wants only to communicate himself.[35]

Montaigne's openness pervades not only his writing but his dealings with everyone in his life. His description of his mode of acting in negotiations between princes is especially relevant here. "Professional negotiators make every effort within their power to conceal their thoughts and to feign a moderate and conciliatory attitude. As for me, I reveal myself by my most vigorous opinions, presented in the form most my own" (VS791; F600). And he has had such good luck with this practice that "few men have passed between one party and another with less suspicion and more favor and privacy" (VS792; F600). He characterizes his way as open: "I have an open way that easily insinuates itself and gives credit on first acquaintance. Pure naturalness and truth, in whatever age, still find their time and their place. . . . My freedom has also easily freed me from any suspicion of dissimulation by its vigor. . . . I am not pressed by any passion either of hate or of love toward the great, nor is my will bound by personal injury or obligation. . . . This is what makes me walk everywhere head high, face and heart open" (VS792; F600–1). And he concludes essay I.5, "Whether the governor of a besieged place should go out to parlay," by turning his gaze back on himself: "I put my trust easily in another man's word. But I should do so reluctantly whenever I would give the impression of acting from despair and want of courage rather than freely and through trust in his honesty" (VS27; F17). That is the courage that he shows in his advice and his actions when he and his fellow commanders are warned of betrayal and rebellion by their troops: he advises that they walk among the men with heads held high and faces open, giving no evidence of doubt or fear, and this confidence engendered a mutual confidence in the troops (VS131; F96). It is the courage that he shows in keeping his house open and unarmed through more than thirty years of civil war, inviting the enemy in even when he suspects a ruse to capture him (VS617; F468).

Once again, it is Oakeshott who describes this character and he does so in his discussion of what he calls "the moralization of pride itself." The character he portrays is that of the man who is not made tame by fear but who seeks peace out of generosity and magnanimity. "What he achieves for himself and what he contributes to a common life is a complete alternative to what others may achieve by means of agreement inspired by fear and dictated by reason."[36] He achieves by courage what others achieve by rational calculation. The "moralization" of pride is shown in Montaigne as carelessness of honor and courageous openness.[37]

The element of the free bond of friendship is clearly seen in Montaigne's uncalculating openness to all men. "Not because Socrates said it, but because it is really my feeling, and perhaps excessively so, I consider all men my compatriots, and embrace a Pole as I do a Frenchman, setting this national bond after the universal and common one.... Friendships purely of our own acquisition usually surpass those to which community of climate or of blood binds us" (VS973; F743). Neither place nor time is a barrier to this friendship: "We embrace both those who have been and those who are not yet, not only the absent" (VS976; F746).

Finally, and not surprisingly, Montaigne's openness is especially manifested in his insistence on open speaking. In "Of presumption" he is vehement in his disapproval of dissimulation: "As for this new-fangled virtue of hypocrisy and dissimulation, which is so highly honored at present, I mortally hate it; and of all vices, I know none that testifies to so much cowardice and baseness of heart. It is a craven and servile idea to disguise ourselves and hide under a mask, and not to dare to show ourselves as we are. In that way our men train for perfidy; being accustomed to speak false words, they have no scruples about breaking their word. A generous heart should not belie its thoughts; it wants to reveal itself even to its inmost depths. There everything is good, or at least everything is human" (VS647; F491).

When Montaigne criticizes hypocrisy and dissimulation, he refers to Aristotle's description of the great-souled man: "Aristotle considers it the function of magnanimity to hate and love openly, to judge, to speak with complete frankness, and to have no regard for the approbation or reprobation of others in comparison with truth" (VS647; F491). His reference is, apparently, to the *Ethics* (1124b25–30), on which I have been relying for my portrait of the great-souled man. But here we can see an important difference between Montaigne and Aristotle's portrait, for Aristotle says that the great-souled man will not talk about himself because he is not interested in hearing himself praised (1125a5). Montaigne, of course, is always speaking about himself. He does not presume to speak about himself because he esteems himself or because his self-love cannot be separated from self-esteem. Rather, he speaks about himself because "not to dare to speak roundly of oneself shows some lack of heart.... We must pass over these common rules of civility in favor of truth and liberty" (VS942; F720).[38]

Montaigne dares to speak roundly of himself because he is willing to risk all for friendship. "An open way of speaking opens up another man's speech and draws it out, as do wine and love" (VS794; F602). Why does the desire to tell his *mœurs* seize him? His openness could not be the result of any rational calculation. By nature, he says, "I find it hard to communicate myself by halves and moderately, and with that servile and suspicious prudence that is prescribed to us" (VS821; F623). Perhaps, then, it is in free and uncalculated self-revelation that we see the contingent image of God.

8

What He Learned in the Nursery

Accidental Moral Philosophy and Montaigne's Reformation

Montaigne writes his *Essays* because he is seized by the desire to tell his *mœurs*. What astonishes him is the fact that his weak and lowly *mœurs* conform to so many philosophical discourses and examples, for he has never deliberately formed himself according to the rules of any philosophical school. His *mœurs* are just what he learned in the nursery. So the circle of his thought simply returns to its starting point: there is no philosophical project of forming or reforming. "Others form man; I tell of him, and portray a particular one, very ill-formed" (VS804; F610).

On the other hand, Montaigne is a new figure and the *Essays* are the public display of a new possibility for human being. Although he denies that he has ever attained the philosophical consistency or constancy of Cato, he does present a "natural movement," a picture of "liberty and license so constant and inflexible" that it cannot be captured in the rule of any philosophical school (VS795; F603). He publishes his *mœurs*, in part, because they are new: "The uniformity and simplicity of my *mœurs* produce an appearance easy to interpret, but because the manner of them is a bit new and unusual, it gives too fine a chance to calumny" (VS980; F749).

What is it that is new in Montaigne's manner of being? Are we entitled to speak about a project of reformation when Montaigne is so insistent that he does not "form" man and that he has no authoritative teaching? In this chapter, I first ask about the kind of reform that a nonauthoritative, accidental philosophy might offer: this is not a reform by means of reason or new opinions but by means of example. Then I examine what is new in the moral picture that Montaigne paints of himself. This entails an elucidation of the distinction that he makes between virtue and goodness or innocence and the way in which goodness moderates the "excesses" of pagan virtue. Finally, we see that what is "a bit new and unusual" in Montaigne's moral philosophy is his reordering of virtues and vices and the centrality and foundational status that he gives to what he learned in the nursery, especially his hatred of cruelty and lying.

The Accidental Authority of Example

The notion of "rational" reform, or reform by "new opinions," is rejected by Montaigne not only as ineffective but even as dangerous: "Those who in my time have tried to correct the world's morals [*mœurs*] by new opinions, reform the superficial vices; the essential ones they leave as they were, if they do not increase them; and increase is to be feared. People are likely to rest from all other well-doing on the strength of these external, arbitrary reforms, which cost us less and bring greater acclaim; and thereby they satisfy at little expense the other natural, consubstantial, and internal vices" (VS811; F615).

Also, if goodness and innocence are essential to Montaigne's portrait of moral perfection, then it is not at all clear that these can be deliberately achieved. Virtue can be aimed at and approached through the practice of deliberate philosophy. But innocence and goodness are "natural," and nature is so variable in us that Montaigne can say that his innocence is "accidental" (VS427; F311). How can goodness be deliberately pursued if it belongs to us only by an occult, natural, and pervasive individual manner of being, "without law, without reason, without example?" (VS428; F312) Could there be any kind of reformation that could possibly affect nature in that most fundamental sense?

In "Of practice" Montaigne gives us some insight into the way in which an example can be instructive and authoritative. After telling the story of his near fatal fall, he explains that he has derived instruction for himself from the experience of being so near to death. "What I write here is not my teaching but my study; it is not a lesson for others, but for me. And yet it should not be held against me if I publish what I write. What is useful to me may also by accident be useful to another" (VS377; F272). Example is the way in which one particular human being can see himself in relation to another particular human being, not through any universal but directly. That relationship has more to do with the imagination than with reason in the abstract sense, for the example is present to the mind by means of the imagination. That is why Montaigne emphasizes the role of the imagination in the way he paints the actions of such men as Cato, elevating them as much as he can.

In "Of diversion" he recounts for us the story of how he diverted a prince from taking vengeance: "Recently, in order to lead a young prince away from [vengeance], I did not tell him that we must turn our cheek to the man who has just struck the other one, for charity's sake, nor did I represent to him the tragic results that poetry attributes to this passion. I let the passion alone and applied myself to making him relish the beauty of a contrary image, the honor, favor, and good will he would acquire by clemency and kindness" (VS835; F634). The *Essays* are full of just such images of clemency. And Montaigne is himself an image of the character of Christian magnanimity.

Montaigne's reformation is a reformation of his judgment, his heart, his will. In defending himself for talking about himself in public he writes: "The pride lies in the thought" (VS379; F274). He says that children must be taught from the very beginning to hate vices and to flee them "not only in their actions but above all in their heart" (VS110; F79). Others, he says, see only his face; they do not see his heart where he is what he is (VS625; F474). And in "On some verses of Virgil," speaking of the chastity of women, he writes: "Now let us confess that the crux in judging this duty lies principally in the will" (VS868; F660). Here he emphasizes the distinction between external actions and purity of will: "One woman may be of loose conduct, and yet have a more reformed will than another who conducts herself in a more regular manner" (VS868; F661). For "their mute sins are the worst" (VS867; F660).

Purity of heart, or judgment, certainly looks like a lesser, lower, and weaker condition than that of heroic virtue. But this is precisely Montaigne's reformation. At the beginning of essay I.37, "Of Cato the Younger," he repeats the claim that he makes so often, that he does not make the common error of judging others according to what he himself is: "My weakness in no way alters my necessarily high regard for the strength and vigor of those who deserve it. . . . Crawling in the slime of the earth, I do not fail to observe, even in the clouds, the inimitable loftiness of certain heroic souls. It is a great deal for me to have my judgment regulated, if my actions cannot be, and to maintain at least this sovereign part free from corruption. It is something to have my will good when my legs fail me" (VS229; F169). Reformation of judgment is perhaps less visible than reformation of outward actions but it is far more thorough because it affects the whole man.

The Excesses of Virtue

The most fundamental distinction for Montaigne's moral philosophy is the distinction that he draws between virtue and innocence (or goodness). Virtue belongs to the deliberate philosophers, like Cato, who conform their lives to philosophical doctrine and who even reform themselves according to the principles of philosophy. Montaigne cannot reach so high. His moral status is one of innocence or goodness, a weaker and lower condition.

How does Montaigne draw this distinction? First, it must be emphasized that, in spite of his acceptance and even affirmation of human and cultural diversity, Montaigne is not a moral relativist.[1] The ground on which he stands when he makes his moral judgments is the prior distinction between the higher and the lower, the noble and the base. So, although the cannibals follow customs that are radically different from the customs of the French, Montaigne judges them by the standards of courage, moderation, and justice. He never wavers in his hatred and condemnation of vice, and he especially resists what he sees as the tendency to elevate some vices to the status of virtues. He does, however, weigh the vices a bit differently from the way others do, judging some to be less grave and others more grave than common or philosophical opinion may allow. He also emphasizes some virtues more than others and perhaps even introduces new virtues or at least understands the foundations of the virtues in a new way. In other words, Montaigne judges from the standpoint of what he was taught in the nursery. Only within that set of standards does he "produce his own example" and exercise his own discretion.

Montaigne assumes the conventional assessment of what counts as virtue and what counts as vice, but he does not merely assume it. He does so knowingly, and that is an instance of his return to the common, of his pulling back to the position of ignorance. The return is a knowing return. We can see this in what he says about vice in "Of repentance": "I consider as vices (but each one according to its measure) not only those that reason and nature condemn, but also those that man's opinion has created, even false and erroneous opinion, if it is authorized by laws and customs" (VS806; F612). He accepts them all as vices, but he can distinguish between the natural and the conventional and even between the true and false.

But Montaigne goes further than acceptance. He sees it as his task to raise virtue to the highest possible plane in the imagination of his readers. He is disgusted by the efforts of his contemporaries to deflate the judgments of the heroic actions of the ancients, attributing vicious intentions to them and interpreting their heroic actions according to their own unworthy motives. "I see most of the wits of my time using their ingenuity to obscure the glory of the beautiful and noble actions of antiquity, giving them some vile interpretation and conjuring up vain occasions and causes for them" (VS230; F170). Cato's suicide, for example, is attributed to his desire for glory. As we saw in Chapter 1, Montaigne's response to this tendency is an openness to the possible, the first moment of the movement of his thought. He elaborates on his task with respect to virtue in "Of Cato the Younger." Those who make every effort to detract from the greatness of the ancients do so because of malice or from "that vice of dragging down their belief to their capacity" or from "not having their sight strong enough and clear enough, or properly trained, to conceive of the splendor of virtue in its native purity" (VS231; F170). Montaigne, on the contrary, wants to make every effort to elevate these ancient heroes: "The same pains that they take to detract from these great names, and the same license, I would willingly take to lend them a shoulder to raise them higher. These great figures, whom the consensus of the wise has selected as examples to the world, I shall not hesitate to restore to their places of honor, as far as my ingenuity allows me to interpret them in a favorable light. But we are forced to believe that our powers of conception are far beneath their merit. It is the duty of good men to portray virtue as being as beautiful as possible; and it would not be unbecoming to us if passion carried us away in favor of such sacred models" (VS231; F170).

What is it about virtue, especially at its heights, that elicits the response of awe? At least in part, it is what we take to be the difficulty of virtue, the difficulty that accounts for why it is rare. In "That the taste of good and evil depends in large part on the opinion we have of them," Montaigne is discussing the way in which we deal with the evils of life, especially pain, "the worst accident of our being" (VS56; F38). Virtue is concerned with remaining firm in the face of pain: "And if this were not so, who would have brought into credit among us virtue, valor, strength, magnanimity, and resolution? Where would these play their part if there were no more pain to defy?" (VS56; F38). The wise actually prefer the more difficult actions so as to exercise virtue: "It is a far cry from fleeing evil and pain to what the sages say, that among equally good actions the most desirable to do is the one in which there is most trouble" (VS57; F38). It is difficulty that gives value to virtue just as price gives value to the diamond (VS62; F43). In "That our desire is increased by difficulty" he says that, in the case of virtue, "of two similar acts we still consider that one fairer and more worthy in which more obstacle and risk [are] offered" (VS615; F466). And with respect to the virtue of chastity he writes that "there is neither continence nor virtue if there is no urge to the contrary" (VS867; F660).

Not only does the philosopher overcome and stand firm in the face of the accidents of life; he deliberately creates occasions for practicing and for strengthening his soul. This is one of the most important features of deliberate philosophy, and Montaigne mentions it often. Among the Stoics and Epicureans, for example, "there were many who judged that it was not enough to have the soul in a good posture, well regulated and well disposed to virtue, that it was not enough to have our resolutions and our ideas set above all the attacks of fortune; but that we also had to seek occasions to put them to the proof. They want to seek pain, need, and contempt, in order to combat them and to keep their soul in trim" (VS423; F307).

Thus far, we have only an incomplete picture of what virtue is. But there is a clear emphasis on struggle and strength, suggesting that the common feature of all virtue is courage of some kind. Virtue is an overcoming of either the external difficulties with which fortune confronts us or the internal difficulties that arise out of our disordered appetites and our imperfections (VS423; F307). The tendency to identify virtue with strength appears from the very beginning of the *Essays*. In "By diverse means we arrive at the same end," the explanation that is put forward as plausible to explain why the avenging conqueror is sometimes moved by defiance when submission has failed to move him is that weak natures (those of women, children, and common people) are moved by pity but strong natures are moved by reverence for virtue: "[H]aving disdained tears and prayers, to surrender simply to reverence for the sacred image of valor [*la vertu*] is the act of a strong and inflexible soul which holds in affection and honor a masculine and obstinate vigor" (VS8; F4). This is not an explanation that Montaigne simply accepts, but it is the first plausible explanation that comes to mind because it accords so well with the very meaning of virtue. At the conclusion of "Of honorary awards," Montaigne makes this connection between virtue and strength explicit: "The Romans took the general term 'virtue' from their word for 'strength.' The proper, the only, the essential form of nobility in France is the military profession. It is probable that the first virtue that manifested itself among men and gave some advantage over others was this one, by which the strongest and most courageous made themselves masters of the weaker and acquired particular rank and reputation; whence it has retained this linguistic honor and dignity. Or else that these nations, being very warlike, gave the prize and the worthiest title to the one virtue which was most familiar to them" (VS384; F277).

The second characteristic of virtue that emerges out of Montaigne's descriptions is the rule of reason within the soul. "Pain, pleasure, love, hatred are the first things that a child feels; if when reason comes they cling to her, that is virtue" (VS1111; F853). All true philosophers try to make their lives correspond to their doctrine (VS705; F533), but the rule of reason manifests itself in a constancy that is extremely rare. "If any man could prescribe and establish definite laws and a definite organization in his head, we should see shining throughout his life an evenness of habits, an order, and an infallible relation between his principles and his practice" (VS333; F240). This constancy comes from directing one's entire life toward a single end (VS337; F243). Montaigne refers to constancy as the utmost perfection of the rule of reason in the soul (VS345; F249), a perfection so rare as to be almost unbelievable (VS706; F533). Once again we see the connection between rarity and difficulty.

To speak of the excesses of virtue is strange from the start. On Aristotle's account, for example, virtue cannot be excessive by definition. True, virtue is a kind of extreme but it is an extreme of excellence that consists in achieving in one's action precisely the midpoint between the two vicious extremes of deficiency and excess. It is impossible to be too courageous. One can only be too fearful or too rash. Montaigne acknowledges this view but rejects it. In "Of moderation" he writes: "Those who say that there is never any excess in virtue, inasmuch as it is no longer virtue if there is excess in it, are playing with words. . . . This is a subtle consideration of philosophy. A man may both love virtue too much and perform excessively in a just action" (VS197; F146).

He goes on to say that "immoderation, even in the direction of the good, if it does not offend me, astonishes me and gives me trouble to name it." He gives two examples of such immoderation. The mother of Pausanias

informed on her son and brought the first stone for his death; the dictator
Posthumius had his son killed because, in his youthful ardor, he had rushed
against the enemy in advance of his rank. These actions seem to Montaigne
"not so much just as strange. And I like neither to advise nor to follow a
virtue so savage and costly" (VS197–98; F146). In "Of drunkenness" these
kinds of actions are attributed to a form of frenzy. When Plutarch considers the fact that Brutus and Torquatus killed their own children, it causes
him to doubt that virtue is the cause. "All actions outside the ordinary limits are subject to sinister interpretation, inasmuch as our taste responds no
more to what is above it than to what is below" (VS346; F250). After going
through a list of examples of philosophers and religious martyrs who ex-
hibited incredible endurance under torture, even joking and taunting their
torturers, Montaigne concludes that "in these souls there is some alteration,
some frenzy, however holy it may be. . . . Who does not judge that these are
the sallies of a runaway courage? Our soul from its abode could not reach so
high. It must leave its dwelling place and rise, and, taking the bit in its teeth,
abduct its man and carry him off so far that afterward he is himself astonished at his deeds" (VS347; F250–51). In "The story of Spurina" Montaigne
tells the story of a young Tuscan man of extraordinary beauty on whom no
one could look with continence. Spurina became furious at himself and deliberately slashed and mutilated himself. Montaigne's judgment is that "it
is much to be able to curb our appetites by the arguments of reason, or to
force our members by violence to stick to their duty." But to do what Spurina
did is excessive: "I wonder at such actions more than I honor them; these
excesses are enemies to my rules" (VS733–34; F555).

In fact, Montaigne is inclined to see a certain kind of weakness in such
actions. "Those who evade the common duties and that infinite number of
thorny and many faceted rules that bind a man of precise probity in civil
life, achieve, in my opinion, a fine saving, whatever point of especial rigor
they may impose on themselves. It is in a sense dying to escape the trouble
of living well. They may have some other prize; but the prize of difficulty it
has never seemed to me they had" (VS734; F555).

Thus, in spite of his great and sincere admiration for Cato, Montaigne's
ultimate judgment of suicide is that it is cowardly: "It is an act of cowardice,
not of virtue, to go and hide in a hole, under a massive tomb, in order
to avoid the blows of fortune" (VS353; F254).[2] Montaigne seems to be in
agreement with Saint Augustine when he says that there is more proof of
constancy and firmness in Regulus, who submitted patiently to domination,
than in Cato, who hid under a tomb. In those chapters of *The City of God*
where Augustine makes this claim, he is discussing the question of whether
suicide is ever a mark of greatness of soul: "Greatness of spirit is not the right
term to apply to one who has killed himself because he lacked strength to
endure hardships or another's wrongdoing. In fact we detect weakness in
a mind that cannot bear physical oppression or the stupid opinion of the

mob."[3] And there is a suggestion in "Of virtue" that the extraordinary flights of the soul are evidence of a failure of constancy. "In the lives of the heroes of times past there are sometimes miraculous moments that seem very far to surpass our natural powers; but they are indeed mere moments; and it is hard to believe that the soul can be dyed and imbued with such exalted qualities as these, so that they become ordinary and, as it were, natural to her" (VS705; F533). Perhaps this is why he refers to Cato's second act of suicide as "savage" (*furieux*).

Moderating Virtue

The excesses of virtue qualify the original portrayal of virtue as high and lofty, implying that the higher and most difficult is sometimes extreme and excessive and thus not really what is best. The second aspect of Montaigne's treatment of virtue that modifies the original portrait is his insistence on pleasure as the aim of virtue, thereby undermining somewhat the emphasis on the difficulty of virtue. In "That to philosophize is to learn to die," he criticizes the philosophers once again for their merely verbal dissensions. Who could listen to a man who told us that pain and discomfort are our goal? "Whatever they say, in virtue itself the ultimate goal we aim at is voluptuousness. I like to beat their ears with that word, which so goes against their grain. And if it means a certain supreme pleasure and excessive contentment, this is due more to the assistance of virtue than to any other assistance. This voluptuousness, for being more lusty, sinewy, robust, and manly, is only the more seriously voluptuous. And we should have given virtue the name of pleasure, a name more favorable, sweet and natural; not that of vigor, as we have named it. That other baser sort of voluptuousness, if it deserved that beautiful name, should have acquired it in competition, not as a privilege" (VS82; F56). In "Of the education of children" he wants the tutor to teach the child this "new lesson": that "the value and height of true virtue lies in the ease, utility, and pleasure of its practice, which is so far from being difficult that children can master it as well as men, the simple as well as the subtle. Virtue's tool is moderation, not strength" (VS162; F120).

It turns out that, in Montaigne's account of virtue, pain, difficulty, and conflict disappear when the heights of virtue are actually achieved. "Of cruelty" begins with a contrast between virtue and goodness. Virtue is said to entail internal conflict by which the appetites are mastered. It is here that he mentions the deliberate preparations of the philosophers who sought occasions to master themselves so as to be ready for the tests of fortune. But then he must stop himself and change the direction of his thought for he remembers the soul of Socrates, "the most perfect" soul he has ever come to know. If virtue necessarily implies struggle and self-mastery, then Socrates would deserve little praise "for I cannot conceive, in that person, any power of vicious lust. In the movement of his virtue I cannot imagine any difficulty or any constraint. I know his reason to be so powerful and so much the master in him that it would never so much as let a vicious appetite be born" (VS423; F308). We cannot be satisfied with imagining Socrates merely free from fear in the face of imprisonment and death. He must have been more than simply firm and constant, for we see a new contentment and "a blithe cheerfulness in his last words and actions" (VS425; F310). So also Cato the Younger. When Montaigne sees him dying and tearing out his entrails, he is not content to believe that Cato is simply free of fear as the rules of Stoic discipline require. "I believe without any doubt that he felt pleasure and bliss in so noble an action, and that he enjoyed himself more in it than in any other action of his life" (VS424; F309).

The heights of virtue are achieved, however, only by way of long and difficult practice. That is, difficulty and self-mastery are stages on the way to perfect virtue, and perfect virtue is extremely rare. So in the discussion of the way the philosophers create occasions to test themselves, he does mention Socrates, who "tested himself . . . roughly" with the malignity of his wife, and Epaminondas, who refused the riches that fortune offered him so as to struggle with poverty (VS423; F307). Perfect virtue is arrived at through "a long exercise of the precepts of philosophy." In Socrates and Cato "the vicious passions that come to life in us can find nowhere to enter; . . . the strength and rigidity of their soul stifles and extinguishes lusts as soon as they begin to stir" (VS426; F310).

The process that leads to perfect virtue, the long exercise of the precepts of philosophy, is what I have been calling "deliberate philosophy" in contrast with Montaigne's "accidental philosophy." The term that Montaigne sometimes uses to refer to this process is "reformation." Reformation implies that there was something evil or vicious in the soul to begin with, something that the long exercise of the precepts of philosophy is intended to master and, finally, to leave behind entirely.

Epaminondas is, in Montaigne's judgment, "the most excellent" man (VS756; F572). He belonged to the Pythagorean sect and, as I noted earlier, he tested himself to prepare for the evils that fortune would bring. Montaigne speaks of "the perfect reformation of *mœurs*" that Epaminondas achieved (VS1109; F851). And he refers to Socrates as "the first of all human beings in reformation" (VS892; F680). Socrates's reformation is attributed explicitly to reason struggling successfully against nature: he "corrected . . . by force of reason" his natural disposition. "This reason, which straightens Socrates from his inclination to vice," makes him obedient and courageous in death (VS1059; F811). "Socrates admitted to those who recognized in his face some inclination to vice that this was in truth his natural propensity, but that he had corrected it by discipline" (VS429; F313).

The picture of reason struggling successfully against nature is, however, complicated by the fact that Montaigne often presents nature as unreformable. As we have seen, he delights in reminding the philosopher that he cannot escape the condition that he shares with even the lowliest men: he will go mad if bitten by a dog, lose his senses to wine, tremble like a child over a precipice. "Nature has willed to reserve to herself these slight marks of her authority, invincible to our reason and to Stoic virtue, in order to teach man his mortality and frailty" (VS346; F250). But habit exercises as much if not more power over us, and it is difficult to draw a sharp line between nature and habit. In "Of custom" Montaigne emphasizes the definitive quality of what we learn in the nursery, where nature speaks in its purest and strongest but most tenuous voice: "I find that our greatest vices take shape from our tenderest childhood, and that our most important training is in the hands of nurses. . . . It is a very dangerous educational policy to excuse our children for these ugly inclinations [to cruelty, tyranny, and treason] on the ground of their tender age and the triviality of the subject" (VS110; F78).

Montaigne does not go so far as to say that reformation of one's nature and earliest habits is absolutely impossible but he does present such reformation as extremely difficult and unlikely. In "Of repentance," where he is concerned precisely with the possibility of reform, he writes: "Natural inclinations gain assistance and strength from education; but they are scarcely to be changed and overcome. A thousand natures, in my time, have escaped toward virtue or toward vice through the lines of a contrary training. . . . We do not root out these original qualities, we cover them up, we conceal them." It is here that Montaigne emphasizes the presence in each man of what he calls "a ruling form," staying within the language of form and reform. "There is no one who, if he listens to himself, does not discover in himself a form all his own, a ruling form, which struggles against education and against the tempest of the passions that oppose it" (VS811; F615).

So, then, is reformation possible or not? Is Montaigne contradicting himself when he talks about the entire reformation of Socrates, Cato, and Epaminondas? Montaigne is making the claim that deliberate reformation is possible only if the nature of the individual is of a certain kind: Socrates and Cato have made virtue the very essence of their souls "by a long exercise of the precepts of philosophy, coming upon a fine rich nature" (VS426; F310). The precepts of philosophy cannot struggle successfully against an evil or vicious nature. The "raw material" must be suitable; nature and second nature, which are there from the nursery, must be good. So Montaigne can say in response to Socrates' claim that his ugliness betrayed what would have been ugliness in his soul if he had not corrected it by education: "But in saying this I hold that he was jesting according to his wont. So excellent a soul was never self-made" (VS1058; F810).

When the precepts of philosophy encounter such a fine rich nature, the result is a kind of virtue that has left difficulty, struggle, and pain behind. In other words, it is virtue that has become "natural." Montaigne says of Cato and Socrates that we see in their souls "so perfect a habituation to virtue that it has passed into their nature. It is no longer a laborious virtue, or one formed by the ordinances of reason and maintained by a deliberate stiffening of the soul; it is the very essence of their soul, its natural and ordinary gait" (VS425–26; F310). His descriptions of Socrates emphasize the naturalness, the artlessness of Socrates' ways of being. Now the lowly and the natural turn out to be the loftiest: "By these vulgar and natural motives, by these ordinary and common ideas, without excitement or fuss, [Socrates] constructed not only the best regulated but the loftiest and most vigorous beliefs, actions and morals that ever were" (VS1038; F793). In Socrates we see "the extreme degree of perfection and difficulty: art cannot reach it" (VS1055; F808). Socrates "was always one and the same, and raised himself, not by sallies but by disposition, to the utmost point of vigor. Or to speak more exactly, he raised nothing, but rather brought vigor, hardships, and difficulties down and back to his own natural and original level, and subjected them to it" (VS1037; F793).

Cato, by comparison, is more strained and "mounted on his high horse" (VS1038; F793). Nevertheless, at the conclusion of "Against do-nothingness," even Cato's death is described as natural: "The extreme degree in treating death courageously, and the most natural, is to see it not only without being stunned, but without concern, continuing the course of life freely right into death. Like Cato, who spent his time sleeping and studying while having present in his head and heart a violent and bloody death, and holding it in his hand" (VS679; F515). The extreme degree of virtue is the point at which virtue becomes "ordinary."

The greatest example of moral character for Montaigne is Epaminondas. Plutarch's "Life" of Epaminondas has not been preserved, but some evidence of his deeds and character have come down to us. He was a Theban by birth and a Pythagorean by education. He was one of the rulers of Thebes in 371 B.C. and participated in the restoration of Theban power. His greatest military achievement was the defeat of the Spartan army at Leuctra. Epaminondas helped both Arcadia and Messenia to achieve independence from Sparta and even challenged the Athenian supremacy at sea. He died in 362 B.C. at Mantinea from wounds suffered after an attempt to seize Sparta by surprise.

Montaigne mentions Epaminondas several times in the *Essays*, including "By diverse means we arrive at the same end." He discusses him at some length in two places. In "Of the most outstanding men" Montaigne gives us his judgment of Homer, Alexander, and Epaminondas. The most outstanding of all is Epaminondas: "I know no form or fortune of man that I regard with so much honor and love" (VS756; F573). Montaigne begins his portrait of Epaminondas by acknowledging that he has not nearly as much glory as Alexander or Caesar, but "of resolution and valor, not that which is sharpened by ambition, but that which wisdom and reason may implant in a well-ordered soul, he had all that can be imagined. As for proof of this virtue of his, he has given as much, in my opinion, as Alexander himself and as Caesar." The virtue that is intended here has to do primarily with military boldness and ability, and Epaminondas is said to be the equal of the others. But he surpasses them in moral character: "But as for his character [*mœurs*] and conscience, he very far surpassed all those who have ever undertaken to manage affairs, for in this respect, which must principally be considered, which alone truly marks what we are, and which I weigh alone against all the others together, he yields to no philosopher, not even to Socrates" (VS756; F572–73).

What is it about Epaminondas that prompts Montaigne's extraordinary admiration and praise and, what is more, even his love? It is here that we begin to see Montaigne's own moral philosophy more distinctly. The character of Epaminondas is composed not only of virtue (in the sense of firmness and valor) but also of "innocence" and "goodness." Immediately following his high praise of the *mœurs* and conscience of Epaminondas, ranking him above even Socrates, Montaigne writes: "In this man innocence is a key quality, sovereign, constant, uniform, incorruptible. In comparison, it appears in Alexander as subordinate, uncertain, streaky, soft, and accidental" (VS756; F573). It seems to be the presence of this constant innocence that Montaigne has in mind when he goes on to say that: "In this man alone can be found a virtue and ability full and equal throughout, which, in all the functions of human life, leaves nothing to be desired, whether in public or private occupation, in peace or war, whether in living or in dying greatly and gloriously" (VS756; F573). Virtue in the full sense, as distinguished from virtue as valor in combat, requires a kind of innocence and goodness. Montaigne concludes this portrait with some of Epaminondas's "opinions" as examples of his "exceeding goodness." Epaminondas said that the sweetest contentment he had in all his life was the pleasure he gave his mother and father by his victory over the Spartans at Leuctra. "It says a lot that he preferred their pleasure to his own." He did not think it permissible to kill a man without full knowledge of the case, even for the sake of recovering the freedom of his country. And he held that a man should avoid encountering a friend in battle and should spare him if he did encounter him. He showed humanity even toward enemy forces, not pursuing them to the death at the battle of Morea. That clemency made him suspect, and he was deposed from the rank of commander-in-chief: "To be dismissed for such a cause did him much honor" (VS757; F574).

The second place where Montaigne elaborates on the example of Epaminondas is at the end of essay III.1, "Of the useful and the honorable," as he is drawing toward the conclusion that "not all things are permissible for an honorable man in the service of his king, or of the common cause, or of the laws" (VS802; F609). These passages describing the character of Epaminondas are, to my mind, among the most beautiful and remarkable passages in the *Essays*. Again, he is emphasizing the goodness and innocence of the great warrior. "I once placed Epaminondas in the first rank of outstanding men, and I do not take this back. To what a height did he raise consideration for his private duty, he who never killed a man he had vanquished, who even for the inestimable good of restoring liberty to his country scrupled to kill a tyrant or his accomplices without due form of justice, and who judged anyone a wicked man, however good a citizen he was, who among his enemies and in battle did not spare his friend and his host. There is a soul of rich composition. To the roughest and most violent of human actions he wedded goodness and humanity, indeed the most deli- cate that can be found in the school of philosophy. That heart, so great, full and obstinate against pain, death, and poverty – was it nature or art that had made it tender to the point of such an extreme gentleness and goodness in disposition? Terrible with blood and iron, he goes breaking and shattering a nation invincible against anyone but himself, and turns aside in the middle of such a melee on meeting his host and his friend. Truly that man was in command of war itself, who made it endure the curb of benignity at the point of its greatest heat, all inflamed as it was and foaming with frenzy and slaughter. It is a miracle to be able to mingle some semblance of justice with such actions; but it belongs only to the strength of Epaminondas to be able to mingle with them the sweetness and ease of the gentlest ways, and pure innocence" (VS801–2; F608–9).

Montaigne calls Epaminondas a "great preceptor" who teaches us that some things are illicit even against an enemy and that the common inter- est ought not to demand all things of all men against private interest. He wants to take away the pretext of reason from the actions of wicked men. "Let us abandon this monstrous and deranged justice and stick to more human imitations." The monstrous and deranged justice that he has in mind is the justice that would reward a man for killing his father or brother in battle. Here he quotes verses from Lucan, who has Caesar exhort his men: "When weapons flash, no pious sentiments, / Though you confront your father, you must feel; / No, slash their venerable face with the steel." Epaminondas, then, is a "more human" example, and it is apparent that Montaigne is recommending him as an example to be imitated. The exam- ple of Epaminondas is an example of virtue but a virtue that is tempered and preserved from excess by innocence and goodness: "If it is greatness of heart and the effect of rare and singular virtue to despise friendship, private obli- gations, our word, and kinship, for the common good and obedience to the magistrate, truly it is enough to excuse us from this that it is a greatness that cannot lodge in the greatness of Epaminondas's heart" (VS802; F609–10).

Natural Goodness and Innocence

The example of Epaminondas is very close to the character of Montaigne himself. This comes out most clearly and fully in "Of cruelty," where Montaigne describes his own "virtue" as a kind of innocence. What does this innocence mean? "Of cruelty" begins with a distinction between virtue and goodness: "It seems to me that virtue is something other and nobler than the inclinations toward goodness that are born in us" (VS422; F306). It is here that he goes through the first part of his description of virtue as entailing difficulty, struggle, and self-mastery. "He who through a natural mildness and easygoingness should despise injuries received would do a very fine and praiseworthy thing; but he who, outraged and stung to the quick by an injury, should arm himself with the arms of reason against this furious appetite for vengeance, and after a great conflict should finally master it, would without doubt do much more. The former would do well [*bien*], and the other virtuously; one action might be called goodness, the other virtue" (VS422; F307). Goodness is associated with nature and thus with ease, lack of effort, and lack of art and education.[4] And the example that Montaigne uses here is especially apt, for goodness is so plainly manifested in forgiveness and gentleness, whereas cruelty is most likely to be provoked in cases of vengeance.

Montaigne repeats the distinction later in the same essay, but the distinction is refined because he has been through the discussion of perfect virtue and perfect reformation that transcends difficulty and struggle. "Now I do not think there is any doubt that it is finer to prevent the birth of temptation by a lofty and divine resolution, and to have so formed oneself to virtue that the very seeds of the vices are rooted out, than to prevent their progress by main force, and, having let oneself be surprised by the first commotion of the passions, to arm and tense oneself to stop their course and conquer them; and that this second action still is finer than to be simply provided with a nature easy and affable and having an inborn distaste for debauchery and vice. For it certainly seems that this third and last type makes a man innocent but not virtuous; exempt from doing ill, but not apt enough to do good" (VS426; F310). This third condition is so close to weakness and imperfection that he hardly knows how to distinguish them: even the names of goodness and innocence are, in some sense, terms of contempt.

In the context of this threefold distinction Montaigne locates himself. "I am so far from having arrived at that first and most perfect degree of excellence where virtue becomes a habit, that even of the second degree I have hardly given any proof. I have not put myself to great effort to curb the desires by which I have found myself pressed. My virtue is a virtue, or should I say an innocence, that is accidental and fortuitous" (VS427; F311). The third condition is weak and lowly but is, in fact, very much like the first and highest condition in which virtue has "passed into ... nature," in which virtue is no longer laborious or difficult or "formed by the ordinances of reason" but rather the "essence" of the soul and "its natural and ordinary gait" (VS425–26; F310). Nevertheless, there are important differences between the two conditions, and the claim that I want to make is that Montaigne's condition of goodness and innocence lacks an ingredient of cruelty that the most lofty condition must either include or transcend. In order to see what this claim means, we have to consider something of what is entailed in Montaigne's description of his *mœurs* as "natural." As we have seen, Montaigne often contrasts the natural with the learned. "My *mœurs* are natural: I have not called in the help of any discipline to build them." And in "To the reader" he tells us that he wants to present himself in his "natural form," that is, "without straining and artifice."

One of the clearest statements concerning his natural *mœurs* occurs in "Of cruelty," immediately following his claim that his virtue is really a kind of innocence that is accidental: "If I had been born with a more unruly disposition, I fear it would have gone pitifully with me. For I have not experienced much firmness in my soul to withstand passions, if they are even the least bit vehement. I do not know how to foster quarrels and conflicts within me. Thus I cannot give myself any great thanks because I find myself free from many vices.... I owe it more to my fortune than to my reason" (VS427–28; F311). Perhaps he inherited his disposition from his father, perhaps it was his earliest education, or perhaps it was for "some other reason" that he was born that way. But in any case, "of myself I hold most vices in horror," and "I hold them in horror . . . from an attitude so natural and so much my own that the same instinct and impression that I brought away from my nurse I have still retained. Nothing has been able to make me alter it, not even my own reasonings, which, having in some things broken away from the common road, would easily give me license for actions which this natural inclination makes me hate" (VS428; F312).[5] He contrasts himself in this regard with Socrates, who claimed to have corrected by discipline his natural inclinations to vice. "On the contrary, what I have of good in me I have by the accident of my birth. I have gotten it neither from law, nor from precept, nor from any other apprenticeship. The innocence that is in me is a natural innocence: little vigor and no art" (VS429; F313).

One aspect that emerges from Montaigne's description of his character is the absence of inner conflict and struggle. This is alluded to not only in "Of cruelty" but throughout the *Essays*. In "Of physiognomy" he makes the same contrast with Socrates: "I have not, like Socrates, corrected my natural disposition by force of reason, and have not troubled my inclination at all by art. I let myself go as I have come. I combat nothing. My two ruling parts, of their own volition, live in peace and good accord. But my nurse's milk, thank God, was moderately healthy and temperate" (VS1059; F811). In some ways, this absence of conflict looks like weakness and even cowardice.

The absence of inner conflict in Montaigne is intended as an important point of contrast with the "deliberate philosophers" who follow the path of difficulty and struggle, forcing their inclinations into subjection to reason. So when Montaigne speaks to himself in the throes of an attack of kidney stones, he says: "Do you remember those men of past times who sought out troubles with such great hunger, to keep their virtue in breath and in practice? Put the case this way, that nature is bearing and pushing you into that glorious school, which you would never have entered of your own free will" (VS1091; F837). His practice is rather to avoid temptation than to fight it: "Passions are as easy for me to avoid as they are hard for me to moderate.... He who cannot attain that noble impassibility of the Stoics, let him take refuge in the bosom of this plebeian stupidity of mine. What those men did by virtue, I train myself to do by disposition" (VS1019–20; F780). And in discussing the constant threat of death in the midst of civil war, he says: "I sometimes derive from nonchalance and laxity a way of strengthening myself against these considerations; they too, to some extent, lead us toward fortitude" (VS971; F742). Virtue can perhaps be thought of as "caused," as the effect of actions deliberately undertaken so as to arrive at an end deliberately pursued, a condition of perfect habituation. But goodness is not susceptible to explanation in terms of causes. In the end, he must ask: "Could it be true that to be wholly good we must be so by some occult, natural, and universal property, without law, without reason, without example?" (VS428; F312).

Montaigne's admiration for virtue, especially the heights of virtue in Cato and Socrates, is, I believe, completely sincere. Nevertheless, he sees in the struggle for virtue the possibility of, or the temptation to, cruelty. Some men through piety and some philosophers through reason attempt to anticipate the accidents of fortune by depriving themselves of good things that are in their hands, seeking pain and poverty, even putting out their own eyes: "These are the acts of an excessive virtue" (VS243; F179). And in describing his conduct during his attacks of kidney stones, he says that he has always found the philosophical requirement of maintaining a good countenance through extreme pain to be formalistic. If philosophy really cares about substance, why does it concern itself so much with external appearances? "In such extreme accidents it is cruelty to require of us so composed a bearing" (VS761; F577). The man who is extremely irascible, who is tormented by the violence and fury of his anger, must constrain himself "cruelly" if he wants to hide it completely (VS718; F543).

The point I am making here is that Montaigne seems to see in the struggle for self-mastery a temptation to cruelty because, in its extreme form, self-mastery entails a kind of cruelty to oneself.[6] Montaigne, then, associates his third, lowly condition of goodness and innocence with his hatred of cruelty. "The innocence that is in me is a childish innocence.... Among other vices, I cruelly hate cruelty, both by nature and by judgment, as the extreme of all vices" (VS429; F313). I do not want to imply that Montaigne is really accusing Cato of cruelty, but it is Cato's "goodness" that moderates his virtue: "And if his goodness [*la bonté*], which made him embrace the public advantage more than his own, did not hold me in check, I should easily fall into this opinion, that he was grateful to fortune for having put his virtue to so beautiful a test and for having favored that brigand [Caesar] in treading underfoot the ancient liberty of his country" (VS424; F309). Goodness not only softens the harshness of virtue but, as it shows itself in this passage, it is more open to others than virtue is.[7] If it is goodness that makes Cato embrace the public good more than his own, then there is a suggestion that goodness has an element of compassion, openness, and generosity.

Cruelty is the extreme of all the vices and the extreme point of cruelty is the torture and murder of a human being for the sole purpose of enjoying the spectacle of his suffering and death. Everyday Montaigne sees examples of monstrous cruelty made possible by the license of civil war. "But that has not accustomed me to it at all" (VS432; F315). When Montaigne discusses the cruelties that he sees everyday, he says that they are so monstrous in inhumanity that he marvels at them almost as much as he detests them. They bear "the mark of vigor and strength of soul as much as of error and disorder" (VS956; F730). But he begins essay II.27, "Cowardice, mother of cruelty," with the observation that he has found by experience "that the bitterness and hardness of a malicious and inhuman heart are usually accompanied by feminine weakness" (VS693; F523). True valor acts only against resistance and therefore "stops on seeing the enemy at its mercy." But pusillanimity tries to show its strength in massacre and bloodshed after true valor has won the victory. It seems, then, that both strength and weakness are involved in cruelty, so that, when we judge the cruel actions of Alexander the Great in "By diverse means we arrive at the same end," we might judge that there is a hint of shameful weakness even in that most valorous soul. Epaminondas, by contrast, gives no evidence of cruelty at all.

Montaigne's presentation of himself as weak, and as good rather than virtuous, is a Christian revaluation of pagan "natural" virtue. We can see this more clearly if we consider Montaigne's weakness against the background of Machiavelli's very powerful criticism of Christianity, namely, that Christianity has made the world weak. This criticism is prompted by Machiavelli's reflections on the fact that in ancient times men loved freedom more than they do in his own day:

Thinking then whence it can arise that in those ancient times peoples were more lovers of freedom than in these, I believe it arises from the same cause that makes men less strong now, which is the difference between our education and the ancient. For our religion, having shown the truth and the true way, makes us esteem less the honor of the world, whereas the Gentiles, esteeming it very much and having placed the highest good in it, were more ferocious in their actions. This can be inferred from many of their institutions, beginning from the magnificence of their sacrifices as against the humility of ours, where there is some pomp more delicate than magnificent but no ferocious or vigorous action. Neither pomp nor magnificence of ceremony was lacking there, but the action of the sacrifice, full of blood and ferocity, was added, with a multitude of animals being killed there. This sight, being terrible, rendered men similar to itself. Besides this, the ancient religion did not beatify men if they were not full of worldly glory, as were captains of armies and princes of republics. Our religion has glorified humble and contemplative more than active men. It has then placed the highest good in humility, abjectness, and contempt of things human; the other placed it in greatness of spirit, strength of body, and all other things capable of making men very strong. And if our religion asks that you have strength in yourself, it wishes you to be capable more of suffering than of doing something strong. This mode of life thus seems to have rendered the world weak and given it in prey to criminal men, who can manage it securely, seeing that the collectivity of men, so as to go to paradise, think more of enduring their beatings than of avenging them. And although the world appears to be made effeminate and heaven disarmed, it arises without doubt more from the cowardice of the men who have interpreted our religion according to idleness and not according to virtue. For if they have considered how it permits us the exaltation and defense of the fatherland, they would see that it wishes us to love and honor it and to prepare ourselves to be such that we can defend it. These educations and false interpretations thus bring it about that not as many republics are seen in the world as were seen in antiquity; nor, as a consequence, is as much love of freedom seen in peoples as was then.[8]

What Machiavelli leaves out of his description of the rites of pagan religions is the practice of human sacrifice. Montaigne, however, discusses it at least twice. He cites numerous instances of the practice in which the altars were filled with "butchery, not only of innocent animals, but also of men, as was the ordinary practice in many nations, among others our own. And I think no nation is innocent of having tried this" (VS521; F387). He refers to the ancient belief "of thinking that we gratify heaven and nature by committing massacre and homicide, a belief universally embraced in all religions," giving as one of his examples the six hundred young Greek men immolated by Amurath for the soul of his father so that their blood would serve as propitiation for his sins. "And in these new lands discovered in our time, still pure and virgin compared with ours, this practice is to some extent accepted everywhere: all their idols are drenched with human blood, often with horrible cruelty." And he tells the story of Indians who were defeated by Cortez and sent offerings to seek peace. The messengers brought three kinds of presents saying, "Lord, here are five slaves; if you are a cruel god that feeds on flesh and blood, eat them, and we will bring you more. If you are a good-natured god, here are incense and plumes. If you are a man, take these birds and fruits" (VS201; F149).

Montaigne's judgment on the practice of human sacrifice is that "it was a strange fancy to try to pay for divine goodness with our affliction....It was a strange impulse to try to gratify the architect by the overthrow of his building,...and to think that poor Iphigenia...would, by her death and sacrifice, clear the army in the eyes of God" (VS201; F149). The unspoken sacrifice here is the crucifixion of Christ. Christianity puts an end to the practice of human sacrifice, a practice that assumes the cruelty of the gods.

Certainly Montaigne does not think that Christianity has transformed the world into a peaceful and gentle place, the kingdom of God on earth. As he says, "There is no hostility that excels Christian hostility" (VS444; F324). His own day is rich in examples of horrible cruelty. But he does seem to suggest a link between cruelty and the kind of fierceness or spiritedness that is characteristic of pagan virtue and that, according to Machiavelli, is also necessary for the love of freedom. The Spartans are a clear example of this. Machiavelli's point is that Christianity has made believers weak and has thereby placed them at the mercy of the strong and cruel. Christian weakness is seen in the loss of the love of freedom: the Christian thinks more of enduring his beatings than of avenging them because his sights are set on the world to come and not on this world.

How does Montaigne respond, directly or indirectly, to Machiavelli's criticism of the weakness brought about by the Christian faith? The substance of his response is the display of his own character together with the moral and political philosophy that is implicit in the *Essays*. At this point, we can say that Montaigne does present himself as "weak," but his weakness is first and foremost a form of gentleness to be contrasted with the harshness and cruelty of vengeance: the first thing he says about himself is that he is "wonderfully lax in the direction of mercy and gentleness" (VS8; F4).[9] On the other hand, he presents himself as loving freedom, practicing the virtues that are necessary for political freedom, and encouraging others to practice those virtues. In other words, the combination that Machiavelli seems to think is impossible – the combination of Christian faith and love of freedom – is actually seen in the character displayed in the *Essays*. Montaigne's weakness, then, is not a sign of indifference and cowardice but is rather his Christian reformation of pagan, natural virtue.[10]

Montaigne's Reformation

What, then, is "a bit new and unusual" in Montaigne's way of life? What are the changes that his *mœurs* and his writings display? In particular, how does his moral philosophy differ from the deliberate philosophy of the ancients?

First, deliberate philosophy (followed by certain forms of pious asceticism) seeks out difficulty, pain, and hardship and even invents occasions for testing one's strength. Montaigne, on the contrary, seeks to avoid temptation. He cites the Our Father, the prayer he loves so much: "Lead us not into temptation, but deliver us from evil." And his interpretation of those words is a commentary on his own life: "We do not pray that our reason may not be combated and overcome by concupiscence, but that it may not even be tested by it, that we may not be brought into a state where we even have to suffer the approaches, solicitations, and temptations of sin; and we supplicate our Lord to keep our conscience tranquil, fully and perfectly delivered from dealing with evil " (VS1016; F777).

Second, Montaigne reorders the vices. Although all vices are equally vices, "they are not equal vices" (VS339; F244). And it is of the greatest importance to weigh them accurately: "Confusion about the order and measurement of sins is dangerous. Murderers, traitors, tyrants gain too much by it. It is not right that their conscience should be relieved because some other man is indolent, or lascivious, or less assiduous in his devotions.... Even our teachers often rank sins badly, in my opinion" (VS340; F244–45).

Thus, Montaigne seems far more tolerant of faults due to weakness than the standards of philosophical and pious asceticism would permit. In "Of the punishment of cowardice" he agrees with the prince who maintained that a soldier should not be put to death for faintheartedness: "In truth it is right to make a great distinction between the faults that come from our weakness and those that come from our malice" (VS70; F48). In "The story of Spurina" he compares the passion of lust with "the passions that are all in the soul," such as ambition and avarice. These latter passions "give the reason much more to do, for it can find no help for them except in its own resources; nor are these appetites capable of satiety, but rather they grow sharper and increase by enjoyment" (VS729; F551). And in "On some verses of Virgil" Montaigne criticizes those men who are more concerned for their wives' chastity than for their own virtue: "There is hardly one of us who is not more afraid of the shame that comes to him for his wife's vices than for his own; who does not take better care (wonderful charity) of his good wife's conscience than of his own; who would not rather be a thief and sacrilegious and have his wife be a murderess and a heretic, than not to have her be more chaste than her husband" (VS860–61; F655).

Montaigne's intention is not the lowering of moral standards. Rather, he is concerned with the proper judgment of vices. So to the men he is addressing in the preceding passage he says: "Iniquitous appraisal of vices! Both we and they are capable of a thousand corruptions more harmful and unnatural than lasciviousness. But we create and weigh vices not according to nature but according to our interest, whereby they assume so many unequal shapes" (VS861; F655). And in the "Apology" he questions the point of punishing the body with mutilation "since the offense is in the will, not in the chest, the eyes, the genitals, the belly, the shoulders or the throat." To him "it seems a great cowardice and treachery to mistreat and corrupt the functions of the body, which are stupid and servile, in order to spare the soul the bother of directing them according to reason"(VS522–23; F388–89).

The nature of Montaigne's concern with the accurate judgment of vices is made explicit in "Of drunkenness." As we have seen, this essay is one in which we can trace out the movement of Montaigne's thought as he reforms his judgment. He begins with the assertion that "drunkenness, among the others, seems to me a gross and brutish vice" (VS340; F245). Whereas other vices have something indefinably noble about them – because they involve valor or skill, for example – drunkenness is "all bodily and earthy" and overturns the understanding. But Montaigne comes to moderate his judgment and his disgust: he finds that this vice "is loose and stupid, but less malicious and harmful than the others, which almost all clash more directly with public society" (VS342; F247).[11]

One of the most important ways in which Montaigne reorders the vices can be seen in his preference for private life over the life of politics and, in the way he deals with the passion of ambition, placing it second only to cruelty as a vice to be avoided. At the beginning of "Of repentance" Montaigne writes: "I set forth a humble and inglorious life; that does not matter. You can tie up all moral philosophy with a common and private life just as well as with a life of richer stuff." The richer stuff of the glorious life is not uniquely relevant for moral philosophy: "Each man bears the entire form of the human condition" (VS805; F611). Later in the same essay, he goes even further in his claims concerning private life: "It is a rare life that remains well-ordered even in private. Any man can play his part in the side show and represent a worthy man on the boards; but to be disciplined within, in his own bosom, where all is permissible, where all is concealed – that's the point. The next step to that is to be so in our own house, in our ordinary actions, for which we need render account to no one, where nothing is studied or artificial" (VS808; F613). The seat of moral action is within, in one's thoughts, and in one's ordinary actions. "The real condemnation, which applies to the common run of men of today, is that even their retirement is full of corruption and filth" (VS811; F615–16).

The defining moment in judging a man is not the ascent out of private life into the public eye, but the descent from the public stage into the hiddenness of one's home. "The people escort this man back to his door, with awe, from a public function. He drops his part with his gown; the higher he has hoisted himself, the lower he falls back; inside, in his home, everything is tumultuous and vile." Montaigne is reforming the order of higher and lower, not lowering the standard of moral action: "To win through a breach, to conduct an embassy, to govern a people, these are dazzling actions. To scold, to laugh, to sell, to pay, to love, to hate, and to deal pleasantly and justly with our household and ourselves, not to let ourselves go, not to be false to ourselves, that is a rarer matter, more difficult and less noticeable." Therefore, "it takes a keen and select judgment" to see the order in these "humble private actions" (VS809; F614).

Montaigne's presentation of the meaning of action and his extension of the location of action can be seen in the portraits that he paints of those three completely reformed, virtuous men: Cato, Epaminondas, and Socrates. In Cato we see "that inimitable straining for virtue that astounds us" and a disposition so severe that it troubles us. But we also see him meekly submit to the laws of Venus and Bacchus. "Epaminondas did not think that to mingle with the dance of the boys of his city, to sing, to play music, and to concentrate attentively on these things, was at all derogatory to the honor of his glorious victories and to the perfect reformation of conduct [*mœurs*] that was in him." Socrates showed his extraordinary valor in saving Alcibiades in battle and in his resistance to the Thirty Tyrants. But "there is nothing more remarkable" in Socrates than the fact that as an old man he thought his time well spent in learning to dance and play instruments. He endured twenty-seven years of poverty and the claws of his wife and, in the end, tyranny, prison, and poison. But "he never refused to play at cobnut with children, or to ride a hobbyhorse with them, and he did so gracefully; for all actions, says philosophy, are equally becoming and honorable in a wise man" (VS1109–10; F851–52). And when Montaigne says of himself that "My philosophy is in action," he immediately adds: "Would I might take pleasure in playing at cobnut or with a top!" (VS842; F639).

The most immediate specifically moral consequence of this reordering of action is Montaigne's attitude toward glory, reputation, and ambition. He confesses that he is tempted toward ambition: "I sometimes feel rising in my soul the fumes of certain temptations toward ambition; but I stiffen and hold firm against them" (VS992; F759). His lowly way of avoiding evil and temptation is not suitable "for those who in well-doing are not content with any profit if no reputation is involved. For in truth, such an action is valued only by each man in himself" (VS1018–19; F779). But Montaigne does not prefer his lowly way simply because he is weak and lax by the standards of heroic virtue. The hidden actions and the humble actions of everyday life are to be valued for themselves. Their hiddenness actually adds to their worth. "To be puffed up at every useful and harmless action is for people with whom they are extraordinary and rare; they want to put them at the price they cost them. In proportion as a good deed is more brilliant, I deduct from its goodness the suspicion I have that it was performed more to be brilliant than to be good: put on display, it is half sold. Those actions have much more grace which escape from the hand of the workman nonchalantly and noiselessly" (VS1023; F783). It is significant that Montaigne uses the term "goodness" rather than "virtue" here. It may well be that he is expressing what Arendt regards as a specifically Christian view, that goodness must be hidden if it is not to be destroyed.[12]

This can be seen especially in the account Montaigne gives of his performance as mayor of Bordeaux. He did not leave undone any action that his duty genuinely required of him, but "I easily forgot those that ambition mixes up with duty and covers with its name. Those are the ones that most often fill the eyes and ears, and satisfy men" (VS1021; F781). Again, his avoidance of ambition and his reluctance to perform acts of ambition are not simply due to his weak and idle temperament. "It is acting for our private reputation and profit, not for the good, to put off and do in the public square what we can do in the council chamber, and at high noon what we could have done the night before, and to be jealous to do ourselves what our colleague does as well" (VS1022; F782). So, in "Of solitude" he sees in the proverb that says "we are not born for our private selves but for the public" a cover for ambition. If those who are "in the midst of the dance" would examine their consciences they would find that they seek titles and offices and the hustle and bustle of "the world" for private gain. Indeed, ambition shuns society, for what she seeks is "elbowroom" (VS237; F174–75).

Montaigne responds to the criticism that his administration passed without a mark or trace because of his inactivity. The men of his time, he says, "are so formed for agitation and ostentation that goodness, moderation, equability, constancy, and such quiet and obscure qualities are no longer felt." He sums up his performance as mayor in this way: "I had nothing to do but conserve and endure, which are noiseless and imperceptible acts. Innovation has great luster, but it is forbidden in these times, when we are hard pressed and have to defend ourselves mainly against innovations. Abstention from doing is often as noble as doing, but it is less open to the light; and the little that I am worth is almost all on that side." Montaigne prefers the good of his people to his own honor and reputation. Shouldn't we whip a doctor who would wish for the plague so that he could practice his art? "I have not had that iniquitous and rather common disposition of wanting the trouble and sickness of the affairs of this city to exalt and honor my government" (VS1023–24; F783). This is just what he says about Cato: if it were not for Cato's goodness, which makes him prefer the common good to his own, he would have thanked fortune for having put his virtue to such a test by favoring Caesar, who trampled on the ancient liberty of his country (VS424; F309). On the other hand, his judgment of Caesar is ultimately determined by Caesar's uncontrolled ambition. He admires Caesar for his great clemency and his extreme "sweetness" in his vengeances, and he sees in him many rare seeds of virtue (VS430; F314; and VS731; F552). But his passion of ambition possessed his soul with complete authority (VS731; F552). All of Caesar's fine inclinations were spoiled by his overwhelming ambition that "controlled the tiller by which all his actions were steered." Montaigne's final judgment is that "this single vice . . . ruined in him the finest and richest nature that ever was, and has made his memory abominable to all good men, because he willed to seek his glory in the ruin of his country and the subversion of the most powerful and flourishing republic that the world will ever see" (VS733; F554).

In "Of cruelty" Montaigne associates his own natural goodness and innocence with his hatred of cruelty, implying that goodness and cruelty are moral opposites. But in Caesar we see an example of someone who is not cruel but extremely mild and even sweet in the way he deals with those who have offended him. It is not cruelty but ambition that destroys Caesar's fine and rich nature. Ambition is at odds with the goodness that would otherwise make him prefer the common good to his own glory. Goodness, then, does have a wider scope than the purely private realm. It reaches into the realm of sociability and there its opposite is ambition.

What, then, did Montaigne learn in the nursery? In "Of cruelty" he says that he holds most vices in horror from an attitude that is natural, that is, his own since the nursery. He hates cruelty "both by nature and by judgment" (VS429; F313). His extreme repugnance to cheating is due to "a natural and unstudied propensity" and, at the same time, he had trained himself in childhood always to walk in his own straight open road (VS110; F79). His soul "by nature" hates lying and hates even to think a lie. He feels an "inward shame and a stinging remorse" if a lie escapes him through surprise (VS648; F491). So he is always candid and says what he thinks "by inclination and by reason" (VS649; F492). As we saw in Chapter 7, he hates dissimulation and, of all vices, he finds none that testifies as much to cowardice and baseness of heart. It is cowardly and servile to disguise oneself and to hide under a mask. "A generous heart should not belie its thoughts; it wants to reveal itself even to its inmost depths. There everything is good, or at least everything is human." Truth is "the first and fundamental part of virtue" (VS647; F491). And "the first stage in the corruption of morals is the banishment of truth" (VS666; F505).[13]

Montaigne makes the connection between truth and sociability explicit. "In truth, lying is an accursed vice. We are men, and hold together only by our word" (VS36; F23). In "Of giving the lie" he makes the same point and elaborates more fully: "Lying is an ugly vice" that gives evidence of contempt for God and fear of men. "Since mutual understanding is brought about solely by way of words, he who breaks his word betrays human society. It is the only instrument by means of which our wills and thoughts communicate, it is the interpreter of our soul. If it fails us, we have no more hold on each other, no more knowledge of each other. If it deceives us, it breaks up all our relations and dissolves all the bonds of our society" (VS666–67; F505).

Montaigne's hatred of cruelty and lying, his stance toward public life and ambition, his moderation of pagan virtue, and the foundational status that he gives to truth are traced back to what he learned in the nursery. But they are also "a bit new and unusual." How are we to understand this? Montaigne's *mœurs* can be seen as a kind of reformation because he is displaying a character that is a bit different from what is recommended by both ancient philosophy and Christian theology insofar as theology accepts the moral categories of the ancients. In other words, Montaigne sees himself as going further than the theologians in his understanding of what it means to believe.

At two places in the *Essays* Montaigne distances himself from his father. These instances show us how his own self-understanding is not simply and entirely an inherited self-understanding but is rather a return to his origins at the end of the circular dialectic. The first place is at the very beginning of the "Apology" where he is explaining how he had received Sebond's book from his father and how he had translated it into French at his father's request "being unable to disobey a command of the best father that ever was"

(VS440; F320). He also explains how his father had been given the book by
Pierre Bunel, who had been a guest at his house. Montaigne's father was "inflamed with that new ardor" for letters and "sought with great diligence and
expense the acquaintance of learned men, receiving them at his house like
holy persons having some particular inspiration of divine wisdom, collecting
their sayings and discourses like oracles, and with all the more reverence
and religion as he was less qualified to judge them; for he had no knowledge
of letters, any more than his predecessors." Although Montaigne shows his
filial piety by translating Sebond's book for his father, he distances himself
from his father's attitude toward letters: "Myself, I like them well enough, but
I do not worship them" (VS439; F319). His apology for Sebond also shows
that his understanding of what it means to believe differs from the one expressed by Sebond and by the learned men who frequented Montaigne's
house.

The second place where Montaigne distances himself from his father is
in "Of husbanding your will." His father had been mayor of Bordeaux and
the son attributes his own subsequent election to the fact that the municipal
council wanted to honor his father's memory. Montaigne tells the magis-
trates that he does not bring the same kind of attitude to the job as his
father had. His father's soul had been cruelly agitated by the public turmoil
and he had grown old and sick, the weight of public affairs having borne
down so heavily upon him. "He was like that; and this disposition in him
sprang from a great goodness of nature: there was never a more kindly and
public-spirited soul." But Montaigne is somewhat different: "This course,
which I commend in others, I do not love to follow, and I am not without
excuse. He [his father] had heard it said that we must forget ourselves for
our neighbor, that the particular was not to be considered at all in comparison with the general" (VS1006; F769). Montaigne seems to be associating
his father's public-spiritedness with a certain interpretation of the second
great commandment, "Love thy neighbor as thyself." And that interpretation is confused or conflated with the values of classical moral and political
philosophy.

Montaigne, then, inherits much from his father, especially his faith and
his goodness. Nevertheless, his *mœurs* are a bit new, for his understanding of
what it means to believe is somewhat different from his father's. His nurse's
milk was the milk of the poor, uneducated village woman who held him
over the baptismal font. Montaigne's reform is not a matter of new opinions
and the pursuit of a new ideal of perfection, but rather a return to and a
deepened understanding of what he learned in the nursery.

Christianity and the Limits of Politics

Modern political philosophy must come to terms with the fundamental issue of the relationship of politics and Christianity, for Christianity, unlike pagan religion, is both universal and otherworldly, whereas the political realm is exclusive and is precisely *this* world. In Book IV of his *Social Contract*, Rousseau provides us with a full and clear statement of what he regards as the problem posed by Christianity, which also expresses many of the concerns found in Machiavelli and Hobbes. I begin this chapter by setting out the main lines of Rousseau's paradigmatic account and then I discuss Montaigne's views against that background. Montaigne, as I understand him, is very much at odds with the prevailing tendencies of modern political philosophy, especially with respect to religion.

Rousseau acknowledges that religion is not only essential but is even the necessary foundation for political society: "A State has never been founded without religion serving as its base." Christianity, however, is "more harmful than useful to the strong constitution of a State."[1] Rousseau takes us through the history of civilization in order to show why Christianity poses such a threat to politics. Ancient political societies all began as theocracies: no distinction existed between the religion and the laws of a people. Each city had its own gods, and the gods of one people had no rights over other peoples. Political war, then, was also theological, but men did not fight for their gods: rather, as in Homer, the gods fought for men.[2] Finally, under the Romans, paganism became a single religion because the Romans spread their cult across the world and, at the same time, adopted the gods of the vanquished.

At this point, Jesus Christ "came to establish a spiritual kingdom on earth." This was "an otherworldly kingdom," and its establishment meant the separation of the theological from the political system: "[T]his brought about the end of the unity of the state, and caused the internal divisions that have never ceased to stir up Christian peoples."[3] The supposedly otherworldly kingdom became "the most violent despotism in this world" under a visible leader, the pope. Now there are two powers, the prince and the pope, the state and the Church. "This double power has resulted in a perpetual conflict of jurisdiction that has made any good polity impossible in Christian States, and no people has been able to figure out whom it was obligated to obey, the master or the priest."[4] This is precisely the difficulty that Hobbes is most concerned to resolve. "For who is there that does not see, to whose benefit it conduceth, to have it believed, that a King hath not his Authority from Christ, unless a Bishop crown him? That a King, if he be a Priest, cannot Marry? That whether a Prince be born in lawfull Marriage, or not must be judged by Authority from *Rome*? That Subjects may be freed from their Alleageance, if by the Court of *Rome*, the King be judged an Heretique? That a King (as *Chilperique* of *France*) may be deposed by a Pope (as Pope *Zachary*,) for no cause; and his Kingdome given to one of his Subjects?"[5] For Hobbes, "the question of the Authority of the Scriptures is reduced to this, Whether Christian Kings, and the soveraigne Assemblies in christian common-wealths, be absolute in their own Territories, immediately under God; or subject to one Vicar of Christ, constituted over the Universall Church; to bee judged, condemned, deposed, and put to death, as hee shall think expedient, or necessary for the common good."[6] So Rousseau says of Hobbes: "Of all Christian authors, the philosopher Hobbes is the only one who correctly saw the evil and the remedy, who dared to propose the reunification of the two heads of the eagle, and the complete return to political unity, without which no State or government will ever be well constituted."[7]

The first problem posed for politics by Christianity, then, is the threat it poses to the power of the state. The second has to do with the otherworldly character of Christianity. In Chapter 7 I discussed Machiavelli's claim that Christianity has made the world weak, that, on account of Christianity, men no longer care so much for freedom and are easily enslaved by the wicked. Rousseau makes the same criticism. "Christianity is a totally spiritual religion, uniquely concerned with heavenly matters. The Christian's homeland is not of this world." Thus, the Christian is indifferent to the fate of his country and is even fearful of being proud of its glory. If a society is to be peaceful and harmonious, all of the citizens must be equally good Christians. "But if unfortunately there is a single ambitious man, a single hypocrite . . . he will very certainly get the better of his pious compatriots." Then the pious Christian simply accepts the tyrant as God's instrument of punishment. It would be against the conscience of the Christian, and it would be "inconsistent with the gentleness of a Christian," to rebel, to use violence, and to shed blood in order to chase out the tyrant. "After all, what does it matter whether one is free or a serf in this vale of tears? The essential thing is to go to heaven, and resignation is but an additional means of doing so." If their country is attacked by a foreign power, Christian soldiers will do their duty but without passion for victory. "They have to know how to die rather than to win. What does it matter if they are victors or vanquished?" So for example: "[W]hen the cross chased out the eagle, all Roman valor disappeared."[8]

Rousseau's views are summed up in this way: "But I am mistaken when I speak of a Christian republic; these two words are mutually exclusive. Christianity preaches nothing but servitude and dependence. Its spirit is so favorable to tyranny that tyranny always profits from it. True Christians are made to be slaves. They know it and are scarcely moved thereby; this brief life is of too little worth in their view."[9]

Now given the fact that Rousseau has acknowledged the foundational role of religion for civil society, he is left with an extremely serious problem of his own: what is the religion of his state to be? I do not pursue this question in detail here, but it is important to point out that Rousseau recognizes what is lost if Christianity is deprived of all visible presence in the world. Whereas Roman Catholicism destroys social unity, "the religion of man, or Christianity . . . of the Gospel" (which is totally different from "historical" Christianity) provides no social cohesion because it is entirely private. "Through this saintly, sublime, true religion, men – children of the same God – all acknowledge one another as brothers, and the society that unites them is not even dissolved by death. But this religion, having no particular relation to the body politic, leaves laws with only their intrinsic force, without adding any other force to them; and because of this, one of the great bonds of particular societies remains without effect. Even worse, far from attaching the citizens' hearts to the State, it detaches them from it as from all worldly things. I know of nothing more contrary to the social spirit."[10]

Rousseau resolves his problem by means of the civil religion, "a purely civil profession of faith, the articles of which are for the sovereign to establish, not exactly as religious dogmas, but as sentiments of sociability, without which it is impossible to be a good citizen or a faithful subject." On the other hand, the religious beliefs of the citizens are a purely private matter. "The subjects, therefore, do not have to account for their opinions to the sovereign. . . . Now it matters greatly to the State that each citizen have a religion that causes him to love his duties; but the dogmas of that religion are of no interest to the State or to its members. . . . Everyone can have whatever opinions he pleases"[11]

If Christianity has a visible form and presence in the world as a universal church, then that church is a threat to the power of particular political societies. If Christianity has no visible presence in the world, it cannot serve the function of creating the social bond. And in either case, the otherworldly character of Christianity makes the Christian indifferent to this world and especially to freedom. As I indicated earlier, Rousseau's formulation is paradigmatic for modern political philosophy, especially for Hobbes and Machiavelli. Each attempts to resolve the problem of Christianity in his own way, but there are three closely related principles that emerge and that are definitive of modern political philosophy.

First, religion is subjected to politics. This means that politics is higher than religion and has ultimate authority over men. Second, faith becomes an entirely private matter. That is how its public voice is silenced and why it can assert no authority in public. For the state, "churches are private associations of individual believers."[12] Third, it is philosophy itself that rules in the name of autonomous reason.[13]

Now I want to elucidate Montaigne's political philosophy by examining where he stands with respect to these three principles and to the criticisms of Christianity that gave rise to these principles. In the first section of this chapter I trace out the limits of politics as Montaigne presents them. These limits are seen in the inability of human reason and art to improve upon the imperfections of chance and custom, and the necessary role of vice in political structures and activities. In the second section I discuss the way in which the Christian is a citizen of two cities, and the way in which Christianity exists in tension with politics. In the final section I attempt to think through the political implications of the publicness of Christianity. What are the possibilities for forms of political association that are suggested by the religious foundations of society? I conclude that Montaigne puts forward the possibility of a Christian republic, based on the kind of equality and freedom that Christianity can support.

The Limits of Politics

Discussion of Montaigne's political philosophy often centers around the question of whether he is to be thought of as a conservative or a liberal.[14] These categories are both inadequate and somewhat misleading when applied to Montaigne because they obscure a deeper division within political philosophy. In *The Politics of Faith and the Politics of Scepticism*, Oakeshott sees the deeper division that exists between those who profess a faith in politics, and thus in human reason, to secure the human good (i.e., perfection) and those who are skeptical concerning the ability of government and who want to limit its power. The categories of liberalism and conservatism do not really capture this distinction. Oakeshott counts Montaigne among the skeptics and this is, I believe, a more accurate (although incomplete) description of Montaigne's position. The skeptic is acutely aware of the dangers and the limits of politics and does not believe that the human good can be secured by political means. He does not place his faith in rational schemes that promise to eliminate the evils of human life. Montaigne's skepticism is evident in his attitude toward the inability of art to overcome or improve upon chance, and toward the ineradicability of vice and injustice from the necessary structures and activities of politics.[15]

The recognition of the limits of politics that is the core of Montaigne's skepticism is, then, inherently conservative insofar as it moderates enthusiasm for change, especially deliberate change based on rational schemes that aim at rational ideals of perfection. Here it should be noted that Montaigne does not seem to regard the French monarchy as oppressive. "In truth, our laws are free enough, and the weight of sovereignty scarcely touches a French nobleman twice in his life. The real and essential subjection is only for those among us who go seeking it and who like to gain honors and riches by such service; for anyone who wants to ensconce himself by his hearth, and who can manage his house without quarrels and lawsuits, is as free as the Doge of Venice" (VS266; F195).

On the other hand, Montaigne also reveals an openness to change. In the very place where he says that the best thing he could do as mayor was "to conserve and endure," he qualifies this by adding that innovation "is forbidden in these times, when we are hard pressed and have to defend ourselves mainly against innovations" (VS1023; F783). That is, he implies that there are times when innovation is not to be feared. And in "Of custom" there is the suggestion that habit can work against change that is beneficial: "Nations brought up to liberty and to ruling themselves consider any other form of government monstrous and contrary to nature. Those who are accustomed to monarchy do the same. And whatever easy chance fortune offers them to change, even when with great difficulties they have rid themselves of the importunity of one master, they run to supplant him with another, with similar difficulties, because they cannot make up their minds to hate domination itself" (VS116; F83–84). The change that is described approvingly is in the direction of liberty and self-rule; the seizing of the chance moment is in keeping with an accidental philosophy. In this discussion of the limits of politics, the skeptical-conservative dimension of Montaigne's thought will be brought out. Later in this chapter, I attempt to show how his account of the conditions of sociality (consistent with his own character) suggests a possibility for change in the direction of liberty.

Those who want to place Montaigne in the line of modern political philosophers from Machiavelli and Hobbes to Rousseau tend to focus, at least in part, on Montaigne's break with classical political philosophy. Like Machiavelli and Hobbes, Montaigne criticizes Plato and Aristotle for their preoccupation with the question of the best form of society. Montaigne writes: "Necessity associates men and brings them together. This accidental link afterward takes the form of laws; for there have been some as savage as any human opinion can produce, which have nevertheless maintained their bodily health and long life as well as those of Plato and Aristotle could do. And indeed all those descriptions of a government imagined by art, prove ridiculous and unfit to put into practice. These great, lengthy altercations about the best form of society and the rules most suitable to bind us, are altercations fit only for the exercise of our minds. . . . Such a description of a government would be applicable in a new world, but we take men already bound and formed to certain customs; we do not create them, like Pyrrha or Cadmus. By whatever means we may have the power to correct and reform them, we can hardly twist them out of their accustomed bent without breaking up everything" (VS956–57; F730).

Unlike Machiavelli and Hobbes, however, Montaigne adopts an Aristotelian defense of tradition and habit: "Not in theory, but in truth, the best and most excellent government for each nation is the one under which it has preserved its existence. Its form and essential fitness depend on habit. We are prone to be discontented with the present state of things. But I maintain, nevertheless, that to wish for the government of a few in a democratic state, or another type of government in a monarchy, is foolish and wrong" (VS957; F731). Further, "Nothing presses a state so hard except innovation; change alone lends shape to injustice and tyranny. When some part is dislocated, we can prop it up; we can fight against letting the alteration and corruption natural to all things carry us too far from our beginnings and principles. But to undertake to recast so great a mass, to change the foundations of so great a structure, that is a job for those who wipe out a picture in order to clean it, who want to reform defects of detail by universal confusion and cure illnesses by death" (VS958; F731). He concludes that "the oldest and best-known evil is always more bearable than an evil that is new and untried" (VS959; F732). It is easy to make a people despise ancient customs, but it is extremely difficult to establish a better state in the place of the one that is ruined (VS656; F498).[16]

Machiavelli, Hobbes, and Rousseau all seek to replace the existing imperfect political condition with a rationally constructed ideal state. Whereas they want to introduce "new modes and orders," Montaigne is quite explicit about his restraint, and denies that he is engaged in any such rational and revolutionary project; whoever undertakes to rule and to change the laws of his country usurps the authority of judging. "The following very vulgar consideration has confirmed me in my position and kept me in check even during my rasher youth: not to burden my shoulders with so heavy a load as the responsibility for a knowledge of such importance." Private fantasy is unstable and private reason has only a private jurisdiction (VS121; F88). Montaigne was a Platonist long before he knew there was a Plato, for Plato does not condone doing violence to the repose of one's country even to cure it. The good man leaves all as it is and prays God to send his help. Is there any evil that is worth combating with the destruction of one's country? No, not even the usurpation of the tyrant (VS1043; F797).

Montaigne's defense of the rule of law is also made in Platonic-Aristotelian terms: "In all things except those that are simply bad, change is to be feared: and no laws are held in their true honor except those to which God has given some ancient duration, so that no one knows their origin or that they were ever different" (VS270; F198). In "Of experience" he elaborates on this basis of authority: "Now laws remain in credit not because they are just, but because they are laws. That is the mystic foundation of their authority; they have no other. And that is a good thing for them. They are often made by fools, more often by people who, in their hatred of equality, are wanting in equity; but always by men, vain and irresolute authors. There is nothing so grossly and widely and ordinarily faulty as the laws. Whoever obeys them because they are just, does not obey them for just the reason he should" (VS1072; F821).

The disorder and chaos of the civil wars lead him to see that "human society holds and is knit together at any cost whatever. Whatever position you set men in, they pile up and arrange themselves by moving and crowding together, just as ill-matched objects, put in a bag without order, find of themselves a way to unite and fall into place together, often better than they could have been arranged by art." He tells the story of King Philip who collected the most wicked men and settled them in a city he had built for them. "I judge that from their very vices they set up a political system among themselves and a workable and regular society" (VS956; F730).

The necessity that is at the origin of society is never eliminated and shows itself in the necessity of vice itself. "Our being is cemented with sickly qualities: ambition, jealousy, envy, vengeance, superstition, despair ... even cruelty, so unnatural a vice. . . . Whoever should remove the seeds of these qualities from men would destroy the fundamental conditions of our life. Likewise in every government there are necessary offices which are not only abject but also vicious. Vices find their place in it and are employed for sewing our society together, as are poisons for the preservation of health. . . . The public welfare requires that a man betray and lie and massacre; let us resign this commission to more obedient and suppler people" (VS790–91; F599–600).

Fortune reserves her authority "above our reasonings" and sometimes presents us with a necessity so urgent that the laws must give way. In these ultimate necessities "there is nothing more to hold on to," and then it may be wiser "to lower your head" and give way than to engage in an impossible struggle that allows violence finally to trample everything: "[I]t would be better to make the laws will what they can do, since they cannot do what they will" (VS122; F89).

Even when there is no urgent necessity pushing us toward dishonorable actions, the laws cannot claim to be perfectly just. "Consider the form of this justice that governs us: it is a true testimony of human imbecility, so full it is of contradiction and error" (VS1070; F819). For example, the innocent are punished while their judges, who are guilty of far worse, are untouched by the laws. "The very laws of justice cannot subsist without some mixture of injustice" (VS675; F511). The justice that belongs to particular nations is "constrained to the need of our governments." And it would be a misunderstanding of the world to think that deception has no place in public affairs (VS795–96; F604).

There is, in the end, no possibility of real innocence in the world of politics: "The virtue assigned to the affairs of the world is a virtue with many bends, angles, and elbows so as to join and adapt itself to human weakness; mixed and artificial, not straight, clean, constant, or purely innocent"

(VS991; F758). Montaigne once tried to apply the rules of "a scholastic and novice virtue" in the public service but he found them "inept and dangerous for such matters" (VS991; F758). And if anyone boasts, in times such as this, that he practices a pure virtue in public affairs, he either does not know what virtue is or he does not notice the thousand things of which his conscience should accuse him. "Civic innocence is measured according to the places and the times"(VS993; F760).

Within this context we can see, in part, the ways in which Montaigne is at odds with the principles of modern political philosophy as I outlined them here. In insisting on the limits of politics in the way that he does, Montaigne is denying that politics is the highest human activity to which everything else must be subordinated and that it can secure the greatest good for man. Machiavelli states his position on the ultimacy of politics: "[W]here one deliberates entirely on the safety of his fatherland, there ought not to enter any consideration of either just or unjust, merciful or cruel, praiseworthy or ignominious; indeed every other concern put aside, one ought to follow entirely the policy that saves its life and maintains its liberty."[17] Montaigne, on the other hand, says that "if there should be a prince with so tender a conscience that no cure seemed to him worth so onerous a remedy [e.g., betrayal or massacre], I would not esteem him the less. . . . What is less possible for him to do than what he cannot do except at the expense of his faith and his honor, things which perhaps should be dearer to him than his own safety, yes, and even the safety of his people?" (VS799; F607). At that point, the prince can only call upon God for help. Montaigne concludes this essay, "Of the useful and the honorable," with his description of the character of Epaminondas, who wedded goodness and humanity to the most violent acts of war. Machiavelli, on the other hand, condemns Scipio's "excessive mercy."[18] He wants the prince "to learn to be able not to be good."[19]

Montaigne's "realism" concerning the vices that are an inevitable part of political life may make him appear to be in agreement with Machiavelli, but the crucial difference lies in the fact that Montaigne recognizes something higher than politics. Francis Slade states the difference between premodern and modern political philosophy in this way: for modern political philosophy, the realization of the ideal state is inherent in reason itself. Therefore, modern political philosophy aims to rule: "It will become a partisan among the parties who vie for supremacy in the city. It will take apart the arguments upon which political men base their claims to exercise rule and show the pretentiousness of these claims. It will advance, in opposition, the only claim worthy of respect, the claim to rule of reason itself, a claim which equalizes and cancels all the other claims." For premodern political philosophy, on the contrary, the role of political philosophy is not to be the instrument of rule but to limit the pretensions of politics and therefore the desire to rule.[20]

Now we can begin to see Montaigne's insistence on the nonauthoritative character of the *Essays* and his preference for private life in a somewhat different light, that is, as his way of resisting that product of autonomous reason, the modern state. In Chapters 7 and 8 I presented Montaigne's defense of private life as neither a mere personal preference nor an argument for liberal individualism, but rather as his revaluation of the virtues associated with private life and his relocation of the great-souled man to the private sphere. Montaigne's defense of private life is his resistance to tyranny, and especially the tyranny represented by the "universal and homogeneous state." In *The Politics of Faith and the Politics of Scepticism*, Oakeshott describes the changes that occurred with the emergence of modern out of medieval Europe. "During the late fifteenth and sixteenth centuries, governments all over Europe were, in varying degrees, acquiring a power to control the activities and destinies of their subjects such as their predecessors had never enjoyed."[21] Now "the tireless, inquisitive, roving hand of government was beginning to be able to reach everywhere, accustoming the subject to the notion that nothing should be beyond its grasp." For Oakeshott, "the most significant of all these changes was . . . the gradual disappearance of the intermediate authorities which had formerly stood between a then weak central government and the subjects, leaving them naked before a power which in its magnitude was becoming comparable to a force of nature."[22] This new power is the state, a specifically modern form of political life.

In his "Rule as Sovereignty: The Universal and Homogeneous State," Francis Slade compares the characteristic forms of political philosophy prior to the Machiavellian turn with modern political philosophy. In discussing the premodern category of *amicitia*, Slade claims that this category "assumes that political societies are associations of human beings related to one another in some kind of concrete community, that political communities include within themselves other kinds of communities which find completion in, but do not take their origin from, the political community, and that the inclusive word covering these various relationships among human beings is friendship."[23]

According to Slade, the state does not want to allow any standing to those institutions that originated independently of the state. "Implicit in the State is the dissolution of social authorities as the oppressors of individuals and groups of individuals of this type and their replacement by State apparatuses." The state is "rule indifferent to the differences among human beings, to forms of human community having their origin in man's natural sociability, to institutions embodying the histories and the traditions of societies and reflecting the experiences of diverse associations of human beings."[24] As Slade points out, Rousseau clearly expresses and endorses this indifference. In Book II, chapter 12, of the *Social Contract*, he says that the relationship of the members to each other should be as small as possible and the relationship to the entire body should be as large as possible "so that each citizen is in a position of perfect independence from all the others and of excessive dependence upon the City."

The nonauthoritative status of the *Essays*, then, is Montaigne's denial of the claims of autonomous reason over the traditions of human communities. His preference for private life – that is, actually bringing private life out of its hiddenness and revealing it as the place of the great-souled man – is his attempt to give philosophical grounding for those intermediate institutions that stand between the individual and the state that claims absolute power over him.[25]

Two Cities

Montaigne is both attached to "the world" and detached from it because he belongs to two different worlds. He grants to public life its claims on him unhesitatingly. "As for me, both my word and my honor are, like the rest, parts of this common body. Their best operation is public service; I take that as presupposed" (VS796; F604). But this does not mean that anything and everything can be asked or required of him. He will not betray anyone or be a party to treachery or fraud and he will not knowingly lie to anyone. There are limits on what one's country can legitimately demand. Montaigne would, of course, prefer not to lose his life in the service of his country, but if necessary, he would die for it: "I will follow the good side right to the fire, but not into it if I can help it" (VS792; F601). And he prefers not to lose everything he has in the civil wars but recognizes that his duty may require this of him: "Let [Château] Montaigne be engulfed in the public ruin, if need be; but if not, I shall be grateful to fortune if it is saved; and as much rope as my duty gives me, I use for its preservation" (VS792; F601). In other words, he grants to public obligation its claim on his life and all he owns, but not any claim on his integrity.

Montaigne has no praise for those who refuse to put themselves at risk for the preservation of their country. "To keep oneself wavering and half-and-half, to keep one's allegiance motionless and without inclination in one's country's troubles and in civil dissensions, I consider neither handsome nor honorable." In domestic affairs, such an attitude would be "a sort of treason" for "one must necessarily take sides." On the other hand, he regards it as excusable for someone to remain uninvolved who has neither responsibility nor direct orders. "Nevertheless," he says, "I am not using this excuse for myself." The important thing is how one conducts oneself: "[E]ven those who espouse a cause completely" can do so with order and moderation, without hatred, revenge, ambition, or avarice (VS793; F601).

Montaigne did not seek to be elected mayor of Bordeaux and did not want the job when told of his election. But "I was told that I was wrong." And the king commanded him to do it (VS1005; F768). His account of his service shows that he preferred the good and the tranquillity of his people to his own reputation, refusing to allow ambition to tempt him into dangerous innovations. He did, however, perform his office wholeheartedly out of affection for his people: "I bestirred myself for them just as I do for myself." If the occasion had arisen, "there is nothing I would have spared for their service" (VS1021; F781).

But as we have seen, Montaigne's attitude is different from his father's: "This course, which I commend in others, I do not love to follow, and I am not without excuse. He [Montaigne's father] had heard it said that we must forget ourselves for our neighbor, that the particular was not to be considered at all in comparison with the general."[26] Montaigne interprets the great commandment differently from the way his father did. He does not believe that public service, "the most honorable occupation," is the highest fulfillment of Christian charity. Rather, ambition is a temptation to be resisted: "Political philosophy may condemn, for all I care, the baseness and sterility of my occupation.... I am of the opinion that the most honorable occupation is to serve the public and to be useful to many.... For my part, I stay out of it; partly out of conscience (for in the same way that I see the weight attached to such employments, I see also what little qualification I have for them; and Plato, a master workman in all political government, nevertheless abstained from it); partly out of laziness" (VS952; F727).

Montaigne attributes his preference for private life to his love of liberty and his hatred of any kind of domination or force: "I am disgusted with mastery, both active and passive" (VS917; F700) and "I hate every sort of tyranny, both in words and acts" (VS931; F711). What kind of liberty does he have in mind? In the first place, he means freedom of movement. "I am so sick for freedom, that if anyone should forbid me access to some corner of the Indies, I should live distinctly less comfortably. And as long as I find earth or air open elsewhere, I shall not lurk in any place where I have to hide.... If [the laws] that I serve threatened even the tip of my finger, I should instantly go and find others, wherever it might be" (VS1072; F820–21). Thus, he sees his bond to his country as conditional, not as absolute. In spite of his great admiration for Socrates, Montaigne notes an important difference between them, a difference that reflects the difference between the classical and the Christian worlds. "What Socrates did near the end of his life, in considering a sentence of exile against him worse than a sentence of death, I shall never, I think, be so broken or so strictly attached to my own country as to do.... That was a very fastidious attitude for a man who considered the world his city" (VS973; F743–44).

Montaigne belongs to two cities. First, to Paris: "I love her tenderly, even to her warts and spots. I am a Frenchman only by this great city: great in population, great in the felicity of her situation, but above all great and incomparable in variety and diversity of the good things of life; the glory of France, and one of the noblest ornaments of the world" (VS972; F743). But the "national bond" is not the most important for him: "Not because Socrates said it, but because it is really my feeling, and perhaps excessively so, I consider all men my compatriots, and embrace a Pole as I do a Frenchman, setting this national bond after the universal and common one" (VS973; F743). This universal and common bond is not imaginary, fanciful, or even philosophical: it is a real city, the city of Rome. The ancient city of Rome, "free, just, and flourishing," interests him passionately. But the Rome that we see now "deserves our love."[27] It is "the only common and universal city. The sovereign magistrate who commands there is acknowledged equally elsewhere. It is the metropolitan city of all Christian nations; the Spaniard and the Frenchman, every man is at home there. To be one of the princes of that state one need only be of Christendom, wherever it may be. There is no place here below that heaven has embraced with such favorable influence and such constancy" (VS997; F763). The distinction that Montaigne is making between the national bond and the universal and common bond is not identical to the theological distinction between the earthly and the heavenly cities, or between this world and the other world. Rome is in *this* world: "what it means to believe" and what it means to be a human being who believes entail a common bond that is in some way experienced in this life. In the terms of the "dialectic" of the "Apology," that bond cannot be experienced as either private inspiration or universal reason.

In "Of coaches" Montaigne describes the extreme cruelty of the Spanish conquerors toward the people of the New World and, within that context, he provides a characterization of the kingdom of God. The conquerors not only admit but even boast of their acts of cruelty and murder. "Would it be as a testimonial to their justice or their zeal for religion? Truly, those are ways too contrary and hostile to so holy an end. If they had proposed to extend our faith, they would have reflected that faith is not spread by possession of territory but by possession of men" (VS913; F697).

Unlike the pagan religions, Christianity is transpolitical and universal, open to all men by virtue of our common and universal condition. The separation of politics and religion in the Christian world opens the way to conflict: the Christian belongs to two cities and Rome has the greater, more fundamental claim on him.[28] How does Montaigne deal with the tension between Christianity and politics? In "Of custom" he writes: "The Christian religion has all the marks of the utmost justice and utility, but none more apparent than the precise recommendation of obedience to the magistrate and maintenance of the government. What a marvelous example of this the divine wisdom has left us, which, to establish the salvation of the human race and to conduct its glorious victory over death and sin, willed to do so only at the mercy of our political order; and subjected its progress, and the conduct of such a lofty and salutary action, to the blindness and injustice of our observances and usages; letting flow the innocent blood of so many of its beloved elect, and suffering a long loss of years in ripening this priceless fruit!" (VS120–21; F87–88). Christ submitted himself and his Church to the injustice and cruelty of men, giving the example of obedience to political authority. Christ before Pilate is the perfect image of that submission. It is noteworthy that the only direct quotation of Christ in the *Essays* (apart from some phrases from the Our Father) occurs in "Of cruelty" within the context of Montaigne's discussion of the cruelty of the Roman tyrants. In the Gospel according to Luke (12.4), Christ says: "Do not be afraid of those who kill the body and after that can do no more" (VS431; F315).

Just as the *Essays* are full of examples of clemency, so are they full of examples of the cruelty of tyrants. From the very first page, the shadow of the tyrant falls across the entire work. The political condition of tyranny is the extreme case of inequality, subjection, and vice. In "Cowardice, mother of cruelty," Montaigne asks: "What makes tyrants so bloodthirsty?" and he answers: "[I]t is concern for their security, and the fact that their cowardly heart furnishes them with no other means of making themselves secure than by exterminating those who can injure them, even to the women, for fear of a scratch" (VS699; F528). Montaigne's character stands at the opposite pole to the tyrant's.

The conflict between the two cities – between politics and Christianity – is inevitable because politics is necessarily the realm of mastery and subjection, inequality, ambition, and pride, whereas Christianity teaches that the meek, lowly, poor, and weak shall confound the strong and powerful, shall inherit the earth, and shall seize the kingdom of heaven.[29] The political realm is the place where the weak are at the mercy of the strong. Further, the life of faith and political life are in such tension with each other because the spiritual kingdom of Christ is not simply "the next world" but this world: the two kingdoms occupy the same space of appearances. That is to say, one and the same deed can be either an act of ambition or an act of charity. This is brought out very forcefully in T. S. Eliot's *Murder in the Cathedral*. Archbishop Thomas Becket, who had been chancellor to the king and the king's friend, now finds himself at odds with the king on account of his determination to defend the prerogatives of the Church. The real struggle in the play (and the level at which the action occurs) is not the struggle between Thomas and Henry II but the struggle within Thomas himself. In Part I, four tempters come to him. The first tempts him with the memory of pleasures, the second with the desire for worldly power and glory, and the third with the desire for liberty. But it is the fourth tempter who is unexpected, who tempts him with his own desires, and who enters most deeply into the hidden depths of Thomas's soul. This is the desire for martyrdom itself so that he can rule from the tomb, the desire for spiritual power. Thomas recognizes this as the greatest temptation: "The last temptation is the greatest treason / To do the right deed for the wrong reason."[30] The greatest treason is to turn spiritual concerns into a political cause, thus using the spiritual for one's own power and glory.

In Part II, when it becomes known that the knights of the king are approaching, the priests bar the doors of the cathedral and comfort themselves that they are safe. But Thomas tells them: "Unbar the doors! Throw open the doors!"[31] The church must remain open even to his enemies who have come to kill him.

After the knights have murdered Thomas, they come before the audience to justify their action. The second knight, who corresponds to the second tempter, says that "had Becket concurred with the King's wishes, we should have had an almost ideal State: a union of spiritual and temporal administration, under the central government." But as soon as Becket became archbishop, he affirmed "that there was a higher order" than the political and that "the two orders were incompatible."[32] The fourth knight accuses Becket of monstrous egotism and of having "determined upon a death by martyrdom. . . . he insisted, while we were still inflamed with wrath, that the doors should be opened."[33]

The simple action of opening the doors can be seen either as an act of faith and charity or as an act of monstrous egotism and ambition – that is, it can really be one of two very different actions, both of which occupy the same space of appearance. "And striving with political men / May make that cause political, not by what they do / But by what they are." The life of faith and the life of ambition and pride do not exist in separate realms apart, and the difference between them is difficult, if not impossible, to tell, even for the agent himself. So the real change that occurs in *Murder in the Cathedral* is "interior" and comes closest to visibility in the "Interlude" between Parts I and II in which Thomas preaches his sermon on Christmas morning: he speaks to his people about what the peace promised by Christ really means.

It seems to me that the idea that one and the same visible deed can display two very different actions is foreign to the notion of action discussed by Arendt. For the ancient Greeks and Romans, the public space is homogeneous; the deed that is done within that space is one and visible, even if its meaning is not fully grasped. There is no nonpolitical nonpublic action (in the strict sense) for the ancients. The difference that Christianity introduces is not simply reducible to an emphasis on the motive of action. For the action, say, the opening of the doors, occurs in the public space and enters into the web of meanings that constitutes public life where it will be interpreted in different ways. What Christianity introduces, then, is "another world," but this does not mean "the world to come." The "other world" is just this world, transformed. That is what it means to say that the Christian is "in the world" but not "of the world."

The Religion of Publicness

In my discussion of the dialectic of faith and reason in the "Apology," I attempted to show that Montaigne rejects the claim that faith is held by particular divine inspiration and the claim that autonomous reason provides a public, common ground. Whereas autonomous reason gives us only a private world of dreams and chimeras, faith gives us the public, common world, the world of truth. Francis Slade states the matter precisely: "Christianity cannot live in the privacy of the heart. It is the religion of publicness. To cease to profess it publicly is 'to lose the Faith.' This is because Christianity is the religion of truth."[34]

What are the implications of the publicness of Christianity for political philosophy? First, I want to claim that, for Montaigne, Christianity provides in a preeminent way the conditions for human association. These conditions are truth, goodness, and beauty. Montaigne's attack on the Reformation is based on his perception of the threat that the Reformation poses to these conditions of sociality. Second, I want to show how Montaigne's discussions of political matters throughout the *Essays* point to a political possibility that is based on a deeper realization of these conditions of sociality. Montaigne's political philosophy is accidental; that is, it is not the rational construction of an ideal state but simply the uncovering of the conditions that are already present and that make human association possible at all, and a working out of the political possibilities inherent in these conditions.

The first condition of sociality is truth. "We are men, and hold together only by our word" (VS36; F23). That is why lying is a vice that Montaigne especially abhors. "Since mutual understanding is brought about solely by way of words, he who breaks his word betrays public society. It is the only instrument by means of which our wills and thoughts communicate, it is the interpreter of our soul. If it fails us, we have no more hold on each other, no more knowledge of each other. If it deceives us, it breaks up all our relations and dissolves all the bonds of our society" (VS666–67; F505). As we saw in Chapter 7, he hates dissimulation and, of all vices, finds none that testifies as much to cowardice and baseness of heart. It is cowardly and servile to disguise oneself and to hide under a mask. "A generous heart should not belie its thoughts; it wants to reveal itself even to its inmost depths. There everything is good, or at least everything is human." Truth is "the first and fundamental part of virtue" (VS647; F491). And "the first stage in the corruption of morals is the banishment of truth" (VS666; F505).

The second condition of sociality is goodness. We have seen that it is Cato's goodness (as distinguished from his virtue) that makes him prefer the common good to the political struggle that gives him the opportunity to display his heroic virtue. And it is goodness that accounts for the kindness and humaneness of Epaminondas in the midst of the fiercest battle.

The third condition of sociality is beauty. Montaigne's emphasis on beauty is of a piece with his impatience with the philosophical tendency to dismiss what it regards as the lowly and base considerations associated with the body. In "Of physiognomy" he discusses the role of beauty in human association:

"I cannot say often enough how much I consider beauty a powerful and advantageous quality.... We have no quality that surpasses it in credit. It holds the first place in human relations; it presents itself before the rest, seduces and prepossesses our judgment with great authority and a wondrous impression." Beauty is closely associated with goodness in language and in Scripture, and Aristotle gives to beauty the right to command (VS1058; F810).

In "Of presumption" Montaigne says of beauty that "the first distinction that existed between men and the first consideration that gave some men preeminence over others, was probably the advantage of beauty" (VS640; F485). Here, then, beauty is said to be at the root of inequality. In the contrast between what he says about beauty as the origin of inequality and what he says about valor in battle as the origin of inequality, we can see the essential difference between sociality and mastery. On the one hand, beauty is a self-communicating, reconciling, social quality and, on the other hand, strength and force are divisive, self-aggrandizing, and potentially tyrannical. It is noteworthy that one of the very few places in the *Essays* where Montaigne makes direct reference to Christ occurs in the discussion of beauty: "Our great, divine, and heavenly King, whose every particular should be carefully, religiously, and reverently noted, did not reject the recommendation of a handsome body: 'fairer than the children of men' [Psalms]" (VS640; F485–86).[35] Goodness, truth, and beauty are the basis of the self-communication that is of the essence of sociality.

It remains now to follow through these conditions of sociality to their presupposition and ultimate foundation. Here we can do no better than to turn to Oakeshott's essay on "The Nature and Meaning of Sociality." For Oakeshott, as for Montaigne, the essence of sociality is friendship. Friendship is "the good," and it is religion that gives us the deepest insight into the nature of love and friendship. Oakeshott's most fundamental claim about the nature and meaning of sociality is that "God is the only principle of sociability which will explain the facts of life. Society becomes possible [only] by religion." Thus, Oakeshott interprets "God is Love" to mean "God is the only principle of sociality."[36]

Montaigne's rejection of the Reformation can be understood in terms of the three conditions of sociality – truth, goodness, and beauty – that are founded in religion. He recognizes that his "sticking to the old ways" looks like "simplicity and stupidity." That is how it appears to those who "follow the first plausible meaning" (VS312; F227). There are those who "in recent years had the habit of reproaching each and every man in whom there gleamed some light of intelligence and who professed the Catholic religion, with dissimulation; and who even maintained, thinking to do him honor, that whatever he said for appearance, he could not help having his belief within reformed according to their measure" (VS320; F231). But Montaigne does not follow the first plausible meaning, which is the way of error. Rather, he comes to see "the mysterious and divine secret of our ecclesiastical polity" (VS313; F227).

To those who insist on holding that no intelligent man can really be a Catholic in his "belief within," Montaigne responds, "they may take my word for it: if anything were to have tempted my youth, ambition for the risk and difficulties that attended this recent enterprise [the Reformation] would have played a good part in it" (VS320; F232). The temptation of the Reformation is for Montaigne the temptation to ambition, to "make that cause political."

The Reformers have tried "to construct for us a system of religious practice that is all contemplative and spiritual." They disdain the role of the body and of the senses in worship. They forget that "it is still a man we are dealing with, and it is a wonder how physical his nature is" (VS930; F710). They want to persuade the people that "religious belief is enough, by itself and without morals, to satisfy divine justice." That is "a ruinous teaching for any society" (VS1059; F811). In these criticisms Montaigne shows the ways in which the Reformation destroys the conditions of sociality. The rejection of the senses in religious practice is the elimination of beauty from the life of faith. The teaching that faith alone is sufficient for salvation is destructive of human community, opens the way to the excesses of ambition, and is, in the end, a misunderstanding of faith itself. In making faith a private matter, it destroys the bond of truth that is the essence of life in common. Montaigne remains a Catholic because the Church is "that great common way" (VS520; F387).

Many of Montaigne's readers – both those who see him as a liberal and those who see him as a conservative – have taken a very different view of his sincerity in matters of religion. David Lewis Schaefer places Montaigne within the tradition of the noble lie, claiming that in reality he is profoundly anti-Christian but that he dissimulates for rhetorical and political motives. "Montaigne's substantive purpose in the *Essays*...is to undermine those moral and religious conventions that obstruct freedom of thought and discourse as well as the freedom to indulge in earthly pleasures." What he seeks is "a radical transformation of the political and social order."[37] He sees himself as one of the very few "strong" souls suited to teach the "nonphilosophic multitude," and that nonphilosophic multitude would do best to follow the "common road." In Schaefer's view, then, if Montaigne hides behind a mask of Christian faith, it is because he thinks that "maintenance of the traditional faith is necessary for civic order."[38] David R. Hiley does not follow every aspect of Schaefer's reading but does agree that Montaigne favors the old religion "for its social utility in the current turmoil not because of any authority conveyed to it by time."[39] Alan Levine claims that Montaigne upholds religion because it is useful. In particular, he upholds Christianity because it is the custom of his time and place, but he himself is not a believer.[40] On the basis of what I believe I have shown with respect to Montaigne's views on religion and faith, especially in Chapter 5, it seems to me, however, that the role of religion for Montaigne is not utilitarian but rather ontologically foundational and essential. That is, Schaefer, Hiley, and Levine see Montaigne as subordinating religion to politics, whereas I believe that, for Montaigne, religion is higher than and ontologically prior to politics.

In his "Notes towards the Definition of Culture," T. S. Eliot describes the conditions for the kind of common culture that Montaigne presupposes: "While we believe that the same religion may inform a variety of cultures, we may ask whether any culture could come into being, or maintain itself, without a religious basis. We may go further and ask whether what we call the culture, and what we call the religion, of a people are not different aspects of the same thing: the culture being, essentially, the incarnation (so to speak) of the religion of a people."[41] The situation that Eliot describes is one in which "the culture of an artist or a philosopher is distinct from that of a mine worker or a field labourer; the culture of a poet will be somewhat different from that of a politician; but in a healthy society these are all parts of the same culture."[42] Specifically, the mode of being of Europe cannot be understood apart from its Christian culture: "It is in Christianity that our arts have developed; it is in Christianity that the laws of Europe have – until recently – been rooted. It is against a background of Christianity that all our thought has significance."[43]

What, then, are the political possibilities that are inherent in the conditions of sociality, especially goodness and truth, as Montaigne presents them? First, I discuss the political implications of goodness, that is, the political possibilities that are based on a deeper realization of goodness as a condition of sociality.

In "Of experience" Montaigne spells out in some detail just what he takes the position of adviser to kings to be and how he would be suited for it: "Sometimes people used to ask me what I would have thought myself good for, if anyone had thought of using me while I was young enough.... 'For nothing,' I said. And I readily excuse myself for not knowing how to do anything that would enslave me to others. But I would have told my master home truths, and watched his conduct, if he had been willing. Not in general, by schoolmasterly lessons, which I do not know – and I see no reform spring from them in those who know them – but by observing his conduct step by step, at every opportunity, judging it with my very own eyes, piece by piece, simply and naturally, making him see how he stands in public opinion, and opposing his flatterers. There is not one of us who would not be worse than the kings if he were as continually corrupted as they are by that rabble" (VS1077–78; F825). He would have had enough fidelity, judgment, and independence for that position. The kind of adviser that he is describing would be a position without a name. It should be held by a man who is content with his own fortune and who is of middle rank because he would have easier communication with all sorts of people. "He would not fear to touch his master's heart deeply and to the quick at the risk of losing his preferment" (VS1078; F826). Montaigne prefaces this description with the claim that criticizing a man frankly and for his own good is "a remarkable act of friendship" and an indication of "a healthy love" for him (VS1077; F825). The king for his part must have the strength and courage to endure the freedom of a friend's criticisms, opposing his flatterers who are seeking to advance themselves. And it is clear that the adviser must also have courage: "[T]he duties of true friendship are hard and dangerous to attempt toward a sovereign; so that there is need, not only of much affection and frankness, but of much courage as well" (VS1078; F826).

In "Of diversion" we have one example of his specific advice to the prince. "Vengeance is a sweet passion, whose impact is great and natural: I see this well enough, though I have no experience of it in myself. Recently, in order to lead a young prince away from it, I did not tell him that we must turn our cheek to the man who has just struck the other one, for charity's sake, nor did I represent to him the tragic results that poetry attributes to this passion. I let the passion alone and applied myself to making him relish the beauty of a contrary image: the honor, favor, and good will he would acquire by clemency and kindness. I diverted him to ambition" (VS835; F634). Montaigne acknowledges and accepts the ambition of the prince, and he recognizes ambition as the passion that might move and divert him. He does not appeal to a principle, not even to the admonition of Christ to turn the other cheek. Rather, he appeals to an image, and he shows the prince a possibility that, in his anger, had not occurred to him. Presumably, that possibility is seen in a particular image of clemency and kindness, in an example such as that of Epaminondas or Caesar or Alexander. One of Montaigne's chief goals is to turn the prince away from vengeance toward mercy and gentleness. And if we look back over the *Essays*, we see that images of mercy and gentleness are among the most frequently presented and highly praised from the very first page.

In "Of the inequality that is between us" he discusses Hiero's complaints about his life as a king: "But above all Hiero emphasizes the fact that he finds himself deprived of all mutual friendship and society, wherein consists the sweetest and most perfect fruit of human life. For what testimony of affection and good will can I extract from a man who, willy-nilly, owes me everything he can do? . . . No one follows me for any friendship there may be between him and me; for no friendship can be knit where there is so little relation and correspondence. My elevation has placed me outside of human association: there is too much disparity and disproportion" (VS266; F195). Montaigne says that he feels pity, not envy, when he sees the king surrounded by a crowd but really all alone (VS265; F194).

In "Of husbanding your will" he writes: "Most of our occupations are low comedy. . . . We must play our part duly, but as the part of a borrowed character. Of the mask and appearance we must not make a real essence,

nor of what is foreign what is our very own. We cannot distinguish the
skin from the shirt. It is enough to make up our face, without making up
our heart. I see some . . . who are prelates to their very liver and intestines,
and drag their position with them even into their privy" (VS1011–12; F773–
74). But Montaigne is different: "The mayor and Montaigne have always
been two, with a very clear separation." A man's being is not exhausted by
his public role or in his public appearance. "The judgment of an emperor
should be above his imperial power, and see and consider it as an extraneous
accident; and he should know how to find pleasure in himself apart, and
to communicate himself like any Jack or Peter, at least to himself" (VS1012;
F774). In "Of the inequality that is between us" he writes: "If we consider a
peasant and a king, a nobleman and a plebeian, a magistrate and a private
citizen, a rich man and a pauper, there immediately appears to our eyes
an extreme disparity between them, though they are different, so to speak,
only in their breeches." And again he compares the spectacle of public life
to comedy: "For like actors in a comedy – you see them on the stage assume
the mien of a duke or an emperor, but immediately afterward, there they
are, turned back into miserable valets and porters, *which is their natural and
original condition.*" On the stage, the emperor's pomp is dazzling. If you see
him behind the curtain, "he is nothing but a common man, and perhaps
viler than the least of his subjects" (VS260–61; F191, emphasis added; see
also VS935; F714).

Thus, Montaigne holds that democratic rule (*domination populaire*) is "the
most natural and equitable" (VS20; F12). And he does not like Plato's advice
always to talk to one's servants in masterful tones without either familiarity or
playfulness. For "it is inhuman and unjust to make so much of this accidental
privilege of fortune. And the governments which admit the least disparity
between servants and masters seem to me the most equitable" (VS821; F623).

My point here is that the thrust of Montaigne's advice to the prince, both
explicit and implicit, is to moderate the elements of mastery and cruelty, to
bring the prince to recognize his common humanity, and thus to lead him in
the direction of equality. It is important to emphasize here that the kind of
political association implicit in the conditions of sociality is not the modern
liberal state. Those who see Montaigne as a liberal point to what they regard
as his liberal individualism. His most striking statement in this regard is
found in "Of glory" where he is discussing the fact that most good actions go
unnoticed and remain hidden from others. "All the glory that I aspire to in
my life is to have lived it tranquilly – tranquilly not according to Metrodorus
or Arcesilaus or Aristippus, but according to me. Since philosophy has not
been able to find a way to tranquillity that is good in common, let each one
seek it individually!" (VS622; F471). There is in Montaigne a new emphasis
on the individual, but this is an individual who is such by virtue of a certain
character: the values that Montaigne's individualism embodies are not those
of modern liberalism. Montaigne acknowledges a bond and community

among men that is precisely the bond that liberalism seeks to dissolve, that is, the bond of religion.

The political possibility inherent in goodness as a condition of sociality, then, is equality. The political possibility inherent in truth as a condition of sociality is freedom.[44] We can begin to examine this by considering the way in which he breaks with the classical tradition of "the noble lie." The philosophers do not always present their opinions openly; they have often hidden them under a mask: "[T]hey sometimes obscure their natural opinions and judgments and falsify them to accommodate themselves to public usage . . . so as not to frighten the children" (VS545; F408). The ancient philosophers "did not want to bare popular opinions to the skin, so as not to breed disorder in people's obedience to the laws and customs of their country" (VS512; F379).

Nowhere does Montaigne's break with the tradition of the noble lie come through more clearly than in matters of religion. All lawgivers have used "lying opinion" and "empty ceremony" to keep the people in their duty. That is why most polities have "fabulous origins and beginnings, enriched with supernatural mysteries. That is what has given credit to bastard religions and brought them into favor with men of understanding" (VS629; F477). Montaigne agrees with Saint Augustine's judgment on the practice of such deception (VS535; F399). In *The City of God*, Augustine discusses the views of the historian Varro and the Roman pontiff Scaevola. Varro openly declares that, on the subject of religious rites, "there are many truths which it is not expedient for the general public to know, and . . . many falsehoods which it is good for the people to believe true," thus revealing "the whole policy of the so-called sages, by whose influence cities and peoples are governed."[45] Scaevola held that "it was expedient for communities to be deceived in matters of religion." Augustine's response to this position is scathingly ironic: "What a splendid religion for the weak to flee to for liberation! He asks for the truth which will set him free; and it is believed that it is expedient for him to be deceived!"[46]

In the "Apology" Montaigne makes a crucial distinction between the laws of politics and the laws of religion. "The most plausible advice that our reason gives us in this matter [of our *mœurs*] is generally for each man to obey the laws of his country, which is the advice of Socrates, inspired, he says, by divine counsel." But this would mean that justice and rectitude are tied to the condition of the customs and fancies of each country. "Truth," on the contrary, "must have one face, the same and universal." When philosophy tells us to follow the laws of our country, she is abandoning us to "the undulating sea of opinions of a people or a prince." Montaigne's response is this: "I cannot have my judgment so flexible."

Here he criticizes the English for changing their laws three or four times during his own lifetime "not only in political matters, in which people want to dispense with constancy, but in the most important subject that can be, to wit, religion." Montaigne acknowledges, then, that in political matters constancy cannot be an absolute rule and may even be undesirable under certain conditions. But matters of religion are more important. The distinction between ancient religion and Christianity is brought into the discussion. The god Apollo declared to those who sought his instruction that "the true cult for each man was that which he found observed according to the practice of the place he was in." Thus he implied that their religion was an invention "suitable to bind their society together." But Christianity is universal: in his revelation to us through Christ, our creator has "freed our belief from the folly of those vagabond and arbitrary devotions and . . . based it on the eternal foundation of his holy word" (VS578–79; F436–37).

One of the few reforms of *mœurs* that Montaigne explicitly proposes in the *Essays* is open and truthful speaking. "Whoever would wean men of the folly of . . . scrupulous verbal superstition would do the world no great harm" (VS888; F677). And "we must pass over these common rules of civility in favor of truth and liberty" (VS942; F720). What are the political implications of this reform? In the first place, the free expression of judgment affects conduct. The context for his assertion that men can be freed from scrupulous verbal superstition without harm concerns the proper weighing of evils and vices: "We see that in places where faults are crimes, crimes are only faults; that in nations where the laws of propriety are rarer and looser, the primitive and common laws are better observed. Application to trivial things draws us away from urgent ones" (VS888; F677). We must pass over the rules of propriety concerning speech because it is a sign of lack of heart not to dare to speak roundly of oneself (VS942; F720). And Montaigne breaks with the custom that prohibits talking about oneself because that is "the supreme remedy" to cure the undiscerning self-love that is the essence of presumption (VS379; F274).

The judgment of princes is an especially important example of the kind of open speaking that Montaigne practices and encourages. It displeases him that such a saintly government as that of the Lacedaemonians should have had the deceitful ceremony of mourning every one of their kings in the same way and saying that he was the best king they had ever had, regardless of what he really was. On the contrary, he praises those nations that observed the practice of honestly examining the actions of princes after their death. "Let us make this concession to the political order: to suffer [princes] patiently if they are unworthy, to conceal their vices, to abet them by commending their indifferent actions if their authority needs our support. But, our dealings over, it is not right to deny to justice and to our liberty the expression of our true feelings, and especially to deny good subjects the glory of having reverently and faithfully served a master whose imperfections were so well known to them, and thus to deprive posterity of such a useful example" (VS16; F9).

Another aspect of Montaigne's reform on the basis of truth is presented in "Of the useful and the honorable," where he discusses several cases in which the useful is at odds with the honorable or in which the honorable man is confronted with only evil choices. For example, should Timoleon kill the tyrant who is his own brother? In this context Montaigne takes up the example that he says is often used in philosophy: robbers seize you and you promise to pay a ransom. Are you then obliged to pay it once you are out of their hands? Montaigne's response is that "people are wrong to say that an honest man will be quit of his word without paying, once he is out of their hands. Nothing of the sort. What fear has once made me will, I am bound still to will when without fear. And even if it has forced only my tongue without my will, I am still bound to make good my word to the last penny.... Otherwise we shall come by degrees to overthrow all the rights that a third person obtains from our promises and oaths. 'As if force could be brought to bear on a brave man' [Cicero]." To say that we are excused from paying is one of the "false and lax rules in philosophy." The only case in which we are excused from keeping a promise is if we have promised something wicked and unjust in itself (VS801; F608).

The claim that I am obliged to do what fear has made me agree to seems to be an anticipation of Hobbes. But Montaigne's intention is to guarantee the condition of mutual trust implied in giving one's word. The best case is that of the brave man who does not keep his word out of fear but who keeps it out of magnanimity. I take it that this is why Oakeshott, in "The Moral Life in the Writings of Thomas Hobbes," claims that, in spite of Hobbes's emphasis on fear as the condition for peace, he really requires at least some men whose pride has not been crushed by fear but rather "moralized." Oakeshott's description of this character includes a reference to Montaigne. The man whose pride has been moralized is "a man whose disposition is to overcome fear not by reason (that is, by seeking a secure condition of external human circumstances) but by his own courage; a man not at all without imperfections and not deceived about himself, but who is proud enough to be spared the sorrow of his imperfections and the illusions of his achievements; not exactly a hero, too negligent for that, but perhaps with a touch of careless heroism about him; a man, in short, who (in Montaigne's phrase) 'knows how to belong to himself,' and who, if fortune turned out so, would feel no shame in the epitaph: 'Par delicatesse / J'ai perdu ma vie.'"[47] The character that Oakeshott is describing is the man who is great enough to make the first move in the act of trust and truthfulness.

Truth as a condition of sociality implies a kind of republican government, perhaps a descendant of the Roman Republic that Montaigne admired so greatly. Montaigne's own character, as I have described it, is the character that is both suited to and necessary for this form of government. Thus, a Christian republic, which Rousseau regards as a contradiction in terms, is precisely the possibility that Montaigne intimates.

Notes

Introduction

1. Jean-François Lyotard, *The Postmodern Condition: A Report on Knowledge*, trans. Geoff Bennington and Brian Massumi (Minneapolis: University of Minnesota Press, 1984), 81.

2. See Rémi Brague, *La sagesse du monde: Histoire de l'expérience humaine de l'univers* (Paris: Librairie Arthème Fayard, 1999), especially 260. Marc Fumaroli, in his review of Brague's book, "First Gentleman of Gascony: Montaigne's Liberal Antidotes to the Hubris of Democracy," *Times Literary Supplement*, 15 October 1999, 9, concludes that Montaigne is much nearer to the Thomist thirteenth century than to liberal modernity.

3. George Steiner, *Real Presences* (Cambridge: Cambridge University Press, 1986), 20–21.

4. Ibid., 19.

5. I have left *mœurs* untranslated because no English translation that I am aware of captures precisely the scope of meaning that Montaigne wants to convey. In the passage in the "Apology" where Montaigne identifies himself as an accidental philosopher, Frame translates *mœurs* as "behavior" (F409), which seems to me too narrow. Screech's "ways of life" (S614) is better but does not necessarily convey the moral dimension that Montaigne intends.

Chapter 1: "That Is Where He Got It !"

1. For the most part, the development or change is thought to be unselfconscious. Pierre Villey, *Les sources et l'évolution des Essais de Montaigne*, vol. 2, *Evolution* (Paris: Librairie Hachette, 1933), 87, claims that Montaigne was never a thoroughgoing skeptic but that Book I of the *Essays* was "colored" by Stoicism, that Book II takes on a different color, and that, finally, in Book III Montaigne's design is to portray himself. Philippe Desan, *Naissance de la méthode* (Paris: Librairie A. G. Nizet, 1987), 117, argues that Montaigne changes but does not evolve: Book III manifests a complete rupture with humanism. According to Richard A. Sayce, *The Essays of Montaigne: A Critical Exploration* (Evanston, Ill.: Northwestern University Press, 1972), 166, "There is an evolution of a kind but it cannot be divided into

242 Notes to pp. 11-12

three clearly demarcated stages: not only are the later attitudes...potentially there from the beginning, but the early ones persist to the end." Marcel Conche, *Montaigne et la philosophie* (Villers-sur-Mer: Editions de Mégare, 1987), 79–80, says that Montaigne's way is not an evolution but a deepening: he moves from the strange to himself and discovers what he has always been. My view is similar to Conche's in this respect. Along similar lines, Floyd Gray, "The Unity of Montaigne in the *Essais*," *Modern Language Quarterly* 22 (1961): 81, notes Montaigne's own claim that he has not changed. Therefore, we should speak of a progressive revelation rather than an evolution. I argue, especially in Chapter 4, that there is a movement of thought in the *Essays* but that it is dialectical, not evolutionary.

2. See Donald M. Frame, *Montaigne's Discovery of Man: The Humanization of a Humanist* (New York: Columbia University Press, 1955), where he describes Montaigne's evolution as a growing awareness of human solidarity (134). Montaigne's words for the common people change from forms of disdain to forms of praise (164–65). In his article "To 'Rise above Humanity' and to 'Escape from the Man': Two Moments in Montaigne's Thought," *Romanic Review* 62 (1971), Frame refers to the pessimistic rhetoric of the early essays and the optimism of the late essays (29). This change is due to "Montaigne's growing sense of the unity of the individual and the race" (31). Patrick Henry supports Frame's position in his *Montaigne in Dialogue* (Stanford, Calif.: ANMA Libri, 1987), 107–8, and cites as evidence "the radical transformation of the image of Socrates" that is, Montaigne's emphasis on the simplicity of Socrates. Also in his "Recognition of the Other and Avoidance of the Double: The Self and the Other in the *Essais* of Montaigne," *Stanford French Review* 6 (1982), Henry notes a "purging of human pride" in the "Apology" and in Book III an experience of human unity through Montaigne's "discovery of the similarity of the other" (175–77). I am in basic agreement with Frame and Henry on this point, but I see this change in Montaigne as the outcome of what I will call his "circular dialectic."

3. Jules Brody, *Lectures de Montaigne* (Lexington, Ky.: French Forum Publishers, 1982), provides an excellent discussion of Villey's "evolution" thesis (93–96), and argues that if there were an evolution, it should be evident not only in Book III but in the additions to and revisions of Books I and II (98). Brody examines "That to philosophize is to learn to die" and finds, not an evolution, but a coherence. Dorothy Gabe Coleman, *Montaigne's Essais* (London: Allen and Unwin, 1987), 35, makes the same point: the revisions and additions do not support the "evolution" thesis. There are, for example, Stoical passages added to essay I.20 (45). Emmanuel Faye, *Philosophie et perfection de l'homme. De la Renaissance à Descartes* (Paris: Vrin, 1998), 236–37, cites the "unpremeditated and accidental philosopher" passage as essential for any interpretation of the *Essays* and as showing that Montaigne does not belong to any ancient sect. Montaigne refuses to identify himself with the figure of the sage characterized by his impassibility.

4. There is ample evidence that skepticism was a philosophical position known and discussed in the Renaissance. With respect to the origins of Montaigne's supposed skepticism, Floyd Gray, "Montaigne's Pyrrhonism," in *O un amy! Essays on Montaigne in Honor of Donald M. Frame*, ed. Raymond C. La Charité

(Lexington, Ky.: French Forum Publishers, 1977), 120–21, claims that Montaigne would have had direct contact with the account of Sextus Empiricus from Henri Étienne's edition of the *Outlines of Pyrrhonism*. Gray notes that there are parallels between the beginning of the "Apology" and Étienne's dedicatory epistle. Elaine Limbrick, "Was Montaigne Really a Pyrrhonian?" *Bibliothèque d'humanisme et renaissance* 39 (1977), concludes that Cicero's *Academica* revealed many different forms of skepticism to Montaigne, so that he abandoned the negative skepticism of Sextus and the Pyrrhonians for the more positive skepticism of Socrates and the Old Academy (80). C. B. Schmitt details the recovery of the ancient texts on skepticism in the fifteenth and sixteenth centuries: "The Rediscovery of Ancient Scepticism in Modern Times" in *The Skeptical Tradition*, ed. Myles Burnyeat (Berkeley: University of California Press, 1983), 225–86. Zachary S. Schiffman, "Montaigne and the Rise of Skepticism in Early Modern Europe: A Reappraisal," *Journal of the History of Ideas* 45 (1984), finds the roots of Montaigne's skepticism in the failure of the humanist program of education and the breakdown of commonplace thought (500–3, 510).

The most definitive and influential claim that Montaigne is a skeptic is put forth by the historian of philosophy Richard Popkin in *The History of Scepticism from Erasmus to Spinoza* (Berkeley: University of California Press, 1979), xvi. Popkin sees Montaigne as the founder of modern skepticism. David Hiley, *Philosophy in Question: Essays on a Pyrrhonian Theme* (Chicago: University of Chicago Press, 1988), 21, writes: "Montaigne can hardly be seen ... as contributing any new arguments to the skeptical literature though his style of presentation makes the arguments unusually compelling." André Tournon, "*Suspense philosophique et ironie: La zététique de l'essai*," *Montaigne Studies* 12 (2000), claims that Montaigne goes further in skepticism: he questions even experience and rejects the principle of resemblances (47).

G. Rodis-Lewis, "Doute pratique et doute spéculatif chez Montaigne et Descartes," *Revue philosophique de la France et de l'étranger* 182 (1992), claims that there is a radical difference between Montaigne and Descartes: Descartes seeks clear and distinct knowledge, whereas Montaigne is content to remain in doubt (441). Hubert Vincent, *Vérité et scepticisme chez Montaigne* (Paris: L'Harmatan, 1998), 6–7, says that the first sense of Montaigne's skepticism is an "innocence of judgment." Emerson's discussion of Montaigne as a skeptic emphasizes the space that the skeptic occupies – the middle ground between the "abstractionist" and the "materialist." See Ralph Waldo Emerson, "Montaigne; or, the Skeptic," in *Representative Men*, ed. Pamela Schirmeister (New York: Marsilio Publishers, 1995), 105.

However, many who regard Montaigne as a skeptic see the need to distinguish his skepticism from ancient Skepticism and to regard it as a kind of transformation of ancient Skepticism. Paul Mathias, in his introduction to *Apologie de Raymond Sebond* (Paris: Flammarion, 1999), especially 27–28, claims that Montaigne's skepticism is a critique of traditional skepticism. Alan Levine, *Sensual Philosophy: Toleration, Skepticism, and Montaigne's Politics of the Self* (Lanham, Md.: Lexington Books, 2001), claims that Montaigne is not a Pyrrhonist because he does not want to eliminate the possibility of judgment (36–38). Rather, Montaigne's position closely resembles Academic skepticism. This is a skepticism concerning all transcendent matters, but allowing for a kind of phenomenological self-knowledge (38, 72–78).

See also Ian Maclean, *Montaigne philosophe* (Paris: Presses Universitaires de France, 1946). Maclean argues that Montaigne *does* begin from "principles" (nature and time, *le moi*, and the principle of language) and that he does follow a kind of method. Thus he is not *simply* a skeptic. Nevertheless, Maclean practically identifies this "method" with skepticism (95–96) and he understands Montaigne's attack on Aristotelianism as a form of Pyrrhonism, that is, he takes Montaigne's sympathetic account of the ancient Pyrrhonian philosophy as a statement of Montaigne's own skepticism (56–58).

Conche, in his *Montaigne et la philosophie*, presents a clear picture of the difficulties involved in the claim that Montaigne is a skeptic. In particular, he recognizes that Montaigne does make assertions, including professions of faith, and that he does make judgments. Conche's solution is to attribute to Montaigne a skepticism of "method" in thought – that is, Montaigne is neither dogmatic nor systematic. Montaigne's Pyrrhonian project shows itself in his not presupposing any stable truth or fixed nature or essence of things. The Pyrrhonian has beliefs and opinions but he does not absolutize them, he does not make them into first principles or dogmas (41). This refusal to absolutize extends to his Christian belief. But Conche's interpretation, it seems to me, fails to take the nonskeptical aspects seriously enough.

Frédéric Brahami, in his *Le scepticisme de Montaigne* (Paris: Presses Universitaires de France, 1997) makes an excellent case for the claim that Montaigne is not a skeptic in the ancient sense. He shows that Montaigne does not accept the ancient Skeptical notion of the human good and that Montaigne's doubt goes even further than Pyrrhonian doubt. Brahami, then, sees Montaigne as engaged in a project that is new, but he describes this project as a "new skepticism,"due to the concept of God introduced by Christianity. There is much that I agree with in Brahami's interpretation, but my own view is that what is new in Montaigne is not a new from of skepticsm but what he calls his "unpremeditated and accidental philosophy." Accidental philosophy includes a skeptical moment but also allows us to account for the nonskeptical aspects of Montaigne's thought.

5. Almost all of those who identify Montaigne as a skeptic do recognize that he makes definitive moral judgments that would seem to be incompatible with a self-conscious and thoroughgoing skepticism. See Fortunat Strowski, *Montaigne* (Paris: Librairie Félix Alcan, 1931): Montaigne's skepticism does not prevent him from making judgments and affirmations (308). Craig Walton, in "Montaigne on The Art of Judgment: The Trial of Montaigne," in *The Sceptical Mode in Modern Philosophy: Essays in Honor of Richard H. Popkin*, ed. Richard A. Watson and James E. Force (Dordrecht: Martinus Nijhoff Publishers, 1988), 89, cites a defense of Montaigne published in 1667 by Guillaume Béranger against the criticisms made in the 1662 Port-Royal *Logique* of Arnauld and Nicole. Béranger defends Montaigne against the charge that he was a Pyrrhonian by claiming that Montaigne talks of forming the judgment, not suspending it. Richard L. Regosin, *The Matter of My Book: Montaigne's Essais as the Book of the Self* (Berkeley: University of California Press, 1977), 57, argues that Montaigne's deep concern with the Delphic command of self-knowledge distinguishes him from the skeptics.

6. See E. Zeller, *The Stoics, Epicureans and Skeptics*, trans. Oswald J. Reichel (London: Longmans, Green, 1892), 521. Zeller provides the history of Pyrrhonian and Academic skepticism and an account of its teachings. See also A. A. Long and D. N. Sedley, *The Hellenistic Philosophers* (Cambridge: Cambridge University Press, 1987), 1:14. This volume presents the most important texts and a commentary that also sets out the history of ancient skepticism.

7. David Hume, *An Enquiry concerning Human Understanding* (Indianapolis: Hackett, 1977) 71 (emphasis added). Villey, *Évolution*, 100–1, says that Plutarch is the true educator of Montaigne's judgment and that he enlarges Montaigne's experience. Guy Mermier, "L'essai *Des cannibales* de Montaigne," *Bulletin de la Société des Amis de Montaigne* 7 (1973), concludes that Montaigne's true and authentic method of investigation is the interview of witnesses (37). Gustave Lanson, *Les Essais de Montaigne* (Paris: Librairie Mellottée, [1947?]), claims that the *Essays* require us to raise this question: in what case and under what conditions does human testimony have any authority, and can we find any certitude in it? (283). Thierry Gontier, *De l'homme à l'animal. Paradoxes sur la nature des animaux. Montaigne et Descartes* (Paris: Vrin, 1998), 74–75, presses the claim of credulity further by arguing that Montaigne is indifferent to Plutarch's own reservations in reporting the incredible animal stories. Also, in the animal stories Montaigne moves the "normal" further and further away, first to the exceptional and then to the fabulous (79). It is also important to note that the notion of the "credible" is a rhetorical concept. When this is taken into account, it becomes possible to distinguish more clearly between the credible and the familiar.

8. I discuss this movement of thought more fully in Chapter 4. Here, I want to indicate that Montaigne's skepticism does not culminate in doubt or suspension of judgment but is incorporated into a dialectic that returns to the most familiar. Others have noted certain aspects of openness in Montaigne's thought. Karl Löwith, *Nature, History, and Existentialism* (Evanston, Ill.: Northwestern University Press, 1966), claims that Montaigne's form of skepticism does not paralyze but rather stimulates the mind: "This kind of *skepsis* opens unexpected perspectives in what seemed commonplace; it questions the traditional distinctions between the rational and the irrational, between truth and error. It knows that there is nothing so improbable that human thinking and acting would not be capable of it" (118). David Sedley, "Sublimity and Skepticism in Montaigne," *Publications of the Modern Language Association* 113 (October 1998): 1079–92, discusses Montaigne's meditation on the ruins of ancient Rome in the *Travel Journal* partly in terms of the aesthetic category of *admiratio*. He describes "the volatility of skepticism – the potential of skepticism to indicate both utter confusion and rapt concentration" (1088). See especially note 22 concerning the "interaction of sublimity and skepticism" in the *Essays*. John O'Neill, *Essaying Montaigne: A Study of the Renaissance Institution of Writing and Reading* (London: Routledge and Kegan Paul, 1982), says that Montaigne's skepticism "opens us to the idea of a totality of truth in which contradiction is a necessary element in our experience of truth" (14). Stanley Cavell, *In Quest of the Ordinary: Lines of Skepticism and Romanticism* (Chicago: University of Chicago Press, 1988), writes that the recovery of the ordinary from skepticism is itself a task dictated by skepticism but requires the contesting of skepticism's own view of the task (27). Gray, "Pyrrhonism," 125, presents Montaigne's skepticism as a theoretical limit

but also as a return to common sense. And in his study of Montaigne's religious thought, Dréano sees Montaigne's skepticism as an openness (e.g., he does not easily accept or reject miracles): Maturin Dréano, *La pensée religieuse de Montaigne* (Paris: Gabriel Beauchesne et Fils, 1936), 298–303. Jan Miernowski, "Le 'beau jeu' de la philosophie," *Montaigne Studies* 12 (2000), claims that for Montaigne skepticism is the most playful form of philosophy and that this makes him different from his ancient antecedents. Hugo Friedrich's view of Montaigne's skepticism is very close to my own. Friedrich says that Montaigne the skeptic pulls down the wall of certainty and delusion and opens up the horizon to the possible (137). Montaigne's skepticism is "eye-opening wisdom, not a desire for destruction. It shows that what is unrecognizable reaches much more deeply into what is immediate to our experience than naïve intellect suspects. It tends and protects it rather than driving it out through the inquisitiveness of our supposed knowledge." Hugo Friedrich, *Montaigne*, ed. Philippe Desan, trans. Dawn Eng (Berkeley: University of California Press, 1991), 128.

9. On this aspect of Montaigne's view of the ancient philosophers, see Carol E. Clark, *The Web of Metaphor: Studies in the Imagery of Montaigne's Essais* (Lexington, Ky.: French Forum Publishers, 1978), 148–50: In the "Apology" Montaigne uses images of philosophical thought that convey not simply understanding but making, constructing, controlling, and exercising authority. Friedrich, *Montaigne*, 61, claims that the Stoics, and especially Seneca, held that man, with his reason, joins himself to the reason of the world order.

10. Many of Montaigne's readers have recognized the way he includes in his picture of the human condition both those aspects of life that escape the control of the mind and the extreme case of madness. James G. Beaudry, "Virtue and Nature in the *Essais*," *Kentucky Romance Quarterly* 1 (1976): 103, writes that "Montaigne seems to differ from all the philosophers of antiquity, including Socrates, by his willingness to take into account in human nature what does not fall under the control of consciousness and the will. Not only is nature individualized in Montaigne . . . but there is a certain recognition of the impossibility of bringing everything in one's nature up to the level of consciousness." W. G. Moore, "Montaigne's Notion of Experience," in *The French Mind: Studies in Honor of Gustave Rudler*, ed. Will Moore, Rhoda Sutherland, and Enid Starkie (Oxford: Clarendon Press, 1952), 43–44, notes that Montaigne treats of matters concerning physical existence that are not usually given serious consideration. He does this "because the most immediate, and least intellectual, apprehension of life is via the body." Both Donald Frame, "Considerations on the Genesis of Montaigne's *Essais*," in *Montaigne: Essays in Memory of Richard Sayce*, ed. I. D. McFarlane and Ian Maclean (Oxford: Clarendon Press, 1982), 4, and Craig B. Brush, "Montaigne Tries Out Self-Study," *L'Esprit Créateur* 20 (1980): 25, refer to Montaigne's condition after his fall ("Of practice") as a clear example of his interest in the borders of the soul. M. A. Screech, *Montaigne and Melancholy: The Wisdom of the Essays* (London: Duckworth, 1983; reprint, London: Penguin, 1991), 65–66, and Friedrich, *Montaigne*, 16, note that in calling his thinking and writing "reveries," Montaigne suggests not merely vague dreaming but mad frenzy, insanity, hallucination, delirium. See also Georges Van den Abbeele,

Travel as Metaphor: From Montaigne to Rousseau (Minneapolis: University of Minnesota Press, 1992), 12. Hassan Melehy, *Writing Cogito: Montaigne, Descartes, and the Institution of the Modern Subject* (Albany: State University of New York Press, 1997), 85, claims that "what the essay offers, as a critical instrument, is an attenuation of the forcefulness of reason; a certain form of reason will attempt to exclude from its procedures the madness to which the essay admits." Alain de Botton, *The Consolations of Philosophy* (New York: Vintage Books, 2001), 126–29, contrasts Montaigne with the conventional portraits of man that leave out much of what we are.

11. Montaigne's emphasis on the body is unusual in the philosophical tradition. Michaël Baraz, *L'être et la connaissance selon Montaigne* (Toulouse: Librairie José Corti, 1968), 195, claims that in discussing his kidney stones in "Of experience," Montaigne turns to the "lowest" in the traditional metaphysical hierarchy. O'Neill, *Essaying Montaigne*, 123, makes the inference to the epistemological conclusion: "Montaigne's humanism is essentially tied to man's condition as a living being, in whom reason and the senses are inseparable, and thereby impose a limit to the excesses of philosophy and Christianity alike." Frederick Kellermann, "Montaigne, Reader of Plato," *Comparative Literature* 8 (1956): 313, writes: "It is against Montaigne's whole conception of man to attempt to divide him into a higher, more spiritual element and a lower, material component." According to Sayce, *Critical*, Montaigne is brought before us "shamelessly" in the *Essays* (61). Montaigne scarcely figures among the philosophers because his thinking is contaminated by the pressure of sheer physical life (180–81). Coleman, *Montaigne's Essays*, 137, points to the earthy and unspiritual analogies that Montaigne uses. And Regosin, *Matter*, 204, paraphrases the last page of the *Essays*: the wise man judges all by the measure of his rump.

12. C. S. Lewis, *God in the Dock: Essays on Theology and Ethics*, ed. Walter Hooper (Grand Rapids, Mich.: William B. Eerdmans, 1970), 159, on the Resurrection: "Something perfectly new in the history of the Universe has happened."

13. T. W. Adorno, "The Essay as Form," *New German Critique* 32 (Spring 1984): 160. See also Fumaroli, review of Brague's *La sagesse du monde*, 9: Brague sees Montaigne as a protophenomenologist.

14. Herbert Luthy, "Montaigne, or the Art of Being Truthful," *Encounter* 1 (1953): 35: Montaigne brings together the conclusions of all philosophies "to display the range and possibility of human thought" and "mark out the borders of human awareness, with all its manifold possibilities."

15. Adorno, "Essay as Form," 163.

16. See Baraz, *L'être*, 128: Montaigne is within the great Hellenic and biblical tradition that assumes the identity of being and thought.

17. Clark, *Web of Metaphor*, 90–91: Montaigne is alone among sixteenth-century writers in using such words as *mol* and *lache* as terms of approbation. See also Michael G. Paulson, *The Possible Influence of Montaigne's Essais on Descartes' "Treatise on the Passions"* (Lanham, Md.: University Press of America, 1988), 50, 85.

18. See Sidney Lee, "Montaigne," in *The French Renaissance in England* (New York: Charles Scribner's Sons, 1910), 166–67: Montaigne's "want of premeditation" leads him to contradict himself.

19. Adorno, "Essay as Form," 166. Bruno Pinchard, "Montaigne: Essai de lecture dialectique," *Montaigne Studies* 12 (2000): 63–73, looks at the subjectivity of the Renaissance and of Montaigne in particular from a Hegelian perspective.
20. Friedrich, *Montaigne*, 239, claims that Montaigne practices his *vita contemplativa* "as something questionable." David Quint, *Montaigne and the Quality of Mercy: Ethical and Political Themes in the Essais* (Princeton, N.J.: Princeton University Press, 1998), 119, says that the *Essays* teach the trial, and especially the error, of human understanding.
21. Michael Oakeshott, *On Human Conduct* (Oxford: Oxford University Press, 1975; reprint, Oxford: Clarendon Press, 1991), vii.
22. Michael Oakeshott, *Religion, Politics and the Moral Life*, ed. Timothy Fuller (New Haven: Yale University Press, 1993), 138–39.
23. Gray, "Pyrrhonism," 124, interprets Montaigne's claim that he is an accidental philosopher to mean that he is the philosopher of the accidental. Marie-Luce Demonet, "Philosopher naturellement," *Montaigne Studies* 12 (2000): 24, says that Montaigne's philosophy is founded on the contingent.

Chapter 2: Bending and Stretching the Categories of Traditional Metaphysics

1. Craig B. Brush, "Reflections on Montaigne's Concept of Being," in *From Marot to Montaigne: Essays in French Renaissance Literature*, ed. Raymond C. La Charité, *Kentucky Romance Quarterly* 19 (1972): 152, notes that the end of the "Apology" is the only place where Montaigne "talks this kind of ontology" of being and becoming. Françoise Joukovsky, *Montaigne et le problème du temps* (Paris: Librairie A. G. Nizet, 1972), 168, claims that the mind forces itself to conceive an unchangeable order but cannot succeed in this.
2. Patrick Henry, "Montaigne and Heraclitus: Pattern and Flux, Continuity and Change in 'Du repentir,'" *Montaigne Studies* 4 (1992), concludes that Montaigne's *forme* is "not a transcendent form, but an individual's distinct, coherent ruling pattern, composed of natural inclinations and habits" – that is, "his own particular acquired stability" (17). Permanence cannot be entirely excluded from Heraclitus: there is a *measure* inherent in change (12–13). Baraz, *L'être*, 92, argues that Montaigne situates himself in the middle, between pure being and pure becoming. Jean Starobinski, *Montaigne in Motion*, trans. Arthur Goldhammer (Chicago: University of Chicago Press, 1985), 14, claims that Montaigne moves from a concept of identity based on principles of constancy, stability and self-consistency to a new concept of identity that does not abandon the original one but alters its content and meaning.
3. Regosin, *Matter*, 227, notes the opposition in Montaigne between philosophy and the way of nature. Alexandre Micha, *Le singulier Montaigne* (Paris: Librairie A. G. Nizet, 1964), 122, says that, for Montaigne, nature is the given and art is the acquired. Brody, *Lectures*, 118, points out that, at the end of "That to philosophize is to learn to die," Montaigne's praise of the learned ignorance of the common people is one of the things signified by the concept "nature." Desan, *Naissance*, 132, discusses Montaigne's interest in the cannibals as his way of discovering man before Aristotle.
4. Joukovsky, *Le problème du temps*, 153, finds evidence in Book II that Montaigne rejects the notion of natural law. Maclean, *Montaigne philosophe*, 69, claims

that, for Montaigne, nature escapes traditional philosophy because traditional philosophy does not allow for nature's dissonances and disorders. Montaigne, on the other hand, does not avoid contradictory, incoherent, plural, and partial uses of the term.

5. Aquinas, *Summa Theologica*. 1.2 q.94 a.4.
6. Ibid., a.6.
7. Blaise Pascal, "Entretien avec M. De Sacy," in *Œuvres complètes*, ed. Jean Mesnard (Paris: Desclée de Brouwer, [c. 1991]), 3:152.
8. See Alan M. Boase, *The Fortunes of Montaigne: A History of the Essays in France, 1580–1669* (London: Methuen, 1935), 363–64. Adorno says of the essay form: "It does not concern itself with any supposed primeval condition in order to contravene society's false sociality." Adorno, "Essay as Form," 159. Jesse V. Mauzey, *Montaigne's Philosophy of Human Nature* (Annandale-on-Hudson, N.Y.: St. Stephen's College, 1933), claims that Montaigne is concerned only with this existence: "[L]egends of Eden provide no vantage point for the survey of human affairs" (46–47). Faye, *Philosophie et perfection de l'homme*, 166–67: Sebond claims that there are two "sciences of man," one of perfect man and the other of man after the Fall. Montaigne modifies this in his translation. Faye argues that "jamais Montaigne n'évoque un état antérieur, jamais il ne distingue deux états de l'homme. En ce sens, Montaigne a 'naturalisé' le thème de la misère" (191–92).
9. The difficulty and even the impossibility of maintaining a clear and consistent distinction between nature and custom in the *Essays* has been remarked by many interpreters, for example, Ian Maclean, "'Le païs au delà': Montaigne and Philosophical Speculation," in *Montaigne: Essays in Memory of Richard Sayce*, ed. I. D. McFarlane and Ian Maclean (Oxford: Clarendon Press, 1982), 112; Jean-Yves Pouilloux, *Montaigne, l'éveil de la pensée* (Paris: Editions Champion, 1995), 175; David Lewis Schaefer, *The Political Philosophy of Montaigne* (Ithaca: Cornell University Press, 1990), 63, 123; Neal Dow, "The Concept and Term 'Nature' in Montaigne's Essays" (Ph.D. diss., University of Pennsylvania, 1940), viii; Adorno, "Essay as Form," 168, says that "under the glance of the essay, second nature becomes conscious of itself as first nature." See André Tournon, "L'humaine condition: Que sais-je? Qui suis-je?" and Jean-Yves Pouilloux, "La forme maîtresse," in *Montaigne et la question de l'homme*, ed. Marie-Luce Demonet (Paris: Presses Universitaires de France, 1999), 16–17 and 34–35, on Montaigne's substitution of "humaine condition" for generic notions such as "human nature." In his *Montaigne: La glose et l'essai* (Lyon: Presses Universitaires de Lyon, 1983), 273, Tournon explains that the term "human condition" is a juridical rather than a metaphysical term. Montaigne is not speaking of essence or nature but rather of extrinsic determinations. I would suggest that "human condition" is a kind of metaphysical term in Montaigne since it is the result of his engagement with traditional metaphysical categories.
10. John O'Brien, "The Eye Perplexed: Aristotle and Montaigne on Seeing and Choosing," *Journal of Medieval and Renaissance Studies* 22 (1992): 298–99: Montaigne disagrees with Aristotle that we can arrive at first causes. See also Ruth M. Calder, "Montaigne, *Des boyteux* and the Question of Causality," *Bibliothèque d'humanisme et renaissance* 45, no. 3 (1983): 445–60, especially 454.

11. See Marianne S. Meijer, "Guesswork or Facts: Connections between Montaigne's Last Three Chapters (III:11, 12 and 13)," *Yale French Studies* 64 (1983): 178. See also Maclean, *Montaigne philosophe:* Montaigne breaks the link between rationality and truth and attaches rationality to opinion (74).

12. Micha, *Le singulier*, 226, refers to the *Essays* as a "book of imperfection."

13. Villey, *Les sources et l'évolution des Essais de Montaigne*, estimates that Aristotle's name occurs in the *Essays* only about fifty times and speculates that Montaigne may not have known all of his works directly (1:69). Screech, *Melancholy*, 76, is critical of Villey for dismissing the influence of Aristotle on Montaigne. See also Gérard Defaux, *Marot, Rabelais, Montaigne: L'écriture comme présence* (Paris: Champion-Slatkine, 1987), 185: Montaigne uses the Aristotelian term *forme* very often in Book III.

14. Screech, *Melancholy*, 104, refers to Montaigne's "quiet revolution" – his interpreting Aristotle's *Metaphysics* so as to "turn long-established notions on their heads," for example, the commonplace concerning individuation within species. Desan, *Naissance*, 135, claims that Montaigne does not seek the laws that explain man but, rather, what is singular and extraordinary in each. Conche, *Montaigne et la philosophie*, 22, sees nature as a differentiating and singularizing principle in Montaigne. Graham Good, *The Observing Self: Rediscovering the Essay* (London: Routledge, 1988), 23: the essay records the particulars of experience accurately as particulars.

15. See Raymond C. La Charité, *The Concept of Judgment in Montaigne* (The Hague: Martinus Nijhoff, 1968), and Jean Chateau, *Montaigne psychologue et pédagogue* (Paris: Librairie Philosophique J. Vrin, 1971), 57 and 274, on the absence of concern with essences in Montaigne.

16. Conche, *Montaigne et la philosophie*, holds that Montaigne is a nominalist. He attributes Montaigne's move away from universals to the idea that universals are ideals; for example, the significance of the question "What is man?" is to discover "un idéal de l'homme" (41). Good, *Observing Self*, 8: Montaigne's personality is offered as a "universal particular." Clark, *Web of Metaphor*, suggests a way in which Montaigne's rejection of universals may be tied to his use of images: images have some power to reveal relations between things, but the patterns disclosed are fragmentary and arbitrary (78–79). Antoine Compagnon, *Nous, Michel de Montaigne* (Paris: Éditions du Seuil, 1980), attempts to reconcile Montaigne's nominalism with his claim to universality through a dialectic of the "je" and "mon estre universel" (especially 12, 22, 32, 143). See also Compagnon's "On ne peut rien dire de si absurde qui n'ait été dit par quelque philosophe," in *Columbia Montaigne Conference Papers*, ed. Donald M. Frame and Mary B. McKinley (Lexington, Ky.: French Forum Publishers, 1981), 47–59.

17. Friedrich, *Montaigne*, calls Montaigne "the philosopher of ambiguity," and says that his aversion to fixing the meaning of terms by definitions is striking (362–63). Ian Maclean, "The Place of Interpretation: Montaigne and Humanist Jurists on Words, Intention and Meaning," in *Neo-Latin and the Vernacular in Renaissance France*, ed. Graham Castor and Terence Cave (Oxford: Clarendon Press, 1984), notes Montaigne's dislike of definitions and attributes it to his belief that definitions are unnecessary (258); in "Philosophical Speculation," he says that Montaigne must use the traditional metaphysical terminology but

he attempts to go beyond it (130). Richard L. Regosin, "Language and the Dialectic of the Self in Montaigne's *Essais*," in *From Marot to Montaigne: Essays in French Renaissance Literature*, ed. Raymond C. La Charité, *Kentucky Romance Quarterly* 19 (1972), claims that, for Montaigne, "language does not communicate truth unequivocally but allows ambiguity and shifting meaning" (169). Pouilloux, *L'éveil de la pensée*, refers to Montaigne's "omnipresent critique" of philosophy. Montaigne denies the possibility of knowledge in the terms of earlier philosophy (67–68). See also Yvonne B. Rollins, "Montaigne et le langage," *Romanic Review* 64 (1973): Montaigne is critical of reform of language and holds to the common discourse (267–69). Clark, *Web of Metaphor*, 86: for Montaigne, "the human soul is not the province of specialist study, but 'un sujet qui nous est familier et connu.' ... Thus while he uses vocabulary drawn from the traditional psychology, it is without any regard for rigor." With respect to specific terms, we see how difficult it is to determine a precise meaning such as we would want for a technical term. La Charité, *Concept of Judgment*, provides an exhaustive analysis of Montaigne's use of the term "judgment," an analysis that shows that it is impossible to distinguish its meaning clearly. See especially 97, 110, 112, 118, 139–40. S. John Holyoake, "The Idea of 'Jugement' in Montaigne," *Modern Language Review* 63 (1968): 340–51, also shows how difficult it is to define this term. Linton C. Stevens, "The Meaning of 'Philosophie' in the *Essais* of Montaigne," *Studies in Philology* 62 (1965), concludes that the term *philosophie* in the *Essays* is ambiguous: "His polysemantic usage comprised most of the important meanings which the concept had inherited from pre-Christian and hellenistic writings" (147).

Chapter 3: The Essay as Philosophical Form

1. Georges Duby, *The Age of Cathedrals: Art and Society, 980–1420*, trans. Eleanor Levieux and Barbara Thompson (Chicago: University of Chicago Press, 1981), 100–4.
2. Jules Brody, "From Teeth to Text in *De l'expérience*: A Philological Reading," *L'Esprit Créateur* 20 (1980): 20. See Harold Bloom, *The Western Canon: The Books and School of the Ages* (New York: Riverhead Books, 1994), 138, 142, on Montaigne's originality. See also Pouilloux, *L'éveil de la pensée*, 75, 137; and Léon Brunschvicg, *Descartes et Pascal, lecteurs de Montaigne* (New York: Brentano's, 1944), 20, on the essay as a new genre.
3. These three characterizations are given in Erich Auerbach "L'humaine condition," in *Mimesis: The Representation of Reality in Western Literature*, trans. Willard R. Trask (Princeton, N.J.: Princeton University Press, 1953), 292; Joseph Epstein, "Reading Montaigne," *Commentary* 95 (March 1993): 36, and Conche, *Montaigne et la philosophie*, 39. Other discussions of Montaigne's title reveal a wide range of meaning that includes the connotation of temptation. Andreas Blinkenberg, "Quel sens Montaigne a-t-il voulu donner au mot *Essais* dans le titre de son œuvre?" in *Mélanges de linguistique et de littérature romanes, offerts à Mario Roques* (Geneva: Slatkine Reprints, 1974), 1:12, claims that Montaigne chose as his title a word that is imprecise and large enough to contain latent meanings. Among its possible meanings are: *mise à l'épreuve*, and trial, conveying a sense of danger

(4, 5, 9). E. V. Telle, "A propos du mot 'essai' chez Montaigne," *Bibliothèque d'humanisme et renaissance* 30 (1968), also specifies the meaning of essay as test (229). In Latin, he says, *essai* is *periculum*, that is, danger (231). Friedrich, *Montaigne*, 340–41: Montaigne reserves the term *essai* for a method of thinking. Among the meanings of *essai* in the sixteenth century are: practice, attempt, and temptation. Also *essaier* can mean "lead into temptation." Frame, *Discovery*, 82: essays are "trials or tests." See also Donald M. Frame, *Montaigne's Essais: A Study* (Englewood Cliffs, N.J.: Prentice Hall, 1969), 34. Sayce, *Critical*, 21–22: *essais* are "experiences," soundings into the mind and its workings. *Essai* also has the sense of trial or testing. See also Alan M. Boase, "The Early History of the *Essai* Title in France and Britain," in *Studies in French Literature, Presented to H. W. Lawton*, ed. J. C. Ireson, I. D. McFarlane, and Garnet Rees (New York: Manchester University Press, Barnes and Noble, 1968), especially 69, 71. Joseph Epstein, "The Personal Essay: A Form of Discovery," in *The Norton Book of Personal Essays*, ed. Joseph Epstein (New York: W. W. Norton, 1997), 15, describes the personal essay as a "form of discovery": one starts out with something one does not understand, without a precise definition; then one discovers where one stands and learns what one really thinks. Georg Lukacs, *Soul and Form*, trans. Anna Bostock (Cambridge, Mass.: MIT Press, 1974), 9, writes of the title *Essays* that "the simple modesty of this word is an arrogant courtesy. The essayist dismisses his own proud hopes which sometimes lead him to believe that he has come close to the ultimate. . . . But he ironically adapts himself to this smallness – the eternal smallness of the most profound work of the intellect in face of life – and even emphasizes it with ironic modesty."

4. Oakeshott, *On Human Conduct*, vii. It is true that Oakeshott's practice of the essay form is rather different from Montaigne's. The same could be said of Bacon and Hume. However, these differences only point up the way in which the form allows for originality while preserving its essential orientation toward truth.

5. Maurice Merleau-Ponty, "Reading Montaigne," in *Signs*, trans. Richard C. McCleary (Evanston, Ill.: Northwestern University Press, 1964), 206. See Jules Brody, "'Du repentir' (III:2): A Philological Reading," *Yale French Studies* 64 (1983): 252, on the philological circularity of Montaigne's writing. R. Lane Kauffmann, "The Skewed Path: Essaying as Un-methodical Method," *Diogenes* 143 (Fall 1988): 90, says that in the essay the familiar is regarded as unknown. He also describes the essay as a "critique of instrumental reason" (72).

6. Blaise Pascal, *Pensées et opuscules*, ed. Léon Brunschvicg, rev. ed. (Paris: Librairie Hachette, 1946), no. 64.

7. Michael O'Loughlin, *The Garlands of Repose: The Literary Celebration of Civic and Retired Leisure* (Chicago: University of Chicago Press, 1978), 255–56, writes with respect to this essay that "the peril of retirement is idleness and idleness is the restless incapacity for leisure." He claims that the writing of the essays transforms idleness into leisure in a problematic and distinctively modern way. The "new leisure" is "the feast without gods with its own reason for being."

8. Virginia Woolf, "Montaigne," in *The Common Reader* (New York: Harcourt, Brace, 1925), 98. She also says that the attempt to paint oneself with the pen "is a matter of profound, mysterious, and overwhelming difficulty." Donald M. Frame, "Specific Motivation for Montaigne's Self-Portrait," in *Columbia Montaigne Conference Papers*, ed. Donald M. Frame and Mary B. McKinley (Lexington,

Ky.: French Forum Publishers, 1981), 61, sees Montaigne's need for truth
and communication as his general motivation for his self-portrait. Also see
Marie-Luce Demonet, "Les propres de l'homme chez Montaigne et Charron,"
in *Montaigne et la question de l'homme*, ed. Marie-Luce Demonet (Paris: Presses
Universitaires de France, 1999), 64.

9. Yves Delègue, *Montaigne et la mauvaise foi: L'écriture de la vérité* (Paris: Honoré
   Champion, 1998), 32.

10. Ibid., 137.

11. H. V. Routh, "The Origins of the Essay Compared in French and English Litera-
    tures," parts 1 and 2, *Modern Language Review* 15 (1920), claims that Montaigne's
    purpose is the reform of the schools (36). That is consistent with my interpre-
    tation of his purpose.

12. Oakeshott, *On Human Conduct*, vii.

13. François Rigolot, "Montaigne's Purloined Letters," *Yale French Studies* 64 (1983):
    145–66, claims that the essays try to approximate as closely as possible the
    idealized epistolary style.

14. David Hume, *Essays: Moral, Political, and Literary*, ed. Eugene F. Miller
    (Indianapolis: Liberty Classics, 1985), 534.

15. Pascal, *Pensées*, Br. no. 18.

16. Auerbach, "L'humaine condition," 308.

17. Michael Oakeshott, *Rationalism in Politics and Other Essays*, ed. Timothy Fuller
    (London: Methuen, 1962; reprint, Indianapolis: Liberty Press, 1991), 491.
    Montaigne's relation to his education and to cultural traditions is often seen
    as a kind of respectful but innovative engagement. Friedrich, *Montaigne*, 38:
    "[O]nly in the incorporation of what is foreign into what is one's own does
    knowledge by memory...ripen into education." Sayce, *Critical*, 28, points to
    Montaigne as an example of the real purpose of books, that is, the enhance-
    ment and enlargement of experience. Dudley M. Marchi, *Montaigne among the
    Moderns: Receptions of the Essais* (Providence, R.I.: Berghahn Books, 1994), 280,
    notes the fact that Montaigne had a library of more than one thousand printed
    volumes. "Montaigne would have perhaps understood Eliot's desperate claim
    in 'The Waste Land' that our inability to live in an organic relationship with
    our cultural traditions can only lead to an imperfect ordering of its contents,
    one that nevertheless helps to avoid psychic disintegration: 'These fragments I
    have shored against my ruin.'" According to Boase, *Fortunes*, 365, Pascal refers
    to Montaigne as "the incomparable author of the Art of Conversation." For
    Starobinski, *Motion*, 12, Montaigne's "turning inward" has as its purpose "the
    discovery of a conversational mirror within oneself." Floyd Gray, *Le style de
    Montaigne* (Paris: Librairie A. G. Nizet, 1958), 244, sees the *Essays* as a perpetual
    dialogue between Montaigne and himself, Montaigne and his book, Montaigne
    and antiquity. Henry, *Montaigne in Dialogue*, 120, suggests that Montaigne intro-
    duces opposing voices from the ancients.

18. Montaigne's relation to his education and to cultural traditions can also be
    seen in the role of quotation in the essays. His practice of quotation leads us
    to ask where his authentic self is located, how it is discovered, and how it is
    expressed. Terence Cave, "Problems of Reading in the *Essais*," in *Montaigne:
    Essays in Memory of Richard Sayce*, ed. I. D. McFarlane and Ian Maclean (Oxford:
    Clarendon Press, 1982), 144, notes that there are approximately thirteen

hundred quotations proper in the *Essays*. But the borderline between proper quotations (the "least digested elements of his discourse") and other forms of borrowing is often quite arbitrary. There is a spectrum from quotation to paraphrase to distant echo, and this is a deliberate strategy on Montaigne's part. Cave also remarks on the fact that Montaigne omits the authors' names in his quotations, an omission that is against the sixteenth-century practice. Gérard Defaux, "Readings of Montaigne," trans. John A. Gallucci, *Yale French Studies* 64 (1983): 91, refers to the *Essays* as a text of many voices and levels. There is a danger of "the confusion of the voices and levels of discourse" in reading the *Essays* because not all of the discourses belong to Montaigne in the same way or to the same degree. This is related to my claim that the stance that Montaigne takes toward levels of discourse reveals his awareness of something like the problem of mediation and the difficulty of locating his own authentic voice. André Tournon, "Self-Interpretation in Montaigne's *Essais*," *Yale French Studies* 64 (1983): 55–56, refers to the quotation marks that belong around the maxims. Donald M. Frame, "Montaigne and the Problem of Consistency," *Kentucky Romance Quarterly* 21, supp. 2 (1974): 160, says that Montaigne often moves from monologue to dialogue with a "they" to which he is responding. Michael Platt, "Interpretation," *Interpretation: A Journal of Political Philosophy* 5 (1975): 114, describes the essay as one half of a dialogue. Good, *Observing Self*, 1, says that "quotation becomes a way of bringing a new voice into the conversation, rather than of providing authoritative support." Further, "quoting in the essay introduces an element of dialogue" (6). Berel Lang, "Plotting Philosophy: Between the Acts of Philosophical Genre," *Philosophy and Literature* 12 (1988): 207, argues that the genre of dialogue presupposes other minds.

19. Chateau, *Montaigne psychologue*, 84, compares Montaigne's practice of quotation with that of the pedant for whom the perspective of others is a constraint. Philippe Desan, *Les commerces de Montaigne: Le discours économique des Essais* (Paris: Librairie A. G. Nizet, 1992), 143, claims that Montaigne's attitude to quotation is radically different from the erudite humanist at the beginning of the Renaissance.

20. Robert Sokolowski, *Pictures, Quotations, and Distinctions: Fourteen Essays in Phenomenology* (Notre Dame, Ind.: University of Notre Dame Press, 1992), 32.

21. Ibid., 41. The way in which Montaigne quotes raises the questions of his relation to the tradition and of the nature of his originality. Timothy Hampton, *Writing from History: The Rhetoric of Exemplarity in Renaissance Literature* (Ithaca: Cornell University Press, 1990), 148 and 150, claims that Montaigne's attitude toward models opens up a space in which he can assert his autonomy and authority. Leno Pertile, "Paper and Ink: The Structure of Unpredictability," in *O un amy! Essays on Montaigne in Honor of Donald M. Frame*, ed. Raymond C. La Charité (Lexington, Ky.: French Forum Publishers, 1977), 198: in contrast to the conventional practice of quoting to support one's views with authority, Montaigne's practice is a questioning of all authority. Pertile also sees Montaigne's break with tradition in not naming his sources as a dissolution of authority through anonymity (203). Melehy, *Writing Cogito*, 70, claims that the works of Virgil, Lucretius, Plutarch, et al. find their way into Montaigne's text "but in a manner that transforms their canonical status." Montaigne's "engagement with the books is a disengagement from their authority." Gisèle Mathieu-Castellani,

Montaigne: L'écriture de l'essai (Paris: Presses Universitaires de France, 1988), 78–82, claims that Montaigne "re-writes" Plutarch and redefines "la Vie" in his appropriation of Plutarch. Brody, *Lectures*, 23, says that Montaigne's first readers would have seen his genius in the radical attitude he takes toward his sources. Desan, *Naissance*, 120, argues that, in order to take his own position, Montaigne must situate himself in relation to the ancients. Claude Blum, "La function du 'déjà dit' dans les 'Essais': Emprunter, alléguer, citer," *Cahiers de l'Association Internationale des Etudes Françaises* 33 (1981): 50, sees the *Essays* as one of the places of transformation from the authoritative tradition to the autonomy of the subject. However, Blum says that Montaigne does accept the divine authority of Scripture (44–45). Maclean, *Montaigne philosophe*, 91, makes the point that Montaigne's practice of quotation makes the quoted author present in his contingency. Francis Goyet, "Tragi-comédie de la certitude: L'argument d'autorité dans les *Essais*," *Bulletin de la Société des Amis de Montaigne* 21–22 (1985): 31, 37, 41, argues convincingly that Montaigne's submission to authority allows the movement of his thought to happen. The essays are a quest for the unexpected, but one cannot hear or see the new except through the old.

22. Sokolowski, *Pictures*, 48. Also see Stephen Toulmin, *Cosmopolis: The Hidden Agenda of Modernity* (New York: Free Press, 1990): Montaigne rejects "in advance the conclusions that Descartes argued for in general, abstract terms in the *Meditations*" (37), and unlike Descartes, Montaigne did not think that he was "locked into his brain" (42).

23. Discussions of Montaigne's engagement with history have focused on the access that history gives him to possibility and to particularity. Steven Rendall, "Of History," *Montaigne Studies* 6, nos. 1–2 (October 1994): 4, claims that the specific role of the historian is "to expand the scope of the possible." Emmanuelle Baillon, "Une critique du jugement," in *Montaigne philosophe*, ed. André Comte-Sponville, *Révue Internationale de Philosophie* 46, no. 181 (1992): 147–49, argues that Montaigne's use of history is on account of its particularity. Cathleen M. Bauschatz, "Montaigne's Conception of Reading in the Context of Renaissance Poetics and Modern Criticism," in *The Reader in the Text*, ed. Susan R. Suleiman and Inge Crosman (Princeton, N.J.: Princeton University Press, 1980), 278: reading history is a kind of experience. Pouilloux, *L'éveil de la pensée*, 133: Montaigne's examples are held not as real but as possible. Starobinski, *Motion*, 18: "exempla point to a world composed of unique, dissimilar entities." Graham Good, "Identity and Form in the Modern Autobiographical Essay," *Prose Studies* 15 (1992): 102, notes that the essay stays close to the particular. Concerning Montaigne's stories in relation to possibility, see also Karl-Heinz Stierle, "Story as Exemplum – Exemplum as Story: On the Pragmatics and Poetics of Narrative Texts," in *New Perspectives in German Literary Criticism*, ed. Richard E. Amacher and Victor Lange (Princeton, N.J.: Princeton University Press, 1979), 409. Alexander Nehamas, *The Art of Living: Socratic Reflections from Plato to Foucault* (Berkeley: University of California Press, 1998), 127, discusses the way in which examples function within "the individualist strain of the art of living." To follow an example is to try to be different from it; "it is to try to realize a new and different possibility." Frank Lestrigant, "Montaigne et la laïcisation de l'histoire: L'exemple du nouveau monde," in *Montaigne et la révolution philosophique du XVI siècle*, ed. Jacques Lemaire (Brussels: Editions de l'Université

de Bruxelles, 1992), 45: Montaigne breaks with a providential conception of history.

24. See Gray, *Le style*, 244: each time Montaigne takes a story from Plutarch, he gives it a form superior to the original. He rarely translates; he adapts and transforms. Randolph Runyon, "Trumpet Variations on an Original Air: Self-Referential Allusion in Montaigne's 'Apology,'" *Romanic Review* 77 (1986): 195–208, discusses the animal stories in the "Apology" and notes that Montaigne adds details that are not found in Plutarch.

25. On the story of Rasias, see O'Loughlin, *Garlands of Repose*, 249. On the cannibal's song, see Quint, *Quality of Mercy*, 84. Michael Wood, "Montaigne and the Mirror of Example," *Philosophy and Literature* 13 (1989): 5, cites the change Montaigne makes in the story about the man from Delos.

26. See Quint, *Quality of Mercy*, 40. Victor Davis Hanson, *The Soul of Battle: From Ancient Times to the Present Day, How Three Great Liberators Vanquished Tyranny* (New York: Free Press, 1999), presents a portrait of the character of Epaminondas which is very similar to Montaigne's portrait of him (see especially 53–59) but also claims that Epaminondas would have preferred to destroy the Spartan survivors of the battle of Leuctra but was persuaded to delay (33, 60, 76). See Marcel Gutwirth, "'By Diverse Means...' (I:1)," *Yale French Studies* 64 (1983): 182, 186. Nehamas, *Art of Living*, 122, claims that, in some sense, Montaigne invented Socrates: "Montaigne finds himself by recreating Socrates."

27. Patrick Henry, "The Rise of the Essay: Montaigne and the Novel," *Montaigne Studies* 6, nos. 1–2 (1994), 124–25: the *Essais* are neither history nor fiction but share attributes of both. Glyn P. Norton, *Montaigne and the Introspective Mind* (The Hague: Mouton, 1975), 201, points to a "curious fusion of literary and non-literary realities" in the *Essays*. See Kellermann, "Reader of Plato," 311, on Montaigne's *furor poeticus*. Also see Manfred Frank, "Toward a Philosophy of Style," *Common Knowledge* 1, no. 1 (1991): 67–68, on the relation of poetry and philosophy. Owen Barfield, *Poetic Diction: A Study in Meaning* (London: Faber and Faber, 1928), discusses the ways in which the poetic involves a change in our consciousness; see especially 48–49, 55, 112, 120, 131, 142. François Rigolot, *Les métamorphoses de Montaigne* (Paris: Presses Universitaires de France, 1988), 11, claims that Montaigne transforms disciplines such as history, politics, and moral philosophy when he writes about them. Rigolot refers to this as "la poétique des *Essais*." I agree that Montaigne transforms what he discusses from various disciplines, but I claim that he transforms them into philosophy.

28. On the necessity of Montaigne's disorder, see Pouilloux, *L'éveil de la pensée*, especially 53, 56, 96; Jules Brody, "Les oreilles de Montaigne," *Romanic Review* 74 (1983): 124; Margaret McGowan, "The Art of Transition in the *Essais*," in *Montaigne: Essays in Memory of Richard Sayce*, ed. I. D. McFarlane and Ian Maclean (Oxford: Clarendon Press, 1982), 37.

29. See Marianne S. Meijer, "De l'honnête, de l'utile et du repentir," *Journal of Medieval and Renaissance Studies* 12, no. 2 (1982): 259–74, for a discussion of the unity of essays III.1, 2, and 3.

30. Pascal, *Pensées*, Br. no. 62.

31. Edouard Ruel, *Du sentiment artistique dans la morale de Montaigne* (Paris: Librairie Hachette, 1901), 38, contrasts Montaigne's poetic order with scientific order. Whereas Descartes seeks the truth in philosophy, Montaigne "dreams about it

as an artist" (233). The artistic principle for Ruel is: only life is able to know life (89). I agree that Montaigne's order is poetic, but I argue that poetry is taken up into philosophy. Gray, *Le style*, refers to Montaigne's "interior order" (206); he places himself at the interior of a poetic or philosophic image (210–11). Richard M. Chadbourne, "Michel de Montaigne," in *Encyclopedia of the Essay*, ed. Tracy Chevalier, (London: Fitzroy Dearborn Publishers, 1997), 570, claims that Montaigne "intended his own prose to be moved by a similar 'demon' [to Plato's]." Desan, *Naissance*, 127, also refers to Montaigne's "internal order." Montaigne's method is "une pratique du quotidien," and the "everyday" has a logic that is not obvious.

32. Here we see something of the relation between daemonic order and the challenge of the necessity of mediation. Those who have commented on the order of the essays have sensed the interplay of spontaneity and opaqueness. With respect to spontaneity, Richard L. Regosin, "Sources and Resources: The 'Pretexts' of Originality in Montaigne's *Essais*," *Sub-Stance* 21 (1978), 110, claims that the *Essays* "undermine notions of external origin." For Lukacs, *Soul and Form*, 11: "[T]he essay has to create from within itself all the preconditions for the effectiveness and validity of its vision." O. B. Hardison, "Binding Proteus: An Essay on the Essay," in *Essays on the Essay: Redefining the Genre*, ed. Alexander J. Butrym (Athens: University of Georgia Press, 1989), 26, characterizes the essay as "thought thinking about itself." Lanson, *Les Essais*, 316–17, also notes the spontaneity of the form. Montaigne rejects the modes of composition of the philosophers of his time, that is, a logical order with its path traced out in advance. He abandons himself to the natural course of thought, which follows the detours of spontaneous association of ideas. Gray, *Le style*, 188, contrasts the immobile with the dynamic way of composition. The immobile way is a plan, ruled in advance by reason. That is an "exterior order." Montaigne's way is dynamic, that is, the images that come to mind modify the flow of thought. Caroline Locher, "Primary and Secondary Themes in Montaigne's 'Des cannibales' (I, 31)," *French Forum* 1 (1976): 120, claims that "Des cannibales" is really "an inquiry into the nature and power of reason." But this spontaneity does not amount to the transparency of the self to itself. Peter Burke, *Montaigne* (Oxford: Oxford University Press, 1981), 62, refers to "the author's attempt to catch himself in the act of thinking." Sayce, *Critical*, 104, describes the order of the essays as the order of "spontaneous thought." But what emerges is a sense of mystery, a "labyrinth" (322–23).

33. Merleau-Ponty, "Reading Montaigne," 200.

34. Frame, *Montaigne's Essais*, 73: "No methodical order could probe the self without distorting it." Carol E. Clark, "Talking about Souls: Montaigne on Human Psychology," in *Montaigne: Essays in Memory of Richard Sayce*, ed. I. D. McFarlane and Ian Maclean (Oxford: Clarendon Press, 1982), 65, says that to know oneself, one has to catch oneself unawares. Henry E. Genz, "Compositional Form in Montaigne's *Essais* and the Self-Portrait," *Kentucky Foreign Language Quarterly* 10 (1963): 135, refers to Montaigne's self-portrait as "oblique," because Montaigne is aware of the limitations of a direct approach. "An indirect view may . . . cast light on those areas of the mind inevitably darkened by the shadow of the mind turning back upon itself." S. John Holyoake, "Montaigne's Attitude to Memory," *French Studies* 25 (1971): 269, notes Montaigne's "awareness that a

chance occurrence, an unexpected detail, an apparently irrelevant digression, might involuntarily lead him to a valuable discovery about himself." Epstein, "Reading Montaigne," 36, says that Montaigne finds himself by accident.

35.   The distinctions between the essay form and the syllogism and the treatise are discussed by Maclean, "Philosophical Speculation," 104: the order of shopboys and shepherds is being contrasted by Montaigne with the syllogism. Montaigne's "particular target" is Aristotle (102). Tzvetan Todorov, "L'être et l'autre: Montaigne," *Yale French Studies* 64 (1983): 142–43: the essay is the genre opposed to the treatise. Moore, "Montaigne's Notion," 49–50, contrasts the artistic plan of the essay with a rational, logical, straight-line progression. The essay form, in contrast to more rigid forms, allows a role to the accidental. See Michael L. Hall, "The Emergence of the Essay and the Idea of Discovery," in *Essays on the Essay: Redefining the Genre*, ed. Alexander J. Butrym (Athens: University of Georgia Press, 1989), 80. John C. Lapp, "Montaigne's 'Negligence' and Some Lines from Virgil," *Romanic Review* 61 (1970): 170, claims that the spontaneity and nonchalance of the essay allow for the role of chance and the impromptu.

Chapter 4: The Circular Dialectic of Self-Knowledge

1.   That there is indeed a dialectical dimension to the *Essays* or to individual essays has been noted by many commentators, although the nature of the dialectic has not received systematic treatment. Daniel Russell, "On Montaigne's Device," *Studi Francesi* 55 (1975): 86, claims that Montaigne's choice of the scales and motto is meant to portray the liberal art of dialectic. Kellermann, "Reader of Plato," 320, says that the essay is "the modern form of Platonic dialectic." Frederick Rider, *The Dialectic of Selfhood in Montaigne* (Stanford, Calif.: Stanford University Press, 1973), sees a kind of dialectic in the essays, but he regards it as unconscious (56, 64). Many who recognize a dialectical movement see it in terms of resolution of contradiction or reversal of opposites. Steven Rendall, "Dialectical Structure and Tactics in Montaigne's 'Of Cannibals,'" *Pacific Coast Philology* 12 (1977): 59, claims that "Montaigne's inversion of the usual oratorical structure makes the reader a participant in a dialectic rather than a passive witness to a demonstration." Rendall's interpretation of "Of cannibals" shows that the reader is led "through a dialectical experience in the course of which he entertains by turns several attitudes, each supplanting the earlier ones and leaving him at the end with an opinion precisely the reverse of that with which he started" (56). Richard L. Regosin, "Figures of the Self: Montaigne's Rhetoric of Portraiture," *L'Esprit Créateur* 20 (1980): 78, says that Montaigne records "the perpetual movement of thought towards its own negation, that is, its movement back to itself." Commenting on "Of experience," Jean Starobinski, "The Body's Moment," trans. John A. Gallucci, *Yale French Studies* 64 (1983): 303, writes that this essay ends in "the alliance of opposites [body and soul]" and a "striking example of contradiction overcome." See also 85, 87. Barry Weller, "The Rhetoric of Friendship in Montaigne's *Essais*," *New Literary History* 9 (1978): 519, refers to the continuous synthesis of apparently conflicting positions" in the *Essays*. Michael L. Hall, "'Drawing Myself for Others': The *Ethos* of the Essayist,"

Explorations in Renaissance Culture 7 (1981): 30, says that one quality of the essay is the subversion of received opinion and of the deductive process. When Friedrich, *Montaigne*, 2, claims that "the *Essais* are essentially an inner dialogue," he means that, for Montaigne, "there is an essential, inherent contradictoriness of the intellect" (125) and that "the intellect has become more interesting to itself than all the materials that start it in motion" (6).

2. Jan Miernowski, *L'ontologie de la contradiction sceptique: Pour l'étude de la métaphysique des Essais* (Paris: Honoré Champion, 1998), 79–81, discusses "Of vain subtleties" in terms of the character of the "middle region." He asks whether the median position is that of a judgment in equilibrium and concludes that it is not. My interpretation differs from Miernowski's in part because I distinguish, within that middle region, two types: those who remain in error and those who reach the "extreme limit of Christian intelligence."

3. See Quint, *Quality of Mercy*, 17.

4. See McGowan, "Art of Transition," 45. See Joseph J. Carpino, "Tractatus Liquorico – Philosophicus," *Interpretation: A Journal of Political Philosophy* 26, no. 3 (1999): 379–89.

5. See Gérard Defaux, "De I.20 ('Que philosopher c'est apprendre à mourir') à III.12 ('De la phisionomie'): Ecriture et *essai* chez Montaigne," in *Montaigne et les Essais 1588–1988*, ed. Claude Blum (Paris: Champion, 1990), 93–118. Defaux provides an account of how the "vulgar method" that seemed to be rejected in I.20 seems entirely reasonable in III.12. This could only happen through the premeditation of the essay itself. I am in agreement with Defaux on this point, but I interpret the essay as dialectical.

6. Sextus Empiricus, *Outlines of Pyrrhonism*, in *Hellenistic Philosophy*, ed. Herman Shapiro and Edwin M. Curley (New York: Modern Library, 1965), 159.

7. Ibid., 163–64.

8. Ibid., 163.

9. Ibid., 213.

10. Hume, *Enquiry*, 111.

11. Ibid., 112.

12. Donald W. Livingston, *Hume's Philosophy of Common Life* (Chicago: University of Chicago Press, 1984), 3. See especially chap. 2, "Hume as Dialectical Thinker." Also see Livingston's *Philosophical Melancholy and Delirium: Hume's Pathology of Philosophy* (Chicago: University of Chicago Press, 1998).

13. Presumption involves a failure to recognize one's ignorance and an assumption of the certitude of one's opinions. Pouilloux, *L'éveil de la pensée*, 155: belief is nothing but an ignorance unknown or denied. To think is to interrogate this belief in order to recognize it as ignorance. Starobinski, *Motion*, 80: Montaigne reproaches language for its "presumption of being." Lanson, *Les Essais*, 266: Montaigne must try to get out of all the bad habits of mind that have led humanity astray, for example, precipitate judgment and credulity (271). Lewis, *God in the Dock*, 198, writes of that temptation which none of us can escape, "the temptation of claiming for our favorite opinions that kind and degree of certainty and authority which really belongs only to our Faith." The fact that everyone is satisfied with his own degree of common sense is evidence of presumption. Brunschvicg, *Descartes et Pascal*, 115, notes that Descartes mentions

Montaigne's name only once (in his correspondence) but that Descartes's contemporaries would not need to be told that the first phrase of the *Discourse on Method* shows his debt to Montaigne.

14. On the starting point of the essay in opinion, see Defaux, *Marot, Rabelais, Montaigne,* 180; Lanson, *Les Essais,* 95; Brody, *Lectures,* 119; Good, *Observing Self,* 13. James B. Atkinson, "Montaigne and *Naïveté,*" *Romanic Review* 64 (1973): 248, notes that Montaigne often pairs *vérité* with *naïveté.* With regard to the circular dialectical movement, see Starobinski, *Motion,* ix–xi: the essays are "a sophisticated return to the world of artifice and appearance repudiated at the outset." Barbara C. Bowen, "What Does Montaigne Mean by 'Marqueterie'?" *Studies in Philology* 67 (1970): 153–54: "Montaigne's way of writing is circular, with the subject somewhere in the center, and the essay constituting a series of circles round the subject." Ian J. Winter, "From Self-Concept to Self-Knowledge: Death and Nature in Montaigne's 'De la phisionomie,'" *Kentucky Romance Quarterly* 21, supp. 2 (1974): 365: "The Moi struggles to penetrate further within itself, journeying as it were, towards its own earlier intuitions, and in so doing it embraces the book retrospectively." Sayce, "La peinture du passage," 34, 53: the circular movement of the essays is the dominant form. Joukovsky, *Le problème du temps,* 191: Montaigne comes back to vulgar trust by way of a detour; he goes to the limit of thought but then recognizes the mystery behind it. Edwin M. Duval, "Montaigne's Conversions: Compositional Strategies in the *Essais,*" *French Forum* 7 (1982), 6, identifies "conversions," that is, dialectical turning points in the essays. See also Regosin, *Matter,* 26–27. Brush, "Self-Study," 32–33, describes a typical movement of the mind as it essays a topic, that is, the successive emergences of the topic as Montaigne circles it. This "rambling method" produces "unexpected insights that take even the author by surprise." Marcel Tetel, "Montaigne: Evolution or Convolution?" in *Authors and Their Centuries,* ed. Philip Grant, French Literature Series, vol. 1 (Columbia: University of South Carolina Press, 1973), 33, discusses the ascending and descending movement of the essay: "[T]he purpose of the ascending movement is to return to the point of departure a bit more assured than before." Michaël Baraz, "Montaigne et l'idéal de l'homme entier," in *O un amy! Essays on Montaigne in Honor of Donald M. Frame,* ed. Raymond C. La Charité (Lexington, Ky.: French Forum Publishers, 1977), 22, also notes the ascending and descending movements that are so characteristic of Montaigne's thought. See also Pouilloux, *L'éveil de la pensée,* 84–85, and Burke, *Montaigne,* 63. Levine, *Sensual Philosophy,* 121, claims that Montaigne's ideal human life is a life of "sophisticated simplicity," that is, a combination of the simplicity and mental tranquillity of the cannibals with the self-reflection of a philosopher. For general descriptions of the essay as a mode of thought, see Desan, *Les commerces,* 145, 260; Good, *Observing Self,* 22, 40–42; Richard A. Sayce, "Montaigne et la peinture du passage," *Saggi e ricerche di letteratura francese* 4 (1963), 15; Steven Rendall, "Mus in Pice: Montaigne and Interpretation," *Modern Language Notes* 94 (1979), 1060–61: the *Essays* are dedicated to those who already know him as a "reminder that functions less to communicate knowledge than to recover or keep alive the knowledge that the reader already has." Jerome Schwartz, "'La conscience d'un homme': Reflections on the Problem of Conscience in the *Essais,*" in *O un amy! Essays on*

Montaigne in Honor of Donald M. Frame, ed. Raymond C. La Charité (Lexington, Ky.: French Forum Publishers, 1977), 261, refers to Montaigne's approach as "phenomenological" rather than logical.

15. On the presumption involved in reducing the mind to memory, see Pouilloux, *L'éveil de la pensée*, 131: we believe that we are thinking for ourselves and we do not notice that we are simply repeating the thoughts we have absorbed from others. Many commentators have noted positive aspects of Montaigne's claim to deficient memory. Marcel Gutwirth, *Michel de Montaigne ou le pari d'exemplarité* (Montreal: Les Presses de L'Université de Montréal, 1977), 94, interprets Montaigne's deficiency of memory as a lack of constraint. Chateau, *Montaigne psychologue*, 73, says that Montaigne's poor memory prevents the fixing of ideas in his mind. Gray, *Le style*, 203, refers to the memory as an obstacle in the attempt to seize the successive states of the soul. Maclean, "Philosophical Speculation," 116–17, argues that Montaigne's slighting references to his memory may be self-affirming if books and their authority are inferior to his own writing. Starobinski, *Motion*, 258, links Montaigne's forgetting everything with his openness to all that is new. Richard L. Regosin, "The Text of Memory: Experience as Narrative in Montaigne's *Essais*," in *The Dialectic of Discovery*, ed. John D. Lyons and Nancy J. Vickers (Lexington, Ky.: French Forum Publishers, 1984), 147: Montaigne's weak memory is tied to his ignorance; weak memory neutralizes the privileged tradition of authoritative books (150). See also Regosin, "Sources and Resources," 106–7; and Holyoake, "Attitude to Memory," 265–67. John Middleton Murry, "Montaigne: The Birth of the Individual" in *Heroes of Thought* (Freeport, N.Y.: Books for Libraries Press, 1938), 58–59: Montaigne's self-discovery is made possible by his self-forgetfulness.

16. See I. D. McFarlane, "Montaigne and the Concept of the Imagination," in *The French Renaissance and Its Heritage*, ed. D. R. Haggis et al. (London: Methuen, 1968), 120: the imagination is generally regarded as an obstacle to truth. Montaigne takes a more positive attitude (122–23, 125, 129, 130–31). Screech, *Melancholy*, 159: the wise melancholic learns to distrust the power of the imagination.

17. See John Kekes, *Moral Wisdom and Good Lives* (Ithaca: Cornell University Press, 1995), chap. 5, on the moral imagination as "the mental exploration of what it would be like to realize particular possibilities" (101).

18. Ernst Cassirer, *Individual and Cosmos in the Philosophy of the Renaissance*, trans. Mario Domandi (Oxford: Basil Blackwell, 1963), 74, describes a "basic disposition and attitude of Renaissance philosophy . . . the view that for human knowledge ideas can only be presented and embodied in the form of images. It may be that this kind of presentation will seem hazy when compared to the eternal, transcendent content of the ideas; nevertheless, it is the only one proper to our thought and to *our* mind." Baraz, *L'être*, 59, asks why Montaigne's vision of the world demands images. He answers that Montaigne wants only "incarnate," not abstract thought. For Montaigne, it is always the entire man who thinks and acts. Montaigne's universe is a universe of analogy (60–61). Norton, *Introspective Mind*, 135, claims that metaphor "communicates the preverbal quality of thought processes." According to Friedrich, *Montaigne*, 370, Montaigne thinks that most words are tropes that have died out; for thinking, the metaphor

represents what is real. Jean-Paul Dumont, "L'imagination philosophique de Montaigne," in *Montaigne philosophe*, ed. André Comte-Sponville, *Revue Internationale de Philosophie* 46, no. 181 (1992): 169–89, discusses the philosophical function of the imagination, especially in Montaigne's representations of stories, and argues that, for Montaigne, imagination is necessary for dialectic.

19. For a profound discussion of the philosophical imagination, see Eva T. H. Brann, *The World of the Imagination: Sum and Substance* (Lanham, Md.: Rowman and Littlefield, 1991), 783: the philosophizing of imaginative reason is "philosophizing *par excellence*" because it is "the exploration of the possible." In the imagination "possibilities are tested." Imagination is "spontaneous in the sense of being open to intimations that present themselves unbidden." It is "the power of the possible." Brann claims that "philosophical reason in confronting any mystery becomes itself imaginative." Dreaming is the "preeminently imaginative activity" (779). This helps us to understand why Montaigne refers so often to his thoughts as dreams and reveries.

20. The way in which Montaigne's lowly starting points often lead into the whole is set out beautifully by Brody, "Teeth to Text," 9: "If . . . Montaigne's claim for his book is to be credited fully, then the meanest detail in his 'vie basse et sans lustre' should refer far enough beyond itself to reflect or somehow give access to a vision of 'la forme entiere de l'humaine condition.'" So, the tooth that he talks about in "Of experience" occupies "the very center of Montaigne's reflections on life and death" (11). See also Jules Brody, "Montaigne: Philosophy, Philology, Literature," *Philosophy and Literature* 22 (1998): 91: Brody's "philological reading" leads from the physical to the metaphysical. Epstein, "The Personal Essay," 20, describes the essay as "turning the small into the large." Barbara C. Bowen, "Montaigne's Anti-*Phaedrus*: 'Sur des vers de Virgile' (*Essais*, III, v)," *Journal of Medieval and Renaissance Studies* 5 (1975): 114, says of that essay that our initial impression is that sex is a frivolous subject, but then we see that it is very serious: "The sexual act becomes a kind of metaphysical center of the universe." With respect to Montaigne's finding the high in the low, see Gutwirth, *Le pari d'exemplarité*, 43, 158; and Roy E. Leake Jr., "Montaigne's Gascon Proverb Again," *Neophilologus* 52 (1968): 252.

21. With respect to the place of the miraculous in the essays, see Baraz, *L'être*, 106: in some sense, everything is a miracle for Montaigne. Strowski, *Montaigne*, 153, claims that Montaigne is less astonished at extraordinary than at ordinary things. Dan Roche, "Familiar Essay," in *Encyclopedia of the Essay*, ed. Tracy Chevalier (London: Fitzroy Dearborn Publishers, 1997), 274, describes the essayist as being "in constant search for the significance of the mundane." The way in which the essay brings us around to the surprising is seen in the essentially comic nature of Montaigne's movement of thought as captured by Craig B. Brush, "Montaigne's Surprises," in *Columbia Montaigne Conference Papers*, ed. Donald M. Frame and Mary B. McKinley (Lexington, Ky.: French Forum Publishers, 1981), 40. Atkinson, "*Naïveté*," 256, notes that "part of the truthfulness of the *Essais* is the almost accidental nature of their 'conclusions.'" The surprising is ultimately Montaigne himself. O'Loughlin, *Garlands of Repose*, 241, sees that, although Montaigne seldom starts with himself, he always comes to himself. Melehy, *Writing Cogito*, 68, claims that the more Montaigne "moves toward the plenitude

of the expression of the self in the book, the more foreign it becomes to itself."
Richard L. Regosin, "Montaigne's Monstrous Confession," *Montaigne Studies* 1
(1989): 79–80: man is "the true miracle" and "the marvelous that man witnesses,
the true miracle he sees, is thus himself, himself in his monstrous emptiness and
vanity and . . . in his ignorance." Further, the novelty of this deformity can never
become familiar. "Astonishment is the sign of lack of understanding, of that
monstrous deformity that is man's ignorance of himself." Pouilloux, "La forme
maîtresse," 42–44: the "forme maîtresse" is mysterious and the self is opaque.

22. Merleau-Ponty, "Reading Montaigne," 198.
23. Ibid., 203.
24. Ibid., 206.
25. Oakeshott, *Rationalism in Politics and Other Essays*, 17.

Chapter 5: "What It Means to Believe"

1. Isak Dinesen, "Babette's Feast," in *Anecdotes of Destiny and Ehrengard* (New York:
Random House, Vintage Books, 1993). See Leon Kass, *The Hungry Soul: Eating
and the Perfecting of Our Nature* (Chicago: University of Chicago Press, 1999),
183–92, for an excellent discussion of the philosophical meaning of this story.
2. Auerbach, "L'humaine condition," 310–11. See also Charles Taylor, *Sources of
the Self: The Making of the Modern Identity* (Cambridge, Mass.: Harvard University
Press, 1989), 178.
3. Friedrich Nietzsche, "Schopenhauer as Educator," trans. William Arrowsmith,
in *Unmodern Observations*, ed. William Arrowsmith (New Haven: Yale University
Press, 1990), 171.
4. Pascal, *Pensées*, Br. no. 63. See Marianne S. Meijer, "Mourir lâchement et
mollement," in *Etudes Montaignistes en hommage à Pierre Michel*, ed. Claude Blum
and François Moureau (Paris: Champion, 1984), 173–82, for a defense of
Montaigne against Pascal's charge. Meijer argues that Montaigne makes a separation between human and divine and is, therefore, not engaged in theology.
5. Saint Augustine, *The Confessions*, trans. F. J. Sheed (Indianapolis: Hackett,
1992), VII.11. Augustine's *Confessions* was apparently not among the books
in Montaigne's library. Nigel Abercrombie, *St. Augustine and French Classical
Thought* (1938; reissued, New York: Atheneum Publishers, Russell and Russell,
1972), 40, argues that Montaigne could not have read the *Confessions* because
he does not seem to know that Augustine had a son. But Elisabeth Caron,
"Saint Augustin dans les *Essais*," *Montaigne Studies* 2, no. 2 (1990), 33, says that
Montaigne may well have heard the *Confessions* discussed, even if he did not
actually read the work. Auerbach, "L'humaine condition," 300, is reminded of
Augustine's self-examination when he considers Montaigne's claim to novelty.
He asserts that "it is not possible that [Montaigne] should not have been aware
at least of the existence and the character of this famous book." I agree that
Montaigne must have been familiar with the content of the *Confessions* even if
he did not actually read the work.
6. Saint Augustine, *Confessions*, IV.7.
7. Ibid., IV.6.
8. Ibid., IV.8.

9. Ibid., IV.10.
10. Ibid., VII.9.
11. Ricardo J. Quiñones, *The Renaissance Discovery of Time* (Cambridge, Mass.: Harvard University Press, 1972), 236, speaks of Montaigne's radical "altering the very substance of attachment." Wisdom, for Montaigne, does not mean "disgust with present things, with the ephemeral, nor does it involve the placement of a superior goal or level of perfection toward which the individual ought to aspire." See also Gutwirth, *Le pari d'exemplarité*, 25; Colin Lyas, "That to Philosophise Is to Learn How to Die," *Philosophical Investigations* 16, no. 2 (April 1993): 123, discusses belief in God as reconciliation to suffering.
12. See Friedrich, *Montaigne*, 39.
13. John Kekes, "Constancy and Purity," *Mind* 92 (1983): 515: Montaigne both lives in the world and resists its corruptions. Clement Sclafert, *L'âme religieuse de Montaigne* (Paris: Nouvelles Editions Latines, 1951), 180, claims that Montaigne's use of the expression "the world" is Christian, not pagan. I would also suggest that Montaigne's treatment of the vice of ambition is Augustinian.
14. Montaigne's attachment to and detachment from this world show themselves in several ways and have been interpreted as both Christian and un-Christian. Friedrich, *Montaigne*, 94–95, discusses Montaigne's abasement and affirmation of man but claims that this viewpoint is not Christian. Nicholas Boyle, "Pascal, Montaigne, and 'J.-C.': The Centre of the *Pensées*," *Journal of European Studies* 12 (1982): 18: "Pascal has accepted from Montaigne that talk about the misery of the self is talk about the totality." Joukovsky, *Le problème du temps*, 71, argues that the "mystery" of a destruction which is, at the same time, a creation, is grounded in Montaigne's experience as a Christian. Margaret McGowan, "Clusterings: Positive and Negative Values in 'De la vanité,'" *Montaigne Studies* 1 (1989): 119: Montaigne uncovers comfort in vanity where one did not expect to find it. He gives a very different gloss on Ecclesiastes from those of other sixteenth-century writers. Similarly, Marianne S. Meijer, "The Significance of 'De la diversion' in Montaigne's *Third Book*," *Romance Notes* 32 (1991): 17, says that diversion, for Montaigne, is intended to accept suffering as a part of life. Margaret McGowan, *Montaigne's Deceits: The Art of Persuasion in the Essais* (Philadelphia: Temple University Press, 1974), 73: Montaigne transforms the Christian paradox "life is death" from a mere truism into "an intense realisation of a state of being."
15. Henry, "Heraclitus," 15: Montaigne does not negate all repentance. "Rather, he distinguishes between valid repentance and hypocrisy."
16. That Montaigne's faith is not obvious on the surface of the essays can be inferred from François Moureau, "Montaigne ecrivain des lumières?" *Diotima* 17 (1989): 16, who points out that Montaigne's travel journal surprised his readers because it shows him to be religious. Craig B. Brush, "The Essayist Is Learned: Montaigne's *Journal de Voyage* and the *Essais*," *Romanic Review* 62 (1971): 16, makes a similar point and adds that in the journal there is a remarkable absence of classical lore. See also Frieda S. Brown, *Religious and Political Conservatism in the Essais of Montaigne* (Geneva: Librairie Droz, 1963), 30–31. As Marc Fumaroli writes in his foreword to *Montaigne and Melancholy*, Screech has discovered the religious dimensions of the *Essays*. So also M. A. Screech, "Montaigne: Some Classical Notions in Their Contexts," in *Montaigne in Cambridge, Proceedings of*

the Cambridge Montaigne Colloquium 1989, ed. Philip Ford et al. (1989), 45–49, claims that it is difficult for many readers to see the Christian contexts for Montaigne's classical allusions. For example, "when Montaigne is treating the philosophical attraction of death (which has, oddly, struck generations of read- ers as somehow anti-Christian or un-Christian) he is as close as possible to in- formed theological opinion within his Church in his day." Screech cites a work by Fray Bartholomaeus that links the text of Saint Paul ("I would be dissolved. . . . ") with philosophically inspired suicide. Both Montaigne and Bartholomaeus are dealing with the rational appetite, which, when not corrected, makes suicide so attractive to the philosopher. Screech's observations here show the extent to which many interpreters are unaffected by the sometimes subtle indications of Catholic sensibilities.

17. Friedrich, *Montaigne*, 81–82.
18. Ibid., 81.
19. In connection with the way faith is present in the *Essays*, Boyle, "Pascal," 2; Richard M. Chadbourne, "Michel de Montaigne," in *Encyclopedia of the Essay*, ed. Tracy Chevalier (London: Fitzroy Dearborn Publishers, 1997), 569; and Cathy Yandell, "*Corps* and *corpus*: Montaigne's 'Sur des vers de Virgile,'" *Modern Language Studies* 16 (1986): 78, all note Montaigne's use of "consubstantial" to characterize his relation to his book. Yandell and Chadbourne note that this is an exclusively theological term. Boyle says that this shows an "explicitly sacra- mental understanding of his self-expression." See also Barry Lydgate, "Mort- gaging One's Work to the World: Publication and the Structure of Montaigne's *Essais*," *Publications of the Modern Language Association of America* 96 (1981): 212: the relationship between the self of lived experience and the literary self of the *Essays* is not mimetic but "incarnational."
20. Friedrich, *Montaigne*, 81.
21. Ibid., 26, claims that, for Montaigne, man no longer requires God or needs grace. It seems to me, however, that the "easy grace" that Friedrich says "hovers over all the pages of Montaigne's *Essais*" (175) and Montaigne's Pauline "boast- ing of his own weakness" are important aspects of Montaigne's way of living the life of faith. See also Baraz, "L'idéal de l'homme entier," 31: Montaigne experiences all of life as sacred.
22. For an excellent summary of the various approaches to making sense of the "Apology," see Marcel Gutwirth, "Montaigne pour et contre Sebond," *Revue des Sciences Humaines* 34 (1969): sec. 1, 1176–81. Among those who see Montaigne as a believer, see Pierre Moreau, *Montaigne: L'homme et l'œuvre* (Paris: Boivin et Cie, 1939), especially 42; Homer Woodridge, "Montaigne, the Friend," *Texas Review* 1 (1915–16): 109; Joseph Coppin, "La morale de Montaigne est-elle purement naturelle?" *Facultés Catholiques de Lille, Memoires et travaux* 32 (1927): 107, 115–16. For the most part, those who defend Montaigne's orthodoxy do so on the basis of "external" evidence, that is, evidence from outside the *Essays*. Henry, *Montaigne in Dialogue*, 27–32, concludes that Montaigne is not an atheist. "It is not Montaigne's Catholicism that should be questioned but the view that he always speaks in accordance with the Church's teaching" (29). See also Patrick Henry, "Les titres façades, la censure et l'écriture défensive chez Montaigne," *Bulletin de la Société des Amis de Montaigne*, ser. 5, no. 24 (1977): 11–28. Friedrich, *Montaigne*, 105, and Brunschvicg, *Descartes and Pascal*, 89,

both view Montaigne as Hellenistic rather than Christian. Lanson, *Les Essais*, regards Montaigne as moderately religious: there is no real effort toward holiness (263). André Gide, *Essai sur Montaigne* (Paris: Jacques Schiffrin, Editions de la Pléiade, n.d.), 41–42, claims that Montaigne speaks of Christianity with an almost malicious impertinence and that he never speaks of Christ and may never have even read the Gospels. Arthur Armaingaud, "Montaigne: Était-il ondoyant et divers? Montaigne était-il inconstant?" *Revue du seizième siècle* 10 (1923): 44, says that Montaigne sometimes hides his meaning. Therefore, his contradictions have to be interpreted by seeing what is real and what is pretended. Armaingaud concludes that only Montaigne's antireligious opinions are sincere. David Schaefer, in both his *Political Philosophy* and his "'To Philosophize Is to Learn How to Die': Montaigne vs. Socrates," *Independent Journal of Philosophy* 5–6 (1988): 23–30, agrees with Armaingaud. Levine in his *Sensual Philosophy*, argues that Montaigne supports religious beliefs for political, not religious reasons (especially 43, 61). Sayce, *Critical*, 228, holds that Montaigne is not really Christian but adheres to Catholicism because he hates civil war.

23. Brahami, *Le scepticisme*, 58, 73.
24. Ibid., 29. Popkin, *History of Scepticism*, 52, describes the skeptic-fideist position as "complete doubt on the rational level, joined with a religion based on faith alone." Herman Janssen, *Montaigne fidéiste* (Nijmegen, Utrecht: N. V. Dekker and Van de Vigt en J. W. Van Leeuwen, 1930), says that an essential element of fideism is the deliberate sacrifice of reason to faith (37, 111) and the complete separation of reason and faith (114). Coleman, *Montaigne's Essais*, 53, describes fideism as the view that the intellect is incapable of attaining knowledge of divine matters. Micha, *Le Singulier*, 172–73, on the other hand, holds that Montaigne is not entirely a fideist, and Sclafert, *L'âme religieuse*, 63, claims that Montaigne is not a fideist: the problem posed by the "Apology" is really the problem of who should interpret Scripture. Mathias, introduction to *Apologie*, argues that Montaigne is neither a fideist nor a skeptic in the traditional sense.
25. See F. L. Lucas, "The Master-Essayist," in *Studies in French and English* (London: Cassell, 1934), 118: "[I]f an essay like that on Prayers, with its casual allusions to his own special fondness for the Paternoster and for the sign of the Cross, is all merely a cunning piece of stagecraft, then instead of the sincerest he was the insincerest of men. And why should he tell us, unless it were true, that he always receives the rites of the Church at the beginning of any attack of illness, to set his mind at rest?" Lucas is attempting to articulate Montaigne's Catholic sensibilities, which I try to incorporate on the theoretical level.
26. Brahami, *Le scepticisme*, 46–47. Terence Penelhum, "Skepticism and Fideism," in *The Skeptical Tradition*, ed., Myles Burnyeat (Berkeley: University of California Press, 1983), 293, describes Montaigne as a "Catholic Pyrrhonist." Montaigne equates faith that comes from grace with the Skeptic's acquiescence in local tradition. Montaigne's faith is tepid: he participates but without really identifying himself with faith. Penelhum offers three objections to fideism: (1) faith would be a groundless choice; (2) Why one faith rather than another? (3) Is such belief even possible? These are among the reasons why I maintain that Montaigne is not a fideist: I believe that each can be answered through an elucidation of the dialectic of faith and reason in the *Essays*. See also Penelhum's

God and Skepticism: A Study in Skepticism and Fideism (Dordrecht: D. Reidel, 1983), 22, 24, 56.

27. See Schaefer, *Political Philosophy*, 48.

28. Brahami, *Le scepticisme*, 23.

29. Saint Anselm, *Proslogion*, trans. M. J. Charlesworth (Notre Dame, Ind.: University of Notre Dame Press, 1979), 117.

30. Friedrich, *Montaigne*, 96: Montaigne simultaneously turned against natural philosophy and the Reformation because he saw in both a common danger: a claim to the autonomy of human reason. I agree with Friedrich here but I attempt to make philosophical sense of why the autonomy of reason is dangerous and how reason is reformed in its dialectic with faith. Dréano, *La pensée religieuse*, 276, refers to those who make the second objection as "rationalists." The Reformers were faithful to Aristotle (252). Dréano claims that the "new doctors" are atheists and Reformers. For Montaigne, atheism was only the Reform pushed to its logical conclusion (263–64). According to Floyd Gray, "The 'Nouveaux Docteurs' and the Problem of Montaigne's Consistency in the *Apologie de Raymond Sebond*," *Symposium* 18 (1964): 27–29, the "new doctors" mentioned by Montaigne in his caution to the princess are the Calvinists whose rationalism he intends to combat. Further, the Reformers appealed to "individual reason." See also Brown, *Religious and Political Conservatism*, 41. Donald M. Frame, "Did Montaigne Betray Sebond?" *Romanic Review* 38 (1947): 303, refers to the reason of the second objection as "isolated." Frame argues that Montaigne was fully aware of his differences from Sebond and that he changed from fondness to coolness (314–15). The "Apology" presents "the analysis of the origin of atheism in unbridled rationalism" (325).

31. Faye, *Philosophie et perfection de l'homme*, 185, claims that, for Montaigne, philosophy does not have to serve theology. I agree with this claim. But Faye bases it on the view that philosophy has no common measure with "la doctrine divine," whereas I take the opposite postition, that is, that accidental philosophy does not assume a conflict between faith and reason (see also 197, 203). Catherine Demure, "Montaigne: The Paradox and the Miracle – Structure and Meaning in 'The Apology of Raymond Sebond' (*Essais* II:12)," *Yale French Studies* 64 (1983): 188–208, is one of the few commentators who argue for the coherence of the "Apology." She argues that the essay manifests the rigor of a maintained contradiction: the need for theology but the impossibility of theology (189). This is a paradox that moves toward transcendence (206). André Tournon, *Montaigne: La glose et l'essai*, 241–42, argues that the movement of the "Apology" is rhetorical. He takes up especially the place of the address to the princess and argues that it marks the end of the first section of the essay. Terence Cave, *Pré-histoires: Textes troublés au seuil de la modernité* (Geneva: Librairie Droz, 1999), 42–43, disagrees with Tournon on that point. He argues that the address to the princess refers both backward and forward, revealing Montaigne's critique of Scholasticism by replacing license with liberty. I do not see a necessary contradiction between the claim that there is a rhetorical movement in the "Apology" and my interpretation of the dialectic.

32. On the distinction between God and creation, see Frame, "Problem of Consistency," 171, and Mary B. McKinley, "The *City of God* and the City of Man: Limits of Language in Montaigne's 'Apologie,' " *Romanic Review* 71 (1980): 125.

33. T. S. Eliot, "The *Pensées* of Pascal," in *Selected Essays* (New York: Harcourt Brace, 1932), 363. See also Walton, "Art of Judgment," 88, 93.

34. Marcel Conche, *Montaigne ou la conscience heureuse* (Paris: Editions Seghers, 1966), 44, emphasizes the fact that those who find Sebond's arguments weak consider themselves strong. Lewis, *God in the Dock*, 46, asks whether Christians on different levels of education "conceal radically different beliefs under an identical form of words?" He answers: "Certainly not. For what they agree on is the substance, and what they differ about is the shadow."

Chapter 6: The Latent Metaphysics of Accidental Philosophy

1. Michael B. Foster, *Mystery and Philosophy* (London: SCM Press, 1957), 92n1, refers to the rejection of Aristotelianism at the end of the Middle Ages as the elimination of the influence of Hellenic thought models. Starobinski, *Motion*, 298: "Montaigne's self-absorption (remotely patterned after Aristotle's God) immediately becomes a way of making contact with others." I would put Starobinski's insight this way: Montaigne's "thought thinking thought" is human and unites him to the lowest. Friedrich, *Montaigne*, 362, characterizes the essay form as the direct presentation of the intellect speaking with itself. O'Loughlin, *Garlands of Repose*, 235: "The Horatian achievement of Montaigne was to transform and appropriate to the Christian imagination the Virgilian kind of free time that a god had granted." What we find in Montaigne is a "provocatively new kind of *vita contemplativa*." O'Loughlin refers to Montaigne's "transformation of the contemplative life from an exercise in metaphysical speculation to the mundane pursuit of self-scrutiny" (269).

2. Regosin, *Matter*, 142: In "Of practice," thought, not deed, becomes "the true indicator of particularity."

3. René Descartes, *Meditations on First Philosophy*, trans. Donald A. Cress (Indianapolis: Hackett, 1993), 19.

4. Richard L. Regosin, "Nemo's Descent: The Rhetoric of Presence in Montaigne's *Essais*," *French Forum* 13, no. 2 (1988): 156. Conche, *La conscience heureuse*, 64: for Montaigne, thought is entirely, radically open to reality.

5. Martin Heidegger, "A Discussion between Ernst Cassirer and Martin Heidegger," trans. Francis Slade, in *The Existentialist Tradition*, ed. Nino Langiulli (Garden City, N.Y.: Anchor Books, Doubleday, 1971), 196. Chadbourne, "Michel de Montaigne," 569: "[T]he self that one finds in his essays is never solipsistic or narcissistic but has been broadened to include many other 'voices.' Dialogue occurs not only with his reader and with the authors he quotes but also with himself." On the connection between falsehood and nonbeing, see Pouilloux, *L'éveil de la pensée*, 159: this connection shows up in the way we are dominated by the authority of commonplaces.

6. Oakeshott, *Religion*, 144.

7. Adorno, "Essay as Form," 162.

8. O'Neill, *Essaying Montaigne*, 12: "Montaigne invented the 'Essays' because he knew that self-knowledge is not gained by standing outside of ourselves metaphysically." Truth "cannot be found apart from men"; therefore Montaigne, like Socrates, does not investigate nature, as the scientist does, but other men (20).

9. On the relation between truth and testimony, see Foster, *Mystery*, 47: Christian thought is more "a kind of witnessing than . . . a kind of speculation." Foster distinguishes between the kind of thinking that consists in solving problems and "another kind of thinking which depends on the revealing of a mystery." Mysteries "remain mysterious even when understood, because, though understood, they exceed our comprehension" (18–19). Thus, Foster concludes that "to recognize holiness is to recognize that God has acted, and this is revelation. But further, it is not possible to specify exactly what God has done nor to locate it precisely" (49). "We can only pray for mysteries, i.e., for objects of which we cannot say beforehand what it would be like to have them granted" (83). Montaigne's openness to mystery has been noted by Friedrich, *Montaigne*, 151, who claims that "for Montaigne, to research man means to lead man back into his mysteriousness." Friedrich also refers to what Montaigne sees as "the mystery of what is given" (66). "Montaigne considers precisely that which healthy reason cannot understand to be possible. His scepticism has a tone of metaphysical awe. It mistrusts any platitude 'that takes away . . . strangeness' (I.27)" (134–35). With respect to Augustine's *Confessions*, Friedrich writes: "[T]o a much greater degree than external things, the unfathomable soul demands explanation from a perspective of divine origin" (215). Brann, *World of the Imagination*, 782, describes mystery as "an ever-attractive focus of wonder, the recognition of which comes through a *docta ignorantia*, a knowing kind of nescience." Pouilloux, *L'éveil de la pensée*, 212, characterizes the essay as an enterprise of seizing, at each present moment, what will never able to be said. It seems to me that what some have called "the sublime" conveys something of the sense of mystery that I am describing here. Catherine Randall, "The Swallow's Nest and the Hermeneutic Quest in the Apologie de Raimond Sebond," *Montaigne Studies* 12 (2000): 137, notes that the sublime is linked to skepticism. Miernowski, *L'ontologie de la contradiction sceptique*, argues that the "Apology" displays a conjunction of skepticism and negative theology that affirms the absolute transcendence of the divine (see especially 37–67). Here I think that Miernowski is attuned to Montaigne's sense of the mystery of God's being but that he misses the relevance of the mystery of the Incarnation.

10. Martin Heidegger, "Letter on Humanism," in *The Existentialist Tradition*, ed. Nino Langiulli (Garden City, N.Y.: Anchor Books, Doubleday, 1971), 212.

11. Ibid., 211.

12. Ibid., 227.

13. Ibid., 229.

14. Ibid., 204.

15. Ibid., 243.

16. Ibid., 235.

17. Ibid., 240–42.

18. Ibid., 218–19.

19. Ibid., 237.

20. Ibid., 217.

21. Ibid., 237–38. Friedrich, *Montaigne*, 18–19: "When Montaigne seeks the reality of what it is to be human, he seeks it in the observation of the most ordinary, the most banal things – in himself as in others." The most banal things can open up the most fertile insight into being. "Thus Montaigne's most content-rich

observations appear bound to the images of what is lowliest. . . . Montaigne's method has the incomparable art of portraying the ordinary such that its mysteriousness begins to shine through." O'Loughlin, *Garlands of Repose*, 273: "The 'descent,' to contemplate the human condition, is thus its own kind of ascent. The natural implicates the supernatural reality which it displaces." Chateau, *Montaigne psychologue*, 59, refers to Montaigne's thought as "une philosophie du quotidien." See also Lewis, *God in the Dock*, 144: God "must be the God not only of the philosophers, but of mystics and savages, not only of the head and heart, but also of the primitive emotions and the spiritual heights beyond all emotion." With respect to our image of God, Lewis writes: "We have always thought of God as being not only 'in,' 'above,' but also 'below' us: as the depth of ground" (184).

22. Foster, *Mystery*, 41.
23. Ibid., 28.
24. Ibid., 46.
25. See Gerald J. Galgan, *Interpreting the Present: Six Philosophical Essays* (Lanham, Md.: University Press of America, 1993), 83: "[T]he [created] world is something unexpected, a complete 'surprise.'" See also R. R. Reno, *The Ordinary Transformed: Karl Rahner and the Christian Vision of Transcendence* (Grand Rapids, Mich.: William B. Eerdmans, 1995), 11: "The Christian view of transcendence is of the ordinary transformed."
26. Conche, *Montaigne et la philosophie*, 78. Georges Pholien, "Montaigne et la science," in *Montaigne et la révolution philosophique du XVI siècle*, ed. Jacques Lemaire (Brussels: Editions de l'Université de Bruxelles, 1992), 62: Montaigne is much closer to the spiritual conception of the universe of the Middle Ages than to the modern rationalist conception.
27. Oakeshott, *On Human Conduct*, 83–84.
28. Ibid., 81.
29. Lewis, *God in the Dock*, 150.
30. Steven Rendall, "The Rhetoric of Montaigne's Self-Portrait: Speaker and Subject," *Studies in Philology* 73 (1976): 285. Rendall also claims that the event of falling off his horse in "Of practice" is "the only one in the *Essais* which resembles the kind of turning point or crisis frequently described in autobiography" (292). Jonathan Rée, "Descartes's Comedy," *Philosophy and Literature* 8 (1984): 156, claims that Montaigne is not really an autobiographer.
31. Georges Poulet, "Montaigne," in *Studies in Human Time*, trans. Elliot Coleman (Baltimore: Johns Hopkins Press, 1956), 39.
32. Ibid., 43. Joukovsky, *Le problème du temps*, 246: time is only the discursive manifestation of nothing. Montaigne loves life because, in all logic, it should not be (213). Regosin, *Matter*, 192: "The feeling of loss of self reappears continually through the essays, expressed both as the inclination of the mind . . . *se perdre*, to *extravaguer*, and in the sense that he is nothing (*rien*), a void, vain or empty." Starobinski, *Motion*, 72: "Truth takes death for its accomplice, as if only a background of nothingness could make it stand out." Sclafert, *L'âme religieuse*, 18, defines the religious soul as the man who knows he is not sufficient to himself and that he needs God.
33. Oakeshott, *Religion*, 32.

34. Friedrich, *Montaigne*, 217.
35. Ibid., 131. For an excellent discussion of the difficulties with the view that possibility rather than necessity is the primary ontological category, see Nino Langiulli, *Possibility, Necessity, and Existence* (Philadelphia: Temple University Press, 1992), chap. 13. My point here is that the ontological priority of possibility can only be grounded in the notion of creation out of nothing: within the created world, necessity may still be prior.
36. Foster, *Mystery*, 34–35.
37. Robert Sokolowski, *The God of Faith and Reason* (Notre Dame, Ind.: University of Notre Dame Press, 1982), 23.
38. Eric Voegelin, "Reason: The Classic Experience," chap. 6 in *Anamnesis*, trans. Gerhart Niemeyer (Notre Dame, Ind.: University of Notre Dame Press, 1978), 95.
39. Joseph J. Carpino, "Three Cosmologies," *Interpretation: A Journal of Political Philosophy* 6, no. 1 (1976): 60. Brush, "Concept of Being," 151n16, refers to "the hierarchical structure of being so essential to Sebond." Desan, *Naissance*, 130, points out that with the destruction of Aristotelian metaphysics, Aristotle's idea of "natural place" is annihilated. Starobinski, *Motion*, 82, claims that "the remoteness of God brings man into greater intimacy with his condition in the very heart of the world of appearances. What had been reduced to nothing in comparison with absolute being recovers the right to presence and existence." Lewis, *God in the Dock*, 85: "What the story of the Incarnation seems to be doing is to flash a new light on a principle in nature, and to show for the first time that this principle of inequality is neither good nor bad." With respect to the hierarchy within human being, Foster, *Mystery*, 88, writes: "The Bible does not picture man as made up of two parts; its basic contrast is not between this and that element in human nature, but between man as a whole and God. This is the way in which St. Paul's dualism of flesh and Spirit is to be understood."
40. Foster, *Mystery*, 90–91.
41. Cassirer, *Individual and Cosmos*, 25–26. Gontier, *De l'homme à l'animal*, 50–64, discusses Montaigne's rejection of a hierarchy based on essences and argues that, if there is a "ladder" of beings, Montaigne sees the need to descend rather than ascend it – that is, man makes himself equal to God and must descend from this illusion. Faye, *Philosophie et perfection de l'homme*, 193: Montaigne rejects the hierarchy of creatures that structures the theology of Sebond.
42. Carpino, "Three Cosmologies," 57.
43. Eliot, "Pascal," 360.
44. See Friedrich, *Montaigne*, 132: "The fundamental knowledge attained by Montaigne's skepticism is that what is known and what is best known is transformed into an unknown as soon as it becomes the object of reflective contemplation. Everything becomes a miracle." Jean Céard, "Miracles et monstres dans les *Essais*," in *La nature et les prodiges: L'insolite au seizième siècle en France* (Geneva: Librairie Droz, 1977), 414, notes that it is lack of faith that demands miracles (i.e., extraordinary occurrences). Montaigne precisely does not seek out the extraordinary. His opposition to divination is based on his refusal to presume that God has put signs in the world (419). For Montaigne, the strange is what is nearest to us and all the real is miracle and mystery (427–34). Richard L. Regosin,

272   *Notes to pp. 166–172*

"Le miroüer vague: Reflections of the Example in Montaigne's *Essais*," *Œuvres and Critiques* 8 (1983): 82: "A leveling takes place by which the miraculous and the marvelous now inhere in familiar, concrete experience." McGowan, *Deceits*, 83: Montaigne does not devalue the extraordinary but "he allows what is commonly termed the 'rare' to pass into ordinary acts of life. He uses the extraordinary to throw light on the riches of man's day to day existence." With respect to the kinds of miracles that Montaigne finds in the world, Arendt's discussion of action is illuminating; "Action, seen from the viewpoint of the automatic processes which seem to determine the course of the world, looks like a miracle." Jesus "likened the power to forgive to the more general power of performing miracles, putting both on the same level and within the reach of man." Hannah Arendt, *The Human Condition* (Chicago: University of Chicago Press, 1958), 246–47.

45. Merleau-Ponty, "Reading Montaigne," 198.
46. Friedrich, *Montaigne*, 212.
47. Lewis, *God in the Dock*, 36.
48. Ibid., 29.
49. Ibid., 81. Lewis notes that if God can be known, it must be by self-revelation on his part, not by our own speculation (144). He also affirms the sensuous aspects of revelation: "There are particular aspects of his love and joy which can be communicated to a created being only by sensuous experience. Something of God which the Seraphim can never quite understand flows into us from the blue of the sky, the taste of honey, the delicious embrace of water whether cold or hot, and even from sleep itself" (216).
50. Oakeshott, *On Human Conduct*, 85.
51. Ibid., 86.
52. Oakeshott, *Religion*, 30.
53. Ibid., 34.
54. Pascal, *Pensées*, Br. no. 789.
55. Lewis, *God in the Dock*, 37.
56. Søren Kierkegaard, *Fear and Trembling*, ed. and trans. Howard V. Hong and Edna V. Hong (Princeton, N.J.: Princeton University Press, 1983), 66.
57. Foster, *Mystery*, 47.

Chapter 7: Montaigne's Character

1. Auerbach, "L'humaine condition," 311.
2. Ibid. See also Frame, *Essais*, 69: Montaigne's view of man is comic, not tragic. Also, Frank M. Chambers, "Pascal's *Montaigne*," *Publications of the Modern Language Association of America* 65 (1950): 802.
3. See Ruth M. Calder, "Montaigne as Satirist," *Sixteenth Century Journal* 17 (1986): 225: Montaigne does not satirize other people but is self-critical.
4. Joseph J. Carpino, "On Laughter," *Interpretation: A Journal of Political Philosophy* 13, no. 1 (1985): 92.
5. Ibid., 100.
6. Merleau-Ponty, "Reading Montaigne," 202.
7. Ibid., 200.

8. Ibid., 205. Also see John O'Neill, "The Essay as a Moral Exercise: Montaigne," *Renaissance and Reformation* 9 (1985): 214: The *Essays* "are consciously an element of universal folly." Ian J. Winter, "'Mon livre et moi': Montaigne's Deepening Evaluation of His Own Work," *Renaissance Quarterly* 25 (1972): 302: the *Essays* are Montaigne's greatest "folly."

9. Ibid., 201. See also Gray, *Le style*, especially 128–33. Walton, "Art of Judgment," 101, refers to Montaigne's philosophy as "laughing." Keith Cameron, "Montaigne and the Mask," *L'Esprit Créateur* 8 (1968): 206, claims that Montaigne's sense of humor "helps him to view the world with a certain detachment." Donald M. Frame, "Montaigne on the Absurdity and Dignity of Man," in *Renaissance Men and Ideas*, ed. Robert Schwoebel (New York: St. Martin's Press, 1971), 123, says that Montaigne takes a comic view of himself and of man but, for Frame, this has no relation to faith. See also Géralde Nakam, "La mélancolie et la folie" in *Montaigne: La manière et la matière* (Paris: Klincksieck, 1991), especially 40.

10. Gutwirth, *Le pari d'exemplarité*, 162–63, refers to laughter as the joyous consciousness of our finitude. For O'Neill, *Essaying*, 109, "Montaigne struggled to hold the middle ground between intellectual ecstasy and its melancholic reversal." Thomas M. Greene, "Montaigne and the Savage Infirmity," *Yale Review* 46 (1956): 194, describes joy as Montaigne's "pervasive state of being." Philo M. Buck, "Que sçais-je? – Montaigne," in *The Golden Thread* (New York: Macmillan, 1931), 351, says that, for Montaigne, philosophy is the joyous science. Henry, "Rise of the Essay," 132, suggests that the essay and the novel have the same origin, the echo of God's laughter. Paul Mathias, "Montaigne: Une philosophie de gai savoir," *Montaigne Studies* 12 (2000): 123–36, emphasizes the joy that characterizes Montaigne's writings.

11. With respect to comedy as "low" style, see Burke, *Montaigne*, 60: comedies are concerned with the private lives of ordinary people. Friedrich, *Montaigne*, 365, refers to the comic style as "the product of an everyday way of thinking." Baraz, *L'être*, 46, says that by using the comic style, Montaigne situates himself at the lowest degree of the hierarchy of men.

12. Auerbach, "L'humaine condition," 290.

13. Quoted in Nicolas Malebranche, *Treatise on Nature and Grace*, trans. Patrick Riley (Oxford: Clarendon Press, 1992), introduction.

14. Nietzsche, "Schopenhauer as Educator," 171.

15. Ullrich Langer, *Vertu du discours, discours de la vertu: Littérature et philosophie morale au xvie siècle en France* (Geneva: Librairie Droz, 1999), 18. Langer provides detailed evidence of the numerous translations of and commentaries on Aristotle and Cicero and of the fact that these constituted the essence of synthetic works of moral philosophy (20–22).

16. Ibid., 173–77.

17. Aristotle, *Nicomachean Ethics*, trans. Martin Ostwald (Indianapolis: Bobbs-Merrill, 1962), 93n18.

18. Albert D. Menut, "Montaigne and the *Nicomachean Ethics*," *Modern Philology* 31 (1933–34), claims that the *Ethics* is the source for Montaigne's notion of the gentleman (226–27, 235). Jean-Pierre Boon, *Montaigne gentilhomme et essayiste* (Paris: Editions Universitaires, 1971), 31, finds the prototype of "l'honnête

homme" in Castiglione's *The Courtesan*. However, Montaigne liberalizes this ideal (32). On Montaigne's "culture of the soul," see Brunschvicg, *Descartes et Pascal*, 26.

19. Lewis, *God in the Dock*, 193–94, distinguishes two kinds of self-hatred "which look rather alike in their earlier stages, but of which one is wrong from the beginning and the other right to the end. When Shelley speaks of self-contempt as the source of cruelty, or when a later poet says that he has no stomach for the man 'who loathes his neighbor as himself,' they are referring to a very real and very un-Christian hatred of the self which may make diabolical a man whom common selfishness would have left (at least, for a while) merely animal." Rendall, "Rhetoric," 296–97: the chief obstacle to self-knowledge is *amour-propre*. Frieda S. Brown, "De la solitude: A Re-examination of Montaigne's Retreat from Public Life," in *From Marot to Montaigne: Essays in French Renaissance Literature*, ed. Raymond C. La Charité, *Kentucky Romance Quarterly* 19 (1972): 146, claims that Montaigne's retreat from public life is self-centered but that later additions to "Of solitude" show movement away from self-centered arguments.

20. Friedrich, *Montaigne*, 227: Montaigne does not believe in the perfectibility of the human essence.

21. Dante, *De Monarchia* 1.13, quoted in Arendt, *Human Condition*, 175.

22. Arendt, *Human Condition*, 194.

23. Ibid., 184.

24. Ibid., 73.

25. Ibid., 180.

26. Niccolò Machiavelli, *Discourses on Livy*, trans. Harvey C. Mansfield Jr. and Nathan Tarcov (Chicago: University of Chicago Press, 1996), 288–89.

27. See David Maskell, "The Evolution of the *Essais*," in *Montaigne: Essays in Memory of Richard Sayce*, ed. I. D. McFarlane and Ian Maclean (Oxford: Clarendon Press, 1982), 19; Baraz, *L'être*, 172; Gutwirth, *Le pari d'exemplarité*, 157.

28. John D. Lyons, "Tacit History," *Montaigne Studies* 6, nos. 1–2 (1994): 41–42: Montaigne *creates* the private sphere by the way he writes about it, giving it recognition, dignity, and discursive structure.

29. Arendt, *Human Condition*, 77.

30. See Oakeshott, *Religion*, 150.

31. Ibid., 34.

32. Ibid., 33.

33. Ibid., 37.

34. Screech, *Melancholy*, 16: Montaigne thought of his wife as a friend. He wrote to her: "I believe that I have none more intimate than you."

35. On the quality of openness in Montaigne, see Judith N. Shklar, *Ordinary Vices* (Cambridge, Mass.: Belknap Press of Harvard University Press, 1984), 166; I. D. McFarlane, "The Concept of Virtue in Montaigne," in *Montaigne: Essays in Memory of Richard Sayce*, ed. I. D. McFarlane and Ian Maclean (Oxford: Clarendon Press, 1982), 93; Luthy, "Art of Being Truthful," 43–44: the best fruit of Montaigne's self-possession is his absolute openness to other things and other men. Montaigne is "open to the whole endless variety of spiritual possibilities." Micha, *Le singulier*, 73, notes the importance of the gratuitous act for Montaigne.

De Botton, *Consolations*, 121, refers to Montaigne's "generous, redemptive philosophy."

36. Oakeshott, *Rationalism in Politics*, 340.

37. Montaigne's love of liberty is inseparable from his integrity. See Shklar, *Ordinary Vices*, 5; Conche, *Montaigne et la philosophie*, 128; Strowski, *Montaigne*, 152; Lanson, *Les Essais*, 217–20; Brunschvicg, *Descartes et Pascal*, 147; Gutwirth, *Le pari d'exemplarité*, 17, 20. Montaigne deemphasizes valor among the virtues: see Alfredo Bonadeo, "Montaigne on War," *Journal of the History of Ideas* 46 (1985): 422–23; but he himself is courageous. See Pouilloux, *L'éveil de la pensée*, 129; Quint, *Quality of Mercy*, 122–23; also see 31–32 on the way in which Montaigne dialectically combines clemency and constancy, submission and bravery. On Montaigne's serenity, see Coleman, *Montaigne's Essais*, 79; Baraz, *L'être*, 19.

38. Kekes, *Moral Wisdom*, shows that "moral depth" has "a specific connection with truth" (166). Moral depth "involves understanding the significance of permanent adversities for the human aspiration to live good lives" (175). Starobinski, *Motion*, 98: "[L]ying is not merely a matter of culpable disloyalty to my neighbor; it is an ontological catastrophe for myself." Mauzey, *Human Nature*, 76, claims that the emphasis on honesty is original with Montaigne and is not simply derived from the ancients.

Chapter 8: What He Learned in the Nursery

1. Neil M. Larkin, "Montaigne's Last Words," *L'Esprit Créateur* 15 (1975): 26: the fact that Montaigne makes no argument to show the moral superiority of noble acts indicates that he "subtly posits the existence of a universally valid moral sense." Gustave Lanson, "La vie morale selon les *Essais* de Montaigne," parts 1 and 2, *Revue des deux mondes* ser. 7, 19 (February 1, 1924): 603–25; (February 15, 1924): 836–58: Montaigne is not a moral relativist (609).

2. Friedrich, *Montaigne*, 273: Montaigne sees the part that suicide may have in heroic death, but he himself wants nothing to do with it. Thus he rejects precisely the "most Roman" of behaviors toward death.

3. Saint Augustine, *The City of God*, Bk. I, chap. 22.

4. Kekes, *Moral Wisdom*, 214, describes innocence as "an open, simple, trusting, guileless, spontaneous manner of conduct that is lacking in artifice and calculation." Montaigne's innocence is prereflective and unreflective, an ignorance of good and evil (216). Quint, *Quality of Mercy*, 50, observes that in the discussion of virtue and goodness in "Of cruelty," "we are led to question what is mirroring what: whether goodness has the same countenance as virtue, or whether virtue finds as the final goal of its striving the replication of a goodness that may be available all along in human nature." Philip P. Hallie, "The Ethics of Montaigne's 'De la cruauté,' " in *O un amy! Essays on Montaigne in Honor of Donald M. Frame*, ed. Raymond C. La Charité (Lexington, Ky.: French Forum Publishers, 1977), 161, argues that by bringing in the goodness of God in "Of cruelty," Montaigne raises doubts about the hierarchy of virtue and goodness. The relationship between innocence and virtue is often seen in terms of striving and nonchalance. Kyriaki Christodoulou, "Socrate chez Montaigne et Pascal," *Diotima* 7 (1979): 42, 46, refers to the spontaneity of Socrates' and Montaigne's virtue. Frederick Kellermann, "The *Essais* and Socrates," *Symposium* 10 (1956):

211, claims that in Book III, the first level of virtue (Socrates' virtue that is due to complete self-correction) and the third level (Montaigne's natural goodness) tend to fuse. Quint, *Quality of Mercy*, 38, claims that Epaminondas achieves constancy through *mollesse*. James B. Atkinson, "Naïveté and Modernity: The French Renaissance Battle for a Literary Vernacular," *Journal of the History of Ideas* 35 (1974): 195, refers to naiveté as an "inward life-center" and Montaigne's *forme maistresse*. With respect to Montaigne's nonchalance, Friedrich, *Montaigne*, 322, says that the conclusion of every experience for Montaigne is to "give up a planning will." Similarly, Ralph W. Trueblood, "Montaigne: The Average Man," *Publications of the Modern Language Association of America* 21 (1906): 219, finds no strained enthusiasm in Montaigne.

5. On the way in which Montaigne's first impressions have remained authoritative for him, see J. B. Schneewind, *The Invention of Autonomy* (Cambridge: Cambridge University Press, 1998), 47: for Montaigne, "an acceptable doctrine must be able to accommodate his own already existing convictions about what is right and wrong, what good and what bad." Montaigne "finds out what his deepest convictions are by trying simply to portray himself honestly over a whole lifetime." Schwartz, "La conscience d'un homme," 251, claims that conscience, for Montaigne, is allied with "the heart" rather than with the reasoning faculty. See Quint, *Quality of Mercy*, 58–59: Montaigne's explanation of his goodness wavers between nature and nurture, but "if nurture played a part, it did so insensibly – not through conscious philosophical discipline." Montaigne's reference to his "nurse's milk blurs the distinction between the gifts of birth and those of nature" (125). On the question of whether the actual facts of Montaigne's biography correspond to the picture presented in the *Essays*, see Roger Trinquet, *La jeunesse de Montaigne* (Paris: A. G. Nizet, 1972), especially chap. 11, where Trinquet discusses Montaigne's father. Trinquet's account corroborates much of what Montaigne tells us at the beginning of the "Apology." See also George Hoffmann, *Montaigne's Career* (Oxford: Clarendon Press, 1998).

6. The connection between self-mastery and cruelty is one of the most widely noted features of Montaigne's moral philosophy. See Donald M. Frame, "Montaigne's Rejection of Inner Conflict and His Chapter 'De la cruauté' (II.11)," in *Mélanges sur la littérature de la Renaissance* (Geneva: Librairie Droz, 1984), 484–86; Starobinski, *Motion*, 134; Quint, *Quality of Mercy*, 57; Schaefer, *Political Philosophy*, 230; Friedrich, *Montaigne*, 173; Villey, *Les Essais*, 122. Also see Lewis, *God in the Dock*, 195. Quint, *Quality of Mercy*, 74; and Shklar, *Ordinary Vices*, 11, hold that Montaigne's hatred of cruelty is not specifically Christian, whereas Friedrich, *Montaigne*, 170–71, sees Montaigne's attitude toward the impassibility of the Stoics as Christian in origin. Quint, *Quality of Mercy*, 9, claims that Montaigne's statement about himself in "By diverse means we arrive at the same end" is, from an ethical standpoint, "the single most important contribution to the self-portrait." He links himself with the weakness of the common people and "calls the very terms of virtue and vice into question." Elizabeth Armstrong, "A Study in Montaigne's Post-1588 Style and Sensibility," in *The Equilibrium of Wit*, ed. Peter Bayley and Dorthy Gabe Coleman (Lexington, Ky.: French Forum Publishers, 1982), 79, notes that Montaigne saw the Stoics as arrogant and inhuman.

7. Hallie, "Ethics," 166, sees the emphasis on the inward government of the moral agent as egocentric. Montaigne takes ethical thought out of this egocentricity. Starobinski, *Motion*, 134–35: in the classical tradition, compassion is not associated with strength of character. Starobinski refers to Cato's "masochistic" enjoyment, which "stops at hermetic perfection; it closes in on itself and includes others only as admirers. This virtue isolates the individual by raising him above all others or by involving him in endless struggle against himself. By contrast, Montaigne's 'innocence' counterbalances, by the extensiveness of his compassion, what was first presented as a lack of moral energy."

8. Machiavelli, *Discourses*, II.2.

9. See Quint, *Quality of Mercy*, especially 20, 41–42, 141–42.

10. Conche, *La conscience heureuse*, 10; Gutwirth, *Le pari d'exemplarité*, 33; Micha, *Le singulier*, 158; Lanson, "La vie morale," 849, all claim that Montaigne's moral life is not Christian.

11. Quint, *Quality of Mercy*, argues that Montaigne's ethical project is the reform of the nobility, especially by making mercy a mark of true nobility, replacing martial valor. See especially ix, 10, 26–27, 45, 61. James J. Supple, *Arms versus Letters: The Military and Literary Ideals in the "Essais" of Montaigne* (Oxford: Clarendon Press, 1984), argues that Montaigne's own ethics can be understood as a questioning of both the military and literary ideals and an incorporation of what is best in both ideals. Supple also emphasizes Montaigne's concentration on everyday, private life. See especially 208, 246–48, 265, 249, where he discusses Montaigne's preference for Epaminondas in terms of Epaminondas's combination of public and private values. Schaefer, *Political Philosophy*, 261, regards the overall rhetorical movement of the *Essays* as the attempt to supplant the Stoic model of virtue with his own self-portrait. Regosin, *Matter*, 132, claims that Montaigne inverts accepted values to impose a new order. Shklar, *Ordinary Vices*, 1: Montaigne stepped outside the traditional seven deadly sins; the philosophers and theologians subsume cruelty under other vices and sins (8).

12. Arendt, *Human Condition*, 74–75.

13. See McFarlane, "Concept of Virtue," 84: it is noteworthy how often the words *vertu* and *vérité* occur together in the *Essais*.

Chapter 9: Christianity and the Limits of Politics

1. Jean-Jacques Rousseau, *On the Social Contract with Geneva Manuscript and Political Economy*, trans. Judith R. Masters, ed. Roger D. Masters (New York: St. Martin's Press, 1978), IV.8.

2. Ibid.

3. Ibid.

4. Ibid.

5. Thomas Hobbes, *Leviathan*, ed. C. B. Macpherson (reprint, London: Penguin Books, 1968), I.12.

6. Ibid., III.33.

7. Rousseau, *Social Contract*, IV.8.

8. Ibid.

9. Ibid.

10. Ibid.

11. Ibid.
12. Francis Slade, "Rule as Sovereignty: The Universal and Homogeneous State," in *The Truthful and the Good: Essays in Honor of Robert Sokolowski*, ed. John J. Drummond and James G. Hart (Dordrecht: Kluwer Academic Publishers, 1996), 176.
13. Ibid., 178–79.
14. Fleuret and Levine see Montaigne as a liberal and trace his liberalism to his emphasis on freedom and individualism. Colette Fleuret, "Montaigne et la société civile," *Europe: Revue Littéraire Mensuelle* 50, nos. 513–14 (1972): 111: Montaigne provides a critique of society and a conception of what it should be, based on human nature defined in terms of liberty (116). In Montaigne, we find the basis for bourgeois individualism. Alan Levine, in his *Sensual Philosophy*, claims that Montaigne is a "protoliberal," that is, he wants to promote all possible freedom without jeopardizing stability (167–68). Also, by making the life of the self attractive, he led the way toward liberalism (240). Among those who see him as a conservative, Lanson, *Les Essais*, 238, argues that Montaigne's conservative doctrine is due to the inevitable imperfections of the social order. The reform of laws is always too costly (241). Friedrich, *Montaigne*, 193, links Montaigne's conservatism to his skepticism. There is danger in allowing theoretical consciousness to draw up guidelines for action. "Scepticism breaks down the ideality of the currently applicable norms, yet it strengthens their actual validity." Jean Starobinski, " 'To Preserve and to Continue': Remarks on Montaigne's Conservatism," trans. R. Scott Walker, *Diogenes* 118 (1982): 96, connects Montaigne's political conservatism to his "phenomenalistic" skepticism: "[T]he standard of the political and moral world is no longer conformity to some hidden norm but the open success of the apparent relations individuals establish among each other." Others, recognizing the apparently contradictory tendencies in the essays, have described his stance as a mixture of liberal and conservative elements. Ermanno Bencivenga, *The Discipline of Subjectivity: An Essay on Montaigne* (Princeton, N.J.: Princeton University Press, 1990), 73, refers to "Montaigne's bewildering mixture of ultraconservatism and radicalism." Francis S. Heck, "Montaigne's Conservatism and Liberalism: A Paradox?" *Romanic Review* 66 (1975): 171, concludes that "the so-called paradox of conservative-liberal in Montaigne is a false interpretation of his independent and very flexible position." Brown, "Religious and Political Conservatism," 21, claims that Montaigne's conservatism is based mostly on his view of the weakness of human reason. But, "Montaigne's steadfast concern for mankind is the point in which his apparently conflicting conservative and liberal tendencies meet and merge their identities" (84).
15. Most commentators agree that Montaigne is skeptical about the possibility of radical reform. Carol E. Clark, "Montaigne and the Imagery of Political Discourse in Sixteenth-Century France," *French Studies* 24 (1970): 353–54, notes the absence of any image of a doctor with respect to the image of the state as a sick body. Clark infers that Montaigne does not admit the possibility of an expert in these matters. See also Clark, *Web of Metaphor*, 77. Luthy, "Art of Being Truthful," 43: "All human order is non-rational." Historical reality is "superior to reason, for it is actual." Shklar, *Ordinary Vices*, 32, says that "Montaigne saw no reason to suppose that changes in belief altered human behavior significantly." Jean-Pierre Dhommeaux, "Les idées politiques de Montaigne," *Bulletin*

de la Société des Amis de Montaigne, ser. 5, no. 17 (1976): 16, argues that the rule of *mœurs* cannot be accomplished by politics alone. The Reformation entails a faith in reason that is ultimately the source of anarchy (23). Nannerl O. Keohane, "Montaigne's Individualism," *Political Theory: An International Journal of Political Philosophy* 5 (1977): 378, finds that Montaigne has no confidence in the use of reason in political matters. Starobinski, " 'To Preserve and to Continue,' " 117, argues that Montaigne does not aim to change the world. David R. Hiley, "The Politics of Scepticism: Reading Montaigne," *History of Philosophy Quarterly* 9, no. 4 (1992): 395–97, claims that Montaigne opposes any total reorganization of society and rejects all utopian ideals. Schaefer, *Political Philosophy*, 32, however, argues that Montaigne seeks "a radical transformation of the political and social order." See also 91 on the relationship of politics and philosophy.

16. In the "Apology" he criticizes the English for changing their laws so often "not only in political matters, in which people want to dispense with constancy" but even in religious matters. Thus, he acknowledges the undesirability of resistance to all change in political matters. Also, we have seen that Montaigne himself does have a public purpose in writing the *Essays*: he wants to encourage a certain break with custom with respect to a free and open way of speaking. And in Chapter 8 we considered his innovation in reordering virtues and vices. There are, then, intimations of political possibilities that Montaigne appears to be open to and even to point to.

17. Machiavelli, *Discourses*, III.41. Pierre Manent, *An Intellectual History of Liberalism*, trans. Rebecca Balinski (Princeton, N.J.: Princeton University Press, 1995), 14: for Machiavelli, the city "is not open to anything beyond itself," and "the political order is now a closed circle having its own foundation within itself" (15). Schneewind, *Invention of Autonomy*, makes a similar point: for Machiavelli, politics is the only possible answer to the question of how the highest individual good can be attained, whereas Montaigne does not believe that politics can provide the good life (57). Machiavelli is the political philosopher with whom Montaigne is often compared. On the similarities between the two, see Marcel Tetel, "Montaigne and Machiavelli: Ethics, Politics and Humanism," *Rivista di Letteratura moderne e comparate* 29 (1976): 165–81, especially 166; Quiñones, *Discovery of Time*, 217; Schaefer, *Political Philosophy* (e.g., 347); S. G. Sanders, "Montaigne et les idées politiques de Machiavel," *Bulletin de la Société des Amis de Montaigne*, ser. 5, nos. 18–19 (1976): 85–98. Some writers emphasize the differences: Keohane, "Individualism," 382–84; Alexander Nicolai, "Le machiavélisme de Montaigne," parts 1–4, *Bulletin de la Société des Amis de Montaigne*, ser. 3, no. 4 (1957): 11–21; nos. 5–6 (1958): 25–47; no. 7 (1958): 2–8; no. 9 (1959): 18–30; Robert J. Collins, "Montaigne's Rejection of Reason of State in 'De l'utile et de l'honneste,' " *Sixteenth Century Journal* 23 (1992): 79; and Quint, *Quality of Mercy*, 39.

18. Niccolò Machiavelli, *The Prince*, trans. Harvey C. Mansfield Jr. (Chicago: University of Chicago Press, 1985), chap. 17.

19. Ibid., chap. 15.

20. Francis Slade, "Was Ist Aufklärung? Notes on Maritain, Rorty, and Bloom with Thanks but No Apologies to Immanuel Kant," in *The Common Things: Essays on Thomism and Education*, ed. Daniel McInerny (N.p.: American Maritain Association, 1999), 58.

21. Michael Oakeshott, *The Politics of Faith and the Politics of Scepticism*, ed. Timothy Fuller (New Haven: Yale University Press, 1996), 48.
22. Ibid., 49.
23. Slade, "Rule as Sovereignty," 167.
24. Ibid., 173–75.
25. See Fumaroli, review of Brague's *La sagesse du monde*, 8: "[T]he pitiless irony he directed against any ambitious exercise of public power rather fueled future resistance to, and private reservations about, the authoritarian State erected by Richelieu and Louis XIV."
26. See Henry, "Recognition of the Other," 179–80.
27. Schaefer, *Political Philosophy*, 176, claims that Montaigne's attachment is "to Rome qua pagan republic [rather] than as the seat of the papacy." McGowan, "Clusterings," however, says that "it is impossible to separate the Rome of Montaigne's imagination from the city which he literally saw. They are fused in a compelling double re-enactment of grandeur and of ruins" (117). Rome is both pagan and Christian, thus mirroring Montaigne's own character.
28. Manent, *Intellectual History of Liberalism*, 4–5, sees the Church's position as contradictory: "The remarkable contradiction embedded in the Catholic Church's doctrine can be summarized in this way: although the Church leaves men free to organize themselves within the temporal sphere as they see fit, it simultaneously tends to impose a theocracy on them. It brings a religious constraint of a previously unheard of scope, and at the same time offers the emancipation of secular life."
29. Sayce, *Critical*, 59, notes that "behind the *Essais* and indeed running through them there is . . . a background of extreme violence." Thomas M. Greene, "Dangerous Parleys – *Essais* I:5 and 6," *Yale French Studies* 64 (1983): 3, comments on essay I.1 that it introduces the reader to terror. Eric Aaron Johnson, *Knowledge and Society: A Social Epistemology of Montaigne's Essais* (Charlottesville, Va.: Rookwood Press, 1994), 21–22, makes a similar point. On the relation of Christianity to politics, see Anthony Wilden, "Par divers moyens on arrive à pareille fin: A Reading of Montaigne," *Modern Language Notes* 83 (1968): 578: the Augustinian notion of a transcendent city of God is totally lacking in Montaigne. See Arendt, *Human Condition*, 53, on charity as an unworldly, nonpolitical bond, and 74–77, on Christian goodness as hidden.
30. T. S. Eliot, *Murder in the Cathedral* (New York: Harcourt Brace Jovanovich, 1935), 44.
31. Ibid., 73.
32. Ibid., 81.
33. Ibid., 83–84.
34. Slade, "Was Ist Aufklärung?," 52.
35. See Quint, *Quality of Mercy*, 131–32: on the face in the crowd to entrust oneself to, Quint says that this is the face of clemency. "This face is the one that the *Essais* have presented to us in their self-portrait."
36. Oakeshott, *Religion*, 59–60.
37. Schaefer, *Political Philosophy*, 32.
38. Ibid., 112.
39. Hiley, "Politics of Scepticism," 394. See also Friedrich, *Montaigne*, 108, 115.

40. Alan Levine, "Skepticism, Self, and Toleration in Montaigne's Political Thought," in *Early Modern Skepticism and the Origins of Toleration*, ed. Alan Levine (Lanham, Md.: Lexington Books, 1999), 55.

41. T. S. Eliot, *Christianity and Culture: The Idea of a Christian Society and Notes towards the Definition of Culture* (New York: Harcourt, Brace and World, 1949), 101.

42. Ibid., 198. See also Lewis, *God in the Dock*, 62, on sixth-rate hymns: "I realized that the hymns (which were just sixth rate music) were, nevertheless, being sung with devotion and benefit by an old saint in elastic-side boots in the opposite pew, and then you realize that you aren't fit to clean those boots."

43. Ibid., 200. Fareed Zakaria, in an article entitled "Money for Mars" in *Newsweek* (Winter 1999), asks "Who is prepared to die for Europe?" now that Europe has been unified economically. Zakaria writes: " 'Europe' was not a term commonly used until the 18th century. Nor was 'Western civilization,' a phrase that became popular only in the early 20th century. In earlier times, when people spoke of the common ideas, institutions and people of the Continent they spoke of – Christianity. Christianity was the central organizing principle of European societies. It was the basis of the educational canon, of art, music and culture. . . . The term used to describe Europe long before 'Europe' was 'Christendom.' " With the secularization of the West, "there is no deep commonality, no cultural resonance to give meaning to the term 'Europe' or 'the West.' " (104). When Montaigne writes of his travels in "Europe" he speaks, for example, of "the baths of Christendom." (I am indebted to Firmin DeBraebander for calling my attention to the Zakaria article.)

44. On the primacy of the value of freedom for Montaigne, see Nannerl O. Keohane, "The Radical Humanism of Etienne de la Boétie," *Journal of the History of Ideas* 38 (1977): 121. Eric MacPhail, "Friendship as a Political Ideal in Montaigne's *Essais*," *Montaigne Studies* 1 (1989): 179, 187, suggests the connection between friendship as a political ideal and liberty. Moreau, *L'homme et l'oeuvre*, 87, notes that Montaigne shows a preference for republics in his examples from history. Lewis, *God in the Dock*, 314, uses Montaigne as an example of "the freeborn mind." Economic independence allows an education not controlled by government and "in adult life it is the man who needs, and asks, nothing of government who can criticize its acts and snap his fingers at its ideology. Read Montaigne; that's the voice of a man with his legs under his own table, eating the mutton and turnips raised on his own land. Who will talk like that when the State is everyone's schoolmaster and employer?"

45. Augustine, *The City of God*, IV.31.

46. Ibid., 27.

47. Oakeshott, *Rationalism in Politics*, 339.

Works Cited

Abercrombie, Nigel. *St. Augustine and French Classical Thought*. 1938. Reissued, New York: Atheneum Publishers, Russell and Russell, 1972.

Adorno, T. W. "The Essay as Form." *New German Critique* 32 (Spring 1984): 151–71.

Anselm, Saint. *Proslogion*. Trans. M. J. Charlesworth. Notre Dame, Ind.: University of Notre Dame Press, 1979.

Aquinas, Saint Thomas. *Treatise on Law: Summa Theologica. Questions 90–97*. Chicago: Henry Regnery, 1970.

Arendt, Hannah. *The Human Condition*. Chicago: University of Chicago Press, 1958.

Aristotle. *The Basic Works of Aristotle*. Ed. Richard McKeon. New York: Random House, 1941.

Nicomachean Ethics. Trans. Martin Ostwald. Indianapolis: Bobbs-Merrill, 1962.

Armaingaud, Arthur. "Montaigne: Etait-il ondoyant et divers? Montaigne était-il inconstant?" *Revue du seizième siècle* 10 (1923): 35–56.

Armstrong, Elizabeth. "A Study in Montaigne's Post-1588 Style and Sensibility." In *The Equilibrium of Wit*, ed. Peter Bayley and Dorothy Gabe Coleman, 77–85. Lexington, Ky.: French Forum Publishers, 1982.

Atkinson, James B. "Montaigne and *Naïveté*." *Romanic Review* 64 (1973): 245–57.

"Naïveté and Modernity: The French Renaissance Battle for a Literary Vernacular." *Journal of the History of Ideas* 35 (1974): 179–96.

Auerbach, Erich. "L'humaine condition." In *Mimesis: The Representation of Reality in Western Literature*, trans. Willard R. Trask, 285–312. Princeton, N.J.: Princeton University Press, 1953.

Augustine, Saint. *The City of God*. Ed. David Knowles. Trans. Henry Bettenson. Middlesex: Penguin Books, 1972.

The Confessions. Trans. F. J. Sheed. Indianapolis: Hackett, 1992.

Baraz, Michaël. *L'être et la connaissance selon Montaigne*. Toulouse: Librairie José Corti, 1968.

"Montaigne et l'idéal de l'homme entier." In *O un amy! Essays on Montaigne in Honor of Donald M. Frame*, ed. Raymond C. La Charité, 18–33. Lexington, Ky.: French Forum Publishers, 1977.

Barfield, Owen. *Poetic Diction: A Study in Meaning*. London: Faber and Faber, 1928.

Bauschatz, Cathleen M. "Montaigne's Conception of Reading in the Context of Renaissance Poetics and Modern Criticism." In *The Reader in the Text*, ed. Susan R. Suleiman and Inge Crosman, 264–91. Princeton, N.J.: Princeton University Press, 1980.

Beaudry, James G. "Virtue and Nature in the *Essais*." *Kentucky Romance Quarterly* 1 (1976): 93–103.

Bencivenga, Ermanno. *The Discipline of Subjectivity: An Essay on Montaigne*. Princeton, N.J.: Princeton University Press, 1990.

Blinkenberg, Andreas. "Quel sens Montaigne a-t-il voulu donner au mot *Essais* dans le titre de son œuvre?" In *Mélanges de linguistique et de littérature romanes, offerts à Mario Roques*, 1: 3–14. Geneva: Slatkine Reprints, 1974.

Bloom, Harold. *The Western Canon: The Books and School of the Ages*. New York: Riverhead Books, 1994.

Blum, Claude. "La fonction du 'déjà dit' dans les 'Essais': Emprunter, alléguer, citer." *Cahiers de l'Association Internationale des Etudes Françaises* 33 (1981): 35–51.

Boase, Alan M. "The Early History of the *Essai* Title in France and Britain." In *Studies in French Literature, Presented to H. W. Lawton*, ed. J. C. Ireson, I. D. McFarlane, and Garnet Rees, 67–74. New York: Manchester University Press, Barnes and Noble, 1968.

The Fortunes of Montaigne: A History of the Essays in France, 1580–1669. London: Methuen, 1935.

Bonadeo, Alfredo. "Montaigne on War." *Journal of the History of Ideas* 46 (1985): 417–26.

Boon, Jean-Pierre. *Montaigne gentilhomme et essayiste*. Paris: Editions Universitaires, 1971.

Bowen, Barbara C. "Montaigne's Anti-*Phaedrus*: 'Sur des vers de Virgile' (*Essais*, II, v)." *Journal of Medieval and Renaissance Studies* 5 (1975): 107–21.

"What Does Montaigne Mean by 'Marqueterie'?" *Studies in Philology* 67 (1970): 147–55.

Boyle, Nicholas. "Pascal, Montaigne, and 'J.-C.': The Centre of the Pensées." *Journal of European Studies* 12 (1982): 1–29.

Brague, Rémi. *La sagesse du monde: Histoire de l'expérience humaine de l'univers*. Paris: Librairie Arthème Fayard, 1999.

Brahami, Frédéric. *Le scepticisme de Montaigne*. Paris: Presses Universitaires de France, 1997.

Brann, Eva T. H. *The World of the Imagination: Sum and Substance*. Lanham, Md.: Rowman and Littlefield, 1991.

Brody, Jules. "'Du repentir' (III:2): A Philological Reading." *Yale French Studies* 64 (1983): 238–72.

"From Teeth to Text in De l'expérience: A Philological Reading." *L'Esprit Créateur* 20 (1980): 7–21.

Lectures de Montaigne. Lexington, Ky.: French Forum Publishers, 1982.

"Montaigne: Philosophy, Philology, Literature." *Philosophy and Literature* 22 (1998): 83–107.

"Les oreilles de Montaigne." *Romanic Review* 74 (1983): 121–35.

Brown, Frieda S. "De la solitude: A Re-examination of Montaigne's Retreat from Public Life." In *From Marot to Montaigne: Essays on French Renaissance Literature*, ed. Raymond C. La Charité. *Kentucky Romance Quarterly* 19 (1972): 137–46.

Religious and Political Conservatism in the Essais of Montaigne. Geneva: Librairie Droz, 1963.

Brunschvicg, Léon. *Descartes et Pascal, lecteurs de Montaigne.* New York: Brentano's, 1944.

Brush, Craig B. "The Essayist Is Learned: Montaigne's *Journal de Voyage* and the *Essais.*" *Romanic Review* 62 (1971): 16–27.

"Montaigne Tries Out Self-Study." *L'Esprit Créateur* 20 (1980): 25–35.

"Montaigne's Surprises." In *Columbia Montaigne Conference Papers,* ed. Donald M. Frame and Mary B. McKinley, 31–46. Lexington, Ky.: French Forum Publishers, 1981.

"Reflections on Montaigne's Concept of Being." In *From Marot to Montaigne: Essays on French Renaissance Literature,* ed. Raymond C. La Charité. *Kentucky Romance Quarterly* 19 (1972): 147–65.

Buck, Philo M. "Que Sçais-Je? – Montaigne." In *The Golden Thread,* 336–68. New York: Macmillan, 1931.

Burke, Peter. *Montaigne.* Oxford: Oxford University Press, 1981.

Burnyeat, Myles, ed. *The Skeptical Tradition.* Berkeley: University of California Press, 1983.

Calder, Ruth M. "Montaigne, *Des boyteux* and the Question of Causality." *Bibliothèque d'humanisme et renaissance* 45, no. 3 (1983): 445–60.

"Montaigne as Satirist." *Sixteenth Century Journal* 17 (1986): 225–35.

Cameron, Keith. "Montaigne and the Mask." *L'Esprit Créateur* 8 (1968): 198–207.

Caron, Elisabeth. "Saint Augustin dans les *Essais.*" *Montaigne Studies* 2, no. 2 (1990): 17–33.

Carpino, Joseph J. "On Laughter." *Interpretation: A Journal of Political Philosophy* 13, no. 1 (1985): 91–102.

"Three Cosmologies." *Interpretation: A Journal of Political Philosophy* 6, no. 1 (1976): 48–64.

"Tractatus Liquorico – Philosophicus." *Interpretation: A Journal of Political Philosophy* 26, no. 3 (1999): 379–89.

Cassirer, Ernst. *Individual and Cosmos in the Philosophy of the Renaissance.* Trans. Mario Domandi. Oxford: Basil Blackwell, 1963.

Cave, Terence. *Pré-histoires: Textes troublés au seuil de la modernité.* Geneva: Librairie Droz, 1999.

"Problems of Reading in the *Essais.*" In *Montaigne: Essays in Memory of Richard Sayce,* ed. I. D. McFarlane and Ian Maclean, 133–66. Oxford: Clarendon Press, 1982.

Cavell, Stanley. *In Quest of the Ordinary: Lines of Skepticism and Romanticism.* Chicago: University of Chicago Press, 1988.

Céard, Jean. "Miracles et monstres dan les *Essais.*" In *La nature et les prodiges: L'insolite au seizième siècle en France,* 409–34. Geneva: Librairie Droz, 1977.

Chambers, Frank M. "Pascal's Montaigne." *Publications of the Modern Language Association of America* 65 (1950): 790–804.

Chateau, Jean. *Montaigne psychologue et pédagogue.* Paris: Libraire Philosophique J. Vrin, 1971.

Chevalier, Tracy, ed. *Encyclopedia of the Essay.* London: Fitzroy Dearborn Publishers, 1997.

Christodoulou, Kyriaki. "Socrate chez Montaigne et Pascal." *Diotima* 7 (1979): 39–50.

Clark, Carol E. "Montaigne and the Imagery of Political Discourse in Sixteenth-Century France." *French Studies* 24 (1970): 337–55.

——— "Talking about Souls: Montaigne on Human Psychology." In *Montaigne: Essays in Memory of Richard Sayce*, ed. I. D. McFarlane and Ian Maclean, 57–76. Oxford: Clarendon Press, 1982.

——— *The Web of Metaphor: Studies in the Imagery of Montaigne's Essais*. Lexington, Ky.: French Forum Publishers, 1978.

Coleman, Dorothy Gabe. *Montaigne's Essais*. London: Allen and Unwin, 1987.

Collins, Robert J. "Montaigne's Rejection of Reason of State in 'De l'utile et de l'honneste.'" *Sixteenth Century Journal* 23 (1992): 71–94.

Compagnon, Antoine. *Nous, Michel de Montaigne*. Paris: Éditions du Seuil, 1980.

Comte-Sponville, André, ed. *Montaigne philosophe*. *Revue Internationale de Philosophie* 46 (1992).

Conche, Marcel. *Montaigne et la philosophie*. Villers-sur-Mer: Editions de Mégare, 1987.

——— *Montaigne ou la conscience heureuse*. Paris: Editions Séghers, 1966.

Coppin, Joseph. "La morale de Montaigne est-elle purement naturelle?" *Facultés Catholiques de Lille, Mémoires et travaux* 32 (1927): 105–20.

Curtius, Quintus. *History of Alexander*. Trans. John C. Rolfe. 2 vols. Loeb Classical Library. Cambridge, Mass.: Harvard University Press, 1946.

de Botton, Alain. *The Consolations of Philosophy*. New York: Vintage Books, 2001.

Defaux, Gérard. "De I.20 ('Que philosopher c'est apprendre à mourir') à III.12 ('De la phisionomie'): Ecriture et *essai* chez Montaigne." In *Montaigne et les Essais 1588–1988*, ed. Claude Blum, 93–118. Paris: Honoré Champion, 1990.

——— *Marot, Rabelais, Montaigne: L'écriture comme présence*. Paris: Champion-Slatkine, 1987.

——— "Readings of Montaigne." Trans. John A. Gallucci. *Yale French Studies* 64 (1983): 73–92.

Delègue, Yves. *Montaigne et la mauvaise foi: L'écriture de la vérité*. Paris: Honoré Champion, 1998.

Demonet, Marie-Luce, ed. *Montaigne et la question de l'homme*. Paris: Presses Universitaires de France, 1999.

——— "Philosopher naturellement." *Montaigne Studies* 12 (2000): 5–24.

Demure, Catherine. "Montaigne: The Paradox and the Miracle – Structure and Meaning in 'The Apology of Raymond Sebond' (*Essais* II:12)." *Yale French Studies* 64 (1983): 188–208.

Desan, Philippe. *Les commerces de Montaigne: Le discours économique des Essais*. Paris: Librairie A. G. Nizet, 1992.

——— *Naissance de la méthode*. Paris: Librairie A. G. Nizet, 1987.

Descartes, René. *Meditations on First Philosophy*. Trans. Donald A. Cress. Indianapolis: Hackett, 1993.

Dhommeaux, Jean-Pierre. "Les idées politiques de Montaigne." *Bulletin de la Société des Amis de Montaigne*, ser. 5, no. 17 (1976): 5–30.

Dinesen, Isak. *Anecdotes of Destiny and Ehrengard*. New York: Random House, Vintage Books, 1993.

Dow, Neal. "The Concept and Term 'Nature' in Montaigne's Essays." Ph.D. diss., University of Pennsylvania, 1940.

Dréano, Maturin. *La pensée religieuse de Montaigne*. Paris: Gabriel Beauchesne et Fils, 1936.

Duby, Georges. *The Age of Cathedrals: Art and Society, 980–1420.* Trans. Eleanor Levieux and Barbara Thompson. Chicago: University of Chicago Press, 1981.

Duval, Edwin M. "Montaigne's Conversions: Compositional Strategies in the *Essais.*" *French Forum* 7 (1982): 5–22.

Eliot, T. S. *Christianity and Culture: The Idea of a Christian Society and Notes towards the Definition of Culture.* New York: Harcourt, Brace and World, 1949.

——— . *Murder in the Cathedral.* New York: Harcourt Brace Jovanovich, 1935.

——— . "The *Pensées* of Pascal." In *Selected Essays.* New York: Harcourt Brace, 1932.

Emerson, Ralph W. "Montaigne; or, the Skeptic." In *Representative Men*, ed. Pamela Schirmeister, 149–86. New York: Marsilio Publishers, 1995.

Epstein, Joseph. "The Personal Essay: A Form of Discovery." In *The Norton Book of Personal Essays*, ed. Joseph Epstein, 11–24. New York: W. W. Norton, 1997.

——— . "Reading Montaigne." *Commentary* 95 (March 1993): 34–40.

Faye, Emmanuel. *Philosophie et perfection de l'homme. De la Renaissance à Descartes.* Paris: Vrin, 1998.

Fleuret, Colette. "Montaigne et la société civile." *Europe: Revue Littéraire Mensuelle* 50, nos. 513–14 (1972): 107–23.

Foster, Michael B. *Mystery and Philosophy.* London: SCM Press, 1957.

Frame, Donald M. "Considerations on the Genesis of Montaigne's *Essais.*" In *Montaigne: Essays in Memory of Richard Sayce*, ed. I. D. McFarlane and Ian Maclean, 1–12. Oxford: Clarendon Press, 1982.

——— . "Did Montaigne Betray Sebond?" *Romanic Review* 38 (1947): 297–329.

——— . "Montaigne and the Problem of Consistency." *Kentucky Romance Quarterly* 21, supp. 2 (1974): 157–72.

——— . "Montaigne on the Absurdity and Dignity of Man." In *Renaissance Men and Ideas*, ed. Robert Schwoebel, 122–35. New York: St. Martin's Press, 1971.

——— . *Montaigne's Discovery of Man: The Humanization of a Humanist.* New York: Columbia University Press, 1955.

——— . *Montaigne's Essais: A Study.* Englewood Cliffs, N.J.: Prentice Hall, 1969.

——— . "Montaigne's Rejection of Inner Conflict and His Chapter 'De la cruauté' (II.11)." In *Mélanges sur la littérature de la Renaissance*, 481–89. Geneva: Librairie Droz, 1984.

——— . "Specific Motivation for Montaigne's Self-Portrait." In *Columbia Montaigne Conference Papers*, ed. Donald M. Frame and Mary B. McKinley, 60–69. Lexington, Ky.: French Forum Publishers, 1981.

——— . "To 'Rise above Humanity' and to 'Escape from the Man': Two Moments in Montaigne's Thought." *Romanic Review* 62 (1971): 28–35.

Frame, Donald M., and Mary B. McKinley, eds. *Columbia Montaigne Conference Papers.* Lexington, Ky.: French Forum Publishers, 1981.

Frank, Manfred. "Toward a Philosophy of Style." *Common Knowledge* 1, no. 1 (1991): 54–77.

Friedrich, Hugo. *Montaigne.* Ed. Philippe Desan. Trans. Dawn Eng. Berkeley: University of California Press, 1991.

Fumaroli, Marc. "First Gentleman of Gascony: Montaigne's Liberal Antidotes to the Hubris of Democracy." Review of *Montaigne and the Quality of Mercy: Ethical and Political Themes in the Essais*, by David Quint, and of *La sagesse du monde: Histoire de l'expérience humaine de l'univers*, by Rémi Brague. *Times Literary Supplement*, 15 October 1999, 8–9.

Galgan, Gerald J. *Interpreting the Present: Six Philosophical Essays.* Lanham, Md.: University Press of America, 1993.

Genz, Henry E. "Compositional Form in Montaigne's *Essais* and the Self-Portrait." *Kentucky Foreign Language Quarterly* 10 (1963): 133–39.

Gide, André. *Essai sur Montaigne.* Paris: Jacques Schiffrin, Editions de la Pléïade, n.d.

Gontier, Thierry. *De l'homme à l'animal. Paradoxes sur la nature des animaux. Montaigne et Descartes.* Paris: Vrin, 1998.

Good, Graham. "Identity and Form in the Modern Autobiographical Essay." *Prose Studies* 15 (1992): 99–117.

———. *The Observing Self: Rediscovering the Essay.* London: Routledge, 1988.

Goyet, Francis. "Tragi-comédie de la certitude: L'argument d'autorité dans les *Essais.*" *Bulletin de la Société des Amis de Montaigne* 21–22 (1985): 21–42.

Gray, Floyd. "Montaigne's Pyrrhonism." In *O un amy! Essays on Montaigne in Honor of Donald M. Frame,* ed. Raymond C. La Charité, 119–36. Lexington, Ky.: French Forum Publishers, 1977.

———. "The 'Nouveaux Docteurs' and the Problem of Montaigne's Consistency in the *Apologie de Raymond Sebond.*" *Symposium* 18 (1964): 22–34.

———. *Le Style de Montaigne.* Paris: Librairie A. G. Nizet, 1958.

———. "The Unity of Montaigne in the *Essais.*" *Modern Language Quarterly* 22 (1961): 79–86.

Greene, Thomas M. "Dangerous Parleys – *Essais* I:5 and 6." *Yale French Studies* 64 (1983): 3–23.

———. "Montaigne and the Savage Infirmity." *Yale Review* 46 (1956): 191–205.

Gutwirth, Marcel. "'By Diverse Means . . .' (I:1)." *Yale French Studies* 64 (1983): 180–87.

———. *Michel de Montaigne ou le pari d'exemplarité.* Montreal: Les Presses de l'Université de Montréal, 1977.

———. "Montaigne pour et contre Sebond." *Revue des sciences humaines* 34 (1969): 175–88.

Hall, Michael L. "'Drawing Myself for Others': The *Ethos* of the Essayist." *Explorations in Renaissance Culture* 7 (1981): 27–35.

———. "The Emergence of the Essay and the Idea of Discovery." In *Essays on the Essay: Redefining the Genre,* ed. Alexander J. Butrym, 73–91. Athens: University of Georgia Press, 1989.

Hallie, Philip P. "The Ethics of Montaigne's 'De la cruauté.'" In *O un amy! Essays on Montaigne in Honor of Donald M. Frame,* ed. Raymond C. La Charité, 156–71. Lexington, Ky.: French Forum Publishers, 1977.

Hampton, Timothy. *Writing from History: The Rhetoric of Exemplarity in Renaissance Literature.* Ithaca: Cornell University Press, 1990.

Hanson, Victor Davis. *The Soul of Battle: From Ancient Times to the Present Day, How Three Great Liberators Vanquished Tyranny.* New York: Free Press, 1999.

Hardison, O. B. "Binding Proteus: An Essay on the Essay." In *Essays on the Essay: Redefining the Genre,* ed. Alexander J. Butrym, 11–28. Athens: University of Georgia Press, 1989.

Heck, Francis S. "Montaigne's Conservatism and Liberalism: A Paradox?" *Romanic Review* 66 (1975): 165–71.

Heidegger, Martin. "A Discussion between Ernst Cassirer and Martin Heidegger." Trans. Francis Slade. In *The Existentialist Tradition,* ed. Nino Langiulli, 192–203. Garden City, N.Y.: Anchor Books, Doubleday, 1971.

"Letter on Humanism." Trans. Edgar Lohner in *The Existentialist Tradition*, ed. Nino Langiulli, 204–45. Garden City, N.Y.: Anchor Books, Doubleday, 1971.

Henderson, Edgar H. "Montaigne and Modern Philosophy." *Personalist* 34 (1953): 278–89.

Henry, Patrick. "Montaigne and Heraclitus: Pattern and Flux, Continuity and Change in 'Du repentir.'" *Montaigne Studies* 4 (1992): 7–18.

Montaigne in Dialogue. Stanford, Calif.: ANMA Libri, 1987.

"Recognition of the Other and Avoidance of the Double: The Self and the Other in the *Essais* of Montaigne." *Stanford French Review* 6 (1982): 175–87.

"The Rise of the Essay: Montaigne and the Novel." *Montaigne Studies* 6, nos. 1–2 (1994): 113–34.

"Les titres façades, la censure et l'écriture défensive chez Montaigne." *Bulletin de la Société des Amis de Montaigne*, ser. 5, no. 24 (1977): 11–28.

Hiley, David R. *Philosophy in Question: Essays on a Pyrrhonian Theme*. Chicago: University of Chicago Press, 1988.

"The Politics of Scepticism: Reading Montaigne." *History of Philosophy Quarterly* 9, no. 4 (1992): 379–99.

Hobbes, Thomas. *Leviathan*. Ed. C. B. Macpherson. Reprint, London: Penguin Books, 1968.

Hoffmann, George. *Montaigne's Career*. Oxford: Clarendon Press, 1998.

Holyoake, S. John. "The Idea of 'Jugement' in Montaigne." *Modern Language Review* 63 (1968): 340–51.

"Montaigne's Attitude to Memory." *French Studies* 25 (1971): 257–70.

Hume, David. *Essays: Moral, Political, and Literary*. Ed. Eugene F. Miller. Indianapolis: Liberty Classics, 1985.

An Enquiry concerning Human Understanding. Indianapolis: Hackett, 1977.

Janssen, Herman. *Montaigne fidéiste*. Nijmegen, Utrecht: N. V. Dekker and Van de Vigt en J. W. Van Leeuwen, 1930.

Johnson, Eric Aaron. *Knowledge and Society: A Social Epistemology of Montaigne's Essais*. Charlottesville, Va.: Rookwood Press, 1994.

Joukovsky, Françoise. *Montaigne et le problème du temps*. Paris: Librairie A. G. Nizet, 1972.

Kass, Leon R. *The Hungry Soul: Eating and the Perfecting of Our Nature*. Chicago: University of Chicago Press, 1999.

Kauffmann, R. Lane. "The Skewed Path: Essaying as Un-methodical Method." *Diogenes* 143 (Fall 1988): 66–92.

Kekes, John. "Constancy and Purity." *Mind* 92 (1983): 499–518.

Moral Wisdom and Good Lives. Ithaca: Cornell University Press, 1995.

Kellermann, Frederick. "The *Essais* and Socrates." *Symposium* 10 (1956): 204–16.

"Montaigne, Reader of Plato." *Comparative Literature* 8 (1956): 307–22.

Keohane, Nannerl O. "Montaigne's Individualism." *Political Theory: An International Journal of Political Philosophy* 5 (1977): 363–90.

"The Radical Humanism of Etienne de la Boétie." *Journal of the History of Ideas* 38 (1977): 119–30.

Kierkegaard, Søren. *Fear and Trembling*. Ed. and trans. Howard V. Hong and Edna V. Hong. Princeton, N.J.: Princeton University Press, 1983.

La Charité, Raymond C. *The Concept of Judgment in Montaigne*. The Hague: Martinus Nijhoff, 1968.

ed. *From Marot to Montaigne: Essays on French Renaissance Literature. Kentucky Romance Quarterly* 19 (1972).

ed. *O un amy! Essays on Montaigne in Honor of Donald M. Frame.* Lexington, Ky.: French Forum Publishers, 1977.

Lang, Berel. "Plotting Philosophy: Between the Acts of Philosophical Genre." *Philosophy and Literature* 12 (1988): 190–210.

Langer, Ullrich. *Vertu du discours, discours de la vertu: Littérature et philosophie morale au xvie siècle en France.* Geneva: Librairie Droz, 1999.

Langiulli, Nino. *Possibility, Necessity and Existence.* Philadelphia: Temple University Press, 1992.

Lanson, Gustave. *L'art de la prose.* Paris: Arthème Fayard et Cie, Editeurs, 1911.

Les Essais de Montaigne. Paris: Librairie Mellottée, n.d.

"La vie morale selon les *Essais* de Montaigne." Parts 1 and 2. *Revue des Deux Mondes*, ser. 7, 19 (February 1, 1924): 603–25; (February 15, 1924): 836–58.

Lapp, John C. "Montaigne's 'Negligence' and Some Lines from Virgil." *Romanic Review* 61 (1970): 167–81.

Larkin, Neil M. "Montaigne's Last Words." *L'Esprit Créateur* 15 (1975): 21–38.

Leake, Roy E., Jr. "Montaigne's Gascon Proverb Again." *Neophilologus* 52 (1968): 248–55.

Lee, Sidney. "Montaigne." In *The French Renaissance in England*, 165–79. New York: Charles Scribner's Sons, 1910.

Lemaire, Jacques, ed. *Montaigne et la révolution philosophique du XVIe siècle.* Brussels: Editions de l'Université de Bruxelles, 1992.

Levine, Alan. "Skepticism, Self, and Toleration in Montaigne's Political Thought." In *Early Modern Skepticism and the Origins of Toleration*, ed. Alan Levine, 51–75. Lanham, Md.: Lexington Books, 1999.

Sensual Philosophy: Toleration, Skepticism, and Montaigne's Politics of the Self. Lanham, Md.: Lexington Books, 2001.

Lewis, C. S. *God in the Dock: Essays on Theology and Ethics.* Ed. Walter Hooper. Grand Rapids, Mich.: William B. Eerdmans, 1970.

Limbrick, Elaine. "Was Montaigne Really a Pyrrhonian?" *Bibliothèque d'humanisme et renaissance* 39 (1977): 67–80.

Livingston, Donald. *Hume's Philosophy of Common Life.* Chicago: University of Chicago Press, 1984.

Philosophical Melancholy and Delirium: Hume's Pathology of Philosophy. Chicago: University of Chicago Press, 1998.

Locher, Caroline. "Primary and Secondary Themes in Montaigne's 'Des cannibales' (I, 31)." *French Forum* 1 (1976): 119–26.

Long, A. A., and D. N. Sedley. *The Hellenistic Philosophers.* 2 vols. Cambridge: Cambridge University Press, 1987.

Lowith, Karl. *Nature, History, and Existentialism.* Evanston, Ill.: Northwestern University Press, 1966.

Lucas, F. L. "The Master-Essayist." In *Studies in French and English*, 115–37. London: Cassell, 1934.

Lukacs, Georg. *Soul and Form.* Trans. Anna Bostock. Cambridge, Mass.: MIT Press, 1974.

Luthy, Herbert. "Montaigne, or the Art of Being Truthful." *Encounter* 1 (1953): 33–44.

Lyas, Colin. "That to Philosophise Is to Learn How to Die." *Philosophical Investigations* 16, no. 2 (April 1993): 116–27.

Lydgate, Barry. "Mortgaging One's Work to the World: Publication and the Structure of Montaigne's *Essais.*" *Publications of the Modern Language Association of America* 96 (1981): 210–23.

Lyons, John D. "Tacit History." *Montaigne Studies* 6, nos. 1–2 (1994): 39–51.

Lyotard, Jean-François. *The Postmodern Condition: A Report on Knowledge.* Trans. Geoff Bennington and Brian Massumi. Minneapolis: University of Minnesota Press, 1984.

Machiavelli, Niccolò. *Discourses on Livy.* Trans. Harvey C. Mansfield Jr. and Nathan Tarcov. Chicago: University of Chicago Press, 1996.

— *The Prince.* Trans. Harvey C. Mansfield Jr. Chicago: University of Chicago Press, 1985.

Maclean, Ian. *Montaigne philosophe.* Paris: Presses Universitaires de France, 1996.

— "'Le païs au delà': Montaigne and Philosophical Speculation." In *Montaigne: Essays in Memory of Richard Sayce*, ed. I. D. McFarlane and Ian Maclean, 101–32. Oxford: Clarendon Press, 1982.

— "The Place of Interpretation: Montaigne and Humanist Jurists on Words, Intention and Meaning." In *Neo-Latin and the Vernacular in Renaissance France*, ed. Graham Castor and Terence Cave, 252–72. Oxford: Clarendon Press, 1984.

MacPhail, Eric. "Friendship as a Political Ideal in Montaigne's *Essais.*" *Montaigne Studies* 1 (1989): 177–87.

Malebranche, Nicolas. *Treatise on Nature and Grace.* Trans. Patrick Riley. Oxford: Clarendon Press, 1992.

Manent, Pierre. *An Intellectual History of Liberalism.* Trans. Rebecca Balinski. Princeton, N.J.: Princeton University Press, 1995.

Marchi, Dudley M. *Montaigne among the Moderns: Receptions of the Essais.* Providence, R.I.: Berghahn Books, 1994.

Maskell, David. "The Evolution of the *Essais.*" In *Montaigne: Essays in Memory of Richard Sayce*, ed. I. D. McFarlane and Ian Maclean, 13–34. Oxford: Clarendon Press, 1982.

Mathias, Paul, ed. *Apologie de Raymond Sebond.* Paris: Flammarion, 1999.

— "Montaigne: Une philosophie de gai savoir." *Montaigne Studies* 12 (2000): 123–36.

Mathieu-Castellani, Gisèle. *Montaigne: L'écriture de l'essai.* Paris: Presses Universitaires de France, 1988.

Mauzey, Jesse V. *Montaigne's Philosophy of Human Nature.* Annandale-on-Hudson, N.Y.: St. Stephen's College, 1933.

McFarlane, I. D. "The Concept of Virtue in Montaigne." In *Montaigne: Essays in Memory of Richard Sayce*, ed. I. D. McFarlane and Ian Maclean, 77–100. Oxford: Clarendon Press, 1982.

— "Montaigne and the Concept of the Imagination." In *The French Renaissance and Its Heritage*, ed. D. R. Haggis et al., 117–37. London: Methuen, 1968.

McFarlane, I. D., and Ian Maclean, eds. *Montaigne: Essays in Memory of Richard Sayce.* Oxford: Clarendon Press, 1982.

McGowan, Margaret. "The Art of Transition in the *Essais.*" In *Montaigne: Essays in Memory of Richard Sayce*, ed. I. D. McFarlane and Ian Maclean, 35–56. Oxford: Clarendon Press, 1982.

"Clusterings: Positive and Negative Values in 'De la vanité'" *Montaigne Studies* 1 (1989): 107–19.

Montaigne's Deceits: The Art of Persuasion in the Essais. Philadelphia: Temple University Press, 1974.

McKinley, Mary B. "The *City of God* and the City of Man: Limits of Language in Montaigne's 'Apologie.'" *Romanic Review* 71 (1980): 122–40.

Meijer, Marianne S. "De l'honnête, de l'utile et du repentir." *Journal of Medieval and Renaissance Studies* 12, no. 2 (1982): 259–74.

"Guesswork or Facts: Connections between Montaigne's Last Three Chapters (III:11, 12 and 13)." *Yale French Studies* 64 (1983): 167–79.

"Mourir lâchement et mollement." In *Etudes Montaignistes en hommage à Pierre Michel*, ed. Claude Blum and François Moureau 173–82. Paris: Champion, 1984.

"The Significance of 'De la diversion' in Montaigne's *Third Book.*" *Romance Notes* 32 (1991): 11–17.

Melehy, Hassan. *Writing Cogito: Montaigne, Descartes, and the Institution of the Modern Subject.* Albany: State University of New York Press, 1997.

Menut, Albert D. "Montaigne and the *Nicomachean Ethics.*" *Modern Philology* 31 (1933–34): 225–42.

Merleau-Ponty, Maurice. "Reading Montaigne." In *Signs*, trans. Richard C. McCleary, 198–210. Evanston, Ill.: Northwestern University Press, 1964.

Mermier, Guy. "L'essai *Des cannibales* de Montaigne," *Bulletin de la Société des Amis de Montaigne* 7 (1973): 27–38.

Micha, Alexandre. *Le singulier Montaigne.* Paris: Librairie A. G. Nizet, 1964.

Miernowski, Jan. "Le 'beau jeu' de la philosophie." *Montaigne Studies* 12 (2000): 25–43.

L'ontologie de la contradiction sceptique: Pour l'étude de la métaphysique des Essais. Paris: Honoré Champion, 1998.

Moore, W. G. "Montaigne's Notion of Experience." In *The French Mind: Studies in Honor of Gustave Rudler*, ed. Will Moore, Rhoda Sutherland, and Enid Starkie, 34–52. Oxford: Clarendon Press, 1952.

Moreau, Pierre. *Montaigne: L'homme et l'œuvre.* Paris: Boivin et Cie, 1939.

Moureau, François. "Montaigne, écrivain des lumières?" *Diotima* 17 (1989): 14–19.

Murry, John Middleton. "Montaigne: The Birth of the Individual." In *Heroes of Thought*, 49–62. Freeport, N.Y.: Books for Libraries Press, 1938.

Nakam, Géralde. *Montaigne. La manière et la matière.* Paris: Klincksieck, 1991.

Nehamas, Alexander. *The Art of Living: Socratic Reflections from Plato to Foucault.* Berkeley: University of California Press, 1998.

Nicolai, Alexander. "Le machiavélisme de Montaigne." Parts 1–4. *Bulletin de la Société des Amis de Montaigne*, ser. 3, no. 4 (1957): 11–21; nos. 5–6 (1958): 25–47; no. 7 (1958): 2–8; no. 9 (1959): 18–30.

Nietzsche, Friedrich. *Schopenhauer as Educator.* Trans. William Arrowsmith. In *Unmodern Observations*, ed. William Arrowsmith, 147–226. New Haven: Yale University Press, 1990.

Norton, Glyn P. *Montaigne and the Introspective Mind.* The Hague: Mouton, 1975.

Oakeshott, Michael. *On Human Conduct.* Oxford: Oxford University Press, 1975. Reprint, Oxford: Clarendon Press, 1991.

The Politics of Faith and the Politics of Scepticism. Ed. Timothy Fuller. New Haven: Yale Universtiy Press, 1996.

Rationalism in Politics and Other Essays. Ed. Timothy Fuller. London: Methuen, 1962. Reprint, Indianapolis: Liberty Press, 1991.

Religion, Politics and the Moral Life. Ed. Timothy Fuller. New Haven: Yale Universtiy Press, 1993.

O'Brien, John. "The Eye Perplexed: Aristotle and Montaigne on Seeing and Choosing." *Journal of Medieval and Renaissance Studies* 22 (1992): 291–305.

O'Loughlin, Michael. *The Garlands of Repose: The Literary Celebration of Civic and Retired Leisure*. Chicago: University of Chicago Press, 1978.

O'Neill, John. "The Essay as a Moral Exercise: Montaigne." *Renaissance and Reformation* 9 (1985): 209–18.

Essaying Montaigne: A Study of the Renaissance Institution of Writing and Reading. London: Routledge and Kegan Paul, 1982.

Pascal, Blaise. "Entretien avec M. De Sacy." In *Œuvres complètes*, ed. Jean Mesnard, 3: 76–157. Paris: Desclée de Brouwer, 1991.

Pensées et opuscules. Ed. Léon Brunschvicg. Rev. ed. Paris: Librairie Hachette, 1946.

Paulson, Michael G. *The Possible Influence of Montaigne's Essais on Descartes' "Treatise on the Passions."* Lanham, Md.: University Press of America, 1988.

Penelhum, Terence. *God and Skepticism: A Study in Skepticism and Fideism*. Dordrecht: D. Reidel, 1983.

Pertile, Leno. "Paper and Ink: The Structure of Unpredicatiblity." In *O Un Amy! Essays on Montaigne in Honor of Donald M. Frame*, ed. Raymond C. La Charité, 190–218. Lexington, Ky.: French Forum Publishers, 1977.

Pinchard, Bruno. "Montaigne: Essai de lecture dialectique." *Montiagne Studies* 12 (2000): 63–73.

Platt, Michael. "Interpretation." *Interpretation: A Journal of Political Philosophy* 5 (1975):109–30.

Popkin, Richard H. *The History of Scepticism from Erasmus to Spinoza*. Berkeley: University of California Press, 1979.

Pouilloux, Jean-Yves. "La forme maîtresse." In *Montaigne et la question de l'homme*, ed. Marie-Luce Demonet, 34–45. Paris: Presses Universitaires de France, 1999.

Montaigne, l'éveil de la pensée. Paris: Editions Champion, 1995.

Poulet, Georges. "Montaigne." In *Studies in Human Time*, trans. Elliot Coleman, 39–49. Baltimore: Johns Hopkins Press, 1956.

Quiñones, Ricardo J. *The Renaissance Discovery of Time*. Cambridge, Mass.: Harvard University Press, 1972.

Quint, David. *Montaigne and the Quality of Mercy: Ethical and Political Themes in the Essais*. Princeton, N.J.: Princeton University Press, 1998.

Randall, Catherine. "The Swallow's Nest and the Hermeneutic Quest in the Apologie de Raimond Sebond." *Montaigne Studies* 12 (2000): 137–45.

Rée, Jonathan. "Descartes's Comedy." *Philosophy and Literature* 8 (1984): 151–66.

Regosin, Richard L. "Figures of the Self: Montaigne's Rhetoric of Portraiture." *L'Esprit Créateur* 20 (1980): 66–80.

"Language and the Dialectic of the Self in Montaigne's *Essais*." In *From Marot to Montaigne: Essays on French Renaissance Literature*, ed. Raymond C. La Charité. *Kentucky Romance Quarterly* 19 (1972): 167–75.

The Matter of My Book: Montaigne's Essais as the Book of the Self. Berkeley: University of California Press, 1977.

"Le miroüer vague: Reflections of the Example in Montaigne's *Essais*." *Œuvres & Critiques* 8 (1983): 73–86.

"Montaigne's Monstrous Confession." *Montaigne Studies* 1 (1989): 73–87.

"Nemo's Descent: The Rhetoric of Presence in Montaigne's *Essais*." *French Forum* 13, no. 2 (1988): 153–66.

"Sources and Resources: The 'Pretexts' of Originality in Montaigne's *Essais*." *SubStance* 21 (1978): 103–15.

"The Text of Memory: Experience as Narrative in Montaigne's *Essais*." In *The Dialectic of Discovery*, ed. John D. Lyons and Nancy J. Vickers, 145–58. Lexington, Ky.: French Forum Publishers, 1984.

Rendall, Steven. "Dialectical Structure and Tactics in Montaigne's 'Of Cannibals.'" *Pacific Coast Philology* 12 (1977): 56–63.

"Mus in Pice: Montaigne and Interpretation." *Modern Language Notes* 94 (1979): 1056–71.

"Of History." *Montaigne Studies* 6, nos. 1–2 (October 1994): 3–5.

"The Rhetoric of Montaigne's Self-Portrait: Speaker and Subject." *Studies in Philology* 73 (1976): 285–301.

Reno, R. R. *The Ordinary Transformed: Karl Rahner and the Christian Vision of Transcendence*. Grand Rapids, Mich.: William B. Eerdmans, 1995.

Rider, Frederick. *The Dialectic of Selfhood in Montaigne*. Stanford, Calif.: Stanford University Press, 1973.

Rigolot, François. *Les métamorphoses de Montaigne*. Paris: Presses Universitaires de France, 1988.

"Montaigne's Purloined Letters." *Yale French Studies* 64 (1983): 145–66.

Rodis-Lewis, G. "Doute pratique et doute spéculatif chez Montaigne et Descartes." *Revue Philosophique de la France et de l'étranger* 182 (1992): 439–49.

Rollins, Yvonne B. "Montaigne et le langage." *Romanic Review* 64 (1973): 258–72.

Rousseau, Jean-Jacques. *On the Social Contract with Geneva Manuscript and Political Economy*. Trans. Judith R. Masters. Ed. Roger D. Masters. New York: St. Martin's Press, 1978.

Routh, H. V. "The Origins of the Essay Compared in French and English Literatures." Parts 1 and 2. *Modern Language Review* 15 (1920): 28–40, 143–51.

Ruel, Edouard. *Du sentiment artistique dans la morale de Montaigne*. Paris: Librairie Hachette, 1901.

Runyon, Randolph. "Trumpet Variations on an Original Air: Self-Referential Allusion in Montaigne's 'Apology.'" *Romanic Review* 77 (1986): 195–208.

Russell, Daniel. "On Montaigne's Device." *Studi Francesi* 55 (1975): 84–88.

Sanders, S. G. "Montaigne et les idées politiques de Machiavel." *Bulletin de la Société des Amis de Montaigne*, ser. 5, nos. 18–19 (1976): 85–98.

Sayce, Richard A. *The Essays of Montaigne: A Critical Exploration*. Evanston, Ill.: Northwestern University Press, 1972.

"Montaigne et la peinture du passage." *Saggi e ricerche di letteratura francese* 4 (1963): 11–59.

Schaefer, David Lewis. *The Political Philosophy of Montaigne*. Ithaca: Cornell University Press, 1990.

"'To Philosophize Is to Learn How to Die': Montaigne vs. Socrates." *Independent Journal of Philosophy* 5–6 (1988): 23–30.

Schiffman, Zachary S. "Montaigne and the Rise of Skepticism in Early Modern Europe: A Reappraisal." *Journal of the History of Ideas* 45 (1984): 499–516.

Schneewind, J. B. *The Invention of Autonomy*. Cambridge: Cambridge University Press, 1998.

Schwartz, Jerome. "'La conscience d'un homme': Reflections on the Problem of Conscience in the *Essais*." In *O Un Amy! Essays on Montaigne in Honor of Donald M. Frame*, ed. Raymond C. La Charité, 242–76. Lexington, Ky.: French Forum Publishers, 1977.

Sclafert, Clement. *L'âme religieuse de Montaigne*. Paris: Nouvelles Editions Latines, 1951.

Screech, M. A. *Montaigne and Melancholy: The Wisdom of the Essays*. London: Duckworth, 1983. Reprint, London: Penguin, 1991.

"Montaigne: Some Classical Notions in Their Contexts." In *Montaigne in Cambridge, Proceedings of the Cambridge Montaigne Colloquium 1989*, ed. Philip Ford et al. (1989): 39–52.

Sedley, David. "Sublimity and Skepticism in Montaigne." *Publications of the Modern Language Association* 113 (October 1998): 1079–92.

Sextus Empiricus. *Outlines of Pyrrhonism*. In *Hellenistic Philosophy*, ed. Herman Shapiro and Edwin M. Curley. New York: Modern Library, 1965.

Shklar, Judith. *Ordinary Vices*. Cambridge, Mass.: Belknap Press of Harvard University Press, 1984.

Slade, Francis. "Rule as Sovereignty: The Universal and Homogeneous State." In *The Truthful and the Good: Essays in Honor of Robert Sokolowski*, ed. John J. Drummond and James G. Hart, 159–80. Dordrecht: Kluwer Academic Publishers, 1996.

"Was Ist Aufklärung? Notes on Maritain, Rorty, and Bloom with Thanks but No Apologies to Immanuel Kant." In *The Common Things: Essays on Thomism and Education*, ed. Daniel McInerny, 48–68. N.p.: American Maritain Association, 1999.

Sokolowski, Robert. *The God of Faith and Reason*. Notre Dame, Ind.: University of Notre Dame Press, 1982.

Pictures, Quotations, and Distinctions: Fourteen Essays in Phenomenology. Notre Dame, Ind.: University of Notre Dame Press, 1992.

Starobinski, Jean. "The Body's Moment." Trans. John A Gallucci. *Yale French Studies* 64 (1983): 273–305.

Montaigne in Motion. Trans. Arthur Goldhammer. Chicago: University of Chicago Press, 1985.

"'To Preserve and to Continue': Remarks on Montaigne's Conservatism." Trans. R. Scott Walker. *Diogenes* 118 (1982): 103–20.

Steiner, George. *Real Presences*. Cambridge: Cambridge University Press, 1986.

Stevens, Linton C. "The Meaning of 'Philosophie' in the *Essais* of Montaigne." *Studies in Philology* 62 (1965): 147–54.

Stierle, Karl-Heinz. "Story as Exemplum – Exemplum as Story: On the Pragmatics and Poetics of Narrative Texts." In *New Perspectives in German Literary Criticism*, ed. Richard E. Amacher and Victor Lange, 389–417. Princeton, N.J.: Princeton University Press, 1979.

Strowski, Fortunat. *Montaigne*. Paris: Librairie Félix Alcan, 1931.

Supple, James J. *Arms versus Letters: The Military and Literary Ideals in the 'Essais' of Montaigne*. Oxford: Clarendon Press, 1984.

Taylor, Charles. *Sources of the Self: The Making of the Modern Identity*. Cambridge, Mass.: Harvard University Press, 1989.

Telle, E. V. "A propos du mot 'essai' chez Montaigne." *Bibliothèque d'humanisme et renaissance* 30 (1968): 225–47.

Tetel, Marcel. "Montaigne: Evolution or Convolution?" In *Authors and Their Centuries*, ed. Philip Grant, 23–39. French Literature Series, vol. 1. Columbia: University of South Carolina Press, 1973.

"Montaigne and Machiavelli: Ethics, Politics and Humanism." *Rivista di Letterature moderne e comparate* 29 (1976): 165–81.

Todorov, Tzvetan. "L'être et l'autre: Montaigne." *Yale French Studies* 64 (1983): 113–44.

Toulmin, Stephen. *Cosmopolis: The Hidden Agenda of Modernity*. New York: Free Press, 1990.

Tournon, André. *Montaigne: La glose et l'essai*. Lyon: Presses Universitaires de Lyon, 1983.

"Self-Interpretation in Montaigne's *Essais*." *Yale French Studies* 64 (1983): 51–72.

"*Suspense* philosophique et ironie: La zététique de l'*essai*." *Montaigne Studies* 12 (2000): 45–62.

Trinquet, Roger. *La jeunesse de Montaigne*. Paris: A. G. Nizet, 1972.

Trueblood, Ralph W. "Montaigne: The Average Man." *Publications of the Modern Language Association of America* 21 (1906): 215–25.

Van den Abbeele, Georges. *Travel as Metaphor: From Montaigne to Rousseau*. Minneapolis: University of Minnesota Press, 1992.

Villey, Pierre. *Les sources et l'évolution des Essais de Montaigne*. 2 vols. Paris: Librairie Hachette, 1933.

Vincent, Hubert. *Vérité et scepticisme chez Montaigne*. Paris: L'Harmatan, 1998.

Voegelin, Eric. "Reason: The Classic Experience." In *Anamnesis*, trans. Gerhart Niemeyer, 89–115. Notre Dame, Ind.: University of Notre Dame Press, 1978.

Walton, Craig. "Montaigne on The Art of Judgment: The Trial of Montaigne." In *The Sceptical Mode in Modern Philosophy: Essays in Honor of Richard H. Popkin*, ed. Richard A. Watson and James E. Force, 87–102. Dordrecht: Martinus Nijhoff Publishers, 1988.

Watson, Richard A., and James E. Force, eds. *The Sceptical Mode in Modern Philosophy: Essays in Honor of Richard H. Popkin*. Dordrecht: Martinus Nijhoff Publishers, 1988.

Weller, Barry. "The Rhetoric of Friendship in Montaigne's *Essais*." *New Literary History* 9 (1978): 503–23.

Wilden, Anthony. "Par divers moyens on arrive à pareille fin: A Reading of Montaigne." *Modern Language Notes* 83 (1968): 577–97.

Winter, Ian J. "From Self-Concept to Self-Knowledge: Death and Nature in Montaigne's 'De la phisionomie.'" *Kentucky Romance Quarterly* 21, supp. 2 (1974): 351–65.

"'Mon Livre et moi': Montaigne's Deepening Evaluation of His Own Work." *Renaissance Quarterly* 25 (1972): 297–307.

Wood, Michael. "Montaigne and the Mirror of Example." *Philosophy and Literature* 13 (1989): 1–15.

Woodridge, Homer E. "Montaigne, the Friend." *Texas Review* 1 (1915–16): 106–19.

Woolf, Virginia. "Montaigne." In *The Common Reader*, 87–100. New York: Harcourt, Brace, 1925.

Yandell, Cathy. "*Corps* and *corpus*: Montaigne's 'Sur des vers de Virgile.'" *Modern Language Studies* 16 (1986): 77–87.

Zeller, E. *The Stoics, Epicureans and Skeptics*. Trans. Oswald J. Reichel. London: Longmans, Green, 1892.

Index

Abercrombie, Nigel, 263n5
Adorno, T. W.: contrast between essay and Hegelian dialectic, 35–6; contrast between Montaigne and Descartes, 34, 153; on essay as phenomenology, 34; on nature, 249n8, n9; on truth, 38
Alcibiades, 180, 213
Alexander the Great: and Betis, 81, 96, 97, 133; clemency of, 235; compared with Epaminondas, 203, 208; as exemplar, 202; and Homer, 81; imperfections of, 101; and sleep, 18; sweat of, 54–5
analogy, 24, 142
Angelus, 131
Annunciation, 131
Anselm, St., 141
Aquinas, St. Thomas, 164; on analogy, 24, 142; on natural law, 42, 46–7; scholastic style of, 75, 137–8; and Sebond's natural theology, 23, 137
Arendt, Hannah, 184, 187, 213, 230, 272n44, 280n29
Aristides, 111
Aristotle, 64, 115; on causality, 4, 56–7, 63; on cripples, 55; *De Anima*, 166; and the divine, 27–8, 162–3; on the divinity of the intellect, 31, 152; in the *Essays*, 250n13; *Ethics*, 46, 151, 174–5, 177–8, 182; on Heraclitus, 155; on madness, 98; on magnanimity, 7, 174–8, 190; *Metaphysics*, 55, 59, 150, 153, 162; on nature, 47; on philosophy as useless, 187; on physics, 45, 153–4; *Poetics*, 82; on poetry and history, 83; political philosophy of, 221; on Solon's saying, 41; on virtue, 197
Armaingaud, Arthur, 266n22
Armstrong, Elizabeth, 276n6
Atkinson, James B., 260n14, 262n21, 276n4

Auerbach, Erich, 63, 73, 123, 171, 174, 263n5
Augustine, St., 164; *City of God*, 129, 147; and created being, 123, 127; on death, 124–5; God-centeredness of, 176; on noble lie, 237; on original nature, 50; on sin, 50–1; on suicide, 198–9; and temporality, 159

Baillon, Emmanuelle, 255n23
baptism, 134
Baraz, Michaël, 274n27, 275n37; on being and becoming, 248n2; on comic style, 273n11; on images, 261n18; on metaphysical hierarchy, 247n11; on the miraculous, 262n21; on Montaigne and tradition, 247n16; on movement of Montaigne's thought, 260n14; on the sacred, 265n21
Barfield, Owen, 256n27
Bauschatz, Cathleen M., 255n23
Beaudry, James G., 246n10
Becket, St. Thomas, 229–30
Bencivenga, Ermanno, 278n14
Béranger, Guillaume, 244n5
Bernard, St., 129
Betis, 96, 97, 133
Blinkenberg, Andreas, 251n3
Bloom, Harold, 251n2
Blum, Claude, 255n21
Boase, Alan M., 249n8, 252n3, 253n17
Bodin, Jean: criticisms of Plutarch, 20–2, 81
Bonadeo, Alfredo, 275n37
Boon, Jean-Pierre, 273–4n18
Bowen, Barbara C., 260n14, 262n20
Boyle, Nicholas, 264n14, 265n19
Brague, Rémi, 241n2, 247n13, 280n25
Brahami, Frédéric, 135, 136, 138, 244n4
Brann, Eva T. H., 262n19, 269n9

302 Index

---

presumption (*cont.*)
  142–3, 181; philosophical, 31; and
  possibility, 161; and the prohibition
  against speaking about oneself, 185; and
  quotation, 78; of reason, 128, 142; and
  self-love, 238; of the simple, 145; and
  skepticism, 24; two forms of, 106
poetry, 4, 78–83
Pompey, 95
Poulet, Georges, 159–60
Protagoras, 158
Pyrrho of Elis, 15, 27

Quiñones, Ricardo J., 264n11, 279n17
Quint, David, 259n3, 277n9, 279n17; on
  distinction between virtue and goodness,
  275n4; on Epaminondas, 82; on *Essays* as
  trial, 248n20; on mercy, 275n37, 276n6,
  280n35; on Montaigne's goodness, 276n5;
  on Montaigne's invention, 256n25; on
  Montaigne's project of reform of nobility,
  277n11

Randall, Catherine, 269n9
rationalism, 72
Rée, Jonathan, 270n30
Reformation: and atheism, 140; Montaigne's
  criticisms of, 6, 8, 128–9, 231, 232–3
Regosin, Richard L., 247n11; on
  astonishment, 263n21; on circular
  movement of Montaigne's thought,
  260n14; on meaning, 152–3; on memory,
  261n15; on the miraculous, 271–2n44; on
  Montaigne's ambiguity, 251n17; on
  Montaigne's reordering of virtues, 277n11;
  on movement of Montaigne's thought,
  258n1; on nature, 248n3; on nothingness,
  270n32; on origins of the *Essays*, 257n32;
  on particularity, 268n2; on self-knowledge
  and skepticism, 244n5
Regulus, 198
Rendall, Steven, 159, 255n23, 258n1,
  260n14, 274n19
Reno, R. R., 270n25
Resurrection (of Christ), 123, 130, 247n12
resurrection (of the body), 32–3, 162
Rider, Frederick, 258n1
Rigolot, François, 253n13, 256n27
Roche, Dan, 262n21
Rodis-Lewis, G., 243n4
Rollins, Yvonne B., 251n17
Rome, 115, 228, 239
Rousseau, Jean-Jacques, 8, 217–19, 221, 222,
  225, 239
Routh, H. V., 253n11
Ruel, Edouard, 256n31
Runyon, Randolph, 256n24
Russell, Daniel, 258n1

sacraments, 129–30
Sanders, S. G., 279n17
Saulnier, V.-L., 16–17, 93, 96, 100–1
Sayce, Richard A.: on circular movement of
  essays, 260n14; on education, 253n17; on
  essay title, 252n3; on evolution in *Essays*,
  241–2n1; Montaigne not Christian,
  266n22; on Montaigne's shamelessness,
  247n11; on order, 257n32; on violence in
  Essays, 280n29
Scaevola, 237
Schaefer, David Lewis, 267n27, 276n6; on
  Montaigne as atheist, 266n22; on
  Montaigne's attachment to Rome,
  280n27; on Montaigne and Machiavelli,
  279n17; on Montaigne's transformation of
  political order, 279n15; on "noble lie,"
  233; on Stoic virtue, 277n11
Schiffman, Zachary S., 243n4
Schmitt, C. B., 243n4
Schneewind, J. B., 276n5, 279n17
Schwartz, Jerome, 260–1n14, 276n5
Scipio, 224
Sclafert, Clement, 264n13, 266n24, 270n32
Screech, M. A.: on Aristotle, 250n13, n14; on
  the daemonic, 156; on essay title, 63; on
  imagination, 261n16; on madness,
  246n10; on Montaigne as Christian,
  264–5n16; on Montaigne's wife, 274n34
Sebond, Raymond, 23, 137
Sechel, George, 133
Sedley, D. N., 245n6
Sedley, David, 245n8
Seneca, 122, 161; and deliberate philosophy,
  27; in Dion's testimony, 79; letter to
  Lucilius, 113; as Montaigne's source, 74; as
  superior to God, 31
Sextus Empiricus, 5, 104, 243n4
Shklar, Judith N., 274n35, 275n37, 276n6,
  277n11, 278n15
skepticism: 12–17, 242–4n4; Academic, 15;
  ancient, 3, 12, 15, 105; Christian, 12, 121,
  135–6; and circular dialectic, 104–5,
  245n8; and credulity, 23; and the divine
  stasis, 28; and fideism, 135–7; as moment
  in Montaigne's thought, 16, 22, 24, 25,
  136; Montaigne's transformation of
  ancient, 13–25, 243–4; and politics, 220
Slade, Francis, 224, 225, 231
sociality: conditions of, 231–9
Socrates: and Athens, 227; daemon of, 66,
  156–7; death of, 124; as exemplar, 79, 180,
  190, 199–200, 203, 207; lowliness of,
  114–15; on obedience to laws, 237;
  reformation of, 200–1, 206, 212–13; and
  self-knowledge, 176; and self-mastery, 30;
  susceptibility to accidents of life, 29; and
  virtue, 200, 201–2